MW00825101

THE CONTEST OVER NATIONAL SECURITY

THE CONTEST OVER
NATIONAL SECURITY

FDR, Conservatives, and the Struggle to Claim
the Most Powerful Phrase in American Politics

PETER ROADY

HARVARD UNIVERSITY PRESS
Cambridge, Massachusetts
London, England
2024

First printing

Publication of this book has been supported through the generous provisions
of the Maurice and Lula Bradley Smith Memorial Fund.

Library of Congress Cataloging-in-Publication Data

Names: Roady, Peter, 1983- author.
Title: The contest over national security : FDR, Conservatives, and the Struggle to
Claim the Most Powerful Phrase in American Politics / Peter Roady.
Description: Cambridge, Massachusetts ; London, England : Harvard
University Press, 2024. | Includes bibliographical references and index.
Identifiers: LCCN 2023029099 | ISBN 9780674291256 (cloth)
Subjects: LCSH: Roosevelt, Franklin D. (Franklin Delano),
1882–1945—Language. | Roosevelt, Franklin D. (Franklin Delano),
1882–1945—Political and social views. | Roosevelt, Franklin D.
(Franklin Delano), 1882–1945—Adversaries. | National security—United
States—History—20th century. | New Deal, 1933–1939. |
Rhetoric—Political aspects—United States—History—20th century. |
Business and politics—United States—History—20th century. | United
States—Politics and government—1933–1945.
Classification: LCC E806 .R7214 2024 | DDC 917.917—dc23/eng/20230727
LC record available at https://lccn.loc.gov/2023029099

Contents

Preface and Acknowledgments

A T A BACKYARD PARTY one afternoon during my childhood in Washington, DC, I found myself standing next to a grown-up neighbor. Unsure of what else to say, I asked the question I had heard so many grown-ups in DC ask each other in similar circumstances: what do you do? He said he "worked in national security." Even at the time, this struck me as intriguing. I understood what it meant to be a teacher or a doctor or a lawyer. What did it mean to work in national security?

The question lingered until I watched the smoke rise from the Pentagon on the morning of September 11, 2001. Amid the fear and foreboding that gripped my hometown that day, I decided to contribute whatever I could to preventing a recurrence of those feelings of insecurity. It seemed only logical to assume that banishing insecurity was the province of national security professionals like my childhood neighbor. I decided to join their ranks. In college, I dedicated myself to learning as much as possible about the various government departments and agencies that did national security work, both their current operations and their histories. The Department of Defense and the Intelligence Community seemed to be at the center of the action and seemed to have been so for a long time. I decided those were the places where I wanted to work.

Almost as soon as I started my job as a nonpolitical civil servant in the Office of the Secretary of Defense in the summer of 2006, it became obvious that working in national security meant power, resources, and deference: power and resources for those on the inside, and deference from those on the outside. A subsequent stint in the Intelligence Community underscored those conclusions, as well as their implication: it clearly mattered what counted as a national security issue. During my time in government under both Republican and Democratic presidents, working in national security entailed a focus on the country's physical security and on foreign policy. Every now and then, someone—usually an outsider—would suggest that some domestic policy issue rose to the level of a national security concern. But national security professionals, including me, often dismissed such suggestions out of hand. There was a clear demarcation between national security work and everything else the government did. I assumed it had always been that way. Researching and writing this book made clear how wrong I was. This book tells the story of how the United States developed the type of national security state in which I worked—a national security state far more narrowly focused than the one with which the country began.

It is a pleasure now to thank the people who supported my work on this book. Matt Jones, Drew Lipman, Richard John, Anders Stephanson, Jeremy Kessler, Ira Katznelson, and Daniel Sargent provided early support and encouragement. Margaret Puskar-Pasewicz, Micah McElroy, Salem Elzway, Celia Roady, Steve Roady, and Michael Sulmeyer read every word of early drafts and improved the manuscript greatly with their comments. The anonymous reviewers for Harvard University Press offered similarly constructive suggestions. Kim Phillips-Fein, Mark Wilson, Darren Dochuk, and anonymous reviewers for *Modern American History* gave me valuable feedback on the portions dealing with the conservative movement. Daniel Rodgers provided helpful advice on the introduction. The final manuscript is immeasurably better for their suggestions. My fantastic colleagues in the History Department at the University of Utah offered encouragement and helped me navigate the publication process. The Defense Office of Prepublication and Security Review orchestrated a prompt and professional review of the manuscript and approved it for public release with the disclaimer that the views expressed in this book are those of the author and do not reflect the official policy or position of the Department of Defense or the U.S. Government.

Archivists across the United States lent their expertise and hospitality over a period of years as I researched the book. At the FDR Library, Christian Belena, Matthew Hanson, Virginia Lewick, Sarah Navins, and—especially—Patrick Fahy provided advice and support during multiple visits. Genevieve Coyle, Kate Donovan, and Bilqees Sayed did likewise at Yale, Harvard, and Princeton, respectively. At the Hagley, Lucas Clawson, Angela Schad, Marsha Mills, and Ashley Williams helped me navigate the enormous NAM collection. Lee Grady and Jennifer Barth helped me make the most of my time at the Wisconsin Historical Society. Bill Maher, Katie Nichols, Linda Stepp, and Jameatris Rimkus did likewise at the University of Illinois Archives. At the Hoover Institution, Sarah Patton and David Sun helped me work through a mountain of material from multiple collections. Finally, at the Truman Library, Tammy Williams, Randy Sowell, Laurie Austin, and Sam Rushay helped me nail down some crucial facts. To all of them, thank you.

Andrew Kinney at Harvard University Press eagerly embraced this project, provided valuable editorial feedback, and expertly steered the book through the many stages of the publication process. Heather Rothman diligently checked facts. Stephanie Vyce helped with permissions. Kathleen Drummy and Jamie Armstrong managed the production process. Thanks to all of them for their work.

This book never would have made it into your hands without the love and support of friends and family. Thank you, Alice, Michael, Micah, Brooks, Sam, John, Salem, Ronit, Alex, Kate, Charley, Katie, Caroline, and Marshall. My parents, Celia and Steve Roady, have encouraged my intellectual curiosity for as long as I can remember. For their love and support, as well as for the gift of education, I am forever grateful. My sister Laura Capito has been among my strongest supporters for four decades now. Thank you, Laura. Sharon Boyce and Jack Woodall welcomed me into their family more than a decade ago and have loved and supported me ever since. Whenever work on this project slowed, the example set by their daughter and my late wife, Lauren, provided motivation to keep going. Among their many accomplishments, Beth and Arthur

Golden can be most proud of producing Eliza. She shaped this project from start to finish with her incisive questions and constant encouragement. I am grateful every day for her love and support. The arrival of our delightful daughters, Schuyler and Nora, provided timely spurs to completion. May they live in a time of real national security.

THE CONTEST OVER NATIONAL SECURITY

Introduction

"NATIONAL SECURITY" ranks among the most powerful phrases in American politics, commanding wide deference, garnering almost unlimited resources, and determining many of the government's priorities.[1] The phrase has a timeless quality that makes it easy to assume that it has always been defined as we understand it today.[2] But it hasn't. Nor has the national security state always focused primarily on foreign affairs and protecting the country against physical attack. The meaning we associate with national security and the tasks we associate with the national security state emerged only after nearly twenty years of intense political struggle. Throughout the 1930s and 1940s, liberals and conservatives fought tooth and nail to define the government's national security responsibilities in law, policy, and the public mind. Words were the decisive weapons in that fight.[3]

On the evening of July 2, 1932, Franklin Roosevelt told the audience gathered at the Democratic National Convention in Chicago that providing "security" ought to be one of the government's primary objectives.[4] He campaigned on that premise in the months that followed. Upon assuming the presidency in the spring of 1933, he told Americans gathered around radios to hear his second fireside chat that expanding the government's domestic responsibilities to ensure economic security was

1

"imperative to our national security."[5] At the end of 1940, with war enveloping the world, Roosevelt told Americans in another fireside chat that expanding the government's international responsibilities too had now become vital for "national security."[6] In his January 1944 State of the Union address, Roosevelt proposed a "second Bill of Rights under which a new basis of security and prosperity can be established for all regardless of station, race, or creed."[7] The objective, he said, should be "not only physical security which provides safety from attacks by aggressors" but "also economic security, social security, moral security."[8]

The language of security was not new.[9] Alexander Hamilton and John Jay used it in *The Federalist* to justify creating a strong and balanced national government under the Constitution.[10] But no American politician had used the language of security to advance their agenda in as deliberate and sustained a manner as Franklin Roosevelt. Roosevelt's embrace of the language of security transformed American politics—but not in the ways he envisioned. Ironically, Roosevelt's success expanding the government's domestic and international responsibilities in the name of security galvanized the forces—namely, the conservative movement and foreign policy establishment—that by the late 1940s defeated his plans for a comprehensive national security state responsible for both economic and physical security. This book tells that story.

Why We Know Only Part of the National Security State's History

Although much has been written about "security" and "national security" in the United States, we know surprisingly little about how the language of security became such a potent force in American politics and how its most powerful expression—the phrase "national security"—came to be defined in the way Americans have understood it since the late 1940s.[11] The problem is one of perspective. Almost everything written about national security in the United States has approached the topic with a present-day understanding of the phrase's meaning in mind. As a result, nearly everyone who has talked or written about national security in the past seven decades has assumed that national security refers to physical security and that national security policymaking is a foreign policy matter.

Operating from those assumptions, it is not surprising that most commentators on national security have used the phrase instrumentally to explain American foreign policies.[12] For Americans who came of age in the 1960s and 1970s, a concept of national security provided the answer to two of their most vexing questions: What explained the origins of the Cold War? And why did the United States get involved in Vietnam?[13] Similarly, a later generation of Americans looked to a concept of national security to explain the country's response to the events of September 2001.[14] While this attentiveness to foreign policy–focused concepts of national security has produced some valuable insights, it has also made it difficult for commentators to see or explain the more expansive national security state designed by Franklin Roosevelt and his advisors in the 1930s, which sought to protect citizens against both economic insecurity and physical attack and which relied on a mix of domestic and foreign policy to do so. With the domestic policy part of the story underdeveloped, disconnected, or missing altogether, the national security state's history remains only half written.[15]

The history of the phrase "national security" itself remains similarly incomplete, despite repeated warnings from scholars about the need to nail this "slippery term" down and several promising attempts to do so.[16] Writing in 1952, Arnold Wolfers cautioned that "national security" was "an ambiguous symbol" that "needed to be scrutinized with particular care."[17] In 1966, P. G. Bock and Morton Berkowitz observed that "the term has been used as a rhetorical phrase by politicians, as a specific military objective by generals, and as a promise of utopia by political evangelists. All this has served to create a blanket of smog that has made disciplined inquiry almost impossible."[18] Daniel Yergin lamented in 1977 that "the amount of literature that invokes 'national security' is vast; the amount that critically explores the concept is in short supply."[19] With a few exceptions, the problem only worsened in subsequent decades. In the 1990s, several scholars even proposed using a fixed concept of national security to investigate the entire sweep of United States history.[20] Historians Emily Rosenberg and Anders Stephanson, among others, pointed out the problems with that ahistorical approach, and little came of the suggestion.[21] Several more promising attempts to historicize national security appeared thereafter, but none of them fully escaped the

foreign relations silo.[22] As a result, our understanding of this most powerful of political phrases remains remarkably limited.

We have also paid a more concrete price for the way people have written about national security. Largely unintentionally, three generations of
commentators have solidified a concept of national security focused on
physical security and foreign policy at the expense of alternatives.[23] In so
doing, they have erased Franklin Roosevelt's quite different concept of
national security from historical memory—and therefore also from our
sense of political possibilities. Economic security and domestic policy,
both central to Roosevelt's concept of national security, have been pushed
further and further from the national security frame.

Toward a Political History of the National Security State

Rather than looking at the past from the narrow perspective of the
present, this book sets aside our contemporary understanding of national
security and instead charts the evolution of the phrase's meaning as historical actors conceived it.[24] Shifting perspective in this way immediately
makes clear that national security has not always been solely a foreign
policy matter and that the meaning of national security familiar to us
emerged from an intense political struggle.[25] In other words, the national
security state's history is political history. Accordingly, this book focuses
on the interrelated processes of public persuasion and state building
through which Americans fought to define the national security state's
purview in law, policy, and the public mind.[26] Centering political history
changes our understanding of the national security state by recovering its
origins in 1930s economic security policies and by revealing the domestic
political reasons for the subsequent exclusion of economic security from
what counted as a national security matter.

To understand how and why political actors succeeded in framing issues as essential to national security, we need to get as close as possible to
what people in the past said and wrote. We must learn how and why they
chose their words, narratives, and frames, treating those things as what
historian David Green calls "historical data."[27] We must also consider
the contexts in which those words, narratives, and frames emerged and
the contests through which they evolved.[28] In both cases, that means

eschewing published primary sources in favor of archival material—including the original audio recordings of Franklin Roosevelt's speeches, since he often deviated from prepared texts.[29] It also means parsing the sources behind the sources, such as the drafts and other artifacts of the speech preparation process. These overlooked materials provide valuable insight into why and how people in the past mobilized the language of security for political ends.[30]

But focusing exclusively on how Americans moved issues into the national security frame would leave much unexplained, including the emergence of separate "national security" and "welfare" states rather than the comprehensive national security state Franklin Roosevelt envisioned. This book therefore also focuses on how Americans removed issues from the national security frame. This approach illuminates the role played by a new group of foreign policy–focused professionals and academics in claiming the mantle of national security exclusively for their work in the 1940s. Their success marked a dramatic shift in which policy areas counted as a national security matter, and a remarkable reduction in status for those working on domestic policy. In the 1930s, senior government officials working on economic security issues—people like Secretary of Labor Frances Perkins—were rightly seen as the country's preeminent national security professionals. But by the time Congress passed the National Security Act in 1947, anyone who suggested that economic security-focused entities like the Social Security Administration ought to have been included in the national security state would have been ridiculed.

Focusing on how and why the accepted meaning of national security narrowed also brings into view the modern American conservative movement, which helped channel the national security state's development in ways overlooked until now. Energized by opposition to Franklin Roosevelt's comprehensive vision for national security, the businessmen leading the nascent conservative movement intensified the large public persuasion campaign they had launched in the 1920s as part of a broader effort to limit the growth of the government's domestic responsibilities.[31] The expanded persuasion campaign became the conservative movement's driving force and provided the rhetorical glue that bound together an assortment of groups into a big tent movement in the 1930s and 1940s.[32] Through this campaign, conservatives worked tirelessly to sell a narrower vision of the government's national security responsibilities that excluded domestic economic security.

It can be difficult to assess the impact of persuasion campaigns on public opinion, and doing so for the 1930s and 1940s presents special challenges. Opinion polling was in its infancy and rarely employed the kinds of sampling methods experts would demand today.[33] As a result, there is a tendency to understate the impact of persuasion campaigns like the one conservatives orchestrated in this period.[34] Focusing on the volume of messaging provides a way around this problem. Psychologists established long ago that the frequent repetition of messages shapes minds.[35] To an extent greater than many of us might like to admit, persuasion campaigns use volume and repetition to provide the dominant narratives we use to make sense of the world and to talk about it.[36] These dominant narratives shape not only what we believe the government *should* do but also what the government actually *can* do. The story in the pages that follow lends credence to historian Brian Balogh's observation that "controlling the way in which the central government's policies were framed, it turned out, could sometimes be more important than the actual impact of those programs."[37]

The conservative persuasion campaign ensured that conservatives supplied the dominant narratives about the government beginning in the 1940s. Conservatives inundated Americans with billions of messages disparaging domestic economic security programs, sowing doubt about the government's competence, and presenting the private sector as best able to provide economic security.[38] Through these messages, the conservative persuasion campaign helped cement a conception of the government's national security responsibilities in the public mind and in law and policy that was far narrower than the one put forward by Franklin Roosevelt. Unable to compete with this deluge of conservative messaging, liberals lost the fight to define national security.

Overview of the Book

Eight chapters chart the American national security state's overlooked origins and contested evolution. Events abroad cast a long shadow throughout. The book begins on the presidential campaign trail in early 1932. Using handwritten notes, speech fragments, and marked-up speech drafts, Chapter 1 shows how Franklin Roosevelt and his closest advisors found in the language of security the answers to their most pressing political problems, which were how to get Roosevelt elected president and how to deal with the Great Depression. In deploying the language of security, Roosevelt and his advisors intuited what social scientists later established. The language of security has intrinsic persuasive power and generates deference to leaders who use it because "security" has what psychologists call a "loss frame" built in: people fear insecurity.[39] The language of security enabled Roosevelt to explain the Great Depression's causes in ways Americans could understand instinctively and to propose remedies Americans would support reflexively. Beginning in 1932, Roosevelt made the promise of security the focal point of the new "liberalism" he championed. Until the 1930s, those who called themselves "liberals" generally had opposed expanding the government's responsibilities.[40] Roosevelt appropriated the term and reversed its meaning, invoking national security to justify expanding the government's domestic responsibilities to deal with rampant economic insecurity.[41]

Before the 1930s, the phrase "national security" had appeared sporadically throughout American history in a vague, usually undefined way.[42] To Roosevelt, the global political upheavals associated with the Great Depression made obvious that national security depended on economic security. As Chapter 2 shows, Roosevelt sought to cement that connection in the public mind and in law and policy after entering office in March 1933. In his first term, Roosevelt used the language of security to reshape public perceptions of what the government should do domestically and to expand those responsibilities in law, laying what he called the "corner stone" of a national security state with the establishment of Social Security in 1935.[43] In so doing, Roosevelt and his advisors believed they had taken an important first step toward solving the central problem of their time, which was how to address the economic insecurity associated with modern industrial capitalism without following the path taken by other countries and abandoning democracy.

Roosevelt's demonstration that the government's domestic responsibilities could be expanded seemingly without limit in the name of national security terrified advocates of limited government. As Chapter 3 shows, these Americans had already begun mobilizing in the 1920s against what they saw as unwarranted expansions of the government's domestic responsibilities. These Americans, who saw themselves as the "real" liberals, fought bitterly against Roosevelt's appropriation of that label and accepted the new "conservative" label for themselves only after a long struggle.[44] The new conservatives agreed with Roosevelt that national security depended on preserving individual liberty, but they disagreed about how best to do that. Roosevelt thought assuring individual liberty under modern industrial capitalism required expanding the government's responsibilities to guarantee economic security. Conservatives defined liberty in what philosopher Isaiah Berlin called its "negative" sense, meaning that individual liberty depended on limiting the government's domestic responsibilities.[45]

Chapter 3 shows how Roosevelt's success using the language of security to expand the government's domestic responsibilities lit a fire under the nascent conservative movement. To erode support for Roosevelt's agenda, conservatives mobilized the full power of the public relations profession to deliver billions of messages disparaging domestic economic security programs and casting doubt on the government's competence. The National Association of Manufacturers spearheaded this large public persuasion campaign in the 1930s and early 1940s, with the ostensibly nonpartisan but conservative-run Advertising Council taking the lead thereafter. The conservative persuasion campaign's architects used volume and repetition to cultivate impressions and make them stick. The campaign relied not only on direct messaging, which those who disagreed with the message might ignore, but also on indirect persuasion through trusted intermediaries. The campaign's architects wooed teachers, religious leaders, women, and other "opinion molders" who could deliver tailored anti-statist messages to trusting audiences over an extended period. Whether they realized it or not, by the late 1930s Americans of all ages received conservative messages from the moment they woke up until the moment they went to sleep. The high-stakes struggle between liberals and conservatives to define the government's national security responsibilities had begun.

Chapter 4 chronicles the vicious battle at the end of the 1930s over Roosevelt's proposals to expand the national security state by establishing a Federal Security Agency and a National Resources Planning Board. Both liberals and conservatives pointed to events in Europe to bolster their arguments for and against these proposals. Roosevelt argued that the rise of dictatorships abroad reflected the failure of those countries' governments to satisfy their citizens' desire for economic security. He presented national planning as essential for ensuring the economic security on which he believed national security—and the survival of individual liberty and American republican democracy—depended. By contrast, conservatives believed that national planning represented a grave threat to individual freedom and argued that expanding the government's economic security initiatives would weaken the United States just as conservatives said had happened to France, which fell to the Nazis in June 1940. Roosevelt won this battle, but the fight over the proper extent of the government's national security responsibilities continued.

Ironically, Roosevelt's subsequent actions helped conservatives exclude economic security programs from the national security state's purview. Chapter 5 shows how Roosevelt invoked national security to persuade Americans and their representatives in Congress to adopt a more internationally engaged foreign policy in the 1940s. Roosevelt's success putting foreign policy into the national security frame helped conservatives push domestic policy out of it. At the same time, the massive increase in government spending that accompanied American entry into World War II in 1941 reduced unemployment and increased economic output. But as Chapter 6 shows, conservatives used their large public persuasion campaign to deny credit to the government for this economic boom. Together, the return of prosperity and the public perception that the government had little to do with it made it harder for liberals to frame economic security programs as necessary for national security.

Contrary to the long-standing consensus that Roosevelt abandoned his domestic agenda with the coming of World War II, however, Chapter 6 also shows that Roosevelt worked in his third term toward a comprehensive national security state with domestic and foreign policy as co-equal domains of national security policymaking. During his long tenure in the White House, Roosevelt had seen that the primary threat to national security could be economic insecurity in one period and physical insecurity in another. He believed the government needed to be responsible for addressing all sources of insecurity—not just the one that had primacy at a particular moment—and therefore that national security policymaking must include both domestic and foreign policy. The fullest articulation of Roosevelt's vision for the government's national security responsibilities came in his 1944 State of the Union address, in which Roosevelt proposed a "second Bill of Rights" that would ensure economic security.[46]

Chapter 7 explains why Roosevelt's vision did not come to fruition. Roosevelt's success reorienting foreign policy in the name of national security gave birth to a powerful foreign policy establishment that claimed the mantle of national security exclusively for its work. Members of this newly empowered foreign policy establishment—many of whom sympathized with conservatives on domestic policy—articulated a concept of national security that focused on physical security from foreign threats. These foreign policy professionals worked to enshrine this concept in law with the National Security Act of 1947 and helped create an academic field of "security studies" that excluded domestic "welfare" policies from its ambit. Roosevelt's successor Harry Truman unintentionally accelerated the removal of domestic policy from the national security frame by distinguishing in speeches and budget requests between the government's "national security" and "welfare" responsibilities. Truman came to regret his contribution to this bifurcation as a foreign policy–focused national security state grew rapidly while the domestic policy–focused welfare state embodied in his proposal for a "Fair Deal" stalled. Ironically, rather than institutionalizing the Rooseveltian vision for national security at home, the United States exported it, helping underwrite and build comprehensive national security states abroad in the same years Americans abandoned that project at home.

Chapter 8 shows how conservatives in the late 1940s and early 1950s delivered the final blows to Roosevelt's vision for national security by using "public service advertising" to further disparage economic security programs and to associate them with socialism. Using amusing examples of domestic policy incompetence unearthed by former President Herbert Hoover's Commission on the Organization of the Executive Branch of the Government, the conservative-led Advertising Council sowed doubt in Americans' minds about the government's competence. As the Cold War took shape, conservatives also portrayed liberal domestic policy proposals as socialistic and therefore as threatening to national security. The guise of "public service advertising" provided the conservative persuasion campaign with a veneer of nonpartisanship and abundant free advertising space. This potent combination helped conservatives cement a derisive rhetoric in mainstream political discourse that shaped the way Americans perceived and talked about the government for decades thereafter. The result was a strand of selective anti-statism that paired disdain for domestic economic security programs with support for a robust military and foreign policy establishment.[47] This selective anti-statism solidified separate and imbalanced "national security" and "welfare" states.

The epilogue explores some of the consequences and ironies associated with the narrowing of the national security agenda after the 1940s. The removal of economic security and domestic policy from the national security state's purview diminished their importance in the eyes of the public and created a cycle in which the government found it more difficult to address domestic problems. These difficulties—coupled with conservatives' success sowing doubt about the government's competence—eroded public confidence in the government, which further reduced public support for economic security programs. The government's apparent domestic policy incapacity reinforced a long-standing tendency to use the military and foreign policy to address problems that might have been more efficiently managed through domestic policy. These outcomes make it tempting to conclude that the country would have been better off with Franklin Roosevelt's comprehensive national security state. But the book ends by discussing the potential problems with making an expansive concept of national security the government's chief objective and raises the question of whether such a concept might work better in conjunction with other goals.

Before coming to that, we need to understand how the language of security became such a powerful force in American politics and how its most powerful expression—national security—came to be defined as most Americans understand it today. The story begins in early 1932 as Franklin Roosevelt sought the Democratic nomination for president.

1

———

Campaigning on the Promise
of Security

"THESE ARE UNPRECEDENTED and unusual times," Franklin Roosevelt told the Democratic National Convention in Chicago on July 2, 1932.[1] It was almost an understatement. In the United States and around the world, widespread suffering inflicted by the Great Depression raised serious doubts about the futures of capitalism and democracy.[2] The Depression had stripped away layer after layer of psychological and material security over the preceding two years until millions of Americans struggled to meet even their most basic needs. Nearly a quarter of the American workforce lacked work.[3] National income fell by more than half.[4] Even the more fortunate feared they too would be dragged under.[5] Recalling a drive through Pittsburgh, Pennsylvania, Roosevelt later said, "I could see mile after mile of this greatest mill and factory area in the world, a dead panorama of silent black structures and smokeless stacks. I saw idleness and hunger instead of the whirl of machinery."[6] Americans had never felt so insecure.

In these hard times, Roosevelt asked the audience in Chicago, "What do the people of America want more than anything else?"[7] Roosevelt said they wanted "work, with all the moral and spiritual values that go with work."[8] But Roosevelt acknowledged that work was only a means to an end. What Americans really wanted, Roosevelt said, was "a reasonable measure of security."[9] As president, Roosevelt promised the government would provide "a new deal for the American people."[10] He made clear that security would be its basis.

Roosevelt chose his words carefully and talked in terms of "security" deliberately. After many intense discussions in the spring of 1932, he and his advisors grasped that security was a policy objective with inherent rhetorical power, and they made security the centerpiece of Roosevelt's presidential campaign. Talking in terms of security solved several problems for Roosevelt. He needed a way of explaining the Depression's causes and remedies that would convince Americans that he understood their problems and could solve them. The language of security met that need. Roosevelt said economic insecurity had caused the Depression and that a government guarantee of economic security would solve it. Roosevelt also needed a flexible and durable justification for expanding the government's responsibilities in the ways he and his advisors believed necessary to solve the economic crisis and prevent a recurrence, all without abandoning democracy. Here again the language of security provided the answer. Framing domestic policy as necessary for security helped elevate it above politics and created space for institutional transformation. Finally, of course, Roosevelt needed to win an election. Talking in terms of security was good politics because it promised people what they wanted most in 1932.

During the 1932 campaign, Roosevelt used the language of security to frame proposals for expanding the government's responsibilities as part of a new "liberalism" that would lead the country out of the Great Depression. Roosevelt believed the Depression had imperiled both the "liberty of the individual" and the "liberty of the community." Under the new liberalism, the government would remove the danger to the individual by guaranteeing economic security and would neutralize the danger to the community through government planning. Roosevelt thought both policies necessary to resolve the crisis and prevent a recurrence. Freedom *from* the government defined the old liberalism. The new liberalism held that freedom *depended on* government action. Roosevelt took the new liberal case directly to the American people, crisscrossing the country by railroad to speak to them in their communities and using radio to chat with them in their homes. The language of security helped Roosevelt win the presidency and gain public backing to expand the government's responsibilities under the new liberalism. But Roosevelt's success also rallied proponents of the old liberalism and opened a new phase in the long-running fight over the government's role in American life.

Franklin Roosevelt's Views on Government

Observers at the time and historians since have differed on Franklin Roosevelt's core political and economic philosophy—even on whether he had one at all.[11] By the time the 1932 presidential campaign began, however, several important aspects of Roosevelt's views had taken shape.[12] At the most basic level, Roosevelt thought the republic's founders intended the government's responsibilities to evolve to meet contemporary needs.[13] While serving as New York governor from 1929 to 1932, Roosevelt said, "We cannot call ourselves either wise or patriotic if we seek to escape the responsibility of remolding government to make it more serviceable to all the people and more responsive to modern needs."[14] Roosevelt made clear that economic security ranked foremost among those needs. He argued that only by addressing the individual economic insecurity that appeared to be a by-product of modern industrial capitalism could Americans regain "economic liberty."[15]

Roosevelt saw two aspects to economic liberty, which he called the "liberty of the individual" and the "liberty of the community." He explained both aspects to an audience in Troy, New York, in March 1912 while serving as a New York state senator. The speech contained the earliest and fullest articulation of Roosevelt's political and economic philosophy.[16] In Roosevelt's view, the increasing interdependence associated with modern life had made the liberty of the individual dependent on the liberty of the community. Liberty of the community, for Roosevelt, depended on sustaining high levels of cooperation—including through government action to ensure individual choices did not harm the community.[17] Roosevelt's thinking about interdependence reflected New York's position at the leading edge of modernity and the importance of both agriculture and industry to the state's economy. Fewer and fewer people in the state raised their own food, and fewer and fewer people controlled their own labor. People were no longer masters of their own economic destinies.

While serving as governor of New York, Roosevelt came to believe that restoring economic liberty required expanding the government's responsibilities in two ways. First, Roosevelt thought the government needed to do more to help citizens make ends meet, thereby restoring their individual liberty. As he told the New York State Legislature in 1931, "modern society, acting through its Government, owes the definite obligation to prevent the starvation or the dire want of any of its fellow men and women who try to maintain themselves but cannot. To these unfortunate citizens aid must be extended by the Government—not as a matter of charity, but as a matter of social duty."[18] Eleanor Roosevelt and Frances Perkins, a longtime social reformer who served as New York's industrial commissioner during Roosevelt's governorship, influenced Roosevelt's thinking on this point, with Perkins pushing Roosevelt to support government-provided insurance against unemployment and old age.[19]

Moving from the individual to the community as a whole, Roosevelt believed ensuring the liberty of the community required a greater level of government stewardship of natural resources and the economy.[20] He had seen the ill effects of the country's haphazard and wasteful growth firsthand while traveling the country during the 1920 campaign as the Democratic vice presidential candidate.[21] He believed such profligacy had become problematic with the closing of the American frontier, which prevented Americans who had fallen on hard times from moving away from ruined land and starting again with abundant resources elsewhere.[22] Since the ratification of the Constitution, the government had played a vital behind-the-scenes role in the country's growth, including through building or underwriting the construction of transportation and communications infrastructure.[23] Roosevelt believed the government now needed to play an even greater role in guiding the country's development, including through some measure of national planning.[24] As he argued in January 1932, "the complete solving of those economic problems which are national in scope is an impossibility without leadership and a plan and action by our national government."[25]

As a presidential candidate, the question for Roosevelt was how to persuade the public to support expanded government responsibility and accompanying institutional growth. The ongoing crisis of the Great Depression made the task easier. The Depression made Americans more open to political and economic change and gave political leaders greater freedom to maneuver, as Governor Roosevelt demonstrated when he delivered his January 1932 annual message to the New York State Legislature. On that occasion, Roosevelt declared that "I come before you at a time of domestic crisis which calls for the complete laying aside of partisanship and for a unity of leadership and action as complete as if we were engaged in war."[26] But as he contemplated the presidency, Roosevelt worried that the emergency of the Depression might not prove sufficient to sustain public support for the "reconstruction" he hoped to orchestrate, a project he knew would take a long time.[27] If he won the presidency and succeeded in pulling the country out of the Depression quickly, the public might resist the changes he thought necessary for the country's long-term well-being. Nevertheless, the Depression had at least created conditions favorable for change.

A shift in American elite opinion also worked to Roosevelt's advantage in the early 1930s. The growth of the managerial and professional classes that accompanied the expansion of business and government in preceding decades made opinion leaders more confident that experts could manage economic and social relations.[28] This shift made Roosevelt's argument about the need to expand the government's responsibilities more palatable, for Americans now believed suitable experts could be found to manage the country's affairs. In the 1930s, national-level planning gained wide support from academics, intellectuals, business leaders, and policymakers.[29] As Roosevelt advisor Frances Perkins recalled, "This was the heyday of the Technocrats. Every magazine that you could pick up . . . was full of articles by Technocrats, or about Technocracy. It had great standing."[30] Like the circumstances of the Great Depression, the public's openness to technocracy made it easier for Roosevelt to build support for expanding the government's responsibilities. But it was not clear the trend toward expert-led planning would last long enough to see Roosevelt's reconstruction through.

Roosevelt needed a way of sustaining public support for his agenda as circumstances changed. He agreed with Eleanor that political change required mobilizing and sustaining broad and deep public backing.[31] He needed the right language to describe and justify what he wanted to do—language that was flexible, persuasive, and universal. His advisors helped him find it.

Roosevelt and His Advisors

Like many politicians, Franklin Roosevelt relied on advisors to help him shape and sell his agenda throughout his time in public life. Louis Howe served as Roosevelt's closest political advisor beginning in 1912.[32] Samuel Rosenman joined the inner circle during Roosevelt's run for the New York governorship in 1928.[33] Both men remained important resources for and influences on Roosevelt during his run for the presidency. But as he intensified his effort to win the Democratic presidential nomination in the spring of 1932, Roosevelt sought counsel on national issues from outside his inner circle. By early April 1932, Roosevelt had assembled what he jokingly called his "privy council," what James Kieran of the *New York Times* dubbed the "brains trust," better known as the "Brain Trust."[34] The original Brain Trust included Rosenman; Basil "Doc" O'Connor, Roosevelt's one-time law partner; Raymond Moley, a professor at Columbia University who had advised Governor Roosevelt on criminal justice issues; Rexford Tugwell, an economics professor at Columbia; and Adolf Berle, a brilliant young New York lawyer and Columbia Law School teacher.[35] They would meet with Roosevelt in Albany, sometimes several times a week, to discuss the Depression's causes and potential remedies.

By mid-April 1932, Moley, Tugwell, and Berle had emerged as the prime movers within the Brain Trust. They had stronger ideas than Rosenman or O'Connor about the causes of the Depression and potential remedies for it, as well as more time to devote to Roosevelt's campaign.[36] Rosenman and O'Connor continued to participate in the Brain Trust discussions, but Moley, Tugwell, and Berle exerted greater influence on Roosevelt. Their influence stemmed both from Roosevelt's conversational learning style, which amplified the impact of their discussions with him, and from their leading role in drafting his campaign speeches. Moley, Tugwell, and Berle understood quite quickly that they would have the sort of influence of which policy-minded intellectuals often only dream.[37] "For an intellectual this was a golden period," Berle recalled. "This was a situation in which any reasonable idea could be presented. You stood a very fair chance of having it adopted."[38]

The Brain Trust discussions came at a crucial moment in Roosevelt's career. To secure the Democratic presidential nomination, Roosevelt needed to be able to explain to the American people how their problems had come about and how they could be fixed. His conversations with Moley, Tugwell, and Berle helped him begin to construct that narrative. The discussions allowed Roosevelt to explore a wide range of ideas through the vigorous verbal give-and-take that suited him.[39] "What he gets is from talking to people," Moley recalled, and "from thinking out loud," Tugwell added.[40] After one of the Brain Trusters finished presenting an idea, Berle remembered that Roosevelt would ask "a whole lot of questions and the questions were good ones."[41] Berle concluded that Roosevelt's willingness "to take any idea and look at it on its merits" was one of the candidate's best attributes.[42] "The amount of intellectual ransacking that Roosevelt could crowd into one evening was a source of constant astonishment to me," Moley remembered.[43] But the ransacking always served a purpose, as Tugwell recognized: "After our longish talks he could feel that what he concluded made sense, was defensible."[44] The visitors persevered through the long sessions because they knew they were contributing to the mosaic in Roosevelt's head. As Moley put it, "When he stores away the net of conversation he never knows what part of what he has kept is what he said himself or what his visitor said."[45]

Moley, Tugwell, and Berle's influence grew further in the process of translating Roosevelt's thinking into campaign speeches. Roosevelt devoted serious attention to his speeches, choosing his words carefully, but relied on his advisors to help him.[46] During his governorship, Roosevelt turned primarily to Samuel Rosenman for speechwriting help. But Roosevelt appointed Rosenman to the New York Supreme Court at around the same time the Brain Trust took shape, leaving the path clear for the mercurial and clever Moley to take over as Roosevelt's lead speechwriter.[47] The speechwriting process Moley orchestrated for Roosevelt beginning in April 1932 provided several opportunities for the Brain Trust to shape what Roosevelt said. The process typically began with a conversation between Roosevelt and Moley about the topic or topics to be covered.[48] Research by the Brain Trust and preparation of a first draft—usually by Moley—followed.[49] During the 1932 campaign, Roosevelt rarely had time to write a first draft himself.[50] Roosevelt and Moley would then revise the draft together, often multiple times, before Roosevelt did a final polishing, usually with Moley again by his side.[51]

Roosevelt made the speeches his own in these final sessions, stamping them with the style that enabled him to reach the average American. Although Moley excelled at imposing order on complicated subjects, a close observer of the Brain Trust concluded that "Moley . . . was no match for the incomparable Mr. Roosevelt as a politician and divining rod of public psychology."[52] Moley had taught a course on public opinion, but Roosevelt was the keener student of it.[53] Roosevelt relied on wide newspaper reading, public opinion polling, vast correspondence, and other informal intelligence reports sent in from friendly sources around the country to inform his rhetoric.[54] He combined his informed opinion on the public mood with what Eleanor called "a gift for simplification. He often insisted on putting in simple stories, drawn from conversations with visitors or friends in Warm Springs[, Georgia,] or Hyde Park[, New York]. . . . These illustrations I think helped him to give many people the feeling that he was talking to them in their own living rooms, and that they knew and understood the complicated problems of government."[55]

Moley forever objected to the "speechwriter" label, and Roosevelt's close involvement in drafting almost all his speeches to some extent justifies Moley's objection.[56] But, as Samuel Rosenman later noted, there is also no escaping that "those who are around when [a speech] is being prepared and while it is going through its many drafts, with numerous changes and insertions and deletions, are in a peculiarly strategic position to help shape . . . policy."[57] Moley, Tugwell, and Berle exemplify the type of overlooked behind-the-scenes figure who transforms the way Americans talk—and think—about politics.[58] Despite his aversion to the title, Moley cemented his place as Roosevelt's lead speechwriter in April 1932 and did not relinquish that position fully for four years.[59]

Moley had a lifelong personal and professional interest in politics. It was, he said later, "the absorbing interest of my life."[60] During Roosevelt's governorship, Moley worked his way into Roosevelt's inner circle, thanks largely to his speechwriting skills.[61] Moley "could write brilliantly," Rosenman later recalled, and he could do it quickly.[62] In addition to that rare combination of talents so valuable in politics, Moley excelled at organizing and distilling complicated material and translating it into language the public not only could understand but would also find persuasive.[63] He was, for a time, precisely what Roosevelt wanted and needed: "a high-grade research assistant and literary secretary, an intelligent reliable man who knew where to get facts and ideas, and how to analyze them and put them in usable form."[64]

The exceptional quality of Moley's service to Roosevelt reflected not only the caliber of Moley's mind and rare blend of talents but also Moley's eagerness to play an influential behind-the-scenes role at an inflection point in American history.[65] The work taxed his delicate constitution but also fueled what he called "Wild days and nights of work."[66] The frenetic intellectual energy of Moley's work for Roosevelt comes through clearly in Moley's papers, which contain countless scraps—the literal backs of envelopes and bits of hotel and railroad stationery—covered with words and half-formed sentences as Moley tried to assemble the work of the Brain Trust and other advisors into a coherent vision Roosevelt could sell to the country.[67] Dozens of letters Moley wrote to his wife Eva during the campaign reveal that Moley found the experience exhilarating, exhausting, and sometimes maddening.[68]

Moley was an asset to the campaign, but his flaws sometimes made him a difficult colleague.[69] He presented the facade of confidence commonly worn by the deeply insecure. Photographers tended to catch him looking slightly down, sporting a smug half smile.[70] Despite, or perhaps because of, his talents, he had a fragile ego. Roosevelt later observed that "Ray was a fellow who needed his hand held often."[71] But Roosevelt held Moley's hand during the 1932 campaign because Moley proved so valuable. Moley cherished the time he spent alone with Roosevelt arguing over policy and wrestling piles of material into final speech form.[72] On election eve, Moley wrote with evident pride to Eva that Roosevelt told him that "he could work with me better than with anyone else."[73]

Finding the Language of Security

Roosevelt's first opportunity to make the case for expanding the government's responsibilities to a national audience, and Moley's first opportunity to showcase his speechwriting skills, came in a short radio speech on April 7, 1932. It was the first campaign speech Moley and Roosevelt wrote together, and it showed the potential power of the partnership.[74] The speech was a remarkable piece of political art. In just ten minutes,

Roosevelt managed not just to preview his views on the government's proper responsibilities and the reasons they needed to expand, but also to portray Herbert Hoover, his potential election opponent, as a negligent and uncaring villain.

Within the first thirty seconds, Roosevelt elevated his speech above politics by telling the audience that "the present condition of our national affairs is too serious to be viewed through partisan eyes for partisan purposes."[75] He compared the crisis the country faced in 1932 to the last "great national emergency—the World War" and said that "in my calm judgment, the nation today faces a more grave emergency than in 1917."[76] Roosevelt then blasted Hoover for failing to meet the emergency with the necessary urgency and accused Hoover of thinking "in terms only of the top of the social and economic structure" at the expense of "the forgotten man at the bottom of the economic pyramid."[77] Roosevelt sketched a few policy proposals he had discussed with his Brain Trust and concluded by arguing that "it is high time to admit with courage that we are in the midst of an emergency at least equal to that of war. Let us mobilize to meet it."[78]

Although in retrospect it might seem unnecessary for Roosevelt to have called the situation an emergency, he had good reasons for doing so. True, the millions of unemployed Americans standing in breadlines and living on ruined farms felt the situation had reached the level of emergency. But not all Americans felt that way, and—more importantly—not all the Americans Roosevelt needed to vote for him and support his agenda felt that way. To persuade them that the government's responsibilities needed to expand, Roosevelt first had to convince them an emergency was at hand. But even if he succeeded in doing so, the circumstance and time-limited language of emergency provided only a temporary solution, and Roosevelt had a long-term project in mind.[79] Roosevelt needed a more durable overarching ideal toward which he could orient his reconstruction proposals and a unifying language with which to give them coherence.

The language of security emerged as a potential answer in Brain Trust discussions in mid-April. Rexford Tugwell and Adolf Berle dominated the conversations in Roosevelt's Albany drawing room in those crucial weeks.[80] Just as Moley was solidifying his place as lead speechwriter, so too were Tugwell and Berle cementing their places as leading idea

generators. Tugwell established himself first, both because his membership in the Brain Trust predated Berle's by a couple of weeks and because
he captured Roosevelt's attention almost immediately during their first
conversation.[81] This reflected not only Tugwell's amiability but also the
unusual passion and energy the forty-two-year-old Columbia economics
professor brought to his subject. "Rex was like a cocktail," Moley recalled.
"His conversation picked you up and made your brain race along."[82]

Roosevelt's receptivity to Tugwell's ideas also reflected the pleasure
that comes with having one's views confirmed by an outside authority.
Tugwell agreed with Roosevelt about the basic interdependence of the
community, whether at the state level or the national level, and expounded
on this point at length in diagnosing the problems facing the country.
Tugwell also shared Roosevelt's passion for conservation and got along
well with the Roosevelt family.[83] For all these reasons, Roosevelt was quite
open to what Tugwell had to say. And Tugwell probably framed key points
in the language of security, for when he began to translate into memo form
what he had told Roosevelt, Tugwell wrote of the need to foster "such a
general security that individuals will find it possible to cooperate rather
than to compete."[84]

When Adolf Berle joined and quickly began to dominate the Brain
Trust conversations during the week of April 10, 1932, he likely continued
in the same vein, picking up the language of security and running with it.[85]
Like Tugwell, Berle had wrestled with the causes of the Depression before he joined the Brain Trust and had well-formed views on the topic.[86]
Over the previous months, Berle—then thirty-seven years old—had been
a leading participant in a coffee klatch of bright young men associated
with the New York financial world. This group met from time to time to
discuss the economic calamity and to devise solutions to it.[87] Berle had
volunteered to write a memo summarizing the group's conclusions and
was working on it when he first joined the Brain Trust.[88] Whether because he had come to it already or because Tugwell prompted him, Berle
placed the language of security at the center of his memo.[89] More and
more, Tugwell's and Berle's thinking blended and came to be reflected,
along with the language of security, in the speeches Moley and Roosevelt
crafted together.

The language of security first appeared in a major Roosevelt speech at a Jefferson Day dinner in St. Paul, Minnesota, on April 18, 1932. Working together, Roosevelt and his advisors crafted an interpretation of Thomas Jefferson's views that supported Roosevelt's belief in the interdependence of all Americans and the importance of planning.[90] In one of the final lines added to the speech, Roosevelt said Jefferson had taught Americans that "only in a large, national unity could real security be found."[91] The line showed how Roosevelt and his advisors were beginning to use the language of security to join together and frame their ideas about how to address the Depression while simultaneously restoring the economic liberty they believed modern industrial capitalism had taken from many Americans. Roosevelt spent the rest of the speech making the case for national planning as the sure way to achieve "real security."[92] He said that "the plans we may make for this emergency, if we plan wisely and rest our structure upon a base sufficiently broad, may show the way to a more permanent safeguarding of our social and economic life. . . . In this sense I favor economic planning, not for this period alone but for our needs for a long time to come."[93]

Roosevelt's framing of security as an overarching policy objective and his argument that security required national planning were both new. Consistent themes and phrases run through Roosevelt's rhetoric from the time he entered politics in 1910, but the use of "security" in this way is not one of them.[94] The term does not appear often in his public remarks before 1932—and only once as an overarching ideal or deliberate rhetorical device, in a November 1930 Armistice Day speech in Boston.[95] But once the language of security emerged in Roosevelt's discussions with the Brain Trust in April 1932, Roosevelt and his advisors grasped its special power as a policy objective with inherent rhetorical force and began to place as much of his program as possible into the security frame.[96]

The language of security appeared more prominently in Brain Trust documents in the weeks that followed. With Roosevelt in Warm Springs, Georgia, for the first three weeks of May 1932, the Brain Trust worked furiously to assemble a rough recovery and reconstruction program and translate it into persuasive language Roosevelt could use in the rest of the campaign.[97] Their drafts emphasized the need for the government "to discover a way to provide security for workers and for businesses."[98] The ideas were largely Tugwell's and Berle's, the language part Tugwell, part Berle, part Moley—a true Brain Trust blend. Moley packaged everything in "several large envelopes" and sent them via Samuel Rosenman to Roosevelt in Georgia on May 19.[99] The material arrived just in time for Roosevelt to read through it as he polished a commencement address scheduled for May 22 at Oglethorpe University.[100]

Roosevelt told the Oglethorpe graduates that the country faced a security crisis because government had failed to play an active enough part in planning the country's growth.[101] He ripped Hoover and his allies for selling a "dazzling chimera" of prosperity that had "vanished."[102] Amid the false, "happy optimism of those days," Roosevelt argued, "there existed lack of plan and a great waste."[103] For "millions of our fellow citizens," the resulting crash had led to the loss of "that sense of security to which they have rightly felt they are entitled in a land abundantly endowed with natural resources and with productive facilities to convert them into the necessities of life for all of our population."[104] Roosevelt argued that more active and intelligent government planning provided the route back to security.

But Roosevelt acknowledged that the public would have to be persuaded to embrace planning. So too, Roosevelt said, would its elected representatives, for "too many so-called leaders of the Nation . . . fail to recognize the vital necessity of planning for definite objectives."[105] The country's next leader, Roosevelt suggested, had to educate and persuade. "True leadership calls for the setting forth of the objectives and the rallying of public opinion in support of these objectives," he declared.[106] "When the Nation becomes substantially united in favor of planning the broad objectives of civilization, then true leadership must unite thought behind definite methods."[107]

Security dominated Brain Trust discussions when Roosevelt returned from the South in late May. Adolf Berle had completed work on a detailed memorandum on "The Nature of the Difficulty" with Louis Faulkner, an analyst at the Bank of New York and Trust Company.[108] Roosevelt and his advisors discussed the memo several times at the end of May.[109] The root of the problem, Berle and Faulkner wrote, was individual economic insecurity, which reflected widespread anxiety about "Security of Savings" and "Security of Work."[110] "Both as a matter of sound economics and decent humanity," Berle and Faulkner wrote, "an economic policy of the government ought to be adopted towards the restoration of individual safety."[111] Berle and Faulkner also offered the crucial insight that "the reality of the security is almost immaterial; the psychological effect of the security is the real force at work."[112] In other words, prioritizing economic security was both good policy and good politics.

The language of security featured prominently in Roosevelt's Democratic nomination acceptance speech, which Moley began drafting in early June. The word "security" appeared seven times in the first draft.[113] The speech went through extensive revisions, with Roosevelt striking sentences and instructing Moley to "boil" paragraphs and entire sections, and then Roosevelt and Rosenman making a final series of edits in the days around the convention.[114] But the language of security retained its prominent place. Roosevelt had needed a narrative to explain to Americans how their problems had come about and how they could be fixed. The language of security gave him that narrative. He said the problem was insecurity and the answer was for the government to provide security. Roosevelt had also wanted to be able to speak to people in all parts of the country in the same terms, and to win them over to his view of the government's proper responsibilities. The language of security enabled him to do that too. It provided a highly-desired overarching objective for the government and a unifying language Roosevelt could use to frame his policy proposals.

Although the 1932 Democratic platform did not make security a focus for the party, Roosevelt made it one with his acceptance speech. Roosevelt appeared on the speakers' platform at the Democratic National Convention in Chicago Stadium at 6:00 p.m. on July 2. He looked fresh and buoyant in his blue suit, untroubled by the bumpy, hours-long airplane ride that had carried him to Chicago.[115] The audience rose and cheered as he made his way to the podium, forgetting their accumulated fatigue from the preceding days and nights.[116] After apologizing for arriving late, he came to the point: "never in history have the interests of all the people been so united in a single economic problem."[117] Agriculture and industry depended on each other, and everyone else depended on agriculture and industry. Therefore, he asked rhetorically, "what is the measure of security of each of those groups?" He answered that the security of one depended on the security of all: "danger to one is danger to all."[118] The liberty of the individual and the liberty of the community depended on each other, and both depended on security.

His program, he said, "is based upon this simple moral principle: the welfare and the soundness of a Nation depend first upon what the great mass of the people wish and need; and secondly, whether or not they are getting it."[119] He continued,

> What do the people of America want more than anything else? In my mind, two things: work—work with all the moral and spiritual values that go with work; and with work, a reasonable measure of security— security for themselves and for their wives and children. Work and security—these are more than words. They are more than facts. They are the spiritual values, the true goal towards which our efforts of reconstruction should lead. These are the values that this program is intended to gain; these are the values we have failed to achieve by the leadership we now have.[120]

What Roosevelt said next showed that he agreed with Berle and Faulkner that insecurity was as much a psychological condition as a material one and that the government had to address both aspects of the problem.[121] The country needed "bold leadership," Roosevelt told the crowd in Chicago, and "action" to "drive out that spectre of insecurity from our midst."[122] He charged that "Republican leaders not only have failed in material things, they have failed in national vision, because in disaster they have held out no hope, they have pointed out no path for the people below to climb back to places of security and of safety in our American life."[123] In closing, Roosevelt promised that the government under his leadership would point out such a path and provide "a new deal for the American people."[124] The speech made clear that the government provision of security would be this new deal's basis.

Campaigning on Security

Roosevelt's first post-nomination campaign speech mattered less for its content—a recapitulation of the Democratic platform—than for its tone and method of delivery.[125] On Saturday night July 30, 1932, Roosevelt took to the airwaves in what he said he hoped would be the first of many such encounters with Americans in their homes during the campaign through the transformative medium of radio.[126] He spent hours with Moley, Rosenman, and Tugwell fine-tuning the speech, working with them until past midnight in the nights leading up to the speech to find the right tone.[127] Speaking in a warm, reassuring voice, he said, "I want you to hear me tonight as I sit here in my own home, away from the excitement of the campaign, and with only a few of the family and a few personal friends present."[128] Roosevelt penciled in the part about family and friends at the last minute to add to the feeling of intimacy he sought to produce in his listeners.[129] As governor of New York, Roosevelt had embraced radio as a way of speaking directly to the people of his state and building a rapport with them.[130] Now he hoped to achieve the same thing on a national level.

The contemporaneous emergence of broadcast radio as a means of reaching most Americans was a stroke of immeasurable good fortune for Roosevelt. The term "broadcasting" emerged in 1921, and NBC and CBS began broadcasting in 1926 and 1928, respectively.[131] By the early 1930s, nearly two-thirds of American households had radios and Americans spent in aggregate nearly a billion hours a week listening.[132] As a result, radio presented an unprecedented opportunity to influence large numbers of Americans.[133]

In addition to the reach radio provided, Roosevelt benefited from the peculiar features of radio that make it uniquely powerful. Radio is a participatory medium whose power derives from listeners having to use their imaginations to visualize what they are hearing.[134] Radio's participatory nature creates openings to shape thoughts, identities, and perceptions of reality.[135] Psychiatrist Anthony Storr argues that, "at an emotional level, there is something 'deeper' about hearing than seeing; and something about hearing other people which fosters human relationships even more than seeing them."[136] Building on Storr's insight, Susan Douglas notes in her history of radio that the medium encourages "us to construct imagined communities."[137] Roosevelt relied on radio to foster an imagined community that he hoped would form the basis of a sweeping and lasting political realignment.[138] Roosevelt also exploited the power of radio to achieve the narrative construction of reality in ways more direct, widespread, and frequent than possible before.[139]

Roosevelt arguably performed even better on radio than in person. Eleanor attributed his success to his voice, which "lent itself remarkably to the radio. It was a natural gift."[140] In many ways, the warm, reassuring Roosevelt made headway simply by appearing on the airwaves because, as Douglas notes, radio "provides people with a sense of security that silence does not."[141] Frances Perkins attributed Roosevelt's success to his ability to visualize the people on the other end of the broadcast: "He saw them gathered in the little parlor, listening with their neighbors. He was conscious of their faces and hands, their clothes and homes. . . . As he talked his head would nod and his hands would move in simple, natural, comfortable gestures. His face would smile and light up as though he were actually sitting on the front porch or in the parlor with them."[142] That this aspect of Roosevelt's personality was natural only made it more effective politically.[143] As one listener put it after Roosevelt's radio performances led him to abandon the Republican Party, "all that man has to do is speak on the radio, and the sound of his voice, his sincerity, and the manner of his delivery, just melts me and I change my mind."[144]

Roosevelt concluded his July 30, 1932, radio address by reminding the audience that at the Democratic convention he had pledged to "recover economic liberty."[145] He elaborated on how he proposed to expand the government's responsibilities toward that end in an August 20, 1932, speech at Columbus, Ohio, sharpening the contrast with the more limited vision for government the Republican Party had endorsed at its recent convention. Herbert Hoover had focused on what the government ought *not* do in his speech accepting the Republican nomination for a second term as president. "It is not the function of the Government," Hoover had declared, "to relieve individuals of their responsibilities to their neighbors, or to relieve private institutions of their responsibilities to the public, or the local government to the States, or the responsibilities of State governments to the Federal Government."[146]

Roosevelt, by contrast, told the Columbus audience what he thought the government *should* do. "I believe that the Government, without becoming a prying bureaucracy, can act as a check or counterbalance to this oligarchy so as to secure the chance to work and the safety of savings to men and women, rather than safety of exploitation to the exploiter, safety of manipulation to the financial manipulators, safety of unlicensed power to those who would speculate to the bitter end with the welfare and property of other people."[147] Roosevelt also charged Hoover with hiding behind the "sacred word" of liberty, adding, "I believe that the individual should have full liberty of action to make the most of himself; but I do not believe that in the name of that sacred word a few powerful interests should be permitted to make industrial cannon-fodder of the lives of half of the population of the United States."[148] The government, Roosevelt implied, should prevent that from happening. Roosevelt ended by accusing Hoover of exacerbating the Depression by weakening Americans' trust in "our National leadership."[149] Roosevelt argued that Americans must be able to trust their leaders because "without that kind of confidence we are forever insecure."[150]

Roosevelt spent September traveling the country, delivering a handful of major speeches and many brief ones from his train's open rear platform. Although in public Roosevelt called it "an educational trip for me," he admitted to a private audience in Denver that he saw the trip as an opportunity to educate the public on a grand scale and thereby build support for his agenda.[151] Roosevelt instructed Moley to put "something new or a new slant in every [speech]," but also insisted the theme of "safety" be ever present.[152] In his coordinating role from his compartment in Roosevelt's train, drowning in half-filled legal pads and piles of reference books and background material, Moley ensured the common denominator was the need for the government to provide security for Americans, including through planning.[153] Roosevelt told a farm audience in Topeka, Kansas, that "national planning in agriculture" provided one of the clearest answers to their troubles.[154] He told a railroad audience in Salt Lake City, Utah, that "one chief cause of the great present railroad problem has been that typical cause of many of our problems—the entire absence of any national planning."[155] Planning, Roosevelt said, represented a crucial part of "the road to economic safety."[156]

Roosevelt told the private audience in Denver that he kept hammering these points because he believed the public was "thinking these days more than ever before about the principles of government."[157] He took advantage of the opening created by the Depression to "teach them some of the fundamentals" of the new political economy he championed.[158] He acknowledged that "the education of the electorate takes a long time. It can't be done even in one campaign."[159] But the potential payoff warranted the effort: "If we once get them in this campaign, we are going to hold them, not for one year, or four years, but for a generation to come."[160] Based on the response he had received so far, Roosevelt predicted that "we are about to enter into a new period of liberalism in the United States."[161]

Roosevelt provided the fullest elaboration of the new liberalism in a speech at the Commonwealth Club in San Francisco, California, on September 23, 1932. He invited the audience "to consider with me in the large, some of the relationships of government and economic life that go deeply into our daily lives, our happiness, our future and our security."[162] He then provided a history lesson, noting that "the Declaration of Independence discusses the problem of government in terms of a contract. . . . Under such a contract rulers were accorded power, and the people consented to that power on consideration that they be accorded certain rights."[163] Turning to his belief in the need for the government's responsibilities to evolve with the times, Roosevelt said "the task of statesmanship has always been the re-definition of these rights in terms of a changing and growing social order. New conditions impose new requirements upon government and those who conduct government."[164]

In the present moment, Roosevelt declared, "the task of government . . . is to assist the development of an economic declaration of rights, an economic constitutional order" and said the government guarantee of these economic rights "is the minimum requirement of a more permanently safe order of things."[165] He argued the United States did not lack abundance, but that "our government formal and informal, political and economic, owes to everyone an avenue to possess himself of a portion of that plenty sufficient for his needs, through his own work."[166] He declared the rights to life and property fundamental but added that "individual liberty and individual happiness mean nothing unless both are ordered in the sense that one man's meat is not another man's poison."[167] This idea was a central pillar of Roosevelt's argument for expanding the government's responsibilities. It was a natural evolution of the point Roosevelt first made in 1912 as a New York state senator when he said the government must ensure the "liberty of the community," not just individual liberty.[168]

Roosevelt concluded by echoing a point he made in his Oglethorpe speech in May: "Government includes the art of formulating a policy, and using the political technique to attain so much of that policy as will receive general support; persuading, leading, sacrificing, teaching always, because the greatest duty of a statesman is to educate."[169] Except Roosevelt wasn't only educating on the campaign trail. He was using the language of security to transform people's perceptions of the proper responsibilities of the government under a new conception of liberalism.[170] Up to that point in American history, "liberals" generally had opposed expanding the government and defined liberty as individual freedom *from* the government. Roosevelt now said liberalism meant expanding the government's responsibilities to guarantee not only individual liberty but also the liberty of the community. In other words, Roosevelt argued that liberty in modern times depended on government action to ensure economic security.

Roosevelt's appropriation and redefinition of the "liberal" label reflected careful political calculation. A marked-up draft of a September 1932 speech in Milwaukee, Wisconsin, shows that Roosevelt and Moley crossed out "progressivism" and "progressive" and replaced them with "liberalism" and "liberal."[171] Roosevelt's use of the "liberal" label allowed him to frame his policies as consistent with American political tradition and deprived his opponents of one of their primary rhetorical weapons. The language of security provided the rationale for expanding the government's responsibilities under Roosevelt's new Democratic Party–led liberalism. With Americans struggling to make ends meet during the Depression, Roosevelt argued that the government needed to take a more active role in ensuring economic security. After all, Roosevelt said in an October 13, 1932, campaign radio address, the government's most basic responsibility was to protect "the very existence of its citizens."[172] Paired with the language of security, the appropriation and redefinition of liberalism proved a powerful—and, for Roosevelt's opponents, infuriating—rhetorical move.[173]

Raymond Moley concluded the combination was working. Moley had accompanied Roosevelt for nearly the entire railroad trip around the country, helping him craft his speeches. In September 1932, Moley sent Democratic National Committee Chairman Jim Farley a telegram reporting that "enthusiasm for the governor and for his policies has increased from state to state. . . . In many of the cities in the Northwest we were told that people came two and three hundred miles from back in the mountains to greet the governor. . . . The governor was literally deluged with telegraphic appeals from almost every station through which the train was scheduled to pass asking for a stop no matter how brief and an opportunity to greet him."[174] Moley concluded that "there is in process of creation in this campaign a great liberal party, made up of persons of all shades of political belie[fs] accepting as the charter of liberalism the Chicago platform and as their leader the nominee of the Democratic convention. We are making political history these days under Franklin D. Roosevelt."[175]

Roosevelt's use of the language of security to build support for expanding the government's responsibilities under a new liberalism touched a nerve among proponents of limited government. On October 31, 1932, Herbert Hoover delivered a nationally broadcast address from Madison Square Garden in New York City in which he pushed back bitterly against Roosevelt's use of the "liberal" label. "It is a false liberalism that interprets itself into Government operation of business," Hoover declared.[176] "Every step in that direction poisons the very roots of liberalism. . . . True liberalism is found not in striving to spread bureaucracy, but in striving to set bounds of it. . . . Liberalism is a force truly of the spirit proceeding from the deep realization that economic freedom cannot be sacrificed if political freedom is to be preserved."[177] Hoover argued that people like Roosevelt "who are going about this country announcing that they are liberals because of their promises to extend the Government are not liberals; they are the reactionaries of the United States."[178]

For Hoover, the only security the government had to guarantee to its citizens was such that they could be "secure in their liberty"—by which he meant freedom from the government.[179] Overlooking the expansion of the government's responsibilities he had initiated in response to the Great Depression and previewing a future mainstay of conservative rhetoric, Hoover also attacked the government itself and argued that expanding it would ruin the country. "No man who has not occupied my position in

Washington can fully realize the constant battle which must be carried on against incompetence, corruption, tyranny of government expanded into business activities."[180] In sum, Hoover declared, the campaign amounted to "a contest between two philosophies of government."[181]

Roosevelt sat in a Boston hotel room listening to Hoover's speech over the radio and, Moley recalls, "raging over what he had heard."[182] Roosevelt spoke soon after Hoover finished, blasting the president's record and articulating again a starkly different vision of the government's responsibilities. Roosevelt turned Hoover's own record of advocating greater government responsibility for managing the economy against him, citing the "Hoover Report" from the early 1920s in which Hoover, then the commerce secretary, outlined measures the government could—but did not—take to prevent economic downturns.[183] Because the Republican administrations of the 1920s did not take those steps, Roosevelt said, "we have two problems: first, to meet the immediate distress; secondly, to build up on a permanent basis of permanent employment."[184] On the first point, Roosevelt reiterated that the "national Government . . . owes a positive duty that no citizen shall be permitted to starve."[185] On the second point, Roosevelt called once more for planning led by the federal government in partnership with state and local governments and the private sector.[186] Roosevelt's speech made clear, as Rexford Tugwell recalled later, that in a Roosevelt presidency "the federal government would accept responsibility for a balanced economic system."[187]

Roosevelt summarized the new liberalism in New York City on November 3, placing "security" again at the center of it: "Reducing it to all the essentials of my speech of acceptance, we want to get for the American people two great human values—work and security. To achieve this end I invite you all. It is no mere party slogan. It is a definition of national need. It is a philosophy of life. I repeat it with a courage lent by the knowledge that I speak a philosophy of government as well—the ideals which have made us and kept us a nation."[188] That same night, longtime Roosevelt advisor Frances Perkins told a crowd at Tremont Temple in Boston that Roosevelt knew that "what the people of the United States want is security—security of life; security of opportunity to earn a living; security to plan their lives."[189] She said Roosevelt, through an expanded government, would provide that security.[190] The "wild, thrilled applause"

Perkins received made clear to her that the new liberals had struck rhetorical gold with the language of security.[191]

THE COMPETING CONCEPTIONS of the government's proper responsibilities Hoover and Roosevelt put forward in the final days of the 1932 campaign confirmed Hoover's claim that it was "a contest between two philosophies of government."[192] The new liberals, led by Roosevelt, argued that ensuring individual liberty and the liberty of the community required expanding the government's responsibilities to guarantee economic security. The new conservatives, led by Hoover, argued that such action on the part of the government threatened individual liberty.

With these fundamental differences drawn, the campaign drew to a close. Roosevelt had visited nearly every state, traveling some twenty-seven thousand miles.[193] The language of security had proven a powerful weapon of political persuasion. "Security" had provided an overarching ideal toward which Roosevelt could orient his reconstruction proposals and a unifying language with which to give them coherence. Three million voters more than in 1928 cast ballots in the 1932 presidential election.[194] Americans provided an unequivocal verdict on which philosophy of government they preferred. Out of 38.5 million votes cast, the candidate who proposed to expand the government's responsibilities in the name of security as part of a new liberalism won by more than seven million votes and carried forty-two out of the then forty-eight states.[195]

2

The Domestic Policy Origins of the National Security State

DURING THE LONG INTERVAL between Franklin Roosevelt's election in November 1932 and inauguration in March 1933, Americans confirmed Roosevelt's and his advisors' belief that a pervasive sense of insecurity was perpetuating the Depression.[1] In the weeks before Roosevelt's inauguration, Americans besieged their banks, desperate to remove whatever fraction of their funds they could for safekeeping under their mattresses or in coffee tins buried in some secret spot.[2] This frantic behavior testified to the "Security of Savings" Americans felt they had in the winter of 1933: none at all.[3] By the end of February 1933, most banks around the country had closed and the stock market had sunk again.[4] Nearly a quarter of the workforce had no "Security of Work" either.[5] As weeks of unemployment stretched into months and years, a growing number of the unemployed had no hope of work. Many others had their hours and wages reduced. Seeing what was happening all around them, they feared their working days, too, were numbered. In all, half the workforce was unemployed or underemployed.[6]

Roosevelt took aim at this pervasive psychological insecurity within moments of taking the oath of office on March 4, 1933. "This great Nation will endure as it has endured, will revive and will prosper," Roosevelt reassured Americans in the opening lines of his inaugural address.[7] To the crowd of 150,000 gathered at the Capitol and the 50 million radio listeners, Roosevelt said, "Let me assert my firm belief that the only thing we have to fear is fear itself,—nameless, unreasoning, unjustified terror which paralyzes needed efforts to convert retreat into advance."[8] Tommy Corcoran, who would later become one of Roosevelt's closest advisors, recalled thinking while listening to the speech that "the moment was like Excalibur being pulled from the stone. . . . You just had a sense, 'this guy can do it. He can lift us up.'"[9]

Roosevelt promised he would provide the leadership the country needed. As talk of turning "retreat into advance" illustrated, he framed his inaugural address as a military change-of-command ceremony—or, more accurately, as an assumption-of-command ceremony, for he suggested there had been no commander of late.[10] He said that "if we are to go forward, we must move as a trained and loyal army willing to sacrifice for the good of a common discipline, because without such discipline no progress is made, no leadership becomes effective."[11] He added that "we are, I know, ready and willing to submit our lives and property to such discipline, because it makes possible a leadership which aims at a larger good."[12] The larger good was national security by another name—"the assurance of a rounded and *permanent* national life"—and Roosevelt made clear it would be ensured by the government.[13]

During his first term, Roosevelt laid the rhetorical and institutional foundations for the national security state, a new entity in American life. Reflecting the greatest danger facing the country at the time, the national security state focused initially on domestic economic security, not defense against foreign enemies. The immediate priority, Roosevelt said, was "to get the economic system to function so that there will be a greater general security."[14] During the eventful first hundred days of his administration, Roosevelt took unprecedented measures to address the twin problems of "Security of Savings" and "Security of Work."[15] He leaned on the language of security in messages justifying these domestic policies, including by arguing that they were "imperative to our national security."[16] Most of these measures aimed at relief and recovery. The administration turned to the deeper work of reconstruction in 1934 when it began developing what became the Social Security Act, which Roosevelt saw as the "corner stone" of the national security state.[17]

Domestic Economic Policy as National Security Policy

Roosevelt and his advisors knew there could be no long-term security without a stable, functioning financial system. It was to the crumbling financial system, therefore, that they turned first. Roosevelt had promised "action, and action now" in his inaugural address.[18] The day after the inauguration, he invoked the Trading with the Enemy Act to freeze all transactions in gold and shut the country's banks for four days.[19] These measures bought time to work with outgoing Hoover administration Treasury Department officials to devise emergency legislation to address the insecurity fueling the banking crisis.[20] Roosevelt presented this legislation to an emergency session of Congress an hour after it convened on March 9. The new Congress passed the Emergency Banking Act that afternoon and Roosevelt signed it into law that evening.[21] The measure legitimated the steps the Roosevelt administration had taken over the preceding week and gave the administration wide latitude to manage the banking crisis.[22] The Emergency Banking Act also kept the banks closed until Monday, March 13, 1933, allowing Roosevelt to address the American people before the banks reopened.[23]

On Sunday night, March 12, Roosevelt took to the airwaves in the first of what would become known as "fireside chats." Roosevelt's primary objective was to restore public confidence in the financial system, for he understood the financial system depended on public confidence to function. But he also seized the opportunity to use the language of security to transform public expectations of the government's proper responsibilities.[24] To a nationwide radio audience numbering in the tens of millions, Roosevelt said the banking crisis had "shock[ed] the people of the United States for a time into a sense of insecurity."[25] He told the public that it was "the Government's job to straighten out this situation and to do it as quickly as possible."[26]

In simple terms and a calm, optimistic voice, Roosevelt assured Americans that the government had resolved the banking crisis and that they could redeposit their money in banks with confidence.[27] The public responded positively to the message, pouring money back into banks and inundating the president with nearly half a million letters, most thanking him for his leadership.[28] With words no less than deeds, Roosevelt ended the multiyear banking crisis within a fortnight and began expanding the government's economic security responsibilities.[29]

Roosevelt's reassuring voice appeared in Americans' homes again on May 7, 1933.[30] The president said he wished to give the American people his "report . . . about what we have been doing and what we are planning to do."[31] As in his first fireside chat, Roosevelt used the language of security to justify the steps the government was taking to address the Depression. He explained that, if the government had not acted to stabilize the economy, "it is easy to see that the result of this course would have not only economic effects of a very serious nature, but social results also that might bring incalculable harm."[32] He said such a failure to act would have "involved not only a further loss of homes, of farms, and savings and wages, but also a loss of spiritual values—the loss of that sense of security for the present and the future that is so necessary to the peace and contentment of the individual and of his family."[33] The result of continued government inaction, he argued, would have had serious long-term repercussions, because "when you destroy those things you find it difficult to establish confidence of any sort in the future. And it was clear that mere appeals coming out of Washington for more confidence and the mere lending of more money to shaky institutions could not stop that downward course."[34] Therefore, Roosevelt said, his administration's actions were "not only justified but imperative to our national security."[35]

Here was something new and important. The term "national security" had appeared occasionally in American history in a vague, undefined way. Now Roosevelt and his advisors sought to define national security in ways that would advance their agenda. Roosevelt said national security depended on economic security.[36] This definition of national security enabled Roosevelt to invoke that powerful term to justify proposals to expand the government's domestic responsibilities to ensure economic security. The use of "national security" in this way was brilliant politics—but it was also sincere. Roosevelt and his advisors believed what they wrote and understood its significance. While working on the May 7 fireside chat together, lead speechwriter Raymond Moley asked Roosevelt, "You realize, then, that you're taking an enormous step away from the philosophy of equalitarianism and laissez-faire?" Roosevelt replied, "If that philosophy hadn't proved to be bankrupt, Herbert

Hoover would be sitting here right now. I never felt surer of anything in my life."[37]

The language of security's greater prominence in Roosevelt's second fireside chat than in his first reflected Moley's larger role in drafting the second address.[38] Moley prepared the initial draft containing the crucial phrase that the administration's actions were "not only justified but imperative to our national security."[39] Moley's draft did other important work for Roosevelt too. It helped Roosevelt convey that he understood the heavy toll insecurity had taken on Americans. It also helped Roosevelt head off charges of radicalism by emphasizing that the administration's actions were "constitutional and in keeping with the past American tradition."[40] Finally, as in many of the campaign speeches Moley and Roosevelt wrote together, the fireside chat included the statement that the country's troubles had "been caused in large part by a complete lack of planning."[41] By contrast, Roosevelt told the country, "the legislation which has been passed or in the process of enactment can properly be considered as part of a well-grounded, well-rounded plan."[42]

The first parts of the plan emerged during the first hundred days of Roosevelt's presidency at a rate that astonished observers at the time and has stood as a benchmark for incoming presidential administrations ever since. In short order, Roosevelt secured legislation that began to provide the "Security of Work" he and his advisors considered essential.[43] On May 12, 1933, Roosevelt signed the Agricultural Adjustment Act, a complicated hodgepodge of a bill that gave the executive branch wide flexibility to address the agricultural elements of the economic crisis.[44] Through the Agricultural Adjustment Act, the Roosevelt administration hoped to increase the economic security of farmers by increasing the prices they received for their output.

A little over a month later, Roosevelt signed the National Industrial Recovery Act, which he hoped would boost the economic security of other large groups of Americans. The legislation created a National Recovery Administration intended to boost businesses' sense of security by fostering cooperation within sectors with the goal of reducing what Roosevelt and his advisors—and many business leaders—saw as excessive competition. The act also gave the government power to set maximum hours and minimum wages and guaranteed labor's right to organize and bargain collectively, thereby boosting workers' sense of security. Finally, the act established a federal public works organization to create work and inject money into the economy, thereby providing the economic stimulus business badly needed and boosting the economic security of everyone the program touched.[45]

Like the measures taken to stabilize the financial system, the Agricultural Adjustment Act and the National Industrial Recovery Act solidified the precedent that the government would assume greater responsibility for Americans' economic security. Together, the two acts also opened the door for Roosevelt and his advisors to experiment with ways of restoring balance between the agricultural and industrial sectors of the economy.[46] In the main, however, all these measures amounted to short-term efforts to promote recovery by stabilizing the economy. Roosevelt and his advisors recognized them as such, but they believed economic recovery was an essential prerequisite for the broader institutional remodeling that would lead to permanent national security. Over the following year, the Roosevelt administration began moving beyond simply trying to ensure the country's survival and set its sights on the loftier goal of modernizing the country's institutions.

Laying the Rhetorical Foundation for the National Security State

As early as January 1932, six months before he had secured the Democratic nomination for president, Roosevelt had said, "Let us not seek merely to restore. Let us restore and at the same time remodel."[47] In April 1932, Roosevelt and his advisors had begun trying to think of ways to explain the need to modernize the country's institutions, scribbling the following during a speech drafting session: "If you live in a house that has been shaken by an earthquake of national proportions and the foundations have cracked and the roof leaks it is right to mend the roof but at the same time your house will not be safe until you have repaired the foundation as well. I want the house to stand through all the years to come as well as to keep the rain out of the top story."[48] Now, in 1934, after more than a year of work on the country's roof, Roosevelt and his advisors were ready to work on its foundation. As Roosevelt told Congress in his annual message on January 3, 1934, the time had come "to build on the ruins of the past a new structure designed better to meet the present problems of modern civilization."[49] This new structure would focus on ensuring economic security.

Roosevelt offered additional details on his plans to institutionalize the government's economic security responsibilities in a series of messages in June 1934. Roosevelt and Moley crafted the messages together in Roosevelt's office.[50] Their notes and drafts show how security continued to serve as both the organizing principle for Roosevelt's approach to the Depression and as the persuasive shorthand to sell his policies to the public.[51] Roosevelt and Moley took as their point of departure the idea that, as Moley wrote in an early draft, "the quest for security is one of the most powerful of human instincts."[52] In another early draft, Moley captured the psychological dimension of security that the Roosevelt administration had worked so hard to address during its first year in office: "Far greater than the desire on the part of the average family to attain great riches is their longing for great security. Already we have taken and are taking steps to prevent the loss of thousands of farms and homes and to enable honest people, willing to work, to obtain new homes or better homes."[53] In so doing, Moley wrote, "we have shown the world that democracy has within it the elements necessary to its own salvation."[54]

The "next phase," Moley scribbled in notes from conversations with Roosevelt while working on the messages, required building a more durable structure of "triple security."[55] An early Moley draft previewed the two main lines of effort the administration planned to follow in its endeavor to build a national security state, as well as the order in which the administration planned to proceed: "Next year the government of the United States w[i]ll undertake two other great tasks, both in furtherance of the security of the family. One of these deals with social insurance—not insurance against one evil contingency alone, but insurance which will cover all the principal risks to which the members of a family may in ordinary course be subjected. The other is . . . the better use of the land and the water which God has given us."[56]

Roosevelt and his advisors hoped that placing reconstruction proposals under the umbrella of "security" would make them more difficult to oppose, create pressure for rapid—and deferential—congressional action, and make it harder for the judiciary to strike them down. Just as in the 1932 campaign and administration's early days, Roosevelt and Moley believed that in "security" they had found a persuasive frame they could use to justify and sustain public support for expanding the government's domestic responsibilities.

Roosevelt prepared the legislative ground in a June 4, 1934, message to Congress on flood control, which he framed as a vital element of a broader program for national security. In a closing paragraph he dictated to Moley, Roosevelt said, "I expect before the final adjournment of this Congress to forward to it a broader outline of national policy in which the subject matter of this message will be presented in conjunction with two other subjects also relating to human welfare and security."[57] Roosevelt scribbled in one final sentence repeating a point from his inaugural address, that "we should proceed toward a rounded policy of national scope."[58] As in his inaugural address, the objective of the "rounded policy of national scope" was national security.

Roosevelt made that objective even more explicit four days later in another message to Congress, saying that "among our objectives I place the security of the men, women and children of the Nation first."[59] He then swept several large areas of domestic policy into the national security frame: "This security for the individual and for the family concerns itself primarily with three factors. People want decent homes to live in; they want to locate them where they can engage in productive work; and they want some safeguard against misfortunes which cannot be wholly eliminated in this man-made world of ours."[60]

Roosevelt also reiterated his belief that, in an interdependent world, individual liberty depended on the liberty of the community—and that the government guarantee of economic security held the key to restoring and maintaining both individual and community liberty. Turning to a narrative he would rely on again and again, Roosevelt noted how in earlier times people could achieve security for themselves, with the help of family members and their communities, but emphasized that times had changed. "The complexities of great communities and of organized industry make less real these simple means of security," Roosevelt said.[61] "Therefore, we are compelled to employ the active interest of the Nation as a whole through government in order to encourage a greater security for each individual who composes it."[62] Individual liberty, in other words, had come to depend on government action.

If, as Roosevelt and his advisors continued to believe, economic insecurity presented the most pressing modern problem, then the government had to provide economic security. Doing so was consistent with the Constitution, Roosevelt said, because "fear and worry based on unknown danger contribute to social unrest and economic demoralization. If, as our Constitution tells us, our Federal Government was established among other things 'to promote the general welfare,' it is our plain duty to provide for that security upon which welfare depends."[63] Roosevelt concluded by arguing that a government guarantee of economic security constituted a right of citizenship in modern times: "These three great objectives—the security of the home, the security of livelihood, and the security of social insurance—are, it seems to me, a minimum of the promise that we can offer to the American people. They constitute a right which belongs to every individual and every family willing to work."[64] By institutionalizing the government's responsibility for economic security, the Roosevelt administration hoped to make this last point—that economic security was a "right"—tangible, thereby solidifying a central element of the new liberalism Roosevelt had sketched on the campaign trail in 1932.

Roosevelt knew proponents of limited government would fight his latest proposal to expand the government's responsibilities for economic security but dismissed such opposition as selfish. He told his National Emergency Council on June 26 to expect "a great deal of shooting at the government during the next few months" and "that a large part of the shooting . . . will come either from merely political sources or will come from people whose toes have been stepped on."[65] The reason, Roosevelt explained, was that "the government is being run less for political purposes and more for the general good than it has been in some time."[66]

As he often did when facing a political persuasion challenge, Roosevelt took his economic security policy proposals directly to the American people. In a fireside chat on June 28, 1934, Roosevelt reiterated the animating goal of his administration: "we seek the security of the men, women and children of the Nation."[67] As he did on the campaign trail in 1932 and in his second fireside chat in May 1933, Roosevelt pushed back against the charge that what his administration proposed amounted to something alien: "A few timid people, who fear progress, will try to give you new and strange names for what we are doing. Sometimes they will call it 'Fascism,' sometimes 'Communism,' sometimes 'Regimentation,' sometimes 'Socialism.' But, in so doing, they are trying to make very complex and theoretical something that is really very simple and very practical. . . . I believe that what we are doing today is a necessary fulfillment of what Americans have always been doing—a fulfillment of old and tested American ideals."[68] Using the simple language for which he was famous, Roosevelt compared his reconstruction proposals to the impending White House renovation, both of which, he said, represented necessary modernization projects carefully designed to bring things up to date without jettisoning the valued past. Roosevelt argued that "it is this combination of the old and the new that marks orderly peaceful progress, not only in building buildings but in building government itself."[69]

On the day following the fireside chat, Roosevelt set that state-building process in motion by issuing Executive Order 6757 "The Initiation of Studies to Achieve a Program of National Social and Economic Security."[70] The executive order established the Committee on Economic Security and the Advisory Council on Economic Security. Roosevelt gave the committee a broad mandate, charging it with studying "problems relating to the economic security of individuals."[71] He appointed Secretary of Labor Frances Perkins to lead the committee and gave the group until December to develop its recommendations.[72]

From the beginning of Roosevelt's presidency, Perkins had led the push to expand the government's economic security responsibilities, just as she had during Roosevelt's governorship. When Perkins met with Roosevelt in February 1933 at his townhouse on East 65th Street in Manhattan to discuss a cabinet role in his administration, she brought a to-do list for his presidency.[73] The list represented Perkins's vision for the government's responsibilities to its citizens and included items such as old-age pensions, unemployment insurance, and medical insurance. Although Roosevelt expressed doubts about some of her proposals, he agreed they warranted study and said he would support her.[74]

After Roosevelt's inauguration and Perkins's swearing-in as labor secretary, Perkins raised the need for unemployment insurance at every other cabinet meeting and made dozens of speeches around the country on the topic.[75] In December 1933, Perkins wrote to Roosevelt assistant Marvin McIntyre suggesting Roosevelt propose unemployment insurance in his 1934 State of the Union address, but Roosevelt demurred.[76] He understood the importance of timing in politics. As he told Perkins on one occasion, voters needed to remember what you had done for them. Better to introduce major initiatives and pass laws closer to election day.[77]

In the meantime, Roosevelt and Perkins encouraged Senator Robert Wagner (D-NY) and Representative David J. Lewis (D-MD) to advance legislation authorizing unemployment insurance.[78] Perkins later recalled that "it was evident to us that any system of social insurance would not relieve the accumulated poverty. Nor would it relieve the sufferings of the presently old and needy. Nevertheless, it was also evident that this was the time, above all times, to be foresighted about future problems of unemployment and unprotected old age."[79] By mid-1934, the Wagner-Lewis bill had stalled. Roosevelt felt the time was right to give the issue a more direct presidential push ahead of the midterm elections and leading up to the 1936 presidential campaign.[80] Roosevelt and his advisors still believed that increasing the government's economic security responsibilities was not only good policy but also good politics.

Just as it had in 1932, the language of security proved a powerful political resource for liberal Democrats in the 1934 midterms. Roosevelt and his advisors knew they still had much work to do codifying the expansion of the government's responsibilities and needed solid majorities in Congress to achieve their goals. To that end, in August 1934 Roosevelt traveled around the Western half of the country rallying support for his policies ahead of the midterms. He visited sites like the Bonneville Dam to highlight the government's contributions to the economic security of people and communities.[81]

Roosevelt continued campaigning after returning to the White House. In a fireside chat at the end of September 1934, Roosevelt quoted Abraham Lincoln to justify the expansion of the government's domestic responsibilities: "I believe with Abraham Lincoln, that 'The legitimate object of Government is to do for a community of people whatever they need to have done but cannot do at all or cannot do so well for themselves in their separate and individual capacities.'"[82] Roosevelt continued, "I am not for a return to that definition of liberty under which for many years a free people were being gradually regimented into the service of the privileged few."[83] Instead, Roosevelt argued for his concept of positive liberty, with the government guarantee of economic security at its center: "I prefer and I am sure you prefer that broader definition of liberty under which we are moving forward to greater freedom, to greater security for the average man than he has ever known before in the history of America."[84] Roosevelt also played on Americans' rivalry with their old colonial overlord, asking rhetorically, "Is it not a fact that ever since the year 1909, Great Britain in many ways has advanced further along lines of social security than the United States?"[85]

In a nationally broadcast October 9, 1934, speech to the Chicago Rotary Club, Roosevelt advisor Donald Richberg invoked the specter of a return to insecurity to explain why the government needed to take further steps to institutionalize responsibility for economic security. "Many of the problems made acute by the depression will persist," Richberg warned, "until we have devised permanent safeguards against destructive economic forces that will perennially threaten individual and national security if left uncontrolled."[86]

Roosevelt and his advisors' use of the language of security to justify their policies put their opponents in the untenable position of arguing against the government providing something many Americans craved. The promise of economic security helped liberal Democrats expand their majorities in Congress in the 1934 midterms.[87] The Democratic gains enabled the Roosevelt administration to pursue more ambitious legislation to construct a national security state. As Roosevelt advisor Harry Hopkins told colleagues shortly after the election, "This is our hour. We've got to get everything we want—a works program, social security, wages and hours, everything—now or never. Get your minds to work on developing a complete ticket to provide security for all the folks of this country up and down and across the board."[88]

The ~~Economic~~ Social Security Act

Frances Perkins convened the National Conference on Economic Security in Washington, DC, a week after the midterms. The conference underscored Perkins's position as the country's preeminent security professional. Since she was now leading the effort to create national-level economic security programs like unemployment insurance and old-age pensions, it could even be said of her that she was the country's first national security professional. At the event, Perkins showed that she shared Roosevelt's talent for linguistic appropriation by laying claim to two of conservatives' favorite words: "liberty" and "freedom." She declared that "there is among us today a new concept of the old doctrines of liberty and equality" and added that "we are today fighting for freedom—freedom from insecurity and uncertainty."[89] She argued that Americans "are looking to the President and to the Congress to take measures to give them that security which has been so woefully lacking in the past."[90] She interpreted the recent midterm results as evidence that the public supported the administration's economic security agenda.[91] As her remarks made clear, the operative assumption of the conference was that government had an essential, constructive role to play in providing economic security.

Perkins and other conference speakers situated the American effort to provide economic security in a global context, noting that for decades industrialized countries had grappled with the economic insecurity that accompanied modern industrial capitalism. As Roosevelt had in his September 30, 1934, fireside chat, Perkins and other speakers acknowledged that the United States had fallen behind other countries in the effort to address this issue.[92] Speakers also rebutted some of the more common criticisms leveled at economic security policy proposals, including that similar efforts had failed abroad. Perkins noted, for instance, that "in no country except Russia has unemployment insurance, once started, been abandoned or even suspended."[93] But, sensitive to domestic politics, conference speakers struck a balance between using international comparison to encourage greater American action while also avoiding the suggestion that the United States simply import some foreign scheme. As Harold Butler put it delicately after providing some instructive international comparisons in his remarks on "International Progress Toward Social Security," "Foreign experiences are useful up to a point, as showing the shoals to be avoided, and perhaps pointing to some channels which are probably safe for navigation, but beyond that I should not be disposed to go. . . . Each nation has got to be its own pilot and chart its own course, taking advantage, of course, of such indications as may safely be derived from the previous experience of others."[94]

When Roosevelt met with the Advisory Council of the Committee on Economic Security on November 14, 1934, he emphasized the need to move forward with economic security proposals. As on so many other occasions, Roosevelt made the case for why individual liberty depended on the liberty of the community. He said, "There can be no security for the individual in the midst of general insecurity."[95] But he also sounded a note of caution: "We cannot work miracles or solve all our problems at once. What we can do is to lay a sound foundation on which we can build a structure to give a greater measure of safety and happiness to the individual than any we have ever known."[96] Roosevelt wanted to make sure the people developing his administration's economic security programs understood that they were playing a long game.

In his January 4, 1935, annual message to Congress, Roosevelt previewed the economic security legislation he would soon propose. He reminded the legislators of his June 1934 message, "in which I said: 'among our objectives I place the security of the men, women and children of the Nation first.' That remains our first and continuing task."[97] Roosevelt added that "in a very real sense every major legislative enactment of this Congress should be a component part of it."[98] He said that soon he would be sending "a broad program designed ultimately to establish all three of these factors of security—a program which because of many lost years will take many future years to fulfill."[99] Roosevelt said that "a comprehensive survey of what has been attempted or accomplished in many Nations and in many States proves to me that the time has come for action by the National Government" to provide "security against the major hazards of life."[100] He promised he would "send to you, in a few days, definite recommendations based on these studies. These recommendations will cover the broad subjects of unemployment insurance and old age insurance, of benefits for children, for mothers, for the handicapped, for maternity care and for other aspects of dependency and illness where a beginning can now be made."[101]

The timeline the president announced for delivery of his economic security legislative proposals spurred the Committee on Economic Security to finish its work.[102] After the president appointed Frances Perkins head of the Committee on Economic Security at the end of June 1934, Perkins had brought in Edwin E. Witte, an economist who had worked on related issues for the state of Wisconsin, as executive director and Thomas H. Eliot, a Labor Department lawyer, as general counsel.[103] In December and January, Witte worked feverishly on the committee's final report while Eliot raced through drafts and redrafts of the legislation Roosevelt intended to send to Congress.[104] The committee formally sent the president its recommendations on January 15, 1935, and the president sent his proposed Economic Security Act, drafted by Eliot, to Congress two days later.[105] In its report, the committee emphasized that "even in the 'normal times' of the prosperous [nineteen] twenties, a large part of our population had little security" and that "throughout the [nineteen] twenties, the number of people dependent upon private and public charity steadily increased."[106] The antidote to the rampant and increasing insecurity associated with modern industrial capitalism, the committee argued, was "an assured income."[107]

In his message to Congress transmitting the Committee's report and his proposed Economic Security Act, Roosevelt noted that "most of the other advanced countries of the world have already adopted it and their experience affords the knowledge that social insurance can be made a sound and workable project."[108] But he also repeated the cautionary point he had made to the Advisory Council of the Committee on Economic Security in November. He emphasized that "it is overwhelmingly important to avoid any danger of permanently discrediting the sound and necessary policy of federal legislation for economic security by attempting to apply it on too ambitious a scale before actual experience has provided guidance for the permanently safe direction of such efforts. The place of such a fundamental in our future civilization is too precious to be jeopardized now by extravagant action."[109] Roosevelt preferred to lay a solid, if somewhat narrow, foundation rather than trying to get everything he and his advisors ultimately wanted—national health insurance, for example—right away.

The Economic Security Act became the Social Security Act as the bill moved through Congress. Committee on Economic Security Executive Director Edwin Witte explains this important rhetorical shift this way: "There was . . . some feeling against the economic security bill precisely because it was an Administration measure and came to Congress fully drafted. That was one reason why the Ways and Means Committee recommended a new bill and gave it a new name."[110] Bill drafter Thomas Eliot offers a simpler explanation: when the Ways and Means Committee came to the part of the bill creating a Social Insurance Board to oversee the entire program, one congressman noted that the board's responsibilities extended beyond insurance and that the name was not quite right. Another congressman agreed and suggested it be renamed the Social Security Board, at which point the committee decided to rename the bill the Social Security Act.[111] "Economic security" became "social security"—and lost some of its rhetorical force.[112]

In a fireside chat on April 28, 1935, a little over a week after the House passed the bill, Roosevelt explained to the American people how the legislation for old-age pensions and unemployment insurance would enable the government to address some of their most pressing economic security problems. In the first place, Roosevelt said, the bill "proposes, by means of old-age pensions, to help those who have reached the age of retirement to give up their jobs and thus give to the younger generation greater opportunities for work."[113] The result, Roosevelt said, would be "to give to all a feeling of security as they look toward old age."[114] Turning to unemployment insurance, Roosevelt said that it "will not only help to guard the individual in future periods of lay-off against dependence upon relief, but it will, by sustaining purchasing power, cushion the shock of economic distress."[115]

Roosevelt ended his fireside chat by noting that the economic recovery under way amounted to

> more than the recovery of the material basis of our individual lives. It is the recovery of confidence in our Democratic processes and institutions. We have survived all of the arduous burdens and the threatening dangers of a great economic calamity. We have in the darkest moments of our national trials retained our faith in our own ability to master our destiny. Fear is vanishing and confidence is growing on every side, faith is being renewed in the vast possibilities of human beings to improve their material and spiritual status through the instrumentality of the democratic form of government.[116]

This was no small achievement at a time when other countries were abandoning democracy. But the idea that the government's responsibilities could be adjusted to address contemporary problems received a crushing blow the following week.

While the Roosevelt administration moved to cement economic security as a right the government had a duty to ensure, the judiciary—to conservatives' delight—threatened to derail the administration's efforts. On May 6, 1935, the Supreme Court struck down the Railroad Retirement Act of 1934. Three weeks later, the Court ruled against the National Industrial Recovery Act.[117] In response, Roosevelt argued that the Supreme Court rulings threatened national security, declaring at a press conference on May 31, "The big issue is this: Does this decision mean that the United States Government has no control over any national economic problem?"[118] Roosevelt called such a conclusion absurd in light of contemporary circumstances and what he said was the obvious necessity of greater government responsibility for ensuring economic security.[119] The drafters of the administration's Economic Security Act had worked hard to construct a measure they believed would survive legal challenges but nevertheless awaited such challenges with trepidation following these rulings.[120]

On August 14, 1935, Roosevelt gathered the architects of the Social Security Act for a signing ceremony to bring into law one of the most consequential pieces of legislation in American history.[121] In brief radio remarks, Roosevelt said the law would address the basic problem of modern industrial capitalism: "the civilization of the past hundred years, with its startling industrial changes, has tended more and more to make life insecure."[122] Although the Social Security Act did not fulfill the administration's goals for economic security, it provided two of the elements the administration wanted most: unemployment insurance and old-age pensions. Health insurance would be left for the future—perhaps a few years hence, some administration officials thought.[123] In his signing statement, Roosevelt called the legislation a

> corner stone in a structure which is being built but is by no means
> complete. It is a structure intended to lessen the force of possible fu-
> ture depressions. It will act as a protection to future Administrations
> against the necessity of going deeply into debt to furnish relief to the

needy. The law will flatten out the peaks and valleys of deflation and
of inflation. It is, in short, a law that will take care of human needs and
at the same time provide the United States an economic structure of
vastly greater soundness.[124]

Although it did not cover all Americans and did not provide the full measure of economic security the Roosevelt administration thought necessary, the Social Security Act nevertheless represented a first large step in
the construction of a national security state.

Americans' response to the passage of the Social Security Act showed
that they understood the act's transformational importance.[125] Some, like
the unemployed lumber worker in Oregon made famous by photographer
Dorothea Lange, had their Social Security numbers tattooed on their
bodies.[126] Others had their numbers engraved on metal, which provided
the tangible solidity the flimsy official Social Security cards lacked.[127]
The objective in both cases was to ensure that the valuable number would
not be lost or forgotten. Historian Sarah Igo argues persuasively that
Americans—including many initially excluded from benefits—saw their
Social Security numbers not only "as the entry point to benefits" but also
to "economic rights."[128] The bill fundamentally altered the relationship
between citizens and the government.[129]

Roosevelt reiterated the reasons for the transformation in an address to
the Young Democratic Clubs of America Convention on August 24, 1935,
reminding the group that "the severity of the recent depression . . . has
taught us that no economic or social class in the community is so richly
endowed, so independent of the general community that it can safeguard
its own security, let alone assure security for the general community."[130]
That had become the job of government. To those who continued to
argue for a return to the principles of Adam Smith and John Stuart Mill,
to a government that resembled the one run by Washington and Jefferson,
Roosevelt replied that the rise of modern industrial capitalism had rendered those views and approaches obsolete. The times had changed.
"Facts are relentless," Roosevelt said.[131] "We must adjust our ideas to the
facts of today."[132]

With the Social Security Act and a handful of other important laws
passed, Roosevelt took a vacation and then hit the road for the Western

trip that had become an end-of-summer tradition. In notes he dictated to speechwriter Raymond Moley before heading West, Roosevelt made clear that he saw a pair of scheduled speeches in Los Angeles and San Diego as an opportunity to connect his economic security policies with his ultimate objective, what he called "a larger security—peace of mind."[133]

In Los Angeles on October 1, 1935, Roosevelt reiterated his belief that the government had to provide economic security: "Just so long as the least among us remain hungry or uncared for or unable to find useful work, just so long must it be the task of government, local, state and Federal, to seek reasonable but progressive means to help the unfortunate."[134] The next day in San Diego, Roosevelt returned to the security theme and elevated it, declaring that because of the Depression, "we came to understand the ultimate national need for more than the necessities and pleasures of life; that which is spiritual in us came forward and taught us to seek security of the spirit—that peace of mind, that confidence in the future, that deep contentment which make life not only possible but full and complete."[135] It was the government's job, Roosevelt implied, to provide that psychological security too.

Roosevelt's Persuasion Challenge Grows

As the 1936 presidential campaign approached, Roosevelt faced a more challenging persuasion task than he had in 1932—and something of a catch-22. As the incumbent, he bore responsibility for the state of the country and therefore stood to benefit from any economic improvement. But if the economy continued to improve, there might be less support for the deeper reconstruction project he and his advisors thought necessary but had only just begun. The question facing Roosevelt and his advisors was how to sustain support for reconstruction amid an economic recovery they hoped would continue. This question became more urgent in 1934 and 1935 as the Roosevelt administration's critics grew bolder and more strident in their criticism of the administration's policies.

Rather than responding to critics directly, Roosevelt addressed his responses to the American people. He relied once more on the language of security and also sought other ways to neutralize potentially damaging lines of attack—including the charge of government incompetence, which conservatives levied with increasing frequency as the government's responsibilities grew. "It must . . . be recognized," Roosevelt said on one occasion, "that when an enterprise of this character is extended over more than three thousand one hundred counties throughout the Nation, there may be occasional instances of inefficiency, bad management, or misuse of funds. When cases of that kind occur," Roosevelt said, lowering his voice and speaking more slowly, "there will be those, of course, who will try to tell you that the exceptional failure is characteristic of the entire endeavor."[136] Roosevelt reminded listeners that "in every big job there are some imperfections. There are chiselers in every walk of life, there are those in every industry who are guilty of unfair practices; every profession has its black sheep."[137] He concluded with an emphatic defense of government: "long experience in Government has taught me that the exceptional instances of wrong-doing in Government are probably less numerous than in almost every other line of endeavor."[138] Roosevelt acknowledged that "the process of the constructive rebuilding of America cannot be done in a day or a year" but added that "it is being done in spite of the few who seek to confuse [Americans] and to profit by their confusion."[139]

While Roosevelt continued to lead liberals' efforts to build public support for the construction of an economic security–focused national security state, other influential liberal voices contributed in their own way. Eleanor Roosevelt launched a syndicated newspaper column in the final days of 1935. The column, called "My Day," appeared six days a week in newspapers around the country. It was a hit. As her biographer Blanche Wiesen Cook writes, "Readers felt directly addressed, included in the affairs of state, and connected to Eleanor Roosevelt."[140] Her column thus accomplished something similar to Franklin Roosevelt's fireside chats. Readers of Eleanor Roosevelt's column benefited from the first lady's lived philosophy to "go out and see for yourself" what was going on in the world.[141] In "My Day," Eleanor Roosevelt succeeded in making others see what she had seen, which often helped sustain support for the Roosevelt administration's efforts to construct a national security state. She proved a subtle and effective evangelist for what she called the "philosophy of security."[142]

The new liberals gained another useful means of sustaining public support for their agenda when Roosevelt created the Resettlement

Administration. Headed by original Brain Trust member Rexford Tug-well, the Resettlement Administration faced intense resistance for its core mission of moving Americans off unproductive lands. Tugwell realized he needed to do more to build public support for his program and hired Roy Stryker, an economist who was also a photographer, to lead the Historical Section within the Resettlement Administration's Information Division. Stryker employed talented filmmakers and photographers like Dorothea Lange and sent them around the country to document the difficulties Americans faced, thereby building public support for government efforts to address their compatriots' economic insecurity.[143] As economic recovery continued, the images and films served as useful reminders that for many Americans life remained perilous and that the administration's reconstruction efforts remained necessary.

None of this went unnoticed. Writing in *The Annals of the American Academy of Political and Social Science* in 1935, Harvard professor E. Pendleton Herring observed that "never before has the Federal Government undertaken on so vast a scale and with such deliberate intent, the task of building a favorable public opinion toward its policies."[144] He added that "deliberately and legally establishing agencies for the creation and stimulation of favorable opinion seems to strike at the basic concepts of popular government" and asked, "Can one speak of government by consent when this consent is manufactured?"[145]

Conservatives thought not. In an article titled "Official Propaganda and the New Deal" in the same journal issue, Elisha Hanson, a conservative-leaning lawyer who served as general counsel for the American Newspaper Publishers Association, railed against the president's and his advisors' efforts to cultivate public opinion.[146] "For the first time in their history," Hanson wrote, "the American people have seen their Government turning to propaganda in myriad forms to win their favor and keep their support."[147] Hanson acknowledged that the administration had succeeded at first in controlling the public narrative but noted that the administration's opponents had begun to rally.[148] He concluded by observing that "propaganda loses its desired effect when it becomes known for what it really is. New Deal methods are now well known. The question is, What will come next?"[149]

3

The Conservative Counteroffensive

L EGENDARY ADVERTISING EXECUTIVE BRUCE BARTON delivered a blunt message to the one thousand businessmen gathered for the National Association of Manufacturers (NAM) annual meeting in December 1935: they had wasted their time for the last three years.[1] "Industry and politics, at the moment, are competitors for the confidence and favor of the same patron, the public," Barton said.[2] "Politics knows it; industry, for three years, has acted as if it did not."[3] Barton argued that business leaders had spent too much time over the preceding years taking trains to New York and Washington to fret among themselves over the growth of the government's domestic responsibilities when they should have focused instead on cultivating public opinion.[4] As a result, Barton said, all they had to show for their efforts was "a lot of Pullman stubs."[5]

If businessmen wanted to halt Roosevelt's state building project, Barton told the crowd, then they needed to "beat politics with its own weapon" by speaking "not to the mind only, but to the heart" and making "people believe that [they are] thinking in terms of their welfare and the happiness of their children."[6] And crucially, businessmen "must make [their] appeal not to . . . [their] own circle, but to Everybody."[7] Specifically, Barton said businessmen needed to use "all the imagination and art of which modern advertising is capable" to convince Americans that businessmen "are more reliable than the politicians; that we will work for them more cheaply and with more satisfaction."[8]

The NAM was already answering Barton's call by constructing a large persuasion campaign to turn the public against Roosevelt's agenda.[9] Barton's fiery speech helped build support for the new campaign among NAM members. After Roosevelt's landslide reelection in 1936, the NAM campaign helped the conservative movement develop the persuasion playbook and the reach to compete with Roosevelt during his second term and thereafter. Although it took time to find persuasive arguments to counter Roosevelt's promise of security, the NAM campaign advanced the conservative cause in the interim by helping develop the shared vocabulary conservatives needed to coalesce as a movement. The NAM campaign also helped grow the conservative movement by cultivating what NAM called "opinion molders," including women, religious leaders, teachers, and public relations professionals. By the late 1930s, these contributions established the NAM campaign as the spearhead of the conservative counteroffensive against Roosevelt's economic security–focused national security state.[10]

The Origins of the Modern American Conservative Movement

Many scholars have argued that the conservative movement formed in reaction to Franklin Roosevelt and the New Deal.[11] Roosevelt and the New Deal undoubtedly contributed to the movement's development and spurred the persuasion campaign that became its animating force. But two facts complicate this origin story. The first is that the businessmen leading the conservative movement began mobilizing before the New Deal, which suggests some larger trend moved them to action.[12] That larger trend was the expansion of the government's domestic responsibilities beginning during the Progressive Era.[13] The second is that the papers of these conservative leaders make clear that even during Roosevelt's presidency they were spurred to action by more than just the New Deal and by more than mere animus for Roosevelt. Something else alarmed these conservatives and accelerated their coalescence into an effective movement. That something was Roosevelt's mobilization of the language of security, which held open the prospect of unlimited government expansion. As one conservative later summarized the challenge they faced, "our opponents, being good propagandists, justified all [their] proposals by means of an idealistic objective which they claimed would result from such government intervention. This idealistic objective was 'security,' something for which the American people were hungering desperately in the middle [nineteen] thirties."[14]

By the time Bruce Barton spoke at the 1935 National Association of Manufacturers convention, some of the nation's most powerful businessmen had indeed spent many hours together in the preceding decade trying to find ways to resist what they saw as the move away from the country's founding principles. Chief among those founding principles in the minds of these pioneers of the modern conservative movement was individual liberty, defined in what philosopher Isaiah Berlin called its "negative" sense, meaning freedom *from* the government.[15] These Americans treasured the Bill of Rights for the prohibitions they felt it placed on the government. They viewed with alarm the trend toward using the government to solve domestic problems. The trend away from limited government, they believed, imperiled individual liberty. It also threatened their power, autonomy, and wealth. Whether for reasons of high philosophy or low selfish interest—or both—these businessmen believed something had to be done to reverse the trend away from limited government.[16]

The battle to repeal the Eighteenth Amendment, which outlawed the production, transport, and sale of alcohol, became an improbable focal point of early conservative mobilization. The interlocking directorate of businessmen who served as the conservative movement's leaders saw the Eighteenth Amendment as what historian Robert Burk calls "The Opening Wedge of Tyranny."[17] In their eyes, Burk writes, the Eighteenth Amendment exemplified "the federal government's growing threat to private property, individual liberty, and personal choice."[18] To meet this threat, William H. Stayton, a conservative-minded wealthy Washington lobbyist, founded the Association Against the Prohibition Amendment (AAPA) in 1918.[19] Stayton's objective with the AAPA was broader than the organization's name implied. Uneasy over what he saw as the trend toward greater centralized government power, he hoped to "educate the public on the broader subject of a 'proper' interpretation of the

Constitution."[20] Despite Stayton's efforts, the AAPA made little progress toward its objectives in the first decade of its existence.

In the final years of the 1920s, however, a group of business leaders led by the brothers Pierre, Irénée, and Lammot du Pont took over the AAPA and expanded its efforts as part of what Pierre du Pont called an effort "to straighten out our political affairs."[21] In addition to an immediate desire to replace corporate and income taxes with taxes on legalized alcohol, the du Ponts hoped an invigorated AAPA could turn public opinion against future expansions of the government's domestic responsibilities.[22] Pierre du Pont's private observation that "the collateral issues outweigh the liquor question" underscored that he, like Stayton, saw the AAPA's work as deeper than its stated focus on Prohibition.[23]

With the generous backing of the du Ponts and the other business leaders who joined the AAPA's leadership ranks, the AAPA became a laboratory for conservatives to experiment with organizational approaches and persuasion techniques to shape public opinion at scale. The AAPA's work marked the beginning of the conservative movement's organized effort to develop a shared vocabulary with which to disparage government domestic programs. The AAPA operated research and information bureaus, which disseminated anti-Prohibition propaganda nationwide emphasizing the dangers of expanded government responsibilities and the expense, corruption, and ineptitude that purportedly followed.[24] The association also cultivated grassroots and grasstops support among women, professional groups, and youth by creating committees and auxiliaries.[25] Between 1928 and 1932, the du Pont brothers contributed $400,000 to the AAPA—a huge sum by the standards of political spending at the time.[26]

Although they eventually succeeded in helping to end Prohibition, the conservative businessmen behind the AAPA had not achieved their larger goal of halting the expansion of the government's domestic responsibilities. On the contrary, the expansion accelerated in the early 1930s. As the Great Depression deepened, the public looked increasingly to government—and to the federal government specifically—to address the country's economic problems. Conservatives struggled over how to respond. The du Pont brothers and many of their counterparts at the head of leading American companies believed they were the country's rightful leaders, but their public standing had plummeted with the Depression.[27] Despite this setback, they did not want to cede power they believed rightfully theirs.[28] Nor were they interested in the fundamental transformations in American political economy that Roosevelt and his supporters proposed, which not only threatened to reduce business leaders' autonomy but also in all likelihood would force them to pay more taxes. Some of them believed that Roosevelt was trying to lead the country toward socialism. They resented his appropriation and redefinition of the "liberal" label with which they, as proponents of limited government, had long defined themselves. Some of them detested Roosevelt personally. But what frightened them most of all was that Roosevelt was unusually persuasive and that in the language of security he seemed to have found a key to unlimited government expansion.[29]

When the AAPA board of directors mothballed the organization in December 1933, they resolved "that the individual members of the Executive Committee . . . continue to meet from time to time and have in view the formation of a group, based on our old membership in the association, which would in the event of danger to the Federal Constitution, stand ready to defend the faith of the fathers."[30] To the du Pont brothers and their longtime colleague John J. Raskob, that danger materialized in June 1934 when Franklin Roosevelt proposed what became known as Social Security.[31] Conservative mobilization efforts gained a greater sense of urgency in the weeks that followed. In a series of intense discussions during July 1934, the du Pont brothers; Raskob; John W. Davis, a leading New York corporate lawyer and 1924 Democratic presidential nominee; executives from General Motors and General Foods, including Colby Chester; and other business leaders decided to try to turn the public against Roosevelt's economic security agenda.[32]

The July 1934 discussions produced the American Liberty League. Headed by former AAPA president Jouett Shouse and launched in August 1934 from the same Washington, DC, office from which Shouse had run the AAPA, the Liberty League said it wanted "to preserve for succeeding generations the principles of the Declaration of Independence, the safeguards of personal liberty and the opportunity for initiative and enterprise provided under the Constitution."[33] The Liberty League's founders chose that purpose carefully and emphasized it at every opportunity to inoculate themselves against criticism. After all, one of the Liberty League's founders noted privately, even though most Americans were only loosely familiar with what the Constitution said, "there is a mighty—though vague—affection for it."[34] In the run-up to its public launch, the group took pains to emphasize its educational rather than oppositional nature.[35] Although ostensibly an inclusive organization intended to advance the interests of all Americans, the Liberty League's dependence on the generous financing of a couple dozen wealthy businessmen made the organization easy to caricature and dismiss.[36] "They have appropriated the Liberty Bell as their symbol," said Columbia University's George S. Counts, "but they apparently think the [American] Revolution was fought to make Long Island safe for polo players."[37]

Despite these political liabilities, the Liberty League boosted the conservative movement's prospects by capitalizing on the recent revolution in advertising and public relations. These professions became much more effective in the first three decades of the twentieth century thanks to a boom in academic psychology and the extensive experience gained manipulating public opinion during World War I.[38] Rather than dry presentations of facts, public relations specialists began cultivating impressions through multichannel repetition and indirect persuasion via opinion leaders.[39] Public relations specialists also learned to provide people with sticky rhetoric they would repeat, amplifying the original message.[40] Although the new liberals used some of these techniques, the conservative movement benefited even more from these advances because leading public relations professionals counted as clients many firms headed by the conservative movement's leaders. The Liberty League's decision to retain leading public relations consultants like Edward Bernays, a pioneer in the field, brought modern persuasion techniques into the conservative persuasion campaign.[41]

But adopting these persuasion techniques did not guarantee success. The campaign's effectiveness also depended on reaching large numbers of Americans. To that end, the Liberty League and its public relations advisors expanded the campaign's reach, sending millions of pamphlets and press releases to thousands of public and college libraries; to hundreds of newspapers and press associations and editorial writers; and to an ever-growing mailing list.[42] By passing its material off as "news," the

Liberty League gained extensive media coverage without having to pay for advertising.[43] The organization even started its own news service, the Western Newspaper Union, to supply news stories and editorials—both written with a conservative slant and without attribution to the Liberty League—to more than 1,600 newspapers in the South, Midwest, and West.[44] The organization also took advantage of free time offered by radio stations to push its conservative message over the airwaves.[45] Finally, the organization published a bulletin featuring not only articles and updates on Liberty League activity but also embarrassing anecdotes about the Roosevelt administration's domestic policy foibles—a continuation of earlier AAPA efforts to sow doubt about the government's ability to solve domestic problems.[46] The Liberty League hoped its extensive efforts would help unseat Roosevelt in the 1936 election, thereby halting his state-building project.

The 1936 Election

The Liberty League provided Franklin Roosevelt with a perfect foil for the 1936 campaign.[47] Accepting renomination as the Democratic Party's candidate for president on June 27, 1936, Roosevelt began his speech by declaring that the election amounted to a referendum on "an attitude towards problems, the determination of which will profoundly affect America."[48] The question, Roosevelt said, was whether the country would have positive government or negative government, whether the nation would solve the "new problems which must be solved if we are to pre-serve to the United States the political and economic freedom for which Washington and Jefferson planned and fought."[49] As was their custom, Roosevelt and his advisors chose these words carefully. The inclusion of the word "planned," which did not appear in early drafts, associated national planning with the Founders.[50] The inclusion of "economic" under-scored that the government had a responsibility to guarantee both political and economic rights. In making the case for positive government, Roosevelt turned the tables on conservatives, appropriating one of their favorite words—"freedom"—and reminding Americans that the American Revolution was a struggle for freedom against the political tyranny of the sort that Roosevelt said a new generation of "economic royalists" had im-posed on the country in the period leading to the Great Depression.[51]

Roosevelt said that in modern times freedom had come to depend on the government guarantee of economic security because "for too many of us, the political equality we once had won was meaningless in the face of economic inequality. A small group had concentrated into their own hands an almost complete control over other people's property, other people's money, other people's labor, other people's lives. For too many of us throughout the land, life was no longer free; liberty no longer real; men could no longer follow the pursuit of happiness."[52] This development, Roosevelt said, made plain the need for positive government, for "against economic tyranny such as this, the American citizen could only appeal to the organized power of Government."[53] He declared that "government in a modern civilization has certain inescapable obligations to its citizens, among which are protection of the family and the home, the establishment of a democracy of opportunity, and aid to those overtaken by disaster."[54] These were the purposes of the national security state Roosevelt was trying to build.

Since the 1932 campaign, Roosevelt had used the economic crisis to frame his domestic policy proposals as essential for national security. He had succeeded. Now, with economic recovery seemingly under way and the crisis fading, Roosevelt previewed a new argument for why his domestic agenda remained essential for national security. Speaking very slowly, he said,

> In other lands, there are some people, who, in times past, have lived and fought for freedom, and seem to have grown too weary to carry on the fight. They have sold their heritage of freedom for the illusion of a living. They have yielded their democracy. I believe in my heart that only our success can stir their ancient hope. They begin to know that here in America we are waging a great and successful war. It is not alone a war against want and destitution and economic demoralization. It Is more than that; it is a war for the survival of democracy. We are fighting, fighting to save a great and precious form of government for ourselves and for the world.[55]

In eerily prescient words, Roosevelt told the crowd and those listening through radio that "there is a mysterious cycle in human events. To some generations much is given. Of other generations much is expected. This generation of Americans has a rendezvous with destiny."[56] Roosevelt would rely increasingly on the worsening international crisis to keep his domestic agenda in the national security frame in the years ahead.

For the moment, however, Roosevelt ran on his record of expanding the government's economic security responsibilities and his proposals to continue in that vein. To conservative critics' great annoyance, the Roosevelt administration launched a "massive media effort"—including films and circulars—during the 1936 presidential campaign to publicize and build support for Social Security.[57] Roosevelt's heavy use of the language and promise of security made his opponents' task all but impossible. How could they run against something Americans wanted?

The gymnastics Republican candidate Alfred M. Landon had to perform in a speech criticizing Social Security illustrated the extent to which liberals had succeeded by 1936 in using the language of security to reshape the debate about the government's responsibilities. A Republican seeking the presidency could no longer argue, as Herbert Hoover had in 1932, that voluntarism was the proper way to meet Americans' economic security needs. Instead, Landon told the crowd in Milwaukee, Wisconsin, on September 26, 1936, that he supported the idea of social security but that the system the Roosevelt administration developed was unworkable and amounted to "paternal government."[58] Landon argued that the Social Security Act "assumes that Americans are irresponsible. It assumes that old-age pensions are necessary because Americans lack the foresight to provide for their old age."[59] He charged further that the Social Security Act "is a glaring example of the bungling and waste that have characterized this administration's attempts to fulfill its benevolent purposes."[60] The speech backfired.[61]

For its part, the Liberty League mocked domestic programs as farcical and ruinously expensive using a recent addition to the American political vocabulary: "boondoggling."[62] The word "boondoggle" originally referred to a crafted leather decoration Boy Scouts produced and wore on their uniforms beginning in the second half of the 1920s.[63] By the mid-1930s, however, conservatives had begun using the term to refer to economic security programs of questionable value.[64] The term burst onto the national political scene in April 1935, when the *Chicago Tribune* and the *Wall Street Journal* pounced on an amusing story about a crafts maker seeking work relief funds to make boondoggles.[65] The *Wall Street*

Journal published a piece the next day decrying "A Nation of Boon-Doggles."[66] The Liberty League amplified these efforts to disparage domestic programs through its multichannel persuasion campaign. In a national radio broadcast in June 1936, Liberty League president Jouett Shouse told Americans that "the New Deal has instituted a series of boondoggling enterprises which are as ridiculous as they are unwise."[67] The Liberty League also distributed lengthy lists of questionable domestic economic security initiatives to millions of Americans in a leaflet called "The New Deal Boondoggling Circus" and in a longer pamphlet.[68] The word—and the negative impression of domestic policy the word fostered—stuck.[69] But with government programs seeming to be helping the economy, Roosevelt had little trouble deflecting this criticism. As he told an audience in New Jersey in 1936, "If we can 'boondoggle' ourselves out of this depression, that word is going to be enshrined in the hearts of the American people for many years to come."[70] Conservative efforts to portray government economic security programs as wasteful fell flat for the moment.

Roosevelt stole the "liberal" label from proponents of limited government during the 1932 campaign, infuriating Herbert Hoover. Now he stole the "conservative" label too and put it in service of his agenda. Roosevelt said, "The true conservative is the man who has a real concern for injustices and takes thought against the day of reckoning. The true conservative seeks to protect the system of private property and free enterprise by correcting such injustices and inequalities as arise from it. The most serious threat to our institutions comes from those who refuse to face the need for change. Liberalism becomes the protection for the far-sighted conservative."[71] He added that "never has a nation made greater strides in the safeguarding of democracy than we have made during these past three years. Wise and prudent men, intelligent conservatives, have long known that in a changing world worthy institutions can be conserved only by adjusting them to the changing time."[72] Roosevelt then quoted the famous British historian, politician, and essayist Thomas Babington Macaulay: "the voice of great events is proclaiming to us: reform if you would preserve."[73] Roosevelt concluded, "I am that kind of a conservative because I am that kind of a liberal."[74] It was another masterstroke of linguistic appropriation and redirection.

As Election Day approached, both Franklin and Eleanor Roosevelt made security the focus of their appeals. Franklin Roosevelt's October 13, 1936, speech in Wichita, Kansas, illustrated the advantages the language of security gave liberals and the predicament their use of it created for conservatives.[75] After charging conservatives with "giving vague lip service to that word 'security' and, at the same time, seeking to block, to thwart, and to annul every measure that we have taken to restrain the kind of individualism which hurts the community itself, individualism run amuck," Roosevelt explained what "security" meant to him:

> I use this word "security" not in the narrower sense of old age pensions and of unemployment insurance, fine as these objectives are. I use it in the broader sense—confidence on the part of men and women willing to carry on normal work, and willing to think of their neighbors as well as themselves, confidence that they will not have to worry about losing their homes, about not having enough to eat, about becoming objects of charity. Add to that one more objective: that all Americans may have full opportunity for education, for reasonable leisure and recreation, for the right to carry on representative Government and for freedom to worship God in their own way. That philosophy has been the philosophy and the practical objective of your national Administration at Washington.[76]

Roosevelt continued to press the attack, arguing that only government could provide the economic security the average American wanted and that conservatives did not want the government to provide it. "There was at one time a school of thought in this country that would have us believe that those vast numbers of average citizens who do not get to the top of the economic ladder do not deserve the security which Government alone can give them. And in the past, unfortunately, that philosophy has had too large a hand in making our national economic policies. That school of thought left Washington on March 4, 1933."[77]

Roosevelt ended his Wichita speech by taking another tentative step—his renomination acceptance speech had been the first—toward placing foreign policy in the national security frame: "There is one final form of security on which I have not yet touched. In addition to security at home and in the home, we have sought for security from war with other

Nations. We have not been content merely to talk about peace. We have done something about it. We are trying to break down the economic barriers, to soften the economic rivalries, to end the economic strife between Nations; for these have been the causes and forerunners of war. We have taken the lead among the Nations of the world in restoring economic peace which is so essential to military peace."[78] He concluded the speech by telling the crowd that "we are gaining peace and security at home. I am confident that I have the support of the American people in seeking peace and security abroad."[79] As in his renomination acceptance speech, the association of foreign policy with security was not Roosevelt's focus—but its inclusion illustrated how Roosevelt's concept of national security was evolving amid changing domestic and international circumstances.

Roosevelt's success campaigning on security left conservatives in dire straits as the election approached. Desperate for an effective counter, conservatives launched an ill-considered propaganda offensive against Social Security in the closing stage of the campaign. Some companies included pamphlets in their employees' pay envelopes framing the Social Security program as a harmful tax. One such insert given to Buick Motor Company employees explained that "the heavy tax thus enacted on the Company, must have an adverse influence on what it might otherwise do in employee benefits of one form or another. Like all taxes, it also has the undesirable effect of increasing selling prices."[80] The conservative campaign against Social Security backfired, for it made it even easier for Roosevelt to portray his opponents as uninterested in the public's well-being. In campaign speeches, Roosevelt delivered a resounding defense of the Social Security Act and denounced the conservative campaign against it and against his administration's policies more broadly.[81] He argued that the pay-envelope campaign against Social Security was worse than mere propaganda, that it amounted to "deceit" because it misled the recipients about the details of the Social Security system.[82] He told an audience in Worcester, Massachusetts, that "your pay envelope may be loaded with suggestions of fear, and your dividend letter may be filled with propaganda. But the American people will be neither bluffed nor bludgeoned."[83]

Roosevelt succeeded in framing the 1936 election as a referendum on positive government and the idea that the government should provide economic security for its citizens. He closed some of his campaign speeches with a variation on what he asked an audience in Detroit in October: "When the smoke and when the dust of this political campaign clear away on the night of November third, history is going to record that the outstanding issue of the campaign was this—Shall the social, shall the economic security and betterment of the masses of the American people be maintained and strengthened or not? My friends, we are—you and I are not afraid of that verdict. It is going to be yes."[84] Roosevelt's confidence was not misplaced. He won every state save Maine and Vermont for a total of 523 electoral votes to Alf Landon's 8, and Democrats added to their commanding majorities in both the House and the Senate.[85]

Roosevelt's crushing victory in 1936 underscored the magnitude of the challenge conservatives faced in trying to turn the public against the national security state Roosevelt was building. Roosevelt's reelection also largely discredited the Liberty League, which folded during his second term. Despite its rapid departure from the political scene, the organization contributed to the conservative movement's development in lasting ways by professionalizing the conservative persuasion campaign and helping popularize disparaging rhetoric about domestic programs.[86] This disdainful way of talking about the government became part of the conservative movement's shared vocabulary, and the conservative persuasion campaign implanted this disparaging rhetoric into mainstream American political discourse.

Nevertheless, Bruce Barton had been right when he told the 1935 National Association of Manufacturers convention that "industry has stuck out its tongue at its political competitor. . . . It has pouted and scolded and sulked . . . [but] the time has come when mere opposition and criticism are not much good."[87] The business executives leading the conservative movement needed a new vehicle, and a refined approach, for their persuasion efforts.

The Revival and Reorientation of the National Association of Manufacturers

With the Liberty League's demise, the National Association of Manufacturers emerged as the unlikely vanguard of the conservative movement in the final years of the 1930s. Founded in 1895 to represent the interests of

American manufacturing companies, the NAM fell on hard times during the Depression.[88] Membership dropped from more than five thousand firms to fewer than two thousand by the early 1930s.[89] The association's influence withered and its viability came into question. During the winter of 1931–1932, however, a group of businessmen calling themselves the "Brass Hats" did to the National Association of Manufacturers what the du Pont brothers had done to the Association Against the Prohibition Amendment, taking over the organization and revitalizing it to advance the conservative cause.[90]

Like the du Ponts, the Brass Hats deplored the recent growth of the government's domestic responsibilities.[91] Led by Thomas Girdler of Republic Steel, Robert Henderson of Pacific Portland Cement, Charles Hook of American Rolling Mill, Ernest Weir of National Steel, and Robert Lund of Lambert Pharmaceutical, the Brass Hats convened a series of discussions in Detroit and New York around the 1932 election.[92] Illustrating the interlocking directorates at the heart of the conservative movement, many of the participants in these discussions had participated in the AAPA fight and would join the Liberty League.[93] Henderson recalled that the group was "groping for the answer" to the problems facing them and that at first "nothing really seemed to be coming out of these meetings."[94] But the discussions continued and began to bear fruit as the Brass Hats took control of the struggling National Association of Manufacturers (NAM).

Beginning in 1932, Lund orchestrated NAM's revival as its new president. By September 1933, Lund believed he had identified the source of the problems conservative businessmen faced—public ignorance: "The public does not understand industry, largely because industry itself has made no real effort to tell its story; to show the people of this country that our high living standards have risen almost altogether from the civilization which industrial activity has set up."[95] Lund noted that industry's relative silence was all the more problematic because "selfish groups, including labor, the socialistic-minded and the radical, have constantly and continuously misrepresented industry to the people, with the result that there is a general misinformation of our industrial economy, which is highly destructive in its effect."[96] Like some of the other savvy businessmen leading the conservative movement, Lund also acknowledged that conservatives had a lot to learn from Roosevelt's persuasion efforts.[97]

To compete with Roosevelt, Lund decided to focus NAM on public relations and to rely on professionals to guide its efforts.[98] NAM decided not merely to retain public relations consultants—as the Liberty League had done—but also to bring public relations specialists in house to run a new persuasion campaign. Lund hired Walter Weisenburger, a former journalist, public relations specialist, and one-time head of the St. Louis Chamber of Commerce, to serve as executive vice president and to run the new persuasion campaign.[99] Weisenburger would lead the NAM campaign for the next thirteen years. Weisenburger hired James P. Selvage, an advertising and business executive and journalist who had spent the previous three years writing for the *Atlanta Constitution,* to serve as the association's public relations director.[100] Weisenburger and Selvage, in turn, retained a leading public opinion research firm to undertake a national survey to inform NAM's efforts.[101] This move signaled that the professionals running the NAM campaign did not intend simply to transmit the same conservative messages again and again and hope for success, as the Liberty League had done, but rather planned to tailor messages to audiences—a more nuanced form of repetition.

The NAM's use of professionals to manage its campaign made the overall conservative persuasion campaign more effective in several ways. First, it introduced a moderating filter between the conservatives financing the campaign, some of whom held extreme views, and the campaign's output. This filter became more effective as Weisenburger gained clout within NAM and helped soften the shrill tone that had characterized the Liberty League's messaging.[102] Second, the professionals running the NAM campaign concluded from the Liberty League's direct messaging failures that shifting public opinion would take time and that conservatives needed to devote more energy to delivering messages indirectly through trusted "opinion molders," among whom NAM counted women, religious leaders, teachers, and public relations professionals.[103] These people had the power to deliver conservative messaging to trusting audiences without arousing suspicion, and they also held sway over what the NAM called the "on-coming generation."[104]

NAM's efforts to cultivate women, religious leaders, and teachers followed a standard pattern: lavish them with attention, supply them with material, and groom them at conferences.[105] These materials and conferences helped develop the shared vocabulary that enabled the conservative movement to coalesce and grow. NAM also courted professional opinion molders, again largely through conferences, and helped grow the public relations profession.[106] Most public relations professionals attended at least one NAM conference.[107] The indirect means of getting the conservative message across through opinion molders proved more powerful than direct appeals. These opinion molders' contributions to the conservative movement's subsequent growth suggests NAM invested wisely.[108]

Finally, the professionals running the NAM campaign paid more attention than the Liberty League to the circumstances in which their messages would land. They used regular opinion polling to understand public attitudes, gauge the effectiveness of their efforts, and adjust their approach as necessary.[109] Based on these surveys, the NAM decided to use the phrase "government intervention" rather than "the more common terms 'government control' or 'government regulation'" because "government intervention" "not only summons up a more graphic picture of actual government management of business, but it has an added semantics value in that fewer people will attempt to defend government intervention than will try to justify either government regulation or government control."[110] Similarly, the NAM emphasized the shortcomings of "bureaucracy," the "symbol which is most illustrative of the public's distaste of undue governmental power."[111] This careful choice of words and framing worked. Over time, "government intervention" appeared more often in discussions of economic policy—used even by people who did not consider themselves conservative—and "bureaucracy" became a byword for government inefficiency.[112] Both phrases reinforced the negative perception of economic security programs conservatives wanted the public to hold.

The NAM's governance structure ensured its messaging would be amplified by the prominent companies whose leaders also served as NAM's leaders, and who also bankrolled and helped lead influential associations like the Chamber of Commerce and, beginning in the 1940s, the Committee on Economic Development.[113] To oversee its campaign—and sustain buy-in from NAM members—NAM formed a public relations committee in 1934 composed of several dozen businessmen, many of whom remained at the forefront of the conservative movement thereafter.[114] The NAM also founded the National Industrial Information Committee in

1935 to raise money for its persuasion campaign.[115] The NAM ensured others would learn its approach and carry its messages by hammering them home at its annual Congress of American Industry, attended by several thousand NAM members.[116] NAM members followed through, running advertisements developed in some cases by the same public relations people advising NAM directly.[117]

NAM's public relations campaign took off when General Foods chairman and former Liberty League leader Colby Chester took over the NAM presidency in 1936.[118] In 1938, Chester and Charles Hook created an "advisory committee" of leading public relations professionals to assist the Public Relations Committee in its work.[119] General Motors Director of Public Relations Paul Garrett headed the Advisory Committee.[120] The creation of this group marked the further professionalization—and moderation—of the conservative persuasion campaign, adding another layer between the conservative company heads who served on the NAM board and on the Public Relations Committee and the output of the NAM campaign. By 1939, NAM spent most of its income on public relations and its campaign had developed remarkable reach.[121] Although the NAM campaign could not claim immediate political results amid a continuing deluge of countervailing messages from Roosevelt and his allies in the late 1930s, the NAM's efforts nevertheless positioned the organization as the central force in the conservative persuasion campaign. "One of the most encouraging things," Weisenburger told the Public Relations Advisory Committee in 1939, "is the fact that more and more we are becoming recognized as conservative headquarters."[122]

Developing the Reach and Techniques to Compete with Roosevelt

The NAM developed an effective persuasion playbook that built on the successes and learned from the mistakes of the Association Against the Prohibition Amendment and the American Liberty League. The playbook emphasized reach and repetition and would prove its value to conservatives again and again. Observers at the time expressed astonishment at the NAM campaign's reach. An unnamed U.S. senator noted—accurately, if perhaps apocryphally—that the NAM "used every possible method of reaching the public but the carrier pigeon."[123] After spending the better part of an afternoon listening to Walter Weisenburger describe NAM's efforts, a member of the NAM's Public Relations Advisory Committee declared, "I am perfectly overwhelmed by the amount of work you people do."[124] The NAM campaign delivered the conservative message to tens of millions of Americans every day, often multiple times per day.[125] A NAM campaign booklet called *A Day in the Life of an Average American* captured the extent to which Americans of all ages—mostly unwittingly—encountered the conservative persuasion campaign from the time they woke up in the morning until the time they went to bed at night.[126] Americans heard the conservative message on the radio upon waking, read it in articles planted in their morning newspapers, encountered it on billboards and public transit ads on the way to work, read it again in publications provided at work or at school, and heard it again in lectures in civic clubs and at the movies in the evening.[127] This daily deluge of conservative messaging mattered because, as psychologists have shown, the frequent repetition of messages shapes what people believe.[128]

The first thing the character in *A Day in the Life of an Average American* heard upon waking was NAM programming on his bedside radio.

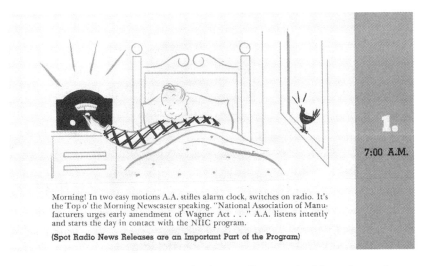

Morning! In two easy motions A.A. stifles alarm clock, switches on radio. It's the Top o' the Morning Newscaster speaking. "National Association of Manufacturers urges early amendment of Wagner Act . . ." A.A. listens intently and starts the day in contact with the NIIC program.

(Spot Radio News Releases are an Important Part of the Program)

7:00 A.M.

1.

FIGURE 3.1 The "Average American" Awakens to Conservative Messaging on the Radio (Courtesy of the National Association of Manufacturers.)

The NAM devoted substantial resources to radio, which it considered one of the most important parts of its persuasion campaign.[129] Whereas Roosevelt thought it best to appear on radio infrequently enough to make each of his addresses a significant event, the NAM took full advantage of free airtime offered to it by many radio stations to get its message on the airwaves as often as possible.[130]

NAM radio programming ranged from news shows hosted by conservative personalities like George Sokolsky to entertainment programs like *The American Family Robinson,* the "nation's largest dramatic radio program."[131] Listeners were often not told that NAM was behind this content.[132] Sokolsky's fifteen-minute weekly program aired on more than 200 stations.[133] Another 250 stations broadcast episodes of *American Family Robinson* on a weekly and semiweekly basis.[134] This popular program presented business leaders as practical and trustworthy and painted government economic policy proposals as radical and harebrained.[135] The NAM also sponsored "Spot Radio News Releases" and foreign-language content designed to carry "the story of the accomplishments of American industry to the millions of Americans who listen to foreign language programs."[136] In addition to developing its own content, the NAM also provided talking points to news commentators and slipped its messaging into other programs, again without attribution.[137]

Over breakfast, the NAM's Average American encountered the organization's conservative message in the newspaper. Since both people running the NAM campaign had worked on newspapers, they knew how to cultivate their former colleagues. They also paid for ads, endearing themselves not only to the advertising agencies who developed the ads but also to newspapers grateful for the advertising revenue (and perhaps more inclined to publish NAM content as a result).[138] The NAM established an "Industrial Press Service" during the 1930s and through it sent "news" stories, editorials, and cartoons to thousands of newspapers around the country, many of which ran them without attribution to the NAM.[139] As with its radio content, the NAM worked hard to ensure its print content appeared as often as possible, preferably as articles indistinguishable from other news coverage, and in multiple languages.[140]

While commuting to work, the Average American saw one of the tens of thousands of billboards that the NAM posted around the country.[141]

Breakfast! And what's this? N.A.M. news story dominating first page of paper. Coffee poised, A.A. reads about Industry's program for national recovery. "Sounds like real horse-sense." As he reads, his toast cools, his interest warms.

(The Nation's Editors Receive Press Releases Regularly)

FIGURE 3.2 The "Average American" Encounters Conservative Messaging in the Press (Courtesy of the National Association of Manufacturers.)

The messages on these billboards trumpeted the superiority of the "American Way" over other forms of political economy because America had the "World's Highest Standard of Living," "World's Shortest Working Hours," and "World's Highest Wages."[142] Lower levels of advertising spending during the Depression meant that many of NAM's billboards remained up and visible to the public far longer than during normal economic times.[143] The NAM put up approximately forty-five thousand billboards around the country and estimated that some sixty-five million people saw them daily.[144]

The Average American encountered NAM messaging in several forms upon arriving at work. NAM public relations strategists recognized that workers on the clock presented a captive audience and a golden persuasion opportunity. As NAM president Frederick Crawford put it to an audience of business leaders, "Did it ever occur to you that you have your workers eight hours a day, and that you pay them money, and that the leaders of the opposition, whether political or labor, or some crackpot scheme, get them only ten minutes on the way home and usually try to take money away from them?"[145] It should be obvious, Crawford argued, that business "has all the advantage" in the battle to persuade workers.[146]

Through its Service for Plant Publications, the NAM distributed content employers could display on bulletin boards and adapt for in-house publications. This material ranged from "The Pocketbook of Knowledge," which conveyed conservative messages in cartoon form, to "news" articles and NAM press releases. Some editions of the Service for Plant Publications also included a section called "The Guide Post" set off in a text box with a version of the disclaimer, "(To House Magazine Editors: 'The Guide Post' is intended for you alone and is not for publication. We hope that the material contained in it will be of help to you. All the other material, outside of this box, is available for your use if you have a place for it.)"[147] As its name implied, "The Guide Post" contained messaging guidance on topics the NAM wanted employers to emphasize.

On his way home from work, the Average American picked up his wife from her Civic and Social Club, which had just finished discussing material NAM provided about the relationship between industry and society.[148] The NAM devoted considerable attention to women, whom it saw as important "opinion molders" and "one of America's most militant crusading groups."[149] The NAM cultivated the leaders of the largest women's organizations and sent booklets and other material to women's

9.

5:20 P.M.

Picks up wife on way home. Asks about meeting of her Tuesday Civic and Social Club, as he should. Replies Mrs. A.A., "You should have seen the girls' amazement at the facts our Chairman brought out in the discussion. Who would have believed that Industry is really owned by thousands and thousands of average people like ourselves. That material the National Association of Manufacturers supplied us certainly opened our eyes."

(Factual Material About Industry is Supplied Speakers and Group Discussional Meetings)

FIGURE 3.3 The "Average American's" Wife Describes Conservative Messaging Discussed in Her Club (Courtesy of the National Association of Manufacturers.)

clubs around the country.[150] The organization left nothing to chance, sending packages to the heads of women's clubs containing everything needed to hold a successful meeting on topics of interest to conservatives: sample meeting invitations and announcement flyers, program outlines, talking points for the discussion leader and other speakers, and even a draft summary of the discussion.[151] This investment paid dividends as women's discussion groups became an important site for conservative mobilization.[152]

On arriving home, the Average American might find a startling letter from the chairman of the board of General Mills, a company in which he owned a small amount of stock, informing him that the expansion of the government's domestic responsibilities threatened his investment: "The government has invaded financial, economic and social fields in competition with private enterprise. It has engaged in the vast program of experimentation, regulation, restriction and regimentation of producer, processor and consumer. It has embarked upon the expenditure of billions of dollars in unproductive works and services. It has imposed discriminatory and burdensome processing taxes which limit consumption, distort competition and restrict profit opportunity."[153] The letter warned that "these measures and policies mean serious impairment, if not the ultimate destruction of your investment in this and other companies."[154] The leaders of the NAM campaign saw these letters as an important part of their overall "public education" effort.[155]

After dinner, the Average American's daughter showed him a *You and Industry* booklet her teacher assigned as homework.[156] The people running the NAM campaign believed "you are doing more lasting public relations work when you do it with the on-coming generation."[157] The organization therefore did all it could to get its materials into the hands of teachers and into the heads of students, succeeding to a remarkable degree. The NAM devoted special attention to teachers, whom it saw as among the most important "opinion molders" in society. Mirroring its efforts with the heads of women's clubs, the NAM tried to make it as easy as possible for teachers to use NAM material by providing lesson plans complete with supporting printed and visual materials. The NAM also distributed a publication called *Trends in Education-Industry Cooperation* to nearly fifty thousand educators each month.[158]

Doris educates papa, abetted by N.A.M. Shows him the "You and Industry" series of eight booklets on the American economic system that many teachers now use for reference purposes.

(2,500,000 "You and Industry" Booklets Have Been Distributed on Request in the Past Year)

FIGURE 3.4 The "Average American's" Daughter Summarizes Conservative Messaging from School (Courtesy of the National Association of Manufacturers.)

NAM executive vice president Walter Weisenburger delighted in teachers' use of the NAM's *You and Industry* booklets in place of textbooks. He noted in 1939 that "we are getting more requests [for this material] than we can possibly fill."[159] By the early 1940s, the NAM reported that "two of every three American high school students" were reading *You and Industry* booklets.[160] The NAM also worked to control the distribution of rival messages by commissioning a study of eight hundred popular school textbooks "so that its members might move against any that are found prejudicial to our form of government, our society or to the system of free enterprise."[161] The NAM also took an active interest in high school and college debate, working through proxies to shape debate topics and providing material with what Weisenburger called "a conservative viewpoint" to debaters.[162] Participants' difficulties obtaining needed material elsewhere only increased the opportunity for influence in Weisenburger's eyes.[163] The NAM rushed to meet the need.

In addition to printed material, the NAM also distributed films for use in schools. "Pictures," NAM Public Relations Director James P. Selvage explained, "have become accepted more and more as the most impressive medium for leaving a lasting impression upon children . . .

during their formative years."[164] Weisenburger reported that, as with printed material, demand from schools for NAM films far outstripped supply.[165] Another official involved in the campaign noted that the "educational films . . . have been conspicuously successful."[166] The NAM took an extra step to ensure its films' messages got through to students: "to improve their effectiveness in schools, we offer a teacher's guide as a basis for an extensive series of classroom projects built around these movies."[167] Like its courting of women, the NAM's efforts to influence young people via teachers greatly expanded the conservative persuasion campaign's influence.

At night, the Average American might go to the movies, where a short NAM film—once again, not always attributed to the organization—trumpeting the virtues and economic contributions of American business might precede the feature presentation.[168] If the Average American did not go to a movie in the evening, he or she might attend a talk by a NAM speaker at a club or community center. Building on the World War I model of "Four-Minute Men," the NAM assembled a speakers bureau that deployed articulate speakers around the country to deliver the NAM's conservative message in person.[169] These speakers augmented the efforts of NAM presidents, who beginning in the mid-1930s spent their one-year terms—as one NAM president put it—"touring the country, appearing before as many business men and other key groups in American life as I can get to listen to me."[170] The goal was not just to persuade these people to embrace the NAM's message but also to get them to spread the conservative gospel in their own communities.

As the NAM's Average American drifted off to sleep after his busy day of interacting—mostly unwittingly—with the conservative persuasion campaign, his "last waking thoughts are pleasant ones. He feels a warm pride in America and a reborn faith in the fundamentals of American progress—the American Way."[171] The Average American's experience shows the NAM campaign's tremendous power to deliver messages to Americans with varying degrees of subtlety in the second half of the 1930s. But this impressive reach did not by itself guarantee that the conservative persuasion campaign would succeed in halting the expansion of the government's responsibilities. Conservatives also needed a persuasive message. They struggled at first to find one.

The Conservative Movement's Search
for a Persuasive Message

When NAM's leaders made public relations the association's focus in 1933, they believed all conservatives needed to do to reverse the trend away from limited government was to educate Americans about how the economy worked—and how much better it worked than any alternative arrangement. Like many conservatives, NAM's leaders believed that Americans supported Roosevelt's proposals out of ignorance because of a "lack of understanding of the central role of business in the economy."[172] The initial phase of the NAM campaign therefore focused on the presentation of "facts" about the American economy and business's positive role in it.

The billboards the Average American saw on the way to work declaring "There's No Way Like the American Way" typified this approach. Even though the country was going through a difficult period, the billboards emphasized, the American "free enterprise" system still provided "those high living standards that dictatorships and planned economies only promise."[173] The implication was that Roosevelt's economic security policies were unnecessary. To reinforce the point, NAM also launched a poster series comparing quality of life in the United States with European countries that had progressed further down the road toward assuring their citizens' economic security.[174] The posters emphasized that "Living is Better in America," citing things like the greater number of automobiles per capita and superior consumer purchasing power.[175]

Over the course of the 1930s, however, NAM shifted focus from presenting facts about the American economy to cultivating favorable impressions of the private sector and negative impressions of the government, which the NAM presented as a wasteful drain on Americans' pocketbooks. As an internal NAM public relations strategy memo from 1939 advised, "Surveys show a tremendous proportion of the people do not realize they pay taxes at all but that, where people do recognize the tax burden, taxes are becoming increasingly unpopular. This would indicate that our efforts should (a) concentrate on 'hidden taxes,' to reach those who do not know they pay taxes and (b) that we should add fuel to the growing fire of resentment among the tax conscious group."[176]

NAM and its member companies also claimed credit for creating wealth and minimized the government's contributions to Americans' financial well-being. To do so, NAM and its companies took a page from Roosevelt's playbook. Just as Roosevelt highlighted the government's contributions to Americans' financial well-being by visiting large public works, so too did NAM companies begin publicizing the role their operations played in sustaining and growing communities around the country. Conservatives took this approach one step further by minimizing or omitting the government's contributions. A General Motors (GM) campaign exemplified this approach. At open houses, in short films, and in newspaper advertisements, GM emphasized that its paychecks enabled local businesses to thrive.[177] The government did not feature. In the years that followed, conservatives continued to downplay the government's contributions to Americans' well-being.

During Roosevelt's second term, the NAM campaign increasingly argued that "private enterprise is the only source of jobs" and therefore the only source of "real security."[178] Many of the conservative movement's leaders sincerely believed that the government could only distribute wealth, not create it. They agreed with former Roosevelt advisor turned critic Raymond Moley that "no politician and no government can make a more abundant life. Government, through law, can divide what is already there. But only in a slight degree can it increase what is there. Government is not a machine for production. It is a mechanism for the adjustment of the elements in production, consumption, and distribution. . . . The creation of new means toward a better life lies with the leaders of business."[179]

To persuade those who disagreed with the premise that the government could not create wealth, conservatives added that even if the government *could* in theory create wealth, the government could not be counted on to do so in practice because it was not merely less competent than the private sector but was to a large degree incompetent. Whether because of inability or ineptitude, the idea that the government could not provide "real" economic security became a central tenet of the conservative persuasion campaign. As Bruce Barton told the audience at the 1935 NAM convention, "On this issue the competition is joined."[180] This argument's power grew as the economy faltered in 1937–1938 and full economic recovery remained elusive.

The NAM campaign also tried to associate liberal economic security proposals with what it called the "isms"—socialism, communism, and fascism—thereby arguing implicitly that those proposals were antithetical to the American political tradition.[181] At first, the NAM generally did not attack the liberal vision directly—unlike similar earlier efforts undertaken by the Liberty League.[182] Instead, much of the NAM's messaging from this early period operated at the level of principle. For example, the first series of the popular *You and Industry* booklets focused on what the NAM described as core American political principles, including that "it is essential, in a free system, that there should be no bureaucratic control of the citizens."[183] The success of the conservative effort to tar liberal policy proposals with the "ism" brush—whether directly or indirectly—depended on the extent to which Americans felt threatened by those ideologies. It therefore fell flat at first but grew more effective as the world descended into a war among competing ideologies.

Another argument that fell flat at first but gained force with the coming of war was the danger of "trading freedom for security." In 1936, James P. Warburg, another former Roosevelt advisor turned critic, had tried unsuccessfully to advance the argument that the continued "feverish quest of national security" defined to include economic security would destroy freedom in the United States just as it had in "Russia, Germany, Austria, and Italy."[184] The argument resonated immediately with conservative leaders and became an article of faith for some of them, including Sun Oil president and NAM board member J. Howard Pew.[185] But the general public remained unmoved until events in Europe took several more dramatic turns for the worse in the late 1930s.

ALTHOUGH THEY MADE little impression independently, all these conservative arguments contained elements that could be combined to amplify their power. To transform these arguments into a persuasive message, however, the leaders of the NAM campaign knew they needed to find an overarching ideal and unifying language comparable to what liberals had found in "security."[186] But that search did not delay their entry into the competition with liberals for the public mind that Bruce Barton urged them to join in his 1935 speech to the NAM convention. Even as the

NAM campaign's leaders searched for their overarching ideal and unifying language, the NAM campaign helped to expand the conservative movement's base through its focus on "opinion molders" and youth. Through those efforts and the rest of its expanding campaign, the NAM picked up where the Liberty League left off in its effort to help conservatives develop the shared vocabulary they needed to coalesce as a movement. The pieces were coming together for the conservative counteroffensive to begin eroding public support for Roosevelt's economic security–focused national security state.

4

The First Battle over the Government's National Security Responsibilities

"IT IS NOT ENOUGH that the wheels turn," Franklin Roosevelt told Congress in his January 6, 1937, annual message.[1] "They must carry us in the direction of a greater satisfaction in life for the average citizen. The deeper purpose of democratic government is to assist as many of its citizens as possible, especially those who need it most, to improve their conditions of life, to retain all personal liberty which does not adversely affect their neighbors, and to pursue the happiness which comes with security and an opportunity for recreation and culture."[2]

In the final days of his first term, Roosevelt thought the country had turned a corner in terms of economic recovery and public acceptance of an expanded government tasked with ensuring economic security. How else could he interpret his overwhelming victory in the 1936 election other than as a ratification of his approach and a mandate to continue building a national security state? In his annual message to Congress, Roosevelt said, "Your task and mine is not ending with the end of the depression. The people of the United States have made it clear that they expect us to continue our active efforts in behalf of their peaceful advancement."[3]

In his second inaugural address, delivered two weeks later on the cold and rainy afternoon of January 20, 1937—the wettest inauguration on record—Roosevelt acknowledged that circumstances had grown less favorable to his state-building project in the four years since he first took the presidential oath. At that time, "advance became imperative under the goad of fear and suffering."[4] Although recovery seemed to be under way, Roosevelt challenged his fellow Americans to aim higher, "to find through government the instrument of our united purpose to solve for the individual the ever-rising problems of a complex civilization."[5]

What were those problems Roosevelt believed it was the government's responsibility to solve? "In this nation," Roosevelt said,

> I see tens of millions of its citizens—a substantial part of its whole population—who at this very moment are denied the greater part of what the very lowest standards of today call the necessities of life. I see millions of families trying to live on incomes so meager that the pall of family disaster hangs over them day by day. I see millions whose daily lives in city and on farm continue under conditions labeled indecent by a so-called polite society half a century ago. I see millions denied education, recreation, and the opportunity to better their lot and the lot of their children. I see millions lacking the means to buy the products of farm and factory and by their poverty denying work and productiveness to many other millions. I see one-third of a nation ill-housed, ill-clad, ill-nourished.[6]

It was these problems that Roosevelt's economic security–focused national security state would solve. Roosevelt believed solving them required more intelligent management of the nation's growth through national planning and the expansion of Social Security to cover more people and more of life's hazards. In both cases, Roosevelt saw administrative weakness as the principal obstacle. Roosevelt therefore focused during his second term on reorganizing the executive branch to increase the managerial capacity of the nascent national security state.

The challenge for Roosevelt as he began his second term was how to sustain support for his agenda amid changing circumstances and stronger conservative opposition. Since 1933, Roosevelt had used the Great Depression to frame economic security programs as imperative for national security. But the power of that framing faded as the economy recovered in 1936 and the sense of crisis waned. More problematic for Roosevelt, the power of that framing continued to fade even after the economy slipped back into recession in the spring of 1937, a result of public loss of confidence—encouraged by conservatives—in the effectiveness of Roosevelt's policies. Roosevelt needed a new argument for why expanding the government's economic security responsibilities remained essential. This need became more urgent as conservative opposition spread to the grassroots and strengthened.

After struggling in 1937, Roosevelt found his answer in events in Europe and the worsening international crisis. These developments provided Roosevelt with a new way of justifying his domestic policy proposals as necessary for national security. Beginning in 1938, Roosevelt argued more often and more persuasively that if Americans did not feel secure economically, the survival of the United States as Americans knew it would be imperiled, either because Americans might abandon their political system in favor of dictatorship, just as citizens in Japan, Italy, and Germany had done, or because the United States would be too weak to resist foreign aggression in an increasingly conflict-ridden world.

But the worsening international crisis provided ammunition for Roosevelt's conservative critics too. They argued that continuing Roosevelt's reconstruction project would lead to dictatorship, the type of catastrophe that had befallen other countries. These dueling interpretations of the mounting international crisis underscored the fundamental difference in how liberals and conservatives understood the relationship between the government and liberty. Liberals saw an expanded government as the essential guarantor of economic security on which they believed liberty depended in modern times. Conservatives saw an expanded government as the destroyer of liberty. The development of Roosevelt's national security state turned on the outcome of this framing battle.

Despite increasingly effective conservative opposition, Roosevelt added two pieces to the national security state during his second term. The National Resources Planning Board provided the national planning Roosevelt considered vital to the country's long-term economic security. The Federal Security Agency built on the economic security "corner stone" laid by the Social Security system and solidified in the public mind the government's economic security responsibilities. Still, Roosevelt believed much remained to be done.

The Push for National Planning

Roosevelt and his advisors entered office in March 1933 convinced that the government needed to take greater responsibility for planning the country's growth.[7] Specifically, they thought the government needed to play a more active role in managing the country's natural resources, which had once seemed infinite but now had obvious limits and were growing scarcer. Roosevelt liked to recall his experience traveling the country as vice presidential candidate during the 1920 election, noting that it was apparent even then that "our country . . . had grown up like Topsy without any particular planning."[8] That may have worked for a time, he said, because seemingly endless available land and resources did not require careful, planned use. He argued that even in 1920, however, "I became impressed with the fact that in these latter days we had come . . . to the end of that limitless opportunity of new places to go to and new sources of wealth to tap, of new industries to start almost anywhere, and new land to take up and that the time was ripe . . . for the beginning of planning, planning to prevent in the future the errors of the past and planning to carry through in the future certain perfectly obvious economic and social needs that were new to the country."[9]

As president, Roosevelt made clear that he believed both short-term economic recovery and the country's long-term economic security depended on planning.[10] In his first inaugural address, Roosevelt pointed to "national planning" as part of the solution to the country's ills.[11] During the packed first hundred days of his presidency, Roosevelt took the first steps toward increasing the government's planning responsibilities, including most visibly through the proposal to create the Tennessee Valley Authority (TVA) to manage that region's development. In his message asking Congress to create the TVA, Roosevelt argued that "it is time to extend planning to a wider field, in this instance comprehending in one great project many States directly concerned with the basin of one of our greatest rivers. This in a true sense is a return to the spirit and vision of the pioneer. If we are successful here we can march on, step by step; in a like development of other great natural territorial units within our borders."[12] His message left no doubt that he saw the TVA as a prototype for greater national planning.

The National Industrial Recovery Act, passed in June 1933, set the wheels of national planning in motion by making possible the establishment of the National Planning Board.[13] The board's original purpose was to help determine which potential public works projects had the greatest value and should be given priority.[14] The dominant strand in economic thought at that time, expressed most clearly by economist and National Planning Board member Wesley C. Mitchell, held that business was cyclical and experienced periodic downturns.[15] To mitigate the economic damage these downturns caused, the government could engage in countercyclical spending through public works projects.[16] But a lack of good information about the country's resources made the board's core task of prioritizing public works projects difficult.[17] On June 24, 1934, the board sent Roosevelt "A Plan for Planning" that went well beyond planning for economic recovery.[18] The board recommended creating a broader planning organization that could both gather the needed information about the country's resources and make recommendations about their wisest use.[19] Roosevelt accepted the proposal, and the focus of planning expanded beyond short-term recovery toward more intelligent long-term management of the country's resources.

On June 30, 1934, the day after creating the Committee on Economic Security to study social insurance and related matters, Roosevelt created a complementary National Resources Board. Together, the two bodies would prepare the blueprints for an economic security–focused national security state. Roosevelt's executive order creating the National Resources Board said, "The functions of the Board shall be to prepare and present to the President a program and plan of procedure dealing with the physical, social, governmental, and economic aspects of public policies for the development and use of land, water, and other national resources, and such related subjects as may from time to time be referred to it by the President."[20] The National Resources Board would be an independent cabinet committee reporting to Roosevelt.[21] He named Interior Secretary Harold Ickes chairman, but also appointed an advisory committee that would do much of the board's work. He appointed his uncle Frederic A. Delano, a longtime champion of government planning, chairman of the advisory committee.[22] Joining Delano on the advisory committee were two academic heavyweights: University of Chicago political scientist Charles E. Merriam and Columbia University economist Wesley C. Mitchell.[23] All three had served on the National Planning Board.

Roosevelt's planners felt that modern circumstances demanded planning and that planning provided the path to the country's long-term economic security. As they wrote in their "Plan for Planning," "Conditions have developed which great masses of people will not tolerate and should not be expected to tolerate over any considerable period of time. Americans are not and should not be convinced that there is no remedy for these calamitous conditions, and experience shows that they will not resign themselves to helpless inaction. Not passive acceptance but violent explosion is the alternative if we fail to develop security and progress by rational and evolutionary methods."[24] In a December 1934 report to Roosevelt, the National Resources Board wrote that "much of the unbalance, insecurity, and suffering which our country has experienced in the past might be avoided in future by a more perfect coordination of the knowledge which we already possess."[25]

Roosevelt's planners rejected the conservative charge that planning reduced individual liberty, arguing that "sound planning on the contrary brings about a fresh release of opportunities rather than a narrowing of choice."[26] The board provided the example of "street planning and traffic regulation," which enable "freer use of the [roads and] highways than unplanned streets and uncontrolled traffic."[27] The board observed tartly that "it may be found that some of those who cry 'regimentation' when public planning is mentioned foresee interference with their own practices of private regimentation and exploitation of otherwise helpless persons under their private control. Those with special privileges to protect and preserve naturally object to any public planning that may dislodge them from a preferred position."[28] The board surmised that "when men express sincere opposition to all governmental planning, it can only mean a grave misunderstanding of what planning really is."[29] The board explained that "planning is not an end, but a means . . . for better use of what we have, a means of emancipation of millions of personalities now fettered, for the enrichment of human life."[30] The board concluded by arguing that it was indeed possible to plan "for fuller liberty."[31]

The board's reports reinforced Roosevelt's belief that increasing the government's economic security responsibilities by embracing national planning would restore individual liberty and achieve the highest purpose assigned to the government in the Declaration of Independence, which was to enable the individual pursuit of happiness. Roosevelt had been reflecting on that lofty purpose in 1934 while reading French literary historian Gilbert Chinard's analysis of Thomas Jefferson and the Declaration of Independence. In the margins, Roosevelt highlighted passages dealing with what Chinard argued was novel about the Declaration of Independence, which Chinard said was its focus on the "pursuit of happiness" and the government's role therein.[32] More and more, Roosevelt believed that economic security constituted the foundation for the psychological security that enabled the pursuit of happiness. And he was convinced that economic security required planning.

Although Roosevelt, with his Brain Trust's help, tried during the 1932 campaign to persuade Americans that national planning dated to the Founding, he and his advisors understood that what they wanted to do constituted a break with the past. Harvard professor E. Pendleton Herring noted in 1935 that "to advocate a planned society under our system of capitalism and democracy is to urge a leopard to change his spots."[33] Roosevelt knew the word "planning" itself generated hostility among some Americans, but he struggled to find an alternative term.[34] In the meantime, Roosevelt and his advisors leaned harder on American icons. Roosevelt told a conference of the nation's governors, for example, that George Washington had "met his problems by patient and informed planning."[35]

Roosevelt's planners developed this continuity narrative more fully in their reports in 1934, writing that "from the beginning of our national life various forms of planning have been in evidence. The industrial situation confronting the founders of this Republic was one of wide-spread distress, insecurity, and depression of the most anxious type. They deliberately planned a way out. The Constitution itself was an economic-political plan on a grand scale."[36] In another report, the board noted that "Hamilton's 'Plan of Manufactures,' Jefferson's and Gallatin's 'Internal Improvements,' [Henry] Clay's 'American System,' the American Homestead Policy, the Conservation Movement, and the 'economic mobilization' of the [First] World War are all examples of national planning."[37] In sum, the board said, "planning is a distinctly American idea."[38] To underscore the point, the board emphasized the tremendous amount of planning already under way in the government and in the private sector.[39] What was missing, the board said, was national-level coordination. "The plans of business, the plans of labor, the plans of agriculture, the plans of science and technology, the plans of social welfare, the plans of government, have not heretofore been aligned in such manner as to promote the general welfare in the highest degree attainable."[40]

In his January 4, 1935, annual message to Congress, Roosevelt used the language of security to impress upon the Congress and the American public the importance of the National Resources Board's work. He explained that "a study of our national resources, more comprehensive than any previously made, shows the vast amount of necessary and practicable work which needs to be done for the development and preservation of our natural wealth for the enjoyment and advantage of our people in generations to come."[41] He argued that "the sound use of land and water is far more comprehensive than the mere planting of trees, building of dams, distributing of electricity or retirement of sub-marginal land."[42] Roosevelt said national planning "recognizes that stranded populations, either in the country or the city, cannot have security under the conditions that now surround them."[43] "The better use of our national resources," Roosevelt argued, was essential to "security of livelihood."[44]

The amount of effort applied to justifying the work of Roosevelt's planners reflected the vehemence of conservative opposition. National Association of Manufacturers chairman Robert Lund presented the conservative argument against national planning in an August 18, 1935, piece in the *Los Angeles Times.* "It grows clearer daily," Lund declared, "that the New Deal's experimental recovery program is a failure."[45] Lund argued that this failure was all the more remarkable because Americans had "accepted . . . many measures and projects new and seemingly alien to American traditions . . . to aid, loyally, 'planned recovery.'"[46] And more remarkable still because "dictatorial authority, complete freedom, the widest cooperation and many billions of dollars—all these were available as aids to those who sought to 'plan' prosperity."[47] After arguing that the New Deal had failed in its basic tasks of reducing unemployment and increasing job security, Lund concluded that "the failure made [by the New Deal to date] certainly does not warrant transforming what we had supposed to be temporary emergency 'planned recovery' into permanent 'planned economy.'"[48]

Lund's piece underscored the conundrum Roosevelt faced with planning. If his "planned" economic recovery programs failed to deliver, then conservative critics would use that failure to discredit planning. If his programs succeeded, then conservatives would argue that further planning was unnecessary. Nevertheless, Roosevelt believed the country needed a greater level of national planning and persisted in his efforts to institutionalize a national planning capability within the executive branch. When the Supreme Court invalidated the National Industrial Recovery Act in mid-1935 and thereby erased the statutory basis for the National Resources Board, Roosevelt reconstituted it under the Emergency Relief Appropriation Act as the National Resources Committee.[49] The nascent national planning capability survived but was far from institutionalized.

The Fight over Executive Branch Reorganization

By the end of 1935, Roosevelt had concluded that insufficient administrative capacity in the executive branch limited the government's ability to deliver national security.[50] When he assumed the presidency, Roosevelt inherited a White House staff structure that granted him only four policy assistants.[51] Since the beginning of his presidency, Roosevelt had tried to work around presidential staffing limitations by appointing key advisors to executive branch positions with limited responsibilities so they could serve primarily as presidential assistants. Hence, Raymond Moley's otherwise nonsensical appointment as assistant secretary of state in 1933.[52] But Roosevelt felt these improvisations hardly suited contemporary needs.

In late 1935, Roosevelt began trying to increase the executive branch's administrative capacity to make possible the increased government planning he believed necessary to prevent future economic crises.[53] In March 1936, Roosevelt told congressional leaders he had established a committee to recommend administrative improvements and asked for their support.[54] Louis Brownlow, a public administration expert at the University of Chicago, served as chairman, with Charles Merriam, who had helped lead Roosevelt's national planning efforts, and Luther Gulick, a public administration specialist at Columbia University, filling out the committee.[55] As he had with the Committee on Economic Security, Roosevelt asked this new committee to prepare recommendations in time for early submission to the next Congress, which would convene in January 1937.[56]

In the meantime, Roosevelt tried to sell national planning as both a basic government function and as vital to national security during the 1936 campaign. At his regular press conference on September 8, 1936, Roosevelt read reporters passages from David Cushman Coyle's book *Waste: The Fight to Save America* about the consequences of the failure to plan: "The money to pay for good things comes out of not having to pay for loss and disaster. Soil erosion losses to date are over ten billion dollars in money values."[57] Roosevelt added that "he is awfully low on that. In the course of 300 years, the soil erosion loss is infinitely more than ten billion dollars."[58] Roosevelt continued reading: "When we look ahead to the future of our country we are forced to decide whether we are willing to invest money in building up the strength and security of the nation. Or shall we insist on holding tight to our money—even though the wealth it is supposed to represent slips away from us?"[59] "It is a grand book," Roosevelt told the reporters gathered in his office. "You ought to read it."[60]

Roosevelt extolled the virtues of planning again during his Western campaign trip the following month. Speaking from his campaign train's rear platform, Roosevelt told a crowd in Olathe, Kansas, on October 13, 1936, that "yes, this year we are planning; and why not? After all, that is one of the things that Government is intended to do, to think not in terms of just this year and the next, but, for the good of the people, to think for many long years ahead."[61] The growing chorus of conservative criticism about government "waste," "bungling," and "boondoggling" during the 1936 campaign further motivated Roosevelt's effort to institutionalize national planning, for institutionalized planning had the potential to inoculate the administration against such charges in the future.

The Committee on Administrative Management sent Roosevelt its report on January 8, 1937. Roosevelt gathered reporters in his office three days later to explain the recommendations. Louis Brownlow and fellow committee members Charles Merriam and Luther Gulick recommended Congress permit the president to submit executive branch reorganization plans and to hire six additional assistants.[62] Previewing what he would ask for if Congress granted him the authority he sought, Roosevelt said creating a permanent national planning board by statute would improve coordination across the government and enable it to happen without the president's continuous involvement in minutiae.[63] Following the template he had used in 1935 to secure passage of his economic security bill, Roosevelt sent Congress the Committee on Administrative Management's report a week after his annual message and asked for legislation implementing its recommendations.[64] Given his and his party's resounding victory in the 1936 elections, he may have expected little resistance.[65] He may even have expected a repeat of what happened in the days after his first inauguration, when his administration drafted legislation that Congress dutifully passed.

There are several reasons why it didn't happen that way. For one, many members of Congress resented what they perceived as Roosevelt's treating their body as a rubber stamp rather than as a coequal branch of government.[66] To peals of laughter in the House, Rep. Charles A. Eaton (R-NJ) captured those feelings colorfully when he reminded his colleagues that "out of 77 major laws passed in the first 4 years of Mr. Roosevelt's administration, only 18 of them originated here, where all ought to have originated, while 59 had an illegitimate birth conceived in sin and shapen in iniquity somewhere downtown and were brought up here, and the bastards laid on our doorstep with the command of the Executive that we acknowledge parentage."[67] The way that Roosevelt sprung his reorganization proposal on Congress in January 1937 did nothing to alleviate these concerns.[68] Many members of Congress also felt the bill would diminish their power relative to the executive branch.[69] Most problematic of all, however, was that Roosevelt submitted a plan to reorganize the judiciary—which critics quickly labeled a "court packing" scheme—at around the same time as his executive branch reorganization bill. Roosevelt's opponents moved quickly to lump the two bills together, citing them as evidence that Roosevelt sought dictatorial powers by reducing the independent power of the other branches of government.[70]

Roosevelt's political troubles increased when the economy worsened in the spring of 1937. The downturn undermined his ability to claim planning had helped bring recovery and, on that record, to push for the institutionalization of planning to ensure future economic security. The downturn presented the administration with one of its toughest challenges yet.

It was a painfully ironic coincidence that the administration had to face the crisis without the national planning capability and executive branch managerial capacity it believed essential to facilitate a speedy recovery.

At the same time, the continuing Depression eroded the elite and popular support for elite-led planning that had marked the early years of Roosevelt's presidency. Walter Lippmann—the same public intellectual who advised Roosevelt in the period before he assumed the presidency that he "might have to assume dictatorial powers"—now used his syndicated newspaper column and a new book to reject planning of the sort the Roosevelt administration had long advocated and wanted to institutionalize.[71] In *Inquiry into the Principles of the Good Society* and in the pages of his widely read newspaper column "Today and Tomorrow," Lippmann argued that the government's chief responsibility was to guarantee freedom of economic transactions, not to guarantee economic security directly.[72]

Roosevelt continued to try to build support for national planning in the fall of 1937, including by highlighting a National Resources Committee report on urban life.[73] Roosevelt explained how "this valuable report takes stock of our urban centers as parts of our national resources, calls attention to a wide range of important urban situations, relates these problems to our national problem, and points out the ways of dealing with many emerging and critical trends of urban life."[74] He concluded by arguing that "the sanitation, the education, the housing, the working and living conditions, the economic security—in brief, the general welfare of all—are American concerns, insofar as they are within the range of Federal power and responsibility under the Constitution."[75] He made little headway.

With Roosevelt struggling, newspaper magnate Frank Gannett organized the National Committee to Uphold Constitutional Government to turn public opinion against the president's proposals.[76] Like nearly all of Roosevelt's opponents at the time, the National Committee focused first on Roosevelt's proposed judiciary reorganization. With "court packing" defeated, the National Committee turned to Roosevelt's executive branch reorganization proposal, declaring that "in our opinion, the time has come when the country should clearly realize that the President is deliberately trying to liquidate our democratic institutions, and set up in their place . . . a political and economic dictatorship."[77]

The effectiveness of the National Committee to Uphold Constitutional Government marked another important evolution in the conservative movement's organization and messaging. Like the revitalized National Association of Manufacturers (NAM), the National Committee to Uphold Constitutional Government learned from the Liberty League's mistakes. The Liberty League's heavy reliance on businessmen for funds made it easy to dismiss as a tool of the rich.[78] Although the wealthy Frank Gannett served as the driving force behind the National Committee, it was a far less expensive operation than the Liberty League and therefore could rely for funds on smaller, less prominent donors. Pierre and Irénée du Pont contributed, but the National Committee's critics could not paint the organization as the Liberty League redux.[79] The National Committee also did a better job than the Liberty League of assembling a leadership group that provided a solid veneer of nonpartisanship.[80]

Like the ongoing NAM persuasion campaign, the National Committee focused its efforts on influencing opinion leaders in communities across the United States. National Committee Executive Secretary Edward A. Rumely called these people "'leadership individuals': doctors, lawyers, clergymen, editors, business executives, farm leaders, educators, members of civic bodies and patriotic organizations, members of women's clubs."[81] Rumely and the National Committee's other leaders believed that "there are about one million men and women, one for every twenty-five families, who give leadership to this nation's thinking."[82]

Direct mail was the National Committee's preferred way of reaching these opinion molders.[83] For some of those groups—lawyers, for instance—Rumely rented commercially available mailing lists. For other groups, Rumely and the National Committee developed its own lists. In total, he estimated that the National Committee sent out "somewhere between six hundred and fifty and seven hundred thousand letters" as part of its direct mailing campaign against Roosevelt's executive branch reorganization plan.[84] Like NAM, Rumely found that cultivating women's groups paid large dividends. He noted that "we ship in bulk responses . . . to people who are interested in the first mailing and want to carry the thing further . . . women are very much given to do that and are very active workers."[85] Through its targeted direct mail campaign, the National Committee to Uphold Constitutional Government contributed to the growth of the conservative network around the country and added an important page to the conservative movement's playbook.[86]

The innovative direct mailing approach proved remarkably effective in mobilizing what appeared to be both grassroots and grasstops opposition to Roosevelt's reorganization plans.[87] Tens of thousands of letters and telegrams flooded the halls of Congress, urging members to vote against reorganization. The success of the National Committee's direct mail campaign aroused the intense ire of the Roosevelt administration. In strong, anger-distorted prose, Roosevelt's Secretary of the Interior Harold Ickes denounced the campaign as "Mail Order Government" in an article in *Collier's*, charging the National Committee with stoking "the mob spirit, that miasmic, bloodthirsty, degrading emanation out of the dim past."[88] He dismissed the movement as the "charge of the light-headed brigade."[89] Ickes's diatribe only confirmed for conservatives that in targeted direct mail they had found an effective technique not just for repeating their message at scale but also for mobilizing public opinion.

The National Committee to Uphold Constitutional Government contributed to the conservative movement's development in other important ways too. The committee's partial success using events abroad to argue against domestic political reform marked the first real progress conservatives had made in pushing Roosevelt's domestic agenda out of the national security frame. In a March 17, 1938, telegram to members of Congress, Frank Gannett urged them to "think seriously of the plight of democracy here and everywhere" and then argued that their votes on the reorganization bill "may mean more than any you have ever cast or are likely to in the future."[90] The reason, Gannett said, was that "in a great many countries the legislators themselves, in order to meet emergencies, have delegated powers which later they have not been able to regain. And soon, democratic control by the people's representatives has disappeared."[91] In this argument conservatives found a compelling counter to Roosevelt's efforts to use events abroad to justify his domestic agenda.

The National Committee also framed Roosevelt's policy proposals as a threat to Americans' liberty. It included in its mailings a copy of a telegram from well-known writer and historian James Truslow Adams—coiner of the phrase "American Dream"—saying that "the preservation of liberty is not a party question" and a piece from widely read columnist

Dorothy Thompson arguing that the bill went "a long way toward estab-lishing authoritarian government in the United States."[92] Denunciations of the reorganization bill from aroused constituents poured into the of-fices of congressmen, persuading some of them of widespread public op-position to the bill.[93] The president's proposal to reorganize the execu-tive branch appeared to suffer a death blow in the House on April 8, 1938, when members voted to recommit the bill to committee.[94]

By the second week of April 1938, the United States seemed to have arrived at a stalemate between competing political philosophies. *The Economist* observed that "an extraordinary change has come over the American political scene since the presidential election of November, 1936. Before that election the President had had to face opposition as bit-ter and as personally venomous as any that even his most unpopular pre-decessors had encountered. He appealed to the country, and the country gave him the largest majority in its history. He seemed to be in impregna-ble position."[95] Now, however, Roosevelt "was charged with planning tyranny because he wished to organize more efficiently the executive branch, for which he has an incontestable mandate from the people."[96] Conservatives continued to fight bitterly against Roosevelt's reorganiza-tion plans, believing that if approved they would solidify the govern-ment's economic security responsibilities. The result, as *The Economist* concluded, was "deadlock."[97]

Roosevelt Regains the Upper Hand

Faced with the most effective opposition he had encountered since be-coming president, Roosevelt took his case directly to the public in an April 14, 1938, fireside chat, leaning once more on the language of secu-rity to build support for his agenda. Roosevelt and his closest advisors knew this fireside chat was important. Missy LeHand, Roosevelt's trusted assistant, asked longtime advisor Samuel Rosenman to come down from New York to work on the address.[98] In the small hours of the morning of April 14, LeHand, Rosenman, Grace Tully—Roosevelt's other trusted assistant—and Tommy Corcoran sat with Roosevelt in his office as he reclined on the sofa and dictated a first draft that contained a powerful new argument for continuing his agenda.[99] Roosevelt said recent events abroad showed that failure to reconstruct government to meet the economic security needs of modern times led to the collapse of democracy and to the loss of individual liberty under dictatorship.[100]

When he appeared via radio in Americans' homes that night, Roosevelt reminded his fellow citizens that "democracy has disappeared in several other great nations—disappeared not because the people of those nations disliked democracy, but because they had grown tired of unemployment and insecurity, of seeing their children hungry while they sat helpless in the face of government confusion, government weakness, weakness through lack of leadership in government. Finally, in desperation, they chose to sacrifice liberty in the hope of getting something to eat."[101] Roosevelt affirmed that "we in America know that our own democratic institutions can be preserved and made to work. But in order to preserve them we need to act together, to meet the problems of the Nation boldly, and to prove that the practical operation of democratic government is equal to the task of protecting the security of the people."[102]

Roosevelt said, "The people of America are in agreement in defending their liberties at any cost" and argued that "the first line of that defense lies in the protection of economic security."[103] "History proves that dictatorships do not grow out of strong and successful governments," Roosevelt said, lowering his voice and emphasizing every word, "but out of weak and helpless governments."[104] He continued, "If by democratic methods people get a government strong enough to protect them from fear and starvation, their democracy succeeds; but if they do not, they grow impatient. Therefore, the only sure bulwark of continuing liberty is a government strong enough to protect the interests of the people."[105] Freedom, in sum, depended on a strong government that guaranteed its citizens' economic security.

Roosevelt reiterated that "security is our greatest need" and warned against demolishing the building blocks of the national security state his administration and Congress had put into place.[106] "Our immediate task," Roosevelt declared, "is to consolidate and maintain the gains achieved."[107] On top of that, Roosevelt said, "all the energies of government and business must be directed to increasing the national income, to putting more people into private jobs, to giving security and a feeling of security to all people in all walks of life."[108] "We are a rich Nation,"

Roosevelt said.[109] "We can afford to pay for security and prosperity without having to sacrifice our liberties into the bargain."[110]

The fireside chat went over well.[111] Even Frank Gannett was impressed, writing to Elisha Hanson that "the President doesn't give up easily, does he? Someone has referred to him as 'resilient' and I think that's a good word for him, for he certainly does bound back."[112] Roosevelt decided to seek authority again to reorganize the executive branch when the next Congress convened early in 1939.[113]

In the meantime, Roosevelt tried to win support for building on the Social Security cornerstone of the national security state. Roosevelt addressed the nation via radio on August 15, 1938, to mark the third anniversary of his signing the Social Security Act into law. He began by rebutting the charge, leveled often by conservatives, that he had expanded the government's responsibilities beyond the bounds of American tradition. He argued, on the contrary, that government provision of economic security was nothing new. Roosevelt pointed out that the government since at least the nineteenth century had ensured some citizens' economic security. He noted that "the first to turn to Government, the first to receive protection from Government, were not the poor and the lowly . . . but the rich and the strong. Beginning in the nineteenth century, the United States passed protective laws designed, in the main, to give security to property owners, to industrialists, to merchants and to bankers."[114]

What was new was the guarantee of economic security to the poor, which, Roosevelt said, changing economic conditions had made necessary—and increasingly urgent as other countries that had failed to do so collapsed into dictatorship. "Because it has become increasingly difficult for individuals to build their own security single-handed," Roosevelt reminded listeners, "Government must now step in and help them lay the foundation stones, just as Government in the past has helped lay the foundation of business and industry. We must face the fact that in this country we have a rich man's security and a poor man's security and that the Government owes equal obligations to both."[115] Roosevelt then returned to a theme he had sounded since his first presidential campaign in 1932, when he argued that "danger to one is danger to all."[116] "National security," he declared forcefully, pausing for a beat, "is not a half and half matter; it is all or none."[117]

This was Roosevelt's second use of the term "national security" in a major address as president, the first since his May 1933 fireside chat. Its appearance was not random. Now, as then, Roosevelt faced a difficult persuasion challenge. In 1933, Roosevelt needed to sell the American people and their representatives on expanding the government's responsibilities for ensuring economic security. Now, as he said in his address, he wanted Congress to "improve and extend the law" to cover more Americans and meet more of their security needs.[118] As he put it, "to be truly national, a social security program must include all those who need its protection."[119] He declared that "we have come a long way. But we still have a long way to go. There is still today a frontier that remains unconquered—an America unreclaimed. This is the great, the nation-wide frontier of insecurity, of human want and human fear. This is the frontier—the America—we have set ourselves to reclaim."[120] When Congress finally amended the Social Security Act in August 1939, Roosevelt issued a statement praising the expansion of the program's coverage and increases in benefits. But he also emphasized that much remained to be done—and that he would continue to seek additional expansions.[121]

Congress finally gave Roosevelt authority to reorganize the executive branch in April 1939, two years after he first sought that authority. On April 3, 1939, Roosevelt signed into law the Reorganization Act of 1939, which enabled him to hire six executive-level assistants and to submit specific reorganization plans to Congress. Three weeks later, he submitted Reorganization Plan No. 1, and Congress quickly approved it.[122] In his transmittal letter, Roosevelt again connected his domestic agenda to the country's ability to survive in a world of disappearing democracies, writing that "we are not free if our administration is weak. But we are free if we know, and others know, that we are strong."[123] Security against foreign enemies, Roosevelt made clear, required domestic economic security. By this logic, domestic policy had become foreign policy.

Under the reorganization authority he gained from Congress, Roosevelt created an Executive Office of the President for the purpose of "strengthening and developing the management arms of the President," which Roosevelt said "deal with (1) budget, and efficiency research, (2) planning, and (3) personnel."[124] To address the first point, he moved the Bureau of the Budget from the Treasury Department to the Executive

Office of the President. To address the second point, he transferred the National Resources Committee to the Executive Office of the President, renamed it the National Resources Planning Board, and "hereby renew[ed] and emphasize[d] my recommendations that the work of this Board be placed upon a permanent statutory basis."[125] Congress had refused to do so as part of the Reorganization Act and continued to express little interest in doing so.[126] On personnel, he named one of his six new administrative assistants "as a liaison agent of the White House on personnel management."[127]

Roosevelt also created a Federal Security Agency composed of "those agencies of the Government, the major purposes of which are to promote social and economic security, educational opportunity and the health of the citizens of the Nation."[128] The choice of name mattered. The Brownlow Committee had recommended creating a "Department of Public Welfare," and a draft executive branch organization chart from 1939 included an entity with that name.[129] But in keeping with his appreciation of the language of security's power, Roosevelt preferred to call the new entity a "security agency."[130] When he had first proposed executive branch reorganization in January 1937 and expected little resistance, Roosevelt told reporters that "on the question of these names . . . I don't think it makes an awful lot of difference."[131] Two years of bitter fighting over reorganization may have led Roosevelt to change his tune. The fact that it was also the *Federal* Security Agency helped solidify the federal government's expanded responsibilities for economic security.[132]

With Congress still refusing to provide a statutory basis for national planning, the president issued an executive order detailing the responsibilities of the National Resources Planning Board:

> (a) To survey, collect data on, and analyze problems pertaining to national resources, both natural and human, and to recommend to the President and the Congress long-time plans and programs for the wise use and fullest development of such resources.
>
> (b) To consult with Federal, regional, state, local, and private agencies in developing orderly programs of public works and to list for the President and the Congress all proposed public works in the order of their relative importance with respect to (1) the greatest good to the greatest number of people, (2) the emergency necessities of the

Nation, and (3) the social, economic, and cultural advancement of the people of the United States.

(c) To inform the President of the general trend of economic conditions and to recommend measures leading to their improvement o[r] stabilization.

(d) To act as a clearing house and means of coordination for planning activities, linking together various levels and fields of planning.[133]

The first and third sets of functions would foster stability and reduce the frequency of economic downturns. The second set of functions empowered the executive branch to use countercyclical public works spending to reduce the impact of downturns. Together, these capabilities represented the missing piece in Roosevelt's strategy for ensuring long-term economic security. As he had with earlier national planning bodies, Roosevelt put his uncle, Frederic Delano, in charge.[134] The National Resources Planning Board was to continue the work begun by its predecessors to plan for a stable and secure future.[135]

But without an act of Congress, the national planning capability Roosevelt thought the country needed still was not institutionalized as solidly as Social Security. Within months, conservatives in Congress tried to slash the board's funding during the 1940 appropriations process. Roosevelt intervened, telling Congress he must "'earnestly plead' for the agency's continuation."[136] Congress acquiesced, despite what the Associated Press called "bitter Republican denunciation of the unit as 'wasteful' and 'vicious.'"[137] Despite conservative hostility, the board set to work, picking up where its predecessors had left off in their efforts to develop a more complete understanding of the country's resources and how they could be best used. Supporters of this work argued that it was essential to economic security and therefore to national security.[138] Conservatives continued to try to kill the board at every opportunity.

THE FIGHT OVER Roosevelt's proposal to reorganize the government and institutionalize national planning had lasted more than two years. The intense struggle led both liberals and conservatives to sharpen their arguments for and against expanding the government's responsibilities.

In the end, Roosevelt's use of the language of security—particularly the argument that events abroad made domestic economic security even more vital—again carried the day. But the battle against reorganization helped conservatives develop promising tactics and strategies that grew more effective as economic and geopolitical circumstances shifted.

Although Roosevelt had regained the upper hand in 1939, conservatives were better positioned to oppose his efforts than at any time since he entered office. Roosevelt's inability to end the Depression—and thereby deliver the economic security he promised—lent force to conservatives' charge that the president had sold the country a bill of goods. At the same time, Roosevelt's accumulation of power while individual freedom collapsed under dictatorships in Europe made arguments about the government's threat to liberty plausible to an audience beyond die-hard conservatives. Roosevelt continued to argue that domestic economic security policies contributed most to national security in the face of growing foreign danger. Ironically, however, the way Roosevelt went about alerting Americans to that growing foreign danger helped conservatives push domestic policy out of the national security frame.

5

Foreign Policy as a National Security Matter

"ALL ABOUT US rage undeclared wars—military and economic," Franklin Roosevelt warned in his 1939 annual message to Congress.[1] "All about us grow more deadly armaments—military and economic. All about us are threats of new aggression—military and economic."[2] These international developments were making the United States less secure by the day, Roosevelt said. Speaking slowly and forcefully, he explained why technological change had rendered America's great oceanic defenses irrelevant: "the world has grown so small and the weapons of attack so swift that no nation can be safe in its will to peace so long as any other powerful nation refuses to settle its grievances at the council table."[3] And he explained why the rise of totalitarian ideologies threatened the country's security: "Storms from abroad directly challenge three institutions indispensable to Americans, now as always. The first is religion. Religion is the source of the other two—democracy and international good faith."[4] He said that "where freedom of religion has been attacked, the attack has come from sources opposed to democracy. Where democracy has been overthrown, the spirit of free worship has disappeared. And where religion and democracy have vanished, good faith and reason in international affairs have given way to strident ambition and brute force."[5]

The message was clear: developments abroad threatened Americans' security. What was to be done? Two things, Roosevelt said. First, the country needed to continue building a national security state that guaranteed Americans' economic security. This, Roosevelt said, was part "of putting our own house in order in the face of storm signals from across the seas."[6] Roosevelt argued that this task remained urgent, because "even a nation well armed and well organized from a strictly military point of view may . . . meet defeat if it is unnerved by self-distrust, endangered by class prejudice, by dissension between capital and labor, by false economy and by other unsolved social problems at home."[7] He concluded that "our nation's program of social and economic reform is therefore a part of defense, a part as basic as armaments themselves."[8]

Just as urgently, Roosevelt said, the country had to adjust its foreign policy to meet the security threat posed by the international crisis. He argued that in a world of hostile, expansionary powers, a policy of strict neutrality no longer worked. He said that "there comes a time in the affairs of men when they must prepare to defend, not their homes alone, but the tenets of faith and humanity on which their churches, their governments and their very foundations are set. The defense of religion, of democracy and of good faith among nations is all the same fight. To save one we must now make up our minds to save all."[9] International affairs, in other words, had now joined economic security as a top national security concern.

The coming of another world war in 1939 greatly influenced both Roosevelt's national security state and the way the public understood the term "national security." Both Roosevelt and his conservative opponents exploited the international crisis by interpreting it to the public in ways that supported their visions for the proper scope of the government's national security responsibilities. In his report on Roosevelt's 1939 annual message to Congress, widely read conservative *New York Times* columnist Arthur Krock identified the principal approaches liberals and conservatives would use to capitalize on the crisis. Liberals would link domestic and foreign policy and argue both were essential to national security. "President Roosevelt publicly argued that national security and the preservation of American democracy depend on the continuation of his economic and social policies, especially spending for recovery," Krock reported.[10] Roosevelt hammered this message home in speeches through-out 1939 and 1940. Krock worried this "ingenious formula" might enable Roosevelt to regain the upper hand just when it seemed that conservatives finally had begun turning public opinion against the president's domestic agenda.[11]

Conservatives' strategy, Krock reported, would be to support increased government spending on physical security programs in the name of national security but to oppose expanding economic security programs.[12] This strategy exemplified the selective anti-statism that would become central to the conservative movement. Conservatives also used France's capitulation to Nazi Germany in June 1940 to warn against continuing Roosevelt's economic security agenda. Conservatives said Roosevelt's economic security policies had not worked and were weakening the country, just as had happened in France. The unsubtle message was that Roosevelt's domestic agenda threatened national security.

Ironically, Roosevelt helped conservatives push domestic policy out of the national security frame through the intensity of his efforts to persuade Americans to abandon a foreign policy based on neutrality. This persuasion challenge was arguably the most difficult Roosevelt had faced as president. Most Americans in 1939 did not believe world events threatened them. To persuade them otherwise, Roosevelt leaned hard on the language of security that had served him so well throughout his presidency. Since the early 1930s, he had called economic insecurity the country's top national security concern. Now he said the physical and ideological threat posed by hostile foreign powers constituted an equally severe threat to national security.[13] Roosevelt repeated this message so often that economic security began to fade from the national security frame despite Roosevelt's attempts to keep it there.

Roosevelt Exploits the International Crisis

As the world edged toward war in 1939, Roosevelt argued in the name of national security for both continuing his domestic agenda and for adopting a more internationally engaged foreign policy. Roosevelt spoke of the need to continue domestic reconstruction in his nationally broadcast June 12, 1939, commencement address at the United States Military

Academy. Roosevelt said that "the military strength of a country can be no greater than its internal economic and moral solidarity, and the task of national defense must concern itself with civilian problems at home, quite as much as with armed forces in the field."[14] Back in Washington, Roosevelt sent a letter to Congress urging speedy revision of neutrality laws that hamstrung American foreign policy.[15] He got nowhere until Nazi Germany invaded Poland on September 1, 1939.[16]

Roosevelt took to the airwaves in a fireside chat two days later, after France and Great Britain declared war on Nazi Germany, and planted the seed of a fundamental shift in the relation of Americans' security to world events.[17] "You must master at the outset a simple but unalterable fact in modern relations between nations," Roosevelt said.[18] "When peace has been broken anywhere, the peace of all countries everywhere is in danger."[19] In other words, as far as the security of the United States was concerned, danger anywhere amounted to danger everywhere—including at home. Modulating his voice and adjusting his cadence for emphasis, he said, "It is easy for you and for me to shrug our shoulders and to say that conflicts taking place thousands of miles from the continental United States, and, indeed, thousands of miles from the whole American Hemisphere, do not seriously affect the Americas—and that all the United States has to do is to ignore them and go about its own business."[20] But he added that "passionately though we may desire detachment, we are forced to realize that every word that comes through the air, every ship that sails the sea, every battle that is fought, does affect the American future."[21]

Roosevelt repeated this new and radically enlarged conception of the relationship between world events and the nation's security a few weeks later when he addressed Congress in person to urge changes to the Neutrality Act. He argued that "any war anywhere necessarily hurts American security and American prosperity" and "any war anywhere retards the progress of morality and religion, and impairs the security of civilization itself."[22] Pressing for legislative action, he declared the embargo provisions of the Neutrality Act inconsistent with what he called "the interest of real American neutrality and security."[23]

Perhaps because conservative *New York Times* columnist Arthur Krock had long observed with dismay Roosevelt's success using the language of security to sell policy proposals, he now pushed for its use in efforts to modify the Neutrality Act—a rare source of agreement between Krock and Roosevelt. In a pair of articles published September 26 and 27, 1939, Krock described Roosevelt's proposed modification of neutrality legislation as "national security insurance," situating it alongside previous Roosevelt administration national security proposals such as unemployment insurance.[24] Krock also suggested renaming the proposed "Neutrality Act of 1939" as the "National Defense and Security Act" to frame debate on the legislation in a way likelier to lead to passage.[25] By mid-October 1939, Krock reported that administration officials had made progress using national security as a framing device to secure congressional repeal of the arms embargo provisions of the Neutrality Act.[26] But Krock and other conservatives continued to fight Roosevelt's effort to link his domestic and foreign policy agendas under the umbrella of national security.

Roosevelt did precisely that again in his January 3, 1940, annual message, telling the country in the opening lines that the growing focus on foreign affairs did not mean "that our Government is abandoning, or even overlooking, the great significance of its domestic policies."[27] Those lines did not appear in the first three drafts of the speech.[28] Their presence and prominent position in the final version illustrate Roosevelt's and his advisors' growing belief that national security could only be achieved through a blend of domestic and foreign policy.

Roosevelt elaborated on the point in a radio address on January 19, 1940, offering one of his clearest explanations of the mix of domestic and foreign policies he believed national security required. He noted that "a succession of world events has shown us that our democracy must be strengthened at every point of strain or weakness."[29] He continued, "All Americans want this country to be a place where children can live in safety and grow in understanding of the part that they are going to play in the future of our American Nation. And on that question, people have come to me and have asked, 'What about defense?' 'Well,' I have said, 'internal defense, external defense are one and the same thing. You cannot have one unless you can have both. Adequate national defense, in the broadest term, calls for adequate—yes, on the one side—munitions and implements of war and, at the same time, it calls for educated, healthy and happy citizens. And neither requisite, taken alone, taken all by itself, without the other, will give us definite national security.'"[30]

Throughout 1940, Arthur Krock continued to voice conservatives' frustration with Roosevelt's success using the international crisis to justify continuing domestic policies the president considered vital to national security. On May 24, Krock filled his column with a fictitious and caustic letter, ostensibly written by a New Deal wordsmith but actually written by Krock, that explained why, in light of the mounting Nazi threat, the Roosevelt administration was centralizing authority in the executive branch to manage the crisis and perpetuate the New Deal. "Dear Country," Krock began,

> The apparent success of the German drive has greatly imperiled our national security, and more suddenly than even the President thought likely. . . . Accordingly, your government is taking immediate steps to organize defense and make it invincible. This will be done principally by members of the President's executive staff. Unlike previous administrations, we, thanks to the high efficiency and broad experience of New Deal statesmen in all pertinent matters—industry, finance, engineering and the military arts—will require only subordinate assistance from outsiders who are the heads of American production.[31]

Krock added sarcastically that "administration heads, who have had long training in politics, law schools and welfare associations, will assume full control of the coordination of technical business matters on which national security and defense depend. Notable among these is Harry Hopkins, whose labors in CWA [Civil Works Administration] and WPA [Works Progress Administration] have brought him the deserved reputation as the finest industrial mind in America."[32] Thus, "it will not be necessary to risk the great social and economic reforms of the New Deal by giving leeway to outside experts."[33] Krock concluded, "Trust us, and listen to the fireside chat."[34]

Most Americans did listen to the fireside chat Roosevelt delivered two nights later. In it, Roosevelt again emphasized that achieving national security required more than military spending and foreign policy—that domestic policy was "just as important to the sound defense of a nation as physical armament itself."[35] The reason, Roosevelt said, was that "while our Navy and our airplanes and our guns and our ships may be our first lines of defense, it is still clear that way down at the bottom, underlying them all, giving them their strength, sustenance and power, are the spirit and the morale of a free people."[36]

Therefore, Roosevelt continued, "we must make sure, in all that we do, that there be no breakdown or cancellation of any of the great social gains which we have made in these past years. We have carried on an offensive on a broad front against social and economic inequalities, against abuses which had made our society weak. That offensive should not now be broken down by the pincers movement of those who would use the present needs of physical military defense to destroy it."[37] The many drafts of this address make clear the importance Roosevelt and his advisors attached to this point.[38] Roosevelt also carried the point further, listing domestic gains such as old-age pensions and unemployment insurance that should be consolidated and extended before declaring that "there is nothing in our present emergency to justify a retreat, any retreat, from any of our social objectives."[39]

A few weeks later, with France buckling in the face of Nazi invasion, Roosevelt and his advisors used that shocking turn of events to underscore that the international crisis required continuing his domestic program. In his speech to the University of Virginia graduating class on June 10, 1940, Roosevelt said, "We need not and we will not, in any way, abandon our continuing effort to make democracy work within our borders."[40] After pausing for applause, he continued: "Yes, we still insist on the need for vast improvements in our own social and economic life."[41] Raising his voice, he declared, "But that—*that*—is a component part of national defense itself."[42]

Campaigning on Security Once Again

The 1940 presidential election marked a crucial moment in the battle between liberals and conservatives over what policies counted as a matter of national security. Both sides understood the stakes. With a change in administration, conservatives believed they could halt and perhaps even reverse the growth of the government's economic security responsibilities. They had been counting the days until Roosevelt's expected departure at the end of his second term. For their part, liberals saw the worsening international crisis as an opportunity to justify an unprecedented third term for Roosevelt in the name of national security. Roosevelt hoped to use another term to deepen government responsibility for a broad conception of national security that included both economic and physical security. Once again, the ever-vigilant Arthur Krock called Roosevelt out, highlighting in a July 12, 1940, column the president's use of the "compulsion" of "national security" to justify seeking a third term.[43]

Roosevelt's speech the following week accepting the Democratic nomination for a third term as president illustrated Krock's point. Roosevelt framed his decision to run again as a reluctant choice made out of a sense of duty because the country's security demanded he continue in office. "The fact which dominates our world is the fact of armed aggression, the fact of successful armed aggression, aimed at the form of Government, the kind of society that we in the United States have chosen and established for ourselves."[44] He continued, "In the face of the danger which confronts our time, no individual retains or can hope to retain, the right of personal choice which free men enjoy in times of peace. He has a first obligation to serve in the defense of our institutions of freedom—a first obligation to serve his country in whatever capacity his country finds him useful."[45] Therefore, he argued, "in the face of that public danger all those who can be of service to the Republic have no choice but to offer themselves for service in those capacities for which they may be fitted."[46] Roosevelt implied that in his case that meant continuing as president.

Roosevelt also sought to use the international crisis and the exigencies of his role as president in directing the country's response to place his candidacy above politics. After explaining why the crisis would force him to curtail his usual campaign trips, he added that "I do expect, of course, during the coming months to make my usual periodic reports to the country through the medium of press conferences and radio talks. I shall not have the time or the inclination to engage in purely political debate. But I shall never be loathe [sic] to call the attention of the nation to deliberate or unwitting falsifications of fact, which are sometimes made by political candidates."[47] In other words, Roosevelt would exploit the power of his position as president to shape public understanding of the crisis—the scale of which he said justified his continuation in office because the country could not, as he put it, risk placing the presidency into "untried hands, inexperienced hands"—while ostensibly remaining above the political fray.[48] Arthur Krock fumed that the president was taking "advantage of his incumbency in a critical time to emphasize that everything he does is official and designed solely to establish national security; that whatever his opponent offers by way of suggestion or criticism is mere 'politics.'"[49] Krock devoted many of his columns during the campaign to rebutting, with little tangible success, what he called the "indispensable man" argument that he believed the president and his supporters were pushing.[50]

In his Democratic nomination acceptance speech, Roosevelt once again connected under the umbrella of national security policies aimed at achieving economic and physical security. Roosevelt leaned on the language of security from his earliest handwritten drafts of the speech.[51] He said that "the task of safeguarding our institutions seems to me to be twofold. One must be accomplished, if it becomes necessary, by the armed defense forces of the nation. The other, by the united effort of the men and women of the country to make our federal and state and local governments responsive to the growing requirements of modern democracy."[52] Roosevelt argued that until the recent international crisis his administration had focused on that latter task. In reviewing his administration's accomplishments, Roosevelt emphasized the greater security Americans now felt thanks to the domestic economic security programs of the still nascent national security state.

Roosevelt said that such progress was under threat not only from Republicans, whom he charged with paying only "lip-service" to the push for security, but also even more "gravely endangered by what is happening on other continents."[53] He repeated the argument that sustaining his domestic agenda provided the best insurance against the collapse of American institutions, noting that "whenever tyranny has replaced a more human form of Government it has been due more to internal causes than external."[54] He said that "Democracy can thrive only when it enlists the devotion of those whom Lincoln called the common people. Democracy can hold that devotion only when it adequately respects their dignity by so ordering society as to assure to the masses of men and women reasonable security and hope for themselves and for their children."[55]

Arthur Krock continued to voice conservatives' complaint that Roosevelt was taking advantage of the international crisis to advance his domestic agenda and using the rhetoric of national security to do so. In an

August 21, 1940, column, Krock accused the Roosevelt administration of invoking national security to pressure Congress into passing a tax bill without taking time to amend it to remove an excess-profits tax the administration sought.[56] Another example showed that the conservative suspicions Krock voiced were not misplaced. Roosevelt had long wanted the government to develop power from the St. Lawrence River but faced consistent resistance from conservatives who did not want the government involved in electricity generation. Now, Roosevelt said, proceeding with the project was imperative for "national security."[57] Conservatives found Roosevelt's tactic infuriating but managed to develop a marginally more effective counter than they had in the 1936 campaign.

Like Roosevelt, Republicans built their 1940 campaign case on events abroad. But they drew different lessons from them. In his speech accepting the Republican nomination for president on August 17, 1940, Wendell Willkie blamed France for its own demise, attributing it to that country's decision to trade individual freedom for economic security and charging the Roosevelt administration with making the same mistake. Willkie argued that in the 1930s, "while Germany was building a great new productive plant, France became absorbed in unfruitful political adventures and flimsy economy theories. Her government was trying desperately to cover the people's nakedness with a garment that was not big enough" when "the free men of France should have been weaving themselves a bigger garment. For in trying to pull the small one around themselves they tore it to pieces."[58] He declared that the Roosevelt administration "does not preach the doctrine of growth. It preaches the doctrine of division. We are not asked to make more for ourselves. We are asked to divide among ourselves that which we already have. The New Deal doctrine does not seek risk, it seeks safety . . . [and] that is exactly the course France followed to her destruction!"[59] Although Willkie himself did not identify as conservative, the dangers of trading individual freedom for economic security became a mainstay of conservative persuasion efforts and grew more effective over time as circumstances changed.

But in the short term, conservatives faced a difficult task arguing against Roosevelt's promise of economic security because most Americans still hungered for it. On September 21, 1940, a man named Albert Culbertson wrote to Eleanor Roosevelt to report that "I get around a good bit and mingle with people of all kinds. It seems to me that one of the very strongest holds [the president] has on the masses of the people is that feeling of security that they have because of what he has stood for and what he has done for them. They feel it, and I believe it offers material for a very strong appeal to the voter and a very damaging blow to the opposition."[60] Wendell Willkie understood that too and knew he could not oppose all the popular things Roosevelt had done in the name of economic security and expect to win.[61]

For months leading up to the 1940 election, conservatives had accused Roosevelt of playing politics with national security. They were absolutely right.[62] But the charge assumed national security and politics were somehow separate. Even though Roosevelt used the language of security to elevate his policy proposals—and his candidacy—above politics, in doing so he was still playing a political game. The problem for conservatives was that in the invocation of national security Roosevelt had found a seemingly unanswerable political weapon. The language of security helped Roosevelt win an unprecedented third term. And it was helping him make headway, albeit slowly, in his effort to shift American foreign policy. But despite repeated efforts to use the international crisis to justify his domestic agenda as imperative to national security, his increasingly frequent use of the language of security to shift the country to a more interventionist foreign policy had begun to nudge domestic policy out of the national security frame. Conservatives gave it a good push as they licked their wounds from the 1940 election.

Conservatives Exploit the International Crisis

Although they again failed to unseat Roosevelt in 1940, conservatives did a better job than in 1936 of constructing persuasive arguments that had the potential to prevent Roosevelt from building on the economic security foundation of the national security state. Conservatives emphasized the ways freedom had disappeared elsewhere, under dictatorship in Nazi Germany and in conquered France, which conservatives said had fatally weakened itself through overzealous efforts to provide economic security to citizens.[63] Conservatives said Americans should learn from those unfolding tragedies. This argument gained force not only from the greater concentration of power in Roosevelt's hands but also from Roosevelt's continuing effort to use the international crisis to justify expanding economic security programs that did not seem to be working.

In October 1940, O. J. Arnold, president of the Northwestern National Life Insurance Company of Minneapolis, delivered a powerful indictment of the Roosevelt administration's approach to national security in a widely circulated speech. As a longtime leading private-sector "security" professional, Arnold was in a unique position to grasp the dramatic recent change in the way Americans talked about security. He marveled at the hold the language of security had taken on American society: "ten or twelve years ago, we seldom thought of security except as a banking term denoting collateral for a loan."[64] Since the 1929 stock market crash, he said, Americans had "been thinking about security, talking about security, and seeking security frantically."[65]

The way the Roosevelt administration had led the pursuit of national security, Arnold said, had been counterproductive. To make his point, Arnold "review[ed] the record of governmental attempts to provide us with national security" in the preceding seven years.[66] "We first went to work to surround our economic house with every form of safeguard against evildoers. In this we apparently succeeded so well that we not only locked the evildoers outside; we locked honest toilers, honest management, and honest capital securely inside in a state of semi-idleness."[67] He continued: "Meanwhile, our normal economic life remained immobilized; so we turned to legislating ourselves the security which by this time we more than ever desperately wanted. And having legislated ourselves security, we then appropriated ourselves funds to pay for it from a treasury to all practical purposes empty, making the generosity of this gift to ourselves at least debatable."[68] And "at the end of this period of trying to give ourselves made-to-order security by law and precept and appropriation, what do we find? Millions of workers still insecure; our *normal* economic activities still largely stagnated; and our government wallowing in a vast sea of debt—while we the people, faced with new and unforeseen threats to our security, feel perhaps less secure than at any time throughout this period."[69]

Roosevelt's policies, Arnold concluded, amounted to nothing more than a "shell game"—a shell game that not only made the country less secure but also imperiled Americans' freedom.[70] "Our national slogan has been benefits and a pseudo-security for everyone at any cost, and in the end such a slogan can only mean security for no one at the greatest possible cost—the cost of our liberties and our way of life."[71] If the United States did not change course quickly, Arnold said, the country might fall just as France had fallen.

Arnold's pointed critique contained the cornerstones of a solidifying conservative case against further expanding the government's economic security responsibilities: it hadn't worked, and it would destroy the country by sapping the strength and will of the American people. Former Roosevelt advisor turned critic Raymond Moley made a similar point in his May 27, 1940, *Newsweek* column, asking rhetorically whether the Roosevelt administration had, "like the Blum government of France, given undue attention to social reform while it neglected the basic necessities of national security? In short, has it pursued the ideal of personal security to the neglect of national security?"[72] This message had real resonance in 1940 with the American economy still struggling and France under Nazi occupation. If this message could be packaged and delivered to the "Average American" through the National Association of Manufacturers' (NAM) ongoing multichannel persuasion campaign, then conservatives might finally compete effectively with Roosevelt and his promise of economic security.

With Roosevelt continuing to use the language of security to frame his domestic agenda, the public relations experts and opinion pollsters helping guide the NAM campaign recognized the need to find "an ideal which has even more public appeal than the ideal of security" in which to wrap conservative proposals.[73] NAM first turned to "opportunity" before settling on the more potent ideal of "freedom."[74] NAM paired the "freedom" frame with a revised persuasion approach that focused less on fact-based appeals and more on cultivating impressions.[75] The objective was to replace the widely held impression, intensively cultivated by Roosevelt since 1932, of the government as rightful guarantor of economic security with the alternative impression of government as a threat to individual freedom.

Beginning in 1940, NAM distributed a booklet aimed at women—whom NAM continued to see as powerful opinion molders—titled

Primer for Americans that demonstrated the power of the revised framing and approach. The *Primer* used Germany and France as examples of "how a nation gradually loses its freedom and surrenders to the idea of dictatorship."[76] For the German case, the authors emphasized the dangers of a country placing too much power in the hands of a persuasive leader who promised something for everybody—an unsubtle attempt to equate Roosevelt with Hitler.[77] With France, the authors listed "some of the many factors contributing to the fall of the French Republic" and encouraged readers to "try to decide which of these bear a resemblance to conditions in the United States."[78] The authors provided helpful cues alongside entries in the list. For example, "the fear of social revolution intensified by the great strike of 1936 and the Blum legislation. This legislation is considered by many to be very similar in its nature to the 'social reform' legislation passed in the United States during the last several years."[79]

With the German and French examples planted in the reader's mind, the authors turned to national planning and declared that "central economic planning means the suppression of civil liberties."[80] The unsubtle "Your Attitude Toward Planning" section opened with a graphic depicting NAM's view of national planning, with the caption "When the hand of state begins to turn the wheels of production, it becomes necessary to gear in one by one the spheres of human activity so that they all move as one."[81] The pamphlet emphasized that "it makes a difference whether you plan for yourself or whether you must accept plans made for you by someone else" and noted that "women in totalitarian countries are constantly interfered with even in running their own households."[82] The authors then offered an "attitude test" full of leading statements for readers to determine their attitudes toward planning, followed by a rosy description of "industrial" and "civic" "voluntary planning" and a dark description of government "arbitrary planning."[83] In the "Arbitrary Planning" section, the authors asserted that

> to put such a plan into operation requires an ever increasing measure
> of control, extending into one area after another of the economic, so-
> cial, intellectual, and cultural life. Such a plan is not accepted volun-
> tarily by all the various groups of people involved. Therefore, it must

be imposed—upon the banks, upon the workers, upon the farmers, upon the industrialists, upon the consumers. To effect the desired objectives, all opposition has to be crushed. Hence, the government establishes control over channels of communication which form public opinion—the press, the radio, the motion picture, the schools, the churches.[84]

By stoking Americans' fears of losing individual freedom, conservatives tried to replace the impression of the government as a source of solutions to problems with a more menacing impression of the government as a source of danger.

The *Primer* cast doubt not only on the desirability of making the government responsible for economic security but also on the plausibility of doing so. The authors sowed doubts in readers' minds about the government's ability to guarantee economic security through planning: "In any discussion of national economic planning, it is well to recognize still other difficulties and dangers. Few men, if any, have the wisdom or the vision to look ahead and to take into account all the factors involved. This is true for each individual concern; it is much more obviously true when you try to visualize a small group planning for a whole nation's industry."[85]

Promoting the *Primer* was one of NAM's top priorities at the beginning of the 1940s.[86] The way NAM approached that promotional task illustrates the important role NAM played in growing the conservative movement. To maximize the *Primer*'s reach, the text provided tips for how women could use the material in the book, "first in your club, and then, if you wish, to promote thought and discussion in your community."[87] Through these suggestions NAM hoped to multiply the opinion-molding effects of the book. For example, NAM suggested that "you will want to bring this material to the attention of your minister or some other leader of activities in your church. In these days when many churches are accepting responsibility for the interpretation of social, economic, and political thought, there is need for such a series of vital topics for weekday meetings, for discussions among young people's groups, or for a planned course of study for adult classes."[88] NAM also encouraged women to "pass this program along" to teachers, who "are no doubt eager for fresh, interesting materials that will help them to interpret to their classes the nature of representative democracy and the principles of the American system."[89]

The *Primer*'s argument that government-promised economic security threatened individual freedom was fast becoming conservatives' preferred weapon in the fight to shape the government's national security responsibilities. This argument posed a serious threat to the economic security foundation of Roosevelt's national security state and grew in power as the international crisis worsened.

Domestic Policy Begins to Fall Out of the National Security Frame

Roosevelt gave conservative efforts to limit the further expansion of the government's economic security responsibilities an inadvertent but substantial boost after the 1940 election by going all in on the effort to sell a non-neutral foreign policy as a national security imperative. In mid-December 1940, Roosevelt decided to deliver a fireside chat in which he could make his case for expanded aid to Britain, then struggling under the weight of the Nazi onslaught. The speech proved decisive in Roosevelt's effort to use the international crisis to shift American foreign policy away from neutrality and marked a turning point in his presidency.

With the radio address scheduled for December 29, 1940, Roosevelt's trusted assistant Missy LeHand called longtime Roosevelt speechwriter Samuel Rosenman and asked him to come to Washington soon after Christmas with Pulitzer Prize–winning playwright Robert Sherwood, who had recently joined the president's speechwriting team.[90] Sherwood had admired Roosevelt for many years, writing to Walter Winchell in October 1938 that the "masses of people everywhere look to the United States + Roosevelt <u>as the sole hope of the human race</u>."[91] The Roosevelts had hosted Sherwood and his wife Madeline for dinner at the White House on January 21, 1940.[92] The next day, Sherwood met with Harry Hopkins, who had succeeded Raymond Moley as Roosevelt's closest confidant and advisor, and volunteered his services to the president.[93] Hopkins said Roosevelt would likely accept. Sherwood sent a letter to Roosevelt on January 25, 1940, formalizing the offer, but nothing came of it right away.[94] By the fall of 1940, however, almost all of the people who had worked with Roosevelt on his speeches since 1932 were gone, with the exception of Rosenman and Hopkins. Roosevelt needed additional speechwriting help and turned to Sherwood.[95] Sherwood proved valuable not only because he was a master wordsmith but also because—like Roosevelt—he grasped the persuasive power gained by placing arguments in the security frame.[96]

Princeton-based psychologist and public opinion expert Hadley Cantril also volunteered his services to Roosevelt in 1940. A passionate interventionist like Sherwood, Cantril angled for influence with the president by peddling his analyses to various people close to Roosevelt.[97] On August 9, 1940, Roosevelt assistant James Rowe forwarded a Cantril report to the president and asked if he would like to see similar analyses in the future. Already a keen student of public opinion, Roosevelt paid even closer attention to it as he sought to use the international crisis to shift American foreign policy away from nonintervention.[98] The president gladly accepted Cantril's offer.[99] Cantril was an expert in both public opinion and framing. In that latter area he benefited from the assistance of Jerome Bruner, who was beginning his career as one of the most influential psychologists of the twentieth century.[100] Cantril served as a valuable source of political intelligence and advice on framing for the president and his advisors for the remainder of Roosevelt's presidency.

The arrival of both Cantril and Sherwood in Roosevelt's inner circle by the second half of 1940 was not a coincidence. Both Cantril and Sherwood happened to be British agents of a kind.[101] The British, of course, were the most passionate advocates of American intervention in World War II. Soon after becoming prime minister in May 1940, Winston Churchill authorized a large covert campaign in the United States to shift American public opinion in favor of intervention.[102] The head of Britain's Secret Intelligence Service, Colonel Stewart Menzies, sent William Stephenson to New York City to run the effort. Stephenson set up shop in June 1940 on the thirty-fifth and thirty-sixth floors of Rockefeller Center under the official cover of the British Passport Control Office. The official purpose of Stephenson's mission, as the British explained it to Roosevelt and to Federal Bureau of Investigation (FBI) Director J. Edgar Hoover, was to build a stronger relationship with the FBI and other elements of the nascent American intelligence apparatus. Stephenson's more important mandate, however, was to counter what the British perceived to be the Nazis' success in "buttressing the wall of traditional isolationism by which the President was encompassed," a success the British attributed to the absence of "organized opposition" to Nazi propaganda in the United States.[103] Stephenson's British Security Coordination (BSC) worked tirelessly behind the scenes to aid Roosevelt's efforts to reorient American foreign policy. As BSC officers recalled in the organization's official history, "the ultimate purpose of all BSC's Political Warfare was to assist Mr. Roosevelt's own campaign."[104]

BSC officers delighted in the ease with which they could manipulate American public opinion, noting that "a country that is extremely heterogeneous in character offers a wide variety of choice in propaganda methods. While it is possibly true to say that all Americans are intensely suspicious of propaganda, it is certain that a great many of them are unusually susceptible to it even in its most patent form."[105] Former BSC officers recalled that "covert propaganda [was] one of the most potent weapons which BSC employed."[106] Among many clever tactics, they succeeded in planting items in American newspapers, covertly operated one of the most powerful short-wave radio stations in the United States, and even supplied material, usually through Robert Sherwood, for some of Roosevelt's speeches.[107]

Roosevelt's December 29, 1940, fireside chat was of particular importance to the British, whose fate depended on the president's persuasiveness. Sherwood and Rosenman arrived in Washington after Christmas and began work on the address with Hopkins.[108] For three days, the president and his wordsmiths searched for the words and arguments that would persuade Americans and their representatives in Congress to support aid to Britain on the scale required to prevent British defeat. The opening paragraphs of the seven drafts of the fireside chat underscore how Roosevelt and his advisors used the invocation of national security to persuade Americans to change policy. These documents also cast doubt on the argument that Roosevelt's use of the term "national security" was anything other than deliberate.[109]

The first draft opened with a flashback to Roosevelt's first fireside chat, during the banking crisis at the beginning of his administration in March 1933.[110] According to Rosenman, the probable author of that opening, Roosevelt wanted to explain "the crisis in as simple terms as he had [explained] the banking crisis in 1933."[111] It therefore made sense to refer to that speech in the opening of this fireside chat.[112] But this first draft was not likely to achieve Roosevelt's objective of persuading Americans to change their foreign policy. It did not make a sufficiently clear connection between the older domestic economic crisis and the current international one.

The opening of the second draft, probably written by Sherwood, tried to address these deficiencies by beginning with an apocalyptical discussion of the threat to "Christian civilization."[113] But Roosevelt had made that point for more than a year without persuading the public that the international crisis demanded an adjustment in American foreign policy. The third and fourth drafts merged the openings from the first and second.[114] Rosenman and Roosevelt might have wanted to retain the opening from the first draft because it equated the international crisis of 1940, which many Americans did not yet feel threatened them, with the domestic crisis of 1933, the severity of which Americans had felt in their bones and that still haunted many of them. Roosevelt had succeeded in labeling that earlier domestic economic crisis a threat to national security, so the connection was worth making. But the speech still needed a more compelling opening.

With the fifth draft, Roosevelt and the speechwriters found one. The first words listeners heard would be "This is not a fireside chat on war; this is a talk on national security and peace."[115] Someone—probably Roosevelt, since the other markings on the sixth draft are in his handwriting—struck the word "peace" from the sentence, leaving national security to stand alone as the subject of the speech.[116] The final version of the opening read, "This is not a fireside chat on war. It is a talk on national security; because the nub of the whole purpose of your President is to keep you now, and your children later, and your grandchildren much later, out of a last-ditch war for the preservation of American independence and all the things that American independence means to you and to me and to ours."[117] Roosevelt spoke those words deliberately, pausing for nearly two seconds after the phrase "national security" to underscore the gravity of the situation.[118]

Although the historical record does not provide a definitive answer, there are several reasons to think Roosevelt dictated the powerful new opening. Chief among them is that the only continuity in speechwriting during Roosevelt's presidency came from Roosevelt himself. He had consistently and profitably used the language of security throughout his time as a candidate for president and once in office. And when the stakes were highest and he needed to sell a fundamental change in policy—as in the spring of 1933—he invoked national security.[119] The folksy tone also points to Roosevelt, as does the reference to "your children, and your grandchildren," which resembled other passages Roosevelt had dictated.[120]

With that stark new opening, Roosevelt had all but guaranteed himself an attentive audience. Roosevelt then equated the mounting international crisis of the 1940s with the domestic crisis of the 1930s, which not only provided an analogy Americans could use to grasp the severity of the situation but also reinforced that when it came to achieving national security, the policymaking toolkit included both domestic and foreign policy. Roosevelt told Americans that in 1933 he had "tried to convey to the great mass of American people what the banking crisis meant to them in their daily lives" and said that "tonight, I want to do the same thing, with the same people, in this new crisis which faces America. We met the issue of 1933 with courage and realism. We face this new crisis—this new threat to the security of our nation—with the same courage and realism."[121]

Lest Americans doubt the seriousness of this new threat, Roosevelt declared with great emphasis that "never before since Jamestown and Plymouth Rock has our American civilization been in such danger as now."[122] To support his claim, Roosevelt cited statements from Adolf Hitler to the effect that the United States and the Axis nations were in implacable ideological competition. More tangibly, Roosevelt argued once again that technology had rendered America's geographic defenses obsolete. Speaking slowly, he said that "some of us like to believe that even if Great Britain falls, we are still safe, because of the broad expanse of the Atlantic and of the Pacific. But the width of those oceans is not what it was in the days of clipper ships."[123] He added, in words he crafted himself and using his tone and cadence to underscore the point, that "at one point between Africa and Brazil the distance is less than from Washington to Denver, Colorado: five hours for the latest type of bomber. And at the North end of the Pacific Ocean America and Asia almost touch each other. Even today we have planes that could fly from the British Isles to New England and back again without refueling. And remember that the range of the modern bomber is ever being increased."[124] In other words, Americans were no longer immune to aerial bombardment, the horror of which had become clear to many Americans in recent years through news coverage of events in Europe and Asia.

Roosevelt's framing of aid to Britain as a matter of national security—and the shift in American foreign policy such a program required—proved persuasive. When Hadley Cantril sent the White House his latest analysis of public opinion in early 1941, the results suggested the president was succeeding in his efforts to use the language of security to reorient foreign policy.[125] One of the poll questions asked, "Suppose the United States does not go into the war, and Germany defeats England—do you think you, personally, would be affected by this German victory?"[126] Most respondents said yes.[127] But answers to a follow-up question asking them to elaborate on the negative effects they anticipated revealed that Roosevelt's invocation of the physical danger posed by the aggressors had proven more persuasive than his efforts to highlight the ideological threat. As Cantril noted in his analysis of the responses, the results suggested that "few people think in terms of personal freedoms and liberties—the things they now take for granted."[128] This finding helped to explain why conservatives had made only limited progress using the language of freedom up to that point. But Roosevelt did not need multiple winning arguments to achieve his immediate objective of shifting American foreign policy toward intervention. He needed only one, and, in the threat to American physical security, he had it. Congress approved Lend-Lease in March 1941. Thanks in part to the increased American aid that followed, Britain survived the German onslaught.[129]

Roosevelt's successful invocation of national security to reorient American foreign policy cemented the phrase's position as one of the most potent weapons in American politics. But Cantril's astute analysis of public opinion suggested the physical security aspect of Roosevelt's conception of national security was beginning to carry greater weight than the economic security component Roosevelt considered equally vital. This insight foreshadowed difficulties to come as the president expanded his efforts to sell and institutionalize a national security state responsible for both economic and physical security. The president said in his fireside chat that "the strength of this nation shall not be diluted by the failure of the Government to protect the economic well-being of its citizens," but that message grew fainter as foreign policy supplanted domestic policy as the focus of national security policymaking.[130]

6

Roosevelt's Unrealized Vision for a Comprehensive National Security State

We have come to a clearer realization of the fact . . . that true individual freedom cannot exist without economic security and independence.[1]

—Franklin Roosevelt, January 1944

It is a strange paradox that the only real national security comes from the risk and venture, daring and opportunity only possible under freedom. While the pursuit of security itself often destroys it.[2]

—National Association of Manufacturers Chairman Fredrick C. Crawford, January 1945

IN HIS 1941 STATE OF THE UNION MESSAGE, Franklin Roosevelt presented a vision for not only the type of country the United States ought to be but also for the type of world in which everyone deserved to live. The "Four Freedoms" Roosevelt proposed—freedom of speech and expression, freedom of worship, freedom from want, freedom from fear—represented a world based on individual liberty and the liberty of the community, both grounded in a sense of security.[3] "That is no vision of a distant millennium," Roosevelt said, pausing for applause.[4] "It is a definite basis for a kind of world attainable in our own time and generation."[5]

Although the "Four Freedoms" justly made the speech famous, the ideas they expressed were not new. Roosevelt had articulated versions of them for years.[6] What was new was Roosevelt's deliberate effort to place not only his vision for a comprehensive national security state in the United States under the heading of freedom but to extend that vision to the world.[7]

Roosevelt's "Four Freedoms" speech represented another masterpiece of linguistic appropriation. Through it, he tried to do for "freedom" what he did for "liberal" during the 1932 campaign—to shift the term's meaning from a negative conception of the government's role to a positive one. The "Four Freedoms" Roosevelt outlined were all examples of rights to be guaranteed by government. Even though Roosevelt presented the last two as "freedom from," they were not freedom from government in the way conservatives defined freedom. They were freedom to thrive, ensured by the United States government and by some form of future world government.[8] Conservatives had hoped to frame their fight with Roosevelt over the government's most basic responsibilities as a contest between security and freedom. Roosevelt tried to make it a fight over competing ideas of freedom. In his version, he said, not only Americans but the entire world would have both freedom and security, made possible by government.

In the early 1940s, Roosevelt and his advisors continued work on a comprehensive national security state responsible for both economic and physical security. This fact has been all but lost amid historians' intense focus on Roosevelt's foreign policy and the Second World War. It is widely believed that Roosevelt basically abandoned his domestic agenda with the coming of war. But he remained committed to guaranteeing economic security, even if circumstances at times required him to subordinate domestic policy to the war effort.[9] Many historians have read too much into Roosevelt's remark at a December 28, 1943, press conference that "Dr. Win-the-War" had supplanted "Dr. New Deal"—a quip Roosevelt probably hoped would deflect conservative criticism that continued focus on his domestic agenda detracted from the war effort. Later in the press conference, Roosevelt said that "when victory comes, the program of the past, of course, has got to be carried on. . . . We must plan for, and help to bring about an expanded economy which will result in more security, in more employment, in more recreation, in more education, in more health, in better housing for all of our citizens, so that the conditions of

1932 and the beginning of 1933 won't come back again."[10] In the final two years of his second term and throughout his third term, Roosevelt continued to argue that his domestic agenda was just as vital to national security as foreign policy.

Several factors explain why Roosevelt made less progress than he hoped toward expanding the economic security part of the national security state. The first was the return of prosperity. Massive government wartime spending paid for a dramatic increase in production and a return to full employment. But because the Roosevelt administration relied on the government-owned, contractor-operated model for most war production, the Americans involved believed they were working for companies, not the government. Conservatives capitalized on that fact to persuade Americans that the private sector, not the government, deserved credit for the return of prosperity even though government contracts created those jobs. Conservatives also argued that the private sector's wartime production record proved its superior competence compared with the government, which—according to conservatives—produced little more than miles of "red tape" during World War II. In these ways, conservatives used the war to cast further doubt on the plausibility and desirability of making the government responsible for economic security, while simultaneously reinforcing the impression that the private sector was the provider of "real security."

Roosevelt's rhetoric also increasingly played into conservatives' hands. His effective use of the language of security to reorient American foreign policy continued to push domestic policy out of the national security frame. And his increasing emphasis on freedom and on the threat to freedom from across the seas buttressed conservatives' efforts to frame the guarantee of freedom—rather than the provision of security—as the government's primary responsibility. As a result, by the time Roosevelt offered his fullest articulation of his vision for national security in his 1944 State of the Union message, the economic security components he considered foundational no longer seemed so vital to many Americans.

Toward a Comprehensive National Security State

The "Four Freedoms" are all most people remember from Roosevelt's 1941 State of the Union message, but the speech was remarkable for the

extent to which Roosevelt wove together his domestic and foreign policies into a coherent whole aimed at achieving national security. As he had
in his fireside chat at the end of December 1940, Roosevelt began with a
bang: "I address you, the Members of the Seventy-seventh Congress, at a
moment unprecedented in the history of the Union. I use the word 'unprecedented,' because at no previous time has American security been as
seriously threatened from without as it is today."[11] Roosevelt then re-
viewed the history of American foreign relations to prove his point, before concluding that "the need of the moment is that our actions and our
policy should be devoted primarily—almost exclusively—to meeting this
foreign peril."[12] Before conservative opponents of his domestic agenda
could cheer, however, in one deft move Roosevelt placed his domestic
agenda into that category of essential actions, "for all our domestic problems are now a part of the great emergency."[13]

The many surviving drafts and fragments of the speech written by
Roosevelt and his advisors make clear that this blending of domestic and
foreign policy under the umbrella of national security was intentional.[14]
Lauchlin Currie, Roosevelt's economic advisor, sent the president draft
language for the speech that argued that we "must . . . push on" with domestic reconstruction because "as men do not live by bread alone, men
do not fight with armaments alone. Not only those who man our defenses,
but those who build our defenses must have grit and courage and a passionate belief in the way of life which they are helping to defend."[15] A few
days before the address, Federal Security Administrator Paul McNutt sent
the president language that explicitly placed economic security programs
under the heading of national security: "At this time, when the Nation is
concentrating on the development of a program of national defense, it becomes increasingly apparent that national security must include social
security. The present Social Security Act goes a long way in providing
security for the people of this country."[16]

Roosevelt incorporated many of these suggestions into the address,
saying that "certainly this is no time for any of us to stop thinking about
the social and economic problems which are the root cause of the social
revolution which is today a supreme factor in the world."[17] Roosevelt
continued,

There is nothing mysterious about the foundations of a healthy and strong democracy. The basic things expected by our people of their political and economic systems are simple. They are: Equality of opportunity for youth and for others. Jobs for those who can work. Security for those who need it. The ending of special privilege for the few. The preservation of civil liberties for all. The enjoyment of the fruits of scientific progress in a wider and constantly rising standard of living.[18]

As he had many times since making the point forcefully in his April 14, 1938, fireside chat, Roosevelt reiterated that "the inner and abiding strength of our economic and political systems is dependent upon the degree to which they fulfill these expectations."[19]

It was not enough simply to continue existing economic security programs, Roosevelt declared in a passage he drafted himself. "Many subjects connected with our social economy call for immediate improvement. As examples: We should bring more citizens under the coverage of old-age pensions and unemployment insurance. We should widen the opportunities for adequate medical care. We should plan a better system by which persons deserving or needing gainful employment may obtain it."[20] Although Roosevelt spent nearly half the speech pressing for greater military preparedness and the reorientation of foreign policy, the other half made clear that Roosevelt believed national security depended equally on continuing his domestic policies.

In the months that followed, however, Roosevelt diverted attention from his domestic agenda with his increasingly fervent efforts to persuade Americans that events abroad threatened their freedom. Roosevelt used the word "freedom" some twenty times in a May 27, 1941, radio address announcing an "Unlimited National Emergency."[21] Roosevelt described in stark terms what would happen if the Nazis prevailed, aiming his words at key groups in American life: "The American laborer would have to compete with slave labor in the rest of the world. Minimum wages, maximum hours? Nonsense! Wages and hours would be fixed by Hitler. The dignity and power and standard of living of the American worker and farmer would be gone. Trade unions would become historical relics, and

collective bargaining a joke."[22] Turning to farmers, he asked, "Farm income? What happens to all farm surpluses without any foreign trade?
The American farmer would get for his products exactly what Hitler
wanted to give. The farmer would face obvious disaster and complete
regimentation."[23] In sum, Roosevelt argued, "the whole fabric of working
life as we know it—business and manufacturing, mining and agriculture—
all would be mangled and crippled under such a system."[24]

If America failed to act now to stop a totalitarian victory, he warned, it
faced a future of permanent mobilization and endless war, reversing the
hard-fought progress of recent years. In that scenario, he said, "to maintain even that crippled independence would require permanent conscrip-
tion of our manpower; it would curtail the funds we could spend on education, on housing, on public works, on flood control, on health and,
instead, we should be permanently pouring our resources into armaments; and, year in and year out, standing day and night watch against the
destruction of our cities."[25] As if all of that was not enough, he added that
"even our right of worship would be threatened."[26] Amid the deluge of
apocalyptic warnings, the importance of continuing his domestic policies
received only two short sentences. "All of us know that we have made
very great social progress in recent years. We propose to maintain that
progress and strengthen it."[27]

But despite the increasing focus on foreign policy in his speeches,
Roosevelt continued work on his domestic agenda behind the scenes.
The National Resources Planning Board sent the president a memo outlining its vision for a comprehensive national security state and met with
Roosevelt at his Hyde Park home on June 29, 1941, to propose an "Economic Bill of Rights" that Roosevelt could submit to Congress to facilitate the necessary institutional expansions.[28] Roosevelt endorsed the
idea and the planners continued work with an eye toward an announcement in a speech at the end of 1941 or in Roosevelt's 1942 State of the
Union.[29] The Atlantic Charter Roosevelt and British Prime Minister
Winston Churchill announced on August 14, 1941, previewed elements
of the new "Economic Bill of Rights." Among other provisions, the fifth
and sixth points in the Charter pledged the signatories to work toward
"greater economic advancement and social security" and "freedom from
fear and want."[30]

The National Resources Planning Board (NRPB) met with Roosevelt again on December 4, 1941, and discussed the possibility of the president proposing the Economic Bill of Rights in a speech scheduled for December 15, 1941.[31] In draft language for the speech, the NRPB focused on the evolution of the meaning of "freedom" in the United States, emphasizing the shift from negative to positive liberty—from "freedom from" to "freedom to"—that had accompanied the rise of modern industrial capitalism.[32] The NRPB draft said "Any new declaration of personal rights, any translation of freedom into modern terms applicable to the people of the United States here and now must include:

1. The right to work, usefully and creatively through the productive years;
2. The right to fair pay, adequate to command the necessities and amenities of life in exchange for work, ideas, thrift, and other socially valuable service;
3. The right to adequate food, clothing, shelter, and medical care;
4. The right to security, with freedom from fear of old age, want, dependency, sickness, unemployment, and accident;
5. The right to live in a system of free enterprise, free from compulsory labor, irresponsible private power, arbitrary public authority, and unregulated monopolies;
6. The right to come and go, to speak or to be silent, free from the spyings of secret political police;
7. The right to equality before the law, with equal access to justice in fact;
8. The right to education, for work, for citizenship, and for personal growth and happiness; and
9. The right to rest, recreation, and adventure; the opportunity to enjoy life and take part in an advancing civilization."[33]

Events delayed the speech. On December 7–8, 1941, Japan attacked several American outposts in the Pacific. Roosevelt's next speech was a declaration of war rather than an articulation of a new Bill of Rights. Roosevelt devoted almost his entire 1942 State of the Union message, delivered a month after the Japanese attacks, to detailing American plans to win the war. Indeed, in his first draft, he wrote that "we need not spend too much time on postwar problems."[34] His domestic agenda appeared only in the guise of the war aims he presented, which amounted to a restatement of the Four Freedoms, and the declaration, spoken slowly for emphasis, that we "are not making all this sacrifice of human effort and human lives to return to the kind of world we had after the last world war. We are fighting today for security"—a word Roosevelt and his advisors added in the third draft—"for progress, and for peace, not only for ourselves but for all men, not only for one generation but for all generations."[35]

Although the deferral of his Economic Bill of Rights speech and the almost total absence of domestic policy from Roosevelt's 1942 State of the Union address would seem to indicate that Roosevelt had indeed set aside his domestic agenda, behind the scenes Roosevelt and his advisors used the war to continue building the economic security–focused parts of the national security state. Before the war, the Tennessee Valley Authority, National Youth Administration, and Federal Security Agency had all argued that investments in regional economic development amounted to investments in national security.[36] Now that the United States had entered the war, the government could decide where the vast new industrial plants it was paying for—and that would bring jobs and economic security to many Americans—should be built. The National Resources Planning Board saw opportunities to foster economic development by locating new war plants in areas "characterized by severe unemployment" and in "predominately agricultural areas."[37] Such moves, the War Production Board noted, would have "important and permanent consequences for the economic development of different parts of the nation."[38]

The National Resources Planning Board also continued to plan for the postwar period on the assumption that the country would need—and have—the comprehensive national security state Roosevelt envisioned. On February 6, 1942, Luther Gulick, who led the NRPB's "post-emergency" planning, circulated an ambitious "Post War Agenda."[39] The document reflected the NRPB drafters' belief that the government would continue to expand its economic security responsibilities. Among the objectives listed, for example, was "adequate medical care for all."[40] But by mid-1942, Roosevelt and his advisors found it increasingly difficult to frame domestic policies as necessary for national security.

Growing Difficulties Selling Domestic Policy
as National Security Policy

The first problem was that as long as the war continued to go badly, any emphasis on domestic policy risked the charge of detracting from the war effort.[41] In March 1942, Commissioner of Works Projects Howard Hunter informed the president that conservatives were making precisely that argument and trying to use the war to justify dismantling domestic programs.[42] Hunter considered it outrageous that in a moment when the country needed to make full use of its human resources, conservatives wanted "to saw off the bottom rungs from the American ladder of opportunity. They are saying to us that the people who are reaching for the bottom rungs are non-essential and that we cannot afford to help them."[43]

The second challenge was that the wartime economic boom that flowed from vast government wartime expenditures also made it much more difficult for Roosevelt to frame economic security programs as essential for national security. Unemployment all but vanished in 1942 as the country mobilized for war.[44] Americans felt more economically secure than at any point in the preceding decade.[45] As a worker in a Virginia shipyard put it, "I felt like something had come down from heaven. . . . After all the hardships of the Depression, the war completely turned my life around."[46]

Facing these headwinds, the NRPB launched a public relations offensive to rebuild support for the economic security–focused part of the national security state. The NRPB sent thousands of pamphlets highlighting the possibilities of postwar planning to people and organizations it thought could boost its initiatives.[47] The NRPB also issued reports outlining plans for government programs to ensure economic security and the country's continued development after the war. Unlike the conservative persuasion campaign, however, the NRPB did not have top advertising and public relations specialists on the payroll, and its efforts paled in comparison.[48] Its materials were both lengthy and dry. For example, one pamphlet titled "After the War—Toward Security," published in September 1942, consisted of sixty-five pages of solid text, written in academic prose useful to the public only as a cure for insomnia.[49]

When Americans voted in the midterm elections on November 3, 1942, the Roosevelt administration had few recent concrete achievements with which to persuade them to stick with the liberal agenda. Poor turnout, even by the low standards of midterm elections, helped Roosevelt's political opponents gain forty-six seats in the House and nine seats in the Senate.[50] These dismal results increased Roosevelt's already robust appetite for information about public opinion and for advice about how best to shape it.

A week after the election, Roosevelt learned of an opportunity to set up a private polling and opinion analysis operation that would work discreetly for the president. The operation would be funded by Gerard Lambert, who had made a fortune in the drug business—in part through clever public relations work—and led by Hadley Cantril, whose work the administration already trusted and valued.[51] The Cantril-Lambert operation represented a substantial upgrade over the public opinion monitoring Emil Hurja had done for the administration previously, and Roosevelt and his advisors frequently used the information supplied by Cantril and Lambert to tailor messaging.[52] Cantril also offered direct political advice, suggesting in December 1942 that the best thing the president could do to increase public confidence in his administration was to understate war production quotas so they could always be exceeded.[53] Cantril's advice was shrewd, but it overlooked that Roosevelt was not the only one who could try to claim credit for war production successes.

In December 1942, publication and wide American newspaper coverage of the Beveridge Report on expanding Britain's economic security programs prompted a flurry of messages encouraging Roosevelt to share the National Resources Planning Board's own plans for expanding American economic security programs in the postwar period.[54] Later that month, Oscar Cox—who, along with Samuel Rosenman, was one of the leading administration advocates for expanding economic security programs—sent Harry Hopkins a pair of memos suggesting that the president elaborate on his domestic agenda in his upcoming State of the Union.[55] Cox argued that "more and more, the public has tended to concentrate on the President as the war leader and as an international statesman. I should think the time has come when he ought to clearly show that he can also more than lead on the home front."[56] Roosevelt agreed.

It is revealing of Roosevelt's continued focus on his domestic agenda that when it came time to prepare his 1943 State of the Union, Roosevelt

dictated the part proposing expansions of the government's economic security responsibilities first even though that part would come toward the
end of the speech.[57] In a letter to Canadian Prime Minister Mackenzie
King on December 29, 1942, Roosevelt wrote, "I am in the middle of preparing the Annual Message and, among other subjects, I am proposing to
speak of jobs and further security for the post-war period. This is contrary to nearly all political advice I receive; nevertheless, it is bound to be
an issue and we might as well get on the right side of it now."[58]

Roosevelt's draft took many of Oscar Cox's points and expanded on
them.[59] The final version of the speech immortalized the objective for
government Roosevelt had spoken in private for years: to provide economic security "from the cradle to the grave."[60] Roosevelt said that,
"when you talk with our young men and women, you will find that with
the opportunity for employment they want assurance against the evils of
all major economic hazards—assurance that will extend from the cradle
to the grave. And this great Government can and must provide this assurance."[61] After pausing for applause, Roosevelt added, in a line he dictated
himself in his first draft, "I have been told that this is no time to speak of a
better America after the war. I am told it is a grave error on my part. I dis-
sent."[62] After pausing again for applause, Roosevelt continued: "And if
the security of the individual citizen, or the family, should become a subject of national debate, the country knows where I stand."[63]

But circumstances were less and less favorable to Roosevelt's efforts to
expand economic security programs. Lewis Schwellenbach, who represented Washington in the Senate from 1935 to 1940, summarized the challenge in a letter to his former colleague Senator Joseph Guffey (D-PA) a
few weeks after Roosevelt's 1943 State of the Union. Schwellenbach noted
that "the people are not interested in Social Security now. It's only when
they need social security that they are interested. No man making from
ten to fifteen dollars a day can be convinced that he needs the help of the
Government in order to be secure in his economic future."[64] The issue,
Schwellenbach continued, was that "these people who were out of work
in 1930 have good jobs now. I'll bet half the people who were on W. P. A.
wouldn't admit that fact if they were asked. Their confidence in their own
ability to support themselves and their families has been restored. Actually, they think it was somebody else who was starving back in 1933."[65]

As a result, Schwellenbach concluded, "I don't believe social security is any better as a nation-wide political promise of 1944 than was Mr. Hoover's assurance that the bankers and industrialists could put the people back to work in 1932."[66]

Guffey forwarded Schwellenbach's letter to Roosevelt, whose administration again faced the conundrum it first encountered in 1936.[67] As long as the economy seemed to be doing well, Americans would not see the need to expand the government's economic security responsibilities.[68] Ironically, public support for economic security programs fell even in the ever-increasing number of places where massive government investment in military equipment had created well-paying jobs.[69] Without public and congressional support for expanding economic security programs—neither of which were forthcoming—the administration could do little. Roosevelt and his advisors spent the rest of 1943 trying to solve that puzzle.[70]

Meantime, the Seventy-Eighth Congress, the most conservative Roosevelt had faced, chipped away at the economic security–focused pieces of Roosevelt's national security state. The National Resources Planning Board (NRPB) and its predecessor entities relied on tenuous, temporary funding arrangements.[71] Now, Congress killed the NRPB once and for all by cutting off its funding.[72] The board's demise infuriated Roosevelt, who still considered national planning both necessary and desirable.[73] Many people at the time and since believed World War II healed the American economy, rendering entities like the NRPB unnecessary.[74] Roosevelt and his advisors disagreed. They worried that once the massive economic stimulus provided by government wartime spending disappeared, the country would face the same problems with which it had struggled since the late 1920s. Their fears ultimately proved correct, but not right away. The lag contributed to a pervasive misunderstanding of postwar American political economy.

With the greater perspective gained from additional distance from World War II and the postwar economic boom, it is clear that the prosperity of those years stemmed primarily from unusual circumstances. Most people agree that the stimulus provided by wartime government spending restored prosperity. Less well appreciated, thanks in part to conservatives' success claiming credit for the private sector for the wartime and postwar booms, is that prosperity continued into the postwar period both because government spending remained high and because the war destroyed so much of the productive capacity of international economic competitors. The relative absence of competition meant that the private-sector beneficiaries of the enormous industrial plant expansions the government financed or paid for during the war had ample markets for their output after the war and therefore did not have to reduce production. When international economic competition returned by the late 1960s, the economic issues the NRPB was designed to alleviate once again became apparent. The board's demise deprived the government of a tool with which to mitigate the resulting problems.

Roosevelt speechwriter Robert Sherwood recalled that "there were few actions of Congress which so struck in [Roosevelt's] craw as the torpedoing of NRPB.... He never let go of it."[75] At the same time, conservatives used the war to gain the upper hand in the battle for public opinion, making it even more difficult for Roosevelt to sustain public support for the economic security components of the national security state.[76]

Conservatives Claim Credit for the World War II "Miracle of Production" and for Providing "Real Security"

Conservatives achieved greater success than liberals in turning the war to political advantage. The ongoing National Association of Manufacturers (NAM) persuasion campaign led the way by applying the public relations insight that "it is easier to replace an established impression with a new one, than it is to convince people that their existing impressions are wrong."[77] The people orchestrating the NAM campaign recognized that the desire for economic security had captured the public imagination and that most Americans had, since the beginning of the Roosevelt administration, looked to the government to provide economic security.[78] NAM used the war to replace the impression that the government was best placed to provide economic security. The enormous wartime production effort, and widespread use of the government-owned, contractor-operated (GOCO) production model, gave NAM the opening to persuade the public that the private sector was better able to provide the economic security Americans sought.[79] NAM seized this opportunity on behalf of conservatives.[80]

NAM Public Relations Director William V. Lawson wrote that his primary objective was "to assure full credit for industry for whatever defense progress is made."[81] This was an urgent task, Lawson said, because "the administration, through various agencies, is claiming for government all the credit."[82] If the private sector succeeded in claiming credit for wartime production successes and the return of prosperity, NAM leaders reasoned, the public would be less amenable to the Roosevelt administration's efforts to expand economic security programs. As an internal NAM overview of the new approach put it, "it cannot be emphasized too strongly that an increased acceptance of this idea of new [business] leadership will make all our other problems simple ones."[83]

In an astonishing public relations triumph, NAM succeeded both in claiming credit for the private sector for the wartime "miracle of production" and—just as important—in denying credit to the government, even though the government financed more than two-thirds of new plant capacity, spent more than twice as much as the private sector on manufacturing machinery and facilities, and ran the wartime economy.[84] NAM accomplished this remarkable persuasive feat not only by touting the superior competence of the private sector but also by sowing doubts about the government's competence.

NAM used the impressive reach developed over the preceding five years to distribute the message that the private sector, not the government, had restored prosperity and deserved credit for winning the war through its production efforts. Beginning in 1941, articles NAM provided as part of its free Industrial Press Service stressed the competence of business and touted the ability of "free enterprise" to meet the country's needs better than "the 'planned economy' of the totalitarian nations"— this last point unsubtly associating liberal proposals for national planning with America's enemies.[85] NAM Executive Chairman Henning Prentis Jr. declared in 1942 that "it is not government that has wrought the miracle that is being accomplished today in the production of war materials. It is the initiative, ingenuity, and organizing genius of private business."[86]

In addition to using its many print outlets, NAM delivered messages about the superiority of private-sector leadership through its radio content. NAM ran a radio program during the war called "This Nation at War" through which Americans "listened to the dramatization of industry's performance and records in the winning of the war" and learned the answer—a resounding "no"—to the question top of mind for many parents: "If the government took over industry, would it get our boy out of his uniform and home any sooner?"[87] According to NAM, the government contributed only "promises, bureaucracy, bungling, and red tape."[88] To further boost the private sector's reputation, NAM also supplied daily "Briefs for Broadcasters" to "617 radio commentators" around the country highlighting "dramatic instances" of "management's ingenuity and foresight in planning for the war and peace."[89]

The NAM succeeded to a remarkable degree during the war in claiming credit for providing "real" economic security to Americans through employment even though government contracts created those jobs. The endless repetition of their messaging helped conservatives deny credit to the government, but the decisive factor was that most Americans engaged in war production felt they worked for companies, not the government. As historian Mark Wilson has shown, this belief was an ironic consequence of the Roosevelt administration's decision to use the government-owned, contractor-operated (GOCO) model for most war production.[90] Under the GOCO model, the government paid for vast new plants like the million-square-foot bomber plant near Dallas, Texas, and leased many of them for $1 a year to companies like North American Aviation to operate.[91] At its peak, thirty-eight thousand people worked at the North American Dallas bomber plant, and they received paychecks from North American, not the government.[92] Relying on the GOCO model for so much war production allowed conservatives to foster the impression that business, not government, deserved credit for the increased economic security many Americans felt.[93] Policies like relying on GOCO made it hard for Americans to see the connection between government spending and their own economic security.[94]

Through the many means it devised to reach the "Average American," NAM lionized the private sector's contributions to war production and omitted the crucial details that the government paid for and supervised the overwhelming majority of it.[95] An October 1943 Service for Plant Publications article circulated by NAM emphasized the leadership of business executives, the "men who equip our fighting forces, men who meet payrolls, pay taxes, employ millions—the men upon whom Americans have always leaned for jobs, for wages, for a higher standard of living."[96] A piece in the March 1944 issue of Service for Plant Publications argued similarly that "Production Is Proof" that "We Run It"—in other words, business runs the country.[97] Using every element of its multichannel campaign, NAM told Americans again and again that the private sector deserved credit for the "miracle of production" and the return of prosperity. By denying credit to the government for both, NAM helped to persuade the public that the private sector was both more competent and better able than the government to provide the economic security Americans sought as they emerged from the Great Depression.[98]

The Government as a Threat to Liberty

The second, related impression NAM cultivated on behalf of conservatives during the war was that the government was a source of danger rather than a source of solutions to problems. This extended beyond accusations of "red-tape" and "bungling" to the more dramatic charge that the government threatened Americans' freedom. In increasingly direct terms, NAM worked to persuade Americans that national security depended on individual freedom and that government provision of economic security—if expanded too far—threatened individual freedom and therefore threatened national security. This clever framing allowed NAM to stimulate public fears that if the government continued to expand economic security programs, the public stood to lose both freedom and national security.

In the early 1940s, NAM drew on events in Europe to try to persuade workers—as NAM was similarly trying to persuade women through its *Primer for Americans*—that lasting "government intervention" in the economy threatened their freedom. The October 1941 issue of NAM's Service for Plant Publications devoted a column to the threat posed by the potential indefinite extension of emergency government management of aspects of the economy. In the article, NAM argued that "although little is said about restrictions on labor at the present time, experience in other countries has shown that labor controls cannot be avoided if industry is regimented permanently. That is what happened in Germany, and today labor there takes orders from the regime just as industry does. . . .

At any time the government can force him out of one job and into another at less pay or for longer hours or both. The dictatorship that promised him security has not only failed to give him security; it has robbed him of his freedom as well."[99]

At the 1943 Congress of American Industry, NAM president Frederick Crawford echoed the long-standing conservative lament that "people seem ready to swap the very freedoms that are the foundation of this country for a false sense of security."[100] To fight this tendency, NAM published a booklet called *A Better America* that blended optimistic notes about a bright future under private-sector economic leadership and ominous warnings about the threat to freedom posed by taking government provision of economic security too far. "The crux of the security problem," the booklet said, "is to reconcile Freedom from Want, with the maintenance of full individual incentives to production."[101] The booklet argued that government provision of economic security would "be a lure to indolence," that "a nation of loafers cannot supply the production necessary to security," and that people would then have to be coerced to work, at which point "will there be anything left of American freedom?"[102]

The booklet then laid out the case against expanding Social Security programs on the grounds that expansion was both economically unworkable and would destroy freedom. Repeating the conservative conviction that the government could only distribute wealth and not create it, the booklet argued that "Social Security programs can never give us an increase of total security. They can only redistribute whatever security is produced; subtracting from the security of some individuals in order to add to the security of others."[103] The booklet warned that "Social Security, seen in its true light, can never be more than a system for providing for the small minority of our people who are unable to achieve their own security through their own efforts. If it becomes our basic method of providing security for all our people, the incentive system is destroyed and we adopt a collectivist economy with compulsory labor."[104] A minimal economic security provision should remain, the booklet concluded, "but let us be sure we do not carry it to an extent which will so weaken individual incentives as to reduce the total amount of security which is voluntarily produced, until it is inadequate to our needs."[105]

NAM argued that maximum individual freedom held the key to the economic security Americans sought. After acknowledging, in an under-handed way, that not everyone valued freedom as highly as it did—"some of us value freedom above a full stomach. Others, probably, do not"—NAM added that "fortunately, we need not make a choice. For the ma-terial ends we seek not only are consistent with freedom, but they can only be attained in America under institutions of personal freedom. . . . That is because our material objectives can be attained only through bountiful production."[106] The implication, of course, was that bountiful production depended on private-sector economic leadership. NAM could only make that argument credibly because it was succeeding in claiming credit for the wartime "miracle of production" and the return of prosperity even though they resulted from government spending and government management. If economic security depended on private-sector leadership, then so-called "government intervention" in the econ-omy could be portrayed as a security threat. And that is exactly what NAM said, warning against "the swelling flood of bureaucratic decrees laid down by administrative officers not chosen by, or even known to, the People or their elected legislative Representatives."[107]

Through its clever exploitation of wartime circumstances, NAM undermined public support for the economic security part of the com-prehensive national security state the Roosevelt administration was try-ing to build. The NAM campaign helped ensure that the private sector, not the government, received credit for the economic security that flowed from mobilization for war. But the NAM campaign did not stop there. It also sowed doubt about the government's competence and portrayed Roosevelt's effort to build a comprehensive national security state as a threat to Americans' freedom—and it supported that charge with plausi-ble-sounding economic arguments.

Roosevelt jotted down some one-liners that reflected his irritation with the campaign: "Vote Republican and Avoid the Strain of Thought!"; "You Want the Best Hoovers: We Have Them in Store!"; "There are those who are in the armed forces and there are those who are in the harm forces." And finally, "A critic is one who could not go as well himself."[108] But Roosevelt knew that he needed a stronger answer. His advisors thought they had one in the speech Roosevelt had planned to deliver back in December 1941, before the Japanese bombs fell.

An Economic Bill of Rights

As victory in the war began to look likely, Roosevelt's advisors encouraged him to make the Economic Bill of Rights that would have been the focus of that December 1941 speech the centerpiece of his 1944 State of the Union. As the lead drafter of that message and with his close relationship with Roosevelt, Samuel Rosenman was in the best position to lobby for including the Economic Bill of Rights—a fact other liberals within the administration recognized. On December 23, 1943, Office of Price Administration Director Chester Bowles, a liberal stalwart, sent Rosenman an outline for the speech, including "a <u>Second</u> Bill of Rights to establish a new basis for security and prosperity for all of us, regardless of wealth, race or creed."[109] Bowles felt circumstances demanded movement on the Economic Bill of Rights because "without economic and social security, it will be impossible to maintain the freedom and liberty for which we are fighting."[110] Rosenman embraced the idea and began lobbying Roosevelt to include it in the speech.

Rosenman used public opinion polling to support his case. Hadley Cantril, the administration's trusted public opinion expert, sent Rosenman a memo on January 6, 1944, with specific recommendations for the speech based on the latest public opinion trends. Cantril said the data provided "another confirmation of the people's desire to have an affirmative leadership on the domestic front, a desire that has mounted in the last few months of domestic trouble."[111] He added a specific suggestion about the "tone to aim for," recommending that "since people think of Roosevelt as the man we need if there is a crisis ahead, convey the impression that the years ahead <u>are</u> critical—on the domestic as well as the international front—the transition years following the war in getting our economy here at home on a solid basis to carry on peace time development."[112] Rosenman forwarded Cantril's conclusions to Roosevelt and the president agreed to include the call for an Economic Bill of Rights in the speech.[113]

To maximize the chance that their message would not be dismissed by those who had grown weary of Roosevelt's domestic agenda, Roosevelt and his advisors did not frame their proposal for an Economic Bill of Rights as a continuation of the New Deal. In his December 23 memo, Chester Bowles noted that "in the proposed speech, I have omitted any direct reference to the achievements of the New Deal, and I have done this for a specific reason."[114] The reason, Bowles explained, was that "a liberal cycle is usually followed by a conservative cycle," and that many people assumed a conservative cycle was coming next because Roosevelt had served as president since 1933.[115] Bowles argued that "actually, it seems to me, we have been in the midst of a conservative cycle . . . since 1938. I believe the time is at hand for a return to the liberal swing of the cycle. This can be more easily achieved if the general public do not see the new liberal program as simply a continuation of the old."[116] It is possible Rosenman discussed Bowles's shrewd memo with Roosevelt before the president gave his famous press conference on the afternoon of December 28 explaining how "Dr. Win-the-War" had replaced "Dr. New Deal," but it is just as possible Roosevelt had come to the same conclusion himself: it was time to look only forward. But looking forward did not mean jettisoning the language of security with which Roosevelt had achieved so many past successes.

During his long tenure in the White House, Roosevelt had seen how the primary threat to national security could in one period be economic insecurity and in another period be physical and ideological insecurity. Although massive government wartime spending restored prosperity by the mid-1940s, Roosevelt did not believe the United States had completed the institutional reconstruction necessary to eliminate the economic insecurity that accompanied modern industrial capitalism. If the government did not permanently guarantee economic security, individual economic insecurity would again one day become the primary national security problem, just as it was when he assumed the presidency. He also understood how insufficient American attention to mounting foreign threats to national security in the 1930s allowed those threats to grow until they reached crisis proportions. He believed the government needed always to be responsible for addressing all sources of insecurity—not just the one that had primacy at a particular moment—and that national security policymaking therefore must include both domestic and foreign policy.

The 1944 State of the Union message represented the culmination of Roosevelt and his advisors' years of careful thinking about the government's responsibilities to citizens. Implicit in Roosevelt's second Bill of Rights was the idea that government had an indispensable role to play in making the first Bill of Rights real—that in modern times individual freedom depended on positive rights to economic security guaranteed by the government. The president argued, contra conservatives, that the government guarantee of freedom and the government provision of economic security were not opposing forces but were in fact mutually dependent.[117] It was a relationship Roosevelt and his advisors had thought about for many years, and even though Roosevelt decided to pare down the part of the speech discussing the Economic Bill of Rights in the final drafts, he wrote "Next Talk" in the margin next to the sections he cut.[118]

In the speech, Roosevelt listed the rights to which the domestic policy parts of the government's national security responsibilities corresponded, telling the American people that "in our day . . . we have accepted, so to speak, a second Bill of Rights under which a new basis of security and prosperity can be established for all—regardless of station or race or creed. Among these are:

> The right to a useful and remunerative job in the industries, or shops or farms or mines of the nation;
>
> The right to earn enough to provide adequate food and clothing and recreation;
>
> The right of farmers to raise and sell their products at a return which will give them and their families a decent living;
>
> The right of every businessman, large and small, to trade in an atmosphere of freedom from unfair competition and domination by monopolies at home or abroad;
>
> The right of every family to a decent home;
>
> The right to adequate medical care and the opportunity to achieve and enjoy good health;

> The right to adequate protection from the economic fears of old age,
> and sickness, and accident and unemployment;

> And finally, the right to a good education."[119]

Summing up the central objective of his presidency, Roosevelt declared that "all of these rights spell security."[120] He added, "And after this war is won we must be prepared to move forward, in the implementation of these rights, to new goals of human happiness and well-being."[121]

In an attempt to appeal over the heads of Congress to the American people, Roosevelt delivered the address by radio to a national audience rather than delivering it in person in the Capitol.[122] Roosevelt said, "I ask the Congress to explore the means for implementing this economic bill of rights," adding, for the public's benefit, the elementary civics reminder that "it is definitely the responsibility of the Congress so to do" and reminding Congress that "the country knows it."[123] Roosevelt then made the public aware that "many of these problems are already before committees of the Congress in the form of proposed legislation" and warned Congress, in a line he wrote himself, that "in the event that no adequate program of progress is evolved, I am certain that the Nation will be conscious of the fact."[124] Turning up the heat still further, Roosevelt declared that "our fighting men abroad—and their families at home—expect such a program and have the right to insist on it. It is to their demands that this Government should pay heed, rather than to the whining demands of selfish pressure groups who seek to feather their nests while young Americans are dying."[125] Not surprisingly, Roosevelt's speech fell flat with the conservative Seventy-Eighth Congress.[126] But Hadley Cantril reported that the speech had a positive effect on public opinion.[127]

Roosevelt continued to think about the Economic Bill of Rights in the months after the speech. A list of proposed messages to Congress for the rest of 1944 demonstrates Roosevelt's desire to expand the economic security–focused part of the national security state. The list included four separate messages on expanding the existing Social Security program to address "permanent disability"; "temporary disability, medical and hospital care"; "unemployment insurance on national basis"; and "increased coverage of workers and increased public assistance."[128] And Roosevelt himself penciled in one final addition to the list of proposed messages, on "planning."[129]

The administration saw the 1944 GI Bill as the "entering wedge" of a new period of expansion of the economic security–focused part of the national security state.[130] As the administration envisioned it, the bill would provide for veterans and their families many of the rights Roosevelt had outlined in his 1944 State of the Union.[131] Roosevelt believed no sane politician could oppose proposals to do right by American service members who had gone to war on the country's behalf.[132] If the administration could not secure timely passage of an Economic Bill of Rights for all Americans, it could at least win many of those rights immediately for veterans. Given the number of veterans, the bill had a dramatic impact on American society, but—like other economic security programs shaped by the Southern-controlled Congress—the bill distributed this impact unevenly because racial and gender discrimination prevented equal access to its provisions.[133]

In many ways, the GI Bill represented the fullest realization of Roosevelt's economic security–focused concept of national security. It would be an enduring irony, however, that the fullest version of what would soon be rebranded as the "welfare state" emerged within the military establishment and would remain confined there.[134] But that outcome lay in the future. Roosevelt had not accepted that the GI Bill would mark the end of the institutionalization of his vision for a comprehensive national security state. Roosevelt concluded his bill signing statement by saying that "there is still much to be done."[135] That feeling contributed to Roosevelt's decision to seek an unprecedented fourth term as president, despite his failing health.

The 1944 Election

The 1944 campaign showed how conservative messaging had evolved and become more effective. In the 1936 campaign, conservatives charged Roosevelt with "boondoggling"—a pejorative Roosevelt wore with pride as he gave speech after speech in "boondoggle" stadiums and other popular public works projects.[136] In 1940, conservatives accused Roosevelt of leading the country to ruin by trading individual freedom for economic security, but Roosevelt achieved greater success arguing that the one depended on the other. Conservatives continued to press that line, but now, in what was becoming an ever more crucial part of the standard conservative message, Republican candidate Thomas Dewey charged that the government, because of its incompetence, could not provide economic security.

The charge of government incompetence, if it stuck, threatened Roosevelt's ability to finish building the national security state he believed the country needed. Public opinion surveys from mid-1944 showed that "the overwhelming majority of people believe the most important problems facing the next President (and themselves) will be domestic, not international."[137] In his acceptance speech at the Republican National Convention in Chicago, Dewey asserted that the Roosevelt administration "had failed utterly" to solve the problem of unemployment.[138] He said a fourth term for Roosevelt held out "only the dreary prospect of . . . interference piled on interference and petty tyrannies rivaling the very regimentation against which we are now at war."[139] In year eleven of the Roosevelt administration, Dewey said, "we have become familiar with the spectacle of wrangling, bungling and confusion."[140] He asked rhetorically, "Does anyone suggest that the present national administration is giving either efficient or competent government?"[141]

Roosevelt defused these attacks for the moment by pointing out that his "incompetent" administration was leading the country to victory in the war. He also deployed his well-developed sense of humor to good effect against the famously stiff Dewey.[142] In a nationally broadcast campaign address at Soldiers Field in Chicago, Roosevelt said, "I must confess to you that this is the strangest campaign I have ever seen. I have listened to the various Republican orators who are urging the people to throw the present Administration out and put them in. And what do they say? Well, they say in effect, just this: 'Those incompetent blunderers and bunglers in Washington have passed a lot of excellent laws about social security and labor and farm relief and soil conservation—and many others—and we promise that if elected we will not change any of them.'"[143] On foreign policy, he continued, they "go on to say, 'Those same quarrelsome, tired old men—they have built the greatest military machine the world has ever known, which is fighting its way to victory, and,' they say, 'if you elect us, we promise not to change any of that, either.'"[144] Roosevelt concluded, to roaring laughter, "'Therefore,' say these Republican orators, 'it is time for a change.'"[145]

Throughout the campaign, Roosevelt reiterated his long-held belief that national security depended on national planning. In his speech accepting the Democratic nomination, Roosevelt acknowledged that "I realize that planning is a word which in some places brings forth sneers" but argued that "before our entry into the war it was planning which made possible the magnificent organization and equipment of the Army and Navy of the United States which are fighting for us and for our civilization today."[146] On another occasion, Roosevelt said, "I cannot resist the temptation to point to the gigantic contribution to our war effort made by the power generated at T.V.A. and Bonneville and Grand Coulee. But, do you remember when the building of these great public works was ridiculed as New Deal 'boondoggling'?"[147] Roosevelt said, "Improvement through planning is the order of the day. . . . If we are to progress in our civilization, improvement is necessary in other fields—in the physical things that are a part of our daily lives, and also in the concepts of social justice at home and abroad."[148]

As Roosevelt pulled ahead in the polls, Dewey revived a charge conservatives had leveled against liberals during the 1930s, declaring flatly that "the Communists are seizing control of the New Deal, through which they aim to control the Government of the United States."[149] In the end, the Communism charge did not prove decisive in the polling booth in 1944. Roosevelt won reelection despite substantially lower turnout than in either of his previous reelection victories.[150] But evidence indicated that the public had grown more concerned about the specter of Communism. Conservatives could therefore look forward to the possibility that the charge would prove more effective in future campaigns.[151]

Conservatives Redouble Their Efforts to Shift Public Opinion

During the 1944 campaign, conservatives thought they had finally figured out why, beyond simple circumstances, Roosevelt had achieved such success selling his policies to the public. The answers came from a book. In

September 1944, Austrian economist Friedrich Hayek published *The Road to Serfdom* in the United States. Hayek viewed his work as a "patient and detailed examination of the reasons why economic planning will produce such unlooked-for results"—totalitarianism—"and of the process by which they come about."[152] The book amounted to an incisive critique of the approach long championed by some members of Roosevelt's Brain Trust and by the National Resources Planning Board and its predecessors. On the process by which totalitarianism comes about, Hayek offered an observation of particular relevance to his American readers. Hayek identified the appropriation and redefinition of terms like "liberal," "freedom," and "liberty" as "the most efficient" and "most effective" means of persuading people to "transfer their allegiance."[153] This, of course, is what Roosevelt had done to great effect since 1932.

Hayek also devoted a chapter to "Security and Freedom" in which he developed into a more cogent argument the feeling many American conservatives had long expressed, that "when security is understood in too absolute a sense"—in other words, in the way Roosevelt conceived of national security—"the general striving for it, far from increasing the chances of freedom, becomes the gravest threat to it."[154] Hayek acknowledged that the relationship between security and freedom was not entirely antithetical: "some security is essential if freedom is to be preserved, because most men are willing to bear the risk which freedom inevitably involves only so long as that risk is not too great."[155] But he added that "while this is a truth of which we must never lose sight, nothing is more fatal than the present fashion among intellectual leaders of extolling security at the expense of freedom."[156]

Thanks to a focused effort by influential American conservatives, Hayek's ideas—or, more precisely, a cherry-picked version of Hayek's ideas—reached a large audience in the United States.[157] *Reader's Digest* led its April 1945 issue with a twenty-page condensation of Hayek's work, prefaced by conservative economist Henry Hazlitt's glowing endorsement of it as "One of the Most Important Books of Our Generation."[158] Not all the words that appeared in the *Reader's Digest* condensation were Hayek's.[159] Max Eastman and DeWitt Wallace, the *Reader's Digest* editors responsible for the condensation as well as for the publication's recent move to the Right, sharpened Hayek's text to a finer polemical edge and eliminated important qualifications.[160] The actual text of *The Road to Serfdom* reveals Hayek's support for a level of government responsibility for economic security, including the principle behind the defunct National Resources Planning Board.[161] In his book, Hayek distinguished between government planning to combat "general fluctuations of economic activity and the recurrent waves of large-scale unemployment which accompany them," which he supported, and government planning "designed to protect individuals or groups against diminutions of their income," which he opposed.[162] The *Reader's Digest* condensation omitted this point.[163]

Reader's Digest was then the most widely circulated magazine in the United States.[164] Millions of Americans had the chance to read the anti-planning polemic derived from Hayek's book when the April 1945 issue arrived. *Reader's Digest* ensured even wider circulation by offering reprints of the condensation of Hayek's "much discussed book" for a nickel apiece through the Book-of-the-Month Club.[165] More than a million reprints of the *Reader's Digest* version of Hayek's work circulated around the country. NAM sent copies to its fourteen thousand members.[166] General Motors and other large companies provided copies to employees.[167] General Electric ran a cartoon version in its company magazine.[168] The book itself became an unexpected success for the University of Chicago Press, selling an initial forty thousand copies.[169] But most people who encountered Hayek's work did so through *Reader's Digest.* Hayek himself complained that there were "far too many people talking about what I am represented to have said rather than about the argument that I have actually used."[170] The *Reader's Digest* anti-government caricature of Hayek became a touchstone for the American conservative movement, providing crucial intellectual support for conservatives' efforts to eject economic security from the national security frame once and for all.

NAM aided in that task when it launched its first national print advertising campaign at the end of 1944 with the help of the Kenyon & Eckhardt advertising agency. In its successful pitch to NAM, Kenyon & Eckhardt argued that "The job is, in a very large measure, a psychological one. Americans turned to Government in the thirties out of fear, and out of the defeatist belief that we had reached the end of expansion. If only we can sell them another feeling about the future it will do as much as anything to change the course of our affairs."[171] This line of reasoning mirrored conclusions many NAM leaders reached about what had happened since the early 1930s, when—as Brown University President Henry Wriston put it at NAM's 1943 annual gathering—many Americans "unconsciously attempt[ed] to exchange freedom for security."[172] Now, Kenyon & Eckhardt proposed replacing the impression many Americans had come to hold about the proper responsibilities of government. Out went the provision of security as the chief governmental responsibility and in came the guarantee of freedom.

The Kenyon & Eckhardt NAM ads began running in December 1944 "in every daily newspaper, both English and foreign-language, published in all cities of over fifty thousand population."[173] Most of the ads started from the assumption that the government could only distribute wealth, not expand it, and therefore could not guarantee economic security. The ads emphasized that building a prosperous future "can't be done by government hand-outs—which are purely artificial (since the government can't give us any more than we can give it). Handouts only result in more taxes, more debt. It can be done only by using our productive capacity to give people more value in the things they buy—so that they can buy more. In this way, more jobs can be created and more earnings paid."[174]

An ad titled "GUTS" narrated a version of American history that erased the government's contributions to the country's development and made the turn to government for economic security seem recent, anomalous, and cowardly. "It took guts to discover this country in the first place. Guts to settle it. Guts to push back the wilderness, weather the icy winters, stand up to savage hate. It took guts to talk back to a king, to fight his paid armies, to set up a nation and go it on our own. It took guts to carry on despite panics, floods, fires, civil war. But we did it. And we built the richest, healthiest, freest, best-fed, best-educated nation in all history. Then came the Big Depression. And we forgot all about guts. We became timid and afraid. We thought we might better entrust our destiny to government."[175] This supposed shift made no sense, the ad argued, because the "government . . . couldn't give us a dime more than we gave it."[176]

NAM may not have succeeded in shaping public opinion on every single question of importance to conservatives during the war through its national advertising campaign and other efforts, but the volume and endless repetition of its messaging helped persuade more Americans to look skeptically on the government and to look to the private sector for economic security.[177] Although conservative Kenyon & Eckhardt president Thomas D'Arcy Brophy found some of the ads "too dull, too stuffy," he was nevertheless delighted by a February 1945 public opinion survey showing favorable public reaction to the ads.[178] Differences of opinion among NAM board members ultimately scuttled this particular ad campaign, but through his ongoing involvement in the conservative movement Brophy ensured the messages featured again in the conservative persuasion campaign in the years to come.[179]

By 1945, conservative public relations experts like Brophy had helped the burgeoning conservative movement sharpen its message to a fine point: national security depended on freedom *from* government and not, as Roosevelt suggested, on government efforts to provide economic security, which conservatives said threatened freedom and therefore threatened national security. "It is a strange paradox," NAM Executive Committee chairman Frederick Crawford declared in January 1945, "that the only real national security comes from the risk and venture, daring and opportunity only possible under freedom. While the pursuit of security itself often destroys it."[180] Crawford said that "the American people in the past decade have been seeking security through laws to make everyone and everything secure—jobs, investments, farmers, old age; and for the first time in a hundred years national progress to greater economic security stops."[181] He argued that "all our efforts at planned security have succeeded only imposing a well nigh perfect 'Birth Control' on new enterprise." He concluded that "<u>opportunity, risk, venture</u> are the first steps to security. And they can <u>exist only with freedom</u>."[182]

Roosevelt's Passing

In his 1939 State of the Union address, Franklin Roosevelt had declared optimistically that "we have now passed the period of internal conflict in the launching of our program of social reform."[183] In fact, effective opposition to Roosevelt's vision for national security blossomed soon after he spoke those words. The Roosevelt administration was quite aware of the ongoing conservative persuasion campaign but struggled to counter it as it grew in effectiveness in the early 1940s.[184] There are several explanations for the administration's struggles. One is that liberals did not take conservatives' efforts seriously until it was too late.[185] The American Liberty League's demise and Roosevelt's election to unprecedented third and then fourth terms may have led liberals to conclude that they had nothing to fear from the conservative persuasion campaign.[186] Another explanation is that the war and the return of prosperity that accompanied wartime government spending made economic security programs seem less vital for national security. Finally, although Roosevelt and his closest advisors remained committed to their domestic agenda and continued to work on it during the war, victory against the Axis Powers was their primary focus during Roosevelt's third term. By the time they turned their attention fully back to building public support for Roosevelt's domestic agenda, conservatives had seized the opening created by the war to erode public support for Roosevelt's vision for national security.

Roosevelt had ambitious plans for 1945 focused on expanding Social Security and establishing a national health program.[187] But he did not live to fight for them. He died at Warm Springs, Georgia, on April 12, 1945. His death left liberals without their most powerful champion. Conservative *New York Times* columnist Arthur Krock had been right to call Roosevelt "the architect of national security."[188] Roosevelt entered office believing the government had a responsibility to protect citizens from hazards against which they could not protect themselves. Throughout his presidency, Roosevelt used the language of security to build support for expanding the government's responsibilities to address hazards as they emerged. He achieved considerable success. But this success also produced unintended consequences that began to undermine Roosevelt's vision for a comprehensive national security state even before Roosevelt died. An energized conservative movement had gained the upper hand in the battle for public opinion. And now the burgeoning foreign policy establishment began to claim the mantle of national security exclusively for themselves and their work.

7

———

Separate National Security
and Welfare States

There are certain programs of Government which have come to be
looked upon as 'welfare programs' in a narrow sense. This has placed
them in an insulated compartment.[1]

—*Harry Truman, January 8, 1947*

On a Monday morning in late October 1945, Secretary of the Navy
James Forrestal appeared before the Senate Military Affairs Committee
to provide his views on the shape of the postwar national security state.
Forrestal said "national security can only be assured on a very broad and
comprehensive front" and "real national security cannot be achieved
without the most careful planning."[2] That sounded Rooseveltian. But the
"broad and comprehensive front" and the type of planning Forrestal proposed differed markedly from what Franklin Roosevelt intended. Forrestal's conception of national security was broad and comprehensive
only in the wide scope of the international commitments it entailed. It did
not include the economic security component foundational to Roosevelt's concept of national security. The partial exception was the need to
ensure the economy could meet military requirements in an emergency.
Rather than a National Resources *Planning* Board tasked with making
the most of the country's resources to ensure economic security, therefore, Forrestal proposed a National *Security* Resources Board tasked with
ensuring the military could make "maximum use of the nation's natural

and industrial resources."[3] Other than this small foray into domestic policy, Forrestal made clear that national security was a matter for foreign policy professionals to manage.

Forrestal received support in his effort to build a foreign policy–focused national security state from a handful of academics, intellectuals, and advisors, including Walter Lippmann, Edward Mead Earle, E. Pendleton Herring, and Ferdinand Eberstadt, and from conservative members of both parties in Congress who opposed many aspects of the liberal domestic agenda.[4] For a variety of personal and professional reasons, these people pushed for a narrow definition of national security that focused solely on physical security and that considered foreign policy the proper domain for national security policymaking.

Roosevelt had hoped to prevent institutionalization of a narrower definition of national security that excluded domestic economic security. Two weeks before his death, for example, he wrote to Forrestal to say that he intended to fold the wartime military research work of the Research Board for National Security into a broader postwar scientific research program.[5] Roosevelt's death left it to his successor, Harry Truman, to continue the fight for a comprehensive national security state responsible for both economic and physical security. Unlike Roosevelt and his advisors, however, Truman and the advisors closest to him did not fully comprehend the language of security's special power and failed to use it consistently to build support for domestic economic security programs. Instead, Truman distinguished in important messages between the government's "national security" and "welfare" responsibilities in ways Roosevelt deliberately did not.

Clark Clifford and George Elsey, the two men who orchestrated much of Truman's speechwriting during the early years of his presidency, both acknowledged later that speechwriting in that crucial transitional period was not on the same level it had been under Roosevelt.[6] Like Truman himself, the speechwriters often found themselves overwhelmed during those momentous months and prioritized tone over framing.[7] Along with the rapid growth of a foreign policy profession that claimed the mantle of national security exclusively for its work, the distinction Truman helped draw between national security and welfare accelerated the removal of domestic policy from the national security frame. Conservatives exploited these developments, expanding their persuasion campaign to cement a narrower definition of national security in the public mind and to persuade Americans that the government's most basic responsibility was to guarantee freedom, not economic security.

Truman's Distinction between "National Security" and "Welfare"

During the remainder of what would have been Roosevelt's fourth term, Harry Truman saw himself as an "acting president" obligated to carry out his responsibilities in ways consistent with Roosevelt's vision.[8] Truman retained longtime Roosevelt advisor and speechwriter Samuel Rosenman as special counsel to aid in this effort.[9] Rosenman recalled that whenever Truman faced a decision, "he would say to himself: 'I wonder what Roosevelt would have done? Would he think this is the right thing?' You know, he had a picture on the wall of Roosevelt that he could see just by turning, and he frequently said to me, 'I'm trying to do what he would like.'"[10] Thus, in the years following World War II Truman sought to expand the government's economic security responsibilities in ways Roosevelt thought necessary for national security.[11] That translated to a push to actualize the Economic Bill of Rights from Roosevelt's 1944 State of the Union.

Truman's September 6, 1945, reconversion message to Congress outlining his program for transitioning the economy back to a peacetime footing illustrates how he tried to continue along the lines Roosevelt would have wanted but undercut that effort by distinguishing between the government's "national security" and "welfare" responsibilities. In the message, Truman said, "a comprehensive and continuous program of national security" included "a universal [military] training program, unification of the armed services, and the use and control of atomic energy."[12] "National welfare," by contrast, meant full employment and full production.[13] The sections of Truman's message where he quoted from Roosevelt's 1944 State of the Union underscored the differences in the way the two presidents framed policy. Roosevelt used the term "security" repeatedly to refer to economic security programs. When Truman used his own words in other parts of his message, however, he substituted the term "welfare."[14]

The drafting of Truman's reconversion message was a major flashpoint in the battle between liberals and conservatives within the Truman administration to shape the president's public statements and the details of policy.[15] With the exception of Rosenman and a few others, Truman's advisors were more conservative than Roosevelt's. As Rosenman recalled, "when President Truman started off in April 1945, he was surrounded by a group of men who did not believe in the New Deal, and who wanted to get away from it as soon as possible. The leader of that group was John Snyder. . . . He really believed, sincerely believed, that the continuation of the New Deal program would be disastrous to the country; and that President Truman ought to resume a middle-of-the-road policy."[16] Clark Clifford, one of Rosenman's liberal allies within the administration, similarly recalled that John Snyder "was openly probusiness and anti-New Deal on every issue."[17] Clifford added that "most of the rest of the Cabinet was conservative as well."[18]

Although Truman's reconversion message was far from the most elegant message Rosenman had helped craft, he saw it as a crucial victory for liberals.[19] He said later that "personally, I think that the most important thing that I did for President Truman, and perhaps through him for the country itself, was to fight without let-up for that twenty-one point message. Although I believe that it really conformed with the President's general policy, and was wholly consistent with his prior senatorial voting record, it committed him publicly to the philosophy of the Fair Deal or its synonym, the New Deal."[20]

It was a hollow victory. The message, which Truman called "one of the most important messages of my administration," made clear that he and his advisors saw a distinction between "welfare" programs and "national security" programs.[21] The distinction ceded the last bits of rhetorical high ground Roosevelt had staked out for a comprehensive national security state. Welfare lacks the intrinsic persuasive power of security, which has a powerful "loss frame" built in because people dread the loss of security. Psychologists have shown that people fear losses more than they look forward to potential gains, and that when trying to persuade it is therefore most effective to place issues in a loss frame.[22] Framing something as necessary for welfare made it optional—a potential gain rather than a definite must. By framing economic security programs as "welfare" programs

rather than "national security" programs, Truman made them easier tar-
gets for conservatives and set the administration on the path of building
separate national security and welfare states.

Nevertheless, liberals' success in shaping the substance of both Truman's reconversion message and his 1946 State of the Union address—in
which he said "there is no question in my mind that the Government . . .
must assume the ultimate responsibility for the economic health of the
Nation"—led John Snyder, head of the administration's conservative faction, to invite the leaders of the ostensibly nonpartisan but conservative-
run Advertising Council for a crisis conference in February 1946 to coordinate a counterattack.[23] Rosenman argued later that "there was no way
that Mr. Snyder, with all of his influence and power could turn the President back to a conservative policy, or even to a middle-of-the-road policy
after that message went up to the Congress."[24] It may not have occurred
to Rosenman that working within the administration was not the only
way for Snyder to achieve his objectives. What Snyder could do, and did
do, was work with conservatives outside government to shift public opinion away from the Rooseveltian vision for national security.

The Advertising Council and the Conservative Movement

John Snyder's turn to the Advertising Council for help in the fight against
the liberal agenda signaled a change in leadership of the conservative
persuasion campaign. The Ad Council, run by influential conservative
public relations experts and business executives, succeeded the National
Association of Manufacturers as the most important player in the conservative persuasion campaign in the late 1940s. The Ad Council developed
out of advertising executives' frustration with negative public perceptions
of their profession in the 1930s and dissatisfaction with Franklin Roosevelt's success expanding the government's domestic responsibilities. At a
joint meeting of the Association of National Advertisers and the American Association of Advertising Agencies in Hot Springs, Virginia, in November 1941, leading advertising executive James W. Young made the
case to his colleagues that they needed to deploy the power of advertising
on behalf of themselves and "free enterprise."[25] The final lines of Young's
speech called his colleagues to arms: "We have within our hands the

greatest aggregate means of mass education and persuasion the world has ever seen—namely, the channels of advertising communication. We have the masters of the techniques of using these channels. We have power. Why do we not use it?"[26] Young's address moved his colleagues to action, but before they could get their effort off the ground Japanese attacks and a German declaration of war brought the United States fully into World War II.[27]

Like the public relations specialists running the National Association of Manufacturers (NAM) campaign, the Ad Council's conservative leaders saw the war as a tremendous persuasion opportunity. Through what they called "public service advertising," advertisers and businesses would aid the war effort and generate public goodwill for themselves while also demonstrating private-sector leadership on national issues and subtly denigrating the government. Although the Ad Council claimed to be a nonpartisan organization, in private its leaders made clear their conservative views and opposition to the Roosevelt and Truman administrations' domestic policies.[28] The Ad Council continued operating after the war because its leaders believed it could play an important role in the coming "ideological battle."[29] At least some Ad Council staffers clearly agreed. When they came across a pamphlet from an organization called The People's Lobby advocating further expansion of economic security programs, the staffers marked up the pamphlet in pink pencil—noting the deliberate use of that color to reflect what they perceived as the pamphlet's socialist tinge—and filed the pamphlet in their Future Plans folder.[30]

Although partisan themselves, the Ad Council's leaders understood that the organization's ability to influence public opinion depended on maintaining a solid veneer of nonpartisanship.[31] The Ad Council's success doing so enabled the organization to sell its work as "public service advertising," making the organization even more valuable to the conservative movement than the continuing NAM campaign. In "public service advertising," the Ad Council developed a subtler and more effective means of indirect persuasion than what the NAM had achieved working through "opinion molders." The nonpartisan image enabled the Ad Council to obtain vast amounts of free advertising content and space from media and advertising companies, giving the organization even greater reach than what the NAM, quite impressively, had managed.[32] Messages delivered by the Ad Council made billions of reader, viewer, and listener "impressions" each year.[33] As a repetition tool, the Ad Council had no match.

In the period after World War II when the extent of the government's economic security responsibilities remained undetermined, the Ad Council helped to foster a selective anti-statism by encouraging Americans to support spending for "national security," defined narrowly to include only foreign policy and physical security, and to oppose spending for economic security programs increasingly saddled with the "welfare" label.[34] The Cold War's onset all but guaranteed substantial investments in military and foreign policy capacity. The question at the time was, Would the country also expand its domestic policy capacity substantially? The conservative persuasion campaign helped ensure the answer would be no. "The essence of the advertising method," Charles Mortimer Jr. reminded his fellow Ad Council board members, "is repetition—of saying basic facts over and over until, like postage stamps, they stick to one thing until they get there."[35] In the years following World War II, the "basic facts" the Ad Council repeated over and over again through every communications medium reflected a conservative view of the proper responsibilities of the government.

The Postwar Conservative Persuasion Campaign

Like their predecessors in the mid-1930s, the people running the postwar conservative persuasion campaign believed Americans were, by and large, "staggeringly ignorant," particularly when it came to matters of political economy, and needed to be schooled.[36] Many conservatives continued to attribute Americans' support for the expansion of the government's economic security responsibilities to this ignorance. They believed they could dampen support for further such expansions by shaping the public's understanding of economics and American history.

Toward the end of the war, longtime conservative activist and financier E. F. Hutton—a former Liberty Leaguer and backer of the National Committee to Uphold Constitutional Government—lobbied his conservative friends on the Ad Council to "re-sell" the original Bill of Rights to Americans.[37] Hutton and other conservatives treasured the Bill of Rights for the prohibitions they believed it placed on government activity. After failing to persuade the Ad Council to take on the project, Hutton launched his own national advertising campaign in 1946.[38] Kenyon & Eckhardt helped develop and place ads under Hutton's name in newspapers around the country.[39]

Kenyon & Eckhardt president and Ad Council director Thomas D'Arcy Brophy agreed with Hutton that more needed to be done to "re-sell" Americans on the negative liberty ideal they believed the first Bill of Rights embodied. But Brophy felt Hutton's ads would not persuade anyone who did not already harbor conservative views.[40] By October 1946, Brophy thought he had identified a more promising approach.[41] Brophy wanted to work with the Ad Council to arrange a nationwide weekly primetime radio program modeled on the "I Am An American" mass patriotic rally that took place in New York in May 1946.[42] The goal of his initiative, Brophy wrote, was to "persuade Americans that the freedoms we now enjoy are endangered, and that only by good citizenship and hard work can they be preserved."[43] Getting that message across would not be difficult, Brophy noted in a memo he circulated among a small group of other conservatives, because "we have at our disposal facilities which, used in concert, can reach every man, woman and child in America. They can be reached on a national scale by magazines and radio; and locally by newspapers, radio, outdoor and transportation advertising."[44] "Salesmanship," Brophy said, "can sell Americanism to Americans as well as it can sell soap and motor cars."[45]

While Brophy brainstormed, conservative government officials in Washington, DC, fretted over how to combat what Attorney General Tom Clark said was "the disintegration of much of our American unity."[46] One day in April 1946, Department of Justice assistant director of public information William Coblenz wandered into the nearby National Archives during his lunch break and walked out with the idea of creating a traveling exhibit of the documents that formed the foundation of Americans' liberties.[47] Attorney General Clark—a leading member of the conservative faction within the Truman administration—embraced the idea, but postwar budget constraints prevented him from bringing what he called the "Bill of Rights Train" to fruition as a government program.[48] Clark thought the project important and made the fateful decision to seek private funding for it.[49] Paramount Pictures president Barney Balaban, who felt so strongly about the Bill of Rights that in 1943 he purchased the original manuscript and donated it to the Library of Congress, jumped at the chance to back the project.[50] With Balaban's involvement, the project expanded from a single railcar and a short tour to an entire train and a yearlong national tour.[51] In December 1946, Clark hosted a luncheon at the Justice Department to present the plan to a wider audience, including representatives of the Ad Council.[52] Brophy attended the meeting and realized that the "Bill of Rights Train" had even more potential to mold public opinion than the radio program he had proposed. Like Balaban, Brophy leapt at the opportunity to lead the effort. Brophy abandoned his radio program idea and turned his full energies to the train.[53]

As he took control of the project, Brophy sought support from the same people who had backed the conservative persuasion campaign from the beginning.[54] In January 1947, he met with representatives of the National Association of Manufacturers, the U.S. Chamber of Commerce, and the American Bankers Association. He also asked prominent banker Winthrop Aldrich to chair the ostensibly nonpartisan foundation that would manage the project.[55] Aldrich agreed. Brophy served as president of the American Heritage Foundation, incorporated in February 1947, and Aldrich chaired the board.[56] The foundation's stated objective was "to give meaning to the American heritage, vitality to its spirit, and validity to its historic mission. Thus may the American body politic be immunized against subversive propaganda and strengthened for the constructive tasks ahead."[57] To that end, the Foundation launched "a national program of rededication to [American] ideals and institutions" using, thanks to Brophy's connection with the Ad Council, "all media of communication, education, and community action in a national program that will emphasize and dramatize the common heritage of every American— our system of democratic government based on individual freedom."[58]

Although the American Heritage Foundation claimed that the American people financed what would be called the "Freedom Train," most of the money came from the same organizations and people who had long bankrolled the conservative persuasion campaign.[59] Aldrich hosted a fundraising lunch for business leaders in New York and secured large pledges from the likes of du Pont, U.S. Steel, General Electric, Standard

Oil, and others.[60] Former Liberty Leaguer John W. Davis agreed to serve on the foundation's board.[61] Brophy used his seat on the Ad Council board to secure the full support of that organization and to gain access to the millions of dollars of free radio airtime and print media space the Ad Council received for its "public service advertising."[62]

The American Heritage Foundation emphasized the attorney general's sponsorship and the president's support for the project, but private-sector conservatives had taken it over.[63] Crucially, however, most Americans continued to believe the Freedom Train was a government initiative.[64] This misperception was the opposite of what happened during the war with government-owned, contractor-operated (GOCO) production facilities, where the government footed the bill and the private sector got the credit.[65] But the result proved just as damaging to Franklin Roosevelt's vision of government-guaranteed economic security as an essential element of national security. Through the Freedom Train, conservatives made further progress in their effort to rewrite American history in ways that minimized the government's constructive role.

Conservatives' influence could be seen clearly in the train's name and slogan. At first, the slogan for the massive Ad Council campaign backing the train was to be "Work at democracy to make democracy work."[66] But the conservatives overseeing the project argued that "we [should] use the word 'freedom' instead of 'democracy' in connection with our publicity."[67] For many conservatives, Franklin Roosevelt's presidency underscored the dangers to individual freedom associated with too much democracy. And Friedrich Hayek's *The Road to Serfdom* explained how democracy could lead to totalitarianism.[68] To address these concerns, Brophy substituted a National Association of Manufacturers tagline: "Freedom Is Everybody's Job."[69] The train itself would be called the "Freedom Train." The booklet that the American Heritage Foundation sent to community leaders made clear that the freedom sought was freedom from the government, from what it called "the panacea of state control."[70] Through the Freedom Train, conservatives framed the government as a potential threat to freedom against which the public must remain vigilant.

The process for selecting the documents to be exhibited further revealed the extent of conservative influence on the project.[71] The American Heritage Foundation said the Freedom Train would be a mobile

"National Shrine to house about 100 original documents of American history upon which the development of American democracy and civil rights is based."[72] But the chosen documents focused on "negative liberty" (freedom from the government) rather than "positive liberty" (freedoms guaranteed by the government) and focused on political rights rather than the fusion of political and economic rights Roosevelt championed.[73] Before private-sector conservatives took over the project, the representatives from the National Archives who helped to compile the original list of documents to be exhibited devoted an entire section to "Economic Rights" that featured a draft of the report that led to the creation of the Social Security system.[74] The conservatives overseeing the document selection process—among them, Winthrop Aldrich, John W. Davis, and John Foster Dulles—vetoed that section.[75] The Freedom Train arrived at its first stop in Philadelphia on September 16, 1947, pulled by a specially painted red, white, and blue American Locomotive Company PA-1 engine numbered 1776, carrying the first Bill of Rights, but not the Fourteenth or Fifteenth Amendments to the Constitution—and certainly not copies of the Social Security Act, National Labor Relations Act, or Roosevelt's proposed Economic Bill of Rights.[76] The Freedom Train celebrated political rights and, by omission, wrote the economic rights central to Roosevelt's vision for national security out of American history.[77] On the Freedom Train, national security meant physical security alone.

The Emergence of National Security as a Foreign Policy–Focused Profession

The National Security Act of 1947 took effect on September 18, 1947, two days after the Freedom Train began its nationwide tour.[78] The Act, passed during the first Republican-controlled Congress since 1932, revealed the extent to which liberals had failed in their efforts to keep alive the dream of a comprehensive national security state that used a mix of domestic and foreign policy to guarantee economic and physical security. The Act did not define the term "national security," but the things the Act left out accomplished much of that definitional work. The word "domestic" appeared only once in the text, and the Act dealt not at all with the economic security institutions Franklin Roosevelt considered the "corner stone" of the national security state.[79] In this moment of political peril at the dawn of the Cold War, no liberal in Congress rose in defense of Roosevelt's broader conception of national security.

Through his successful efforts to frame foreign policy as a national security problem, Roosevelt had set in motion the processes that culminated in the codification of a concept of national security that excluded domestic economic security.[80] There were indications that the forces championing a foreign policy–focused concept of national security had grown beyond Roosevelt's control even before his death in April 1945. In 1943, widely read columnist Walter Lippmann published a book on national security whose very title—*U.S. Foreign Policy: Shield of the Republic*—implied that foreign policy was the key to national security. Like Lippmann's 1937 *Inquiry into the Principles of the Good Society,* which helped undercut public support for national planning at the precise moment when Roosevelt sought to institutionalize it, Lippmann's latest book appeared just as the Roosevelt administration was trying to reinvigorate the domestic economic security–focused parts of the national security state.[81] Lippmann's book received wide attention.[82] *Reader's Digest* ran a condensation and *Ladies' Home Journal,* published by NAM leader Walter Fuller's Curtis Publishing Company, featured a patronizing cartoon-strip version.[83] Ironically, Lippmann's actual argument—that achieving national security required a restrained foreign policy balancing interests and commitments with power and capabilities—gained little traction.[84] The book's main contribution was to add to the growing impression that national security was exclusively a foreign policy matter.

From his academic perch at the Institute for Advanced Studies in Princeton, New Jersey, Edward Mead Earle worked as hard as anyone to define the government's national security responsibilities in a way that excluded domestic policy.[85] Beginning in the fall of 1939, Earle organized a seminar for Institute for Advanced Studies and Princeton University scholars. They called themselves the Princeton Military Studies Group and met weekly at the Institute for Advanced Studies.[86] The group spent 1941 trying to define national security.[87] Leaning on his diplomatic history background, Earle focused on the balance of power between states, avoiding the politically fraught question of the relationship between domestic economic policies and national security. In a memo to seminar participants, Earle wrote that "it is obvious that the definition of 'security' must not include its domestic economic meanings."[88] In most of his published work, Earle omitted—as he put it in one instance—"security in the domestic sense, important as that is."[89] Although Earle had a much smaller platform than Walter Lippmann, he proselytized tirelessly for his narrow conception of the government's national security responsibilities. He wrote stacks of letters pushing his ideas on influential people, published journal articles and a short book, and gave talks throughout North America.[90]

But Earle's significance in the history of the American national security state lies less in his influence on policymakers and opinion leaders and more in his contributions to the emergence of a foreign policy–focused academic field of "security studies" that excluded domestic policy from its ambit.[91] The subsequent international relations–focused output of "security studies" hardened the link between national security and foreign policy and helped erase from memory the national security state's domestic policy origins.[92] Earle and other "security studies" scholars thus provided conceptual support to those, including an increasing number of conservatives, who sought to distinguish between a foreign policy–focused national security state and a domestic policy–focused welfare state.

Harvard professor E. Pendleton Herring had a more direct hand than either Lippmann or Earle in shaping the institutional evolution of the national security state. Herring believed centralized administrative power was essential to maximizing the nation's war-making potential, but he preferred to centralize that power in the hands of professionals within the executive branch who could provide the range of needed expertise rather than in a single chief executive.[93] Herring thus provided the conceptual rationale for sustaining and growing the foreign policy–focused "national security" profession that began taking shape during World War II.[94] And through his close work with Ferdinand Eberstadt on the report, commissioned by Secretary of the Navy James Forrestal, that provided the blueprint for the National Security Act of 1947, Herring helped to design a foreign policy–focused national security state that dealt hardly at all with the economic security issues Roosevelt considered of central importance.[95]

The Eberstadt Report's recommendation to create a National Security Resources Board exemplified the shift in focus away from the economic

security concerns central to Roosevelt's national security state. Like the
Roosevelt-era National Resources Planning Board, the new National Security Resources Board would live in the Executive Office of the President. Unlike the old National Resources Planning Board, however, the
new National Security Resources Board did not deal with economic security except in the context of sustaining the country's war-making potential.[96] The board's membership would consist of the "Secretaries of
War, Navy and Air and of the heads of the agencies now charged with
important civilian mobilization functions."[97] The board would "Implement military plans in the industrial mobilization and civilian fields,"
"Formulate such plans and programs and keep them up to date," and
"Take an inventory of our resources and keep our national balance sheet
of resources solvent through supervising disposal of present surpluses,
advocating sound policies of conservation, guarding against shortages in
strategic materials, and developing and maintaining adequate information
on the manpower, resources, and productive facilities of the nation."[98]

The Eberstadt Report's outline for a physical security and foreign
policy-focused national security state provided Secretary of the Navy
James Forrestal with the ammunition with which to save his service—
and himself—from extinction. When Forrestal appeared before the Senate Military Affairs Committee on the morning of Monday, October 22,
1945, he sought to persuade the gathered senators that unification of the
armed services, under which Forrestal believed the navy would suffer,
was a mistake.[99] Just as Franklin Roosevelt invoked national security
when facing his toughest persuasion challenges, so too did Forrestal do
likewise now with the fate of his service on the line.[100] He opened his
testimony by declaring, "I do not appear here simply in opposition to
unification of the War and Navy Departments. I prefer to appear here to
present a comprehensive and dynamic program to save and strengthen
our national security. I do not feel that unification of the services meets
these requirements. It falls short on two counts. In the first place, current
proposals for unification fail to deal with the vital problems within each
of the military departments. Second, they fail to give adequate attention
to an effective coordination of all the departments concerned with national security."[101] Deviating from his prepared statement, he added,
"I am using the word 'security' here consistently and continuously rather

than 'defense.'"[102] Forrestal devoted the bulk of his testimony to outlining plans for a national security state that focused solely on international affairs.

Conservatives from both parties in Congress jumped at Forrestal's proposal for a national security state that excluded domestic policy. During the discussion following Forrestal's statement, conservative Senator Edwin Johnson (D-CO) told the secretary, "I like your words 'national security.'"[103] Many historians who have written about the hearing end the quotation there, but what Johnson said next underscored the contested politics of national security.[104] The reason he liked that phrase, Johnson continued, was that he thought it important to distinguish between "military security" and "social security" and had therefore proposed creating a "Department of Military Security" rather than a "Department of National Defense."[105] As Johnson put it, "Military security certainly makes a distinction between social security, that we hear so much about, and military security."[106] As a longtime critic of the Roosevelt administration, Johnson found congenial the narrower physical security and foreign policy–focused national security state Forrestal proposed. As Arthur Krock had recommended back when Franklin Roosevelt first started trying to link his domestic and foreign policies under the umbrella of national security, a conservative coalition in Congress continued to support the foreign policy–focused parts of the national security state while opposing the domestic policy components liberals considered just as important. This selective anti-statism became ever more apparent over the course of Truman's presidency.[107]

Historians have singled out Forrestal, largely based on his October 1945 Senate testimony, as what Daniel Yergin influentially called the "chief apostle" of a new "gospel of national security."[108] This claim is factually accurate, but not in the way that most historians intend. The term "national security" was not new, nor was the proposal to create a national security state. What was new was Forrestal's effort to institutionalize a more limited—in terms of policy scope—national security state than what Franklin Roosevelt pushed during his presidency. Through his advocacy for the ideas in the Eberstadt Report that ultimately shaped the National Security Act, Forrestal led the successful effort to claim the mantle of national security exclusively for the work of foreign policy and physical security specialists.[109] Progress came quickly. In his March 21, 1946, column, Walter Lippmann used the term "national security" to refer to an area of professional responsibility dealing primarily with physical security and foreign policy.[110] Passage of the National Security Act the following year solidified the connection between national security and foreign policy and physical security work.[111] The emergence of a host of other institutions like "think tanks" and architectures like the security clearance system under this narrowed conception of national security further reinforced and perpetuated it.[112]

The striking speed with which the newly defined national security profession took hold reflected not only the circumstances of the time but also the power of the people involved.[113] The leadership ranks of the new national security professionals included many well-connected veterans of the New York financial and legal world, such as Forrestal, head of the Office of Strategic Services William Donovan, and assistant secretaries of war Robert Lovett and John McCloy.[114] To help them run American foreign policy, these men brought in other people they knew from the private sector, including banker Paul Nitze and the lawyers Allen and John Foster Dulles.[115] This was an altogether different group in terms of social and economic status than the earlier generation of national security professionals exemplified and led by Frances Perkins.[116] And unlike that earlier group, the new national security professionals consisted almost entirely of men.[117] Indeed, Ferdinand Eberstadt maintained what he called the "Good Man" list, and it was to a remarkable degree the men on that list who appropriated the mantle of national security for foreign policy and physical security work.[118]

Although some of these new national security professionals, including Forrestal, identified as Democrats, their personal and professional backgrounds generally made them more conservative than liberal. They were something of a Trojan horse within the Roosevelt and Truman administrations, undermining liberals' efforts to construct a comprehensive national security state. Forrestal was the archetype. He reinforced conservative messaging during the war, attributing practically all credit for the "miracle of production" to the private sector. "That sometimes abused sphere of activity known as business," Forrestal said in a 1944 speech, "produced an industrial organization and a productive machine which have been able to pour out the torrent of weapons which today is swamping our enemies. Those vulgar people known as business men, those brash and indecent characters who write advertising to stimulate consumption and create customers—they had created demands and markets which had developed American factories to a productive power that even the national socialism of Hitler with the full might of his government back of him could not match."[119] Forrestal did not point out that the government financed the factories responsible for the vast majority of American war production.[120]

After the war, Forrestal questioned the wisdom of liberal domestic policy proposals during cabinet meetings and echoed conservative warnings about the potentially destructive effects of national planning in public.[121] In a radio broadcast in November 1946, he acknowledged "in our complicated and strained modern society some planning is necessary in certain areas" but added that "every man charged with such planning should have above his desk a reminder that this is a country built through free effort, not by the paternal wisdom of centralized authority and that anything which weakens the vigor and vitality of local responsibility in the long run must slacken the muscles of our whole society."[122]

Forrestal and the other self-proclaimed national security professionals quickly dwarfed their economic security–focused counterparts in size, resources, and influence. They enjoyed their new line of work immensely, many of them finding it more interesting than what they had done on Wall Street.[123] They found the power, the secrecy, and the feeling of being at the center of events intoxicating. As John McCloy contemplated a return to the private sector at the end of World War II, he wrote that it would be hard "to get back to humdrum things."[124] His colleague Robert Lovett recalled their time working in the War Department during World War II as "one of the most exciting and happiest of my life."[125] A member of Forrestal's staff later suggested that his boss "had become addicted to the pace, the excitement, and the exercise of governmental power."[126] This group did not want to share with their domestic policy counterparts the power that accompanied "national security" work.

The rapid growth of a foreign policy–focused national security profession helped solidify the distinction between the government's national security and welfare responsibilities and boosted conservatives' efforts to prevent further expansion of economic security programs. By the time the National Security Act of 1947 emerged from the conservative-controlled Eightieth Congress, anyone who suggested that the Social Security Administration and Federal Security Agency ought to have been included in an act dealing with national security would have been ridiculed.

The Liberal Vision for National Security on Life Support

As the 1948 election approached, the exclusion of economic security from what counted as a national security matter was nearly complete. Not coincidentally, Truman had made little progress actualizing Roosevelt's proposed Economic Bill of Rights. Truman's distinction between national security and welfare, foreign policy specialists' success claiming the mantle of national security exclusively for their work, and the conservative persuasion campaign's progress convincing Americans that the government's job was to guarantee freedom—and not economic security—left the liberal vision for national security on life support. The creation of separate and unequal "national security" and "welfare" states was well under way. This split would have profound consequences for public perceptions of economic security programs and resource flows to them.

Truman himself continued to contribute to this split. With the exception of a paragraph defining national security in broad Rooseveltian terms inserted in Truman's 1947 State of the Union message by Samuel Rosenman, the distinction between national security and welfare became even more common in Truman's rhetoric and in his administration's budget messages, which distinguished between "social welfare" or "domestic programs" on the one hand and "national security" or "foreign affairs" programs on the other.[127] The distinction began trickling into government departments and agencies and shaped the language they used to describe their activities.[128] Economic security fell further and further from the national security frame, and the distinction between the national security state and the welfare state hardened.

Ironically, Truman and his advisors demonstrated a belated awareness of the power of language to influence public perceptions of government programs and resource flows to them. In a special message to Congress on January 8, 1947, Truman lamented that "there are certain programs of

Government which have come to be looked upon as 'welfare programs' in a narrow sense. This has placed them in an insulated compartment," which Truman and his advisors saw as problematic because it meant many Americans did not see these programs as essential.[129] But awareness of this fact did not stop Truman and his advisors from distinguishing between national security programs and welfare programs in speeches and official documents. In a January 1948 report to Congress, Truman again distinguished between "programs related to national security and foreign policy" and those related to "protection of our natural and human resources against serious economic hazards."[130] Truman noted the wide disparity in the allocation of resources budgeted for "national security" programs (79 percent) and everything else the government had to do (21 percent), including "welfare."[131] This disparity increased over the course of Truman's presidency and his advisors grew somewhat defensive about their contributions to it.[132]

Conservatives pressed the advantage, using the Freedom Train to hammer home their message that the government's core responsibility was to guarantee individual freedom, not economic security. At many of the Freedom Train's 322 stops around the country, thousands of people waited hours in line to climb aboard.[133] In total, three-and-a-half million Americans explored the train's exhibits, and as many as fifty million Americans—nearly a third of the country—participated in related activities, such as "Rededication Weeks."[134] At rallies during these Rededication Weeks, members of the emerging class of national security professionals spoke in stark terms about threats to freedom.[135] In a nationwide radio broadcast timed with the beginning of the Freedom Train's tour, future secretary of state John Foster Dulles warned that "powerful forces seek to penetrate and disrupt the societies which cling to free institutions. . . . Before humanity there yawns a black and bottomless pit into which concepts of personal dignity and the sacredness of the human personality threaten to sink without a trace."[136] In remarks like these, Dulles and other national security professionals counseled constant vigilance against threats to individual freedom, from enemies abroad and from enemies within who proposed trading individual freedom for economic security.

The Ad Council campaign supporting the Freedom Train flooded the country with this type of conservative messaging, taking a page from the

NAM persuasion playbook and its emphasis on volume and repetition across all communications channels. Thousands of newspaper and magazine articles, editorials, and advertisements carried the Ad Council's message, along with nationwide billboards and public transit ads.[137] Radio spots generated 6 billion listener impressions.[138] The Ad Council also "distributed over 1.5 million copies of a booklet on the 'duties and privileges' of citizenship."[139] The "staggering" public response thrilled American Heritage Foundation officials.[140] By the summer of 1948, Foundation president Thomas D'Arcy Brophy considered the Freedom Train a resounding success, including with audiences who were otherwise difficult for conservatives to persuade, such as labor.[141]

Meanwhile, the continuing NAM persuasion campaign made explicit the Freedom Train's implied message that government-provided economic security threatened individual freedom. A 1948 illustrated NAM pamphlet called "Real Security" trumpeted the progress individuals had made in recent years to build security for themselves and said that "we hear a lot of talk these days about how the government ought to guarantee 'security' for everyone. But, most people in this country prefer to plan their own future security—through savings and insurance, to mention just two ways."[142] The pamphlet then provided graphical depictions of dramatic growth in the amounts of personal savings and life insurance from 1940 to 1948. "But that's not all," the pamphlet concluded. "Much more important than insurance policies or savings accounts or even expansion of industry is the security found in our way of life—a way of life that gives us *personal freedom*. . . . Which provides security against someone taking our property away from us. . . . Which provides security against the government or anyone else telling us how we must live our lives—ordering us into certain jobs, for instance, or putting a ceiling on how far we can climb. We shall not let this *real* security slip away. We shall not trade any part of our freedom for phony promises of 'cradle-to-grave' care."[143]

Conservatives believed public opinion was shifting in their favor as the 1948 presidential election approached. They looked forward to regaining control of the executive branch and, under Republican candidate Thomas Dewey's leadership, halting the further growth of the government's domestic economic security responsibilities.

But Harry Truman had not given up. He spent the final months of the 1948 campaign barnstorming the country, traveling nearly twenty-two thousand miles by train and talking to everyone he could get to listen to him.[144] In his speeches, he leaned on arguments Roosevelt used successfully in 1936 and 1940. Truman told a crowd in Milwaukee that "I believe from the bottom of my heart that we are engaged in a great crusade to determine whether the powers of government will be used for the benefit of all the people or for the benefit of just a privileged few."[145] In a carefully planned speech in Oklahoma City, Truman accused conservatives of "trying to create the false impression that communism is a powerful force in American life" to divert attention from "their failure to deal with the big practical issues of American life, such as housing, price control, and education."[146] Truman also argued, as Roosevelt had in 1940, that conservatives were playing politics with national security. Conservatives "ought to realize," Truman said, "that their reckless tactics are not helping our national security; they are hurting our national security."[147]

Truman's Oklahoma City speech was one of the sharpest of his campaign. It might have been sharper still had he said explicitly, as Roosevelt had, that national security depended on the economic security programs increasingly branded as "welfare." Instead, Truman relied on his audience to make the connection between "liberal programs" and "national security." Nevertheless, Truman persuaded a majority of Americans that they stood to lose under a Dewey administration, "that the gains they had made under the New Deal were going to be taken away."[148] Compared with Dewey's empty promise that "your future lies ahead of you," this proved a winning argument.[149] A week after the Freedom Train made its penultimate stop in Havre-de-Grace, Maryland, Truman shocked conservatives by winning the 1948 presidential election.

Conservatives had been counting on a Dewey victory to prevent a repeat of what they believed the Roosevelt administration had done, which was to use election victories and worsening international tensions to claim both a public mandate and urgent necessity for expanding economic security programs in the name of national security. A 1948 talking point from the National Association of Manufacturers laid bare the conservative fear that liberal "DoGooders see a bright new hope for every one of the discarded New Deal objectives . . . federal housing, federalized medicine, federal aid to education, federal this and federal that: One federal project after another will be offered—with much waving of flags—as measures to 'Strengthen national security and the common defense.'"[150] Truman's victory did not divert conservatives from their goal of halting the expansion of the government's domestic economic security responsibilities. It simply forced them to continue to find ways of doing so from outside the White House.

8

Cementing a Foreign Policy–Focused National Security State

They know that they cannot persuade the people to give up the gains of the last 20 years. But they think they can undermine those gains by attacking the men and women who have the job of carrying out the programs of the Government. And so they have launched a campaign to make people think that the Government service as a whole is lazy, inefficient, corrupt, and even disloyal.[1]

—*Harry Truman, 1952*

WHEN HARRY TRUMAN DELIVERED his State of the Union address on January 5, 1949, he assumed that by electing him president and restoring Democratic majorities in both houses of Congress, the public had given him a mandate to proceed with the domestic policy proposals on which he had campaigned. Truman therefore focused on his domestic agenda in his address and proposed what he called a "Fair Deal" for the American people. He began by describing the type of country he believed Americans wanted: "In this society, we are conservative about the values and principles which we cherish; but we are forward-looking in protecting those values and principles and in extending their benefits. . . . We have abandoned the 'trickledown' concept of national prosperity. Instead, we believe that our economic system should rest on a democratic foundation and that wealth should be created for the benefit of all."[2] He added that "the recent election shows that the people of the United States are in favor of this kind of society and want to go on improving it" and declared that "the attainment of this kind of society demands the best efforts of every citizen in every walk of life, and it imposes increasing responsibilities on the Government."[3]

Truman got almost none of what he asked for from Congress on the economic security front.[4] Most commentators portray Truman's domestic agenda as a casualty of unfavorable circumstances, with the Cold War under way and the economy booming.[5] Circumstances mattered, of course, but they had to be interpreted, and as the interpretive fights during Roosevelt's presidency showed, dominant interpretations help determine what is politically possible. Thanks to the greater volume of messaging delivered through their well-funded and pervasive persuasion campaign, conservatives did most of the interpreting during Truman's term. The result was the consolidation of separate and unequal—in resources and public esteem—"national security" and "welfare" states, as well as the removal of Roosevelt's vision for a comprehensive national security state from the realm of political possibility.

By the time Truman proposed the Fair Deal, conservatives had inundated Americans for more than a decade with messages designed to dampen the public appetite for expanding the government's economic security responsibilities. Now conservatives pressed their advantage. They had little difficulty framing Truman's proposals as inconsistent with the American political tradition because the flood of conservative messaging, delivered most prominently through the Freedom Train, shaped the way many Americans understood American history. To kill the liberal vision for national security once and for all, conservatives sowed further doubt about the government's competence, tarred liberal domestic policy proposals with the communist brush, and argued that together government incompetence and "creeping socialism" threatened national security.

During Truman's term, the Advertising Council mobilized the full power of the advertising industry to sow doubt about the government's competence through several of its national "public service advertising" campaigns. The most damaging of these campaigns publicized the findings of former president Herbert Hoover's Commission on the Organization of the Executive Branch of the Government. The campaign highlighted amusing and memorable examples of government "waste" and "bungling" that made the government the butt of jokes. Conservatives' persistent efforts to sow doubt about the government's competence ushered in a new era of government bashing that continues to reverberate and, though we lack confirmatory polling data—the famous "trust in government" question was not a regular feature of opinion surveys until the 1950s—probably diminished public confidence in government.[6]

At the same time, the Soviet Union's shift from ally to enemy finally enabled conservatives to succeed in tarring liberal economic security proposals with the communist brush. The conservative persuasion campaign stoked fears of communism and associated liberal policy proposals with the communist enemy.[7] Conservatives argued that constructing the comprehensive national security state liberals proposed not only threatened Americans' freedom but also amounted to surrender to a hostile ideology. On that basis, conservatives argued that the liberal vision for national security threatened national security itself.

As they had during Truman's period as "acting president," conservatives benefited from the distinction Truman drew between national security and welfare programs. Truman's effort to sell economic security programs—his "Fair Deal"—not as vital for national security but less persuasively as a matter of welfare helped seal them in the "insulated compartment" he lamented in 1947.[8] At the same time, ascendant foreign policy–focused national security professionals argued for and benefited from the continued primacy of foreign threats after World War II, solidifying their power at the expense of economic security–focused counterparts. In many respects, the new national security professionals' efforts to channel the government's institutional development comported with conservatives' efforts to halt the growth of the government's economic security responsibilities. That synergy, combined with the conservative leanings of many leading national security professionals, contributed to collaborations that helped kill Roosevelt's vision for a comprehensive national security state once and for all.

Fostering the Impression of Government Incompetence

On the Friday afternoon following Harry Truman's unexpected victory in the 1948 presidential election, General Foods chairman Clarence

Francis brought his top public relations expert to former president Herbert Hoover's suite at the Waldorf-Astoria Hotel in New York for an introductory chat.[9] Hoover was wrapping up work as chairman of the Commission on the Organization of the Executive Branch of the Government, which the conservative Eightieth Congress created in 1947 to provide the template for shrinking the government ahead of the anticipated Republican victory in the 1948 presidential election.[10] Hoover's leadership of the commission that came to bear his name reflected the considerable rehabilitation the former president's reputation underwent in the 1940s.[11] Hoover's resurrection delighted conservatives like leading advertising executive Bruce Barton, who wrote to Hoover in August 1948 that "every day more millions of Americans realize all over again how great and how right you have been and are. May you live long in the glory and joy of your second coming."[12]

Hoover and other conservatives saw the commission as an opportunity to reduce the government's economic security responsibilities. In a statement released after the commission's third meeting, Hoover declared that "at no time has there been such a public desire for a complete reconsideration of the province of the Federal government and overhaul of the business methods of Federal administration and their relationship to the citizen. The need is much greater than at any time in the past. The huge expansion of the Executive Branch during the past twenty years has been made in an atmosphere of hurry and emergency which now calls for calm challenge."[13] Although the Hoover Commission had the nonpartisan veneer conservatives had learned was essential, most of the Democrats who served on the commission were not what Samuel Rosenman would have called "real liberals."[14] It was Hoover's show, and he made no secret of the political philosophy he brought to his work, declaring that "the government can't do it all" and that Americans could not "retire from the voluntary field if [they] wish our American civilization to survive."[15]

Hoover realized even before Truman's surprise victory denied conservatives the opportunity to implement the commission's recommendations directly that it would be important to sell them to the public. An internal Hoover Commission memo from January 1948 underscored the importance of making "people see the entire meaning of the whole report in terms they can understand," such as "the hope for freedom and lasting good government," "removal of the fear of bureaucratic control," and "inviting them to fight waste, duplication, and the cancerous growth of bureaucracy."[16] But conservatives' effort to sell the Hoover Report gained greater urgency with Truman's victory and Democratic gains in the House and Senate, which meant conservatives would have to rely on persuasion rather than fiat to rein in the government. One of Hoover's assistants recalled that "when we woke up the morning after the election and came into the [Hoover] Commission offices, it was a terribly frigid atmosphere."[17]

Without conservative control of the White House and Congress, Hoover realized he needed a public relations expert to build support for his commission's recommendations. Clarence Francis recalled that Hoover "made some investigations" and developed a favorable impression of Charles Coates, who worked for Francis at General Foods as assistant director of public relations.[18] Like many other members of the burgeoning public relations profession, Coates had worked as a journalist before joining General Foods in 1945. He had won several awards for his work and had caught the eye of prominent business leaders like Charles E. Wilson and Donald M. Nelson, both of whom asked Coates to ghostwrite articles for them.[19] Hoover called Francis, a longtime Republican stalwart, and asked to borrow Coates.[20] Francis agreed. After a brief and successful interview in Hoover's suite at the Waldorf, Coates began work as the head of public relations for the Hoover Commission the following Monday. It marked the beginning of a long and influential career at the heart of the conservative persuasion campaign.[21]

Coates and the other conservative public relations experts advising the Hoover Commission devised a simple and devastating strategy for publicizing the commission's findings. The campaign trumpeted examples of government folly unearthed by the commission and worked to persuade the public that the examples were representative of endemic incompetence, calling into question the wisdom of entrusting the government with responsibility for guaranteeing economic security. The explicit rationale for this approach was to build support for the commission's recommendations. But the campaign's messaging implied that the "bungling bureaucrats" in the government did not deserve high levels of either tax dollars or public respect. Leadership of the country belonged in the much more competent private sector—and, conservatives began to argue, national security depended on reining in the government.

Conservatives did not want the Hoover Commission to share the fate of so many other blue-ribbon panels that faded into irrelevance soon after completing their work. To keep pressure on the White House and Congress, and to keep the commission's findings top of the public's mind ahead of the 1950 midterms and the 1952 presidential election, in March 1949 a group of conservatives launched and generously endowed the Citizens Committee for Reorganization of the Executive Branch of the Government.[22] The Citizens Committee for the Hoover Report, as it came to be known, drew on lessons learned during earlier phases of the conservative movement's development about how to inoculate itself against criticism. The Citizens Committee billed its efforts as "educational," just like the Liberty League, the National Association of Manufacturers, and—most successfully—the Ad Council. This framing had the additional benefit of making donations to the Citizens Committee tax deductible.[23]

Like the more successful pieces of the conservative persuasion campaign, the Citizens Committee also tried to maintain a veneer of bipartisanship to increase its effectiveness. But the Democrats asked to serve on the board were more conservative than liberal and included people like former vice president John Garner, who had fallen out with Roosevelt, and Oveta Culp Hobby, then in the process of shifting her political allegiance to the Republican Party.[24] The day-to-day leaders of the Citizens Committee were well-networked conservatives. Robert Johnson served as president and Robert McCormick served as research director.[25] Former Liberty Leaguer and National Association of Manufacturers president Colby Chester served as Citizens Committee campaign chairman.[26] John Wesley Hanes II, another disaffected former Democrat, chaired the finance committee.[27] There were also indications of growing connections between the conservative movement and the new foreign policy–focused national security profession, with former Office of Strategic Services head William Donovan serving on the Citizens Committee board.[28]

The Citizens Committee used two enduringly significant approaches to accomplish its objectives.[29] First, it developed a detailed legislative program and drafted model bills to make it as easy as possible for Congress to act.[30] Citizens Committee research director Robert McCormick called the Citizens Committee's bill drafting effort "the most extensive body of legislation ever prepared by a private enterprise."[31] The drafting and provision of model legislation at scale was an important innovation for the conservative movement and remains a staple of conservative political activism.[32] Second, the Citizens Committee nurtured public skepticism about domestic policy by fostering the impression of government incompetence in the domestic sphere. In a fundraising letter to the heads of top companies, Citizens Committee Campaign Chairman Colby Chester made clear the bottom-line benefits businesses would reap from the campaign: "the long-range value of an educated, tax-conscious, civically-alert public cannot be estimated in dollars and cents."[33]

Charles Coates moved over from the Hoover Commission staff to lead the Citizens Committee's public relations effort, which drew on and expanded the persuasion playbook developed by public relations professionals for the National Association of Manufacturers. It was a big operation. A speaker's bureau supplied speakers for appearances around the country and equipped them with "startling facts" that underscored "the absurdities of poor [government] management."[34] Advertising across all media, a touring exhibition, and a series of conferences reinforced this derisive way of talking about the government.[35] By 1950, the Citizens Committee had "a staff of 60-odd" people, including a very active research department that conveyed its findings through newsletters like *Washington Watchdog* to those it believed could help lobby for enactment of the Hoover Commission's recommendations.[36] The committee also maintained an impressive letter-writing operation and placed articles in newspapers and magazines. These industrious efforts were just the beginning. To get its message across at greater scale, the committee also launched major national advertising campaigns with the assistance of the Ad Council and the J. Walter Thompson agency, one of the leading advertising firms of the time.[37]

The Citizens Committee also cultivated grassroots support, both in fact and in appearance, building on the earlier success of the National Committee to Uphold Constitutional Government.[38] The Citizens Committee orchestrated the establishment of state and local organizations supporting the Hoover Report and provided constant guidance and encouragement to them.[39] Based on personnel rosters, business executives led many of these committees.[40] These state and local committees helped both to shape public opinion and to pressure Congress to act on the Hoover Report's recommendations. They also helped to grow the conservative movement itself.

The Citizens Committee continued the conservative movement's efforts to shape young minds, sending materials to schools and universities and setting up student committees on campuses.[41] The Citizens Committee commissioned a high school teacher to develop a module other teachers could use to teach the Hoover Report.[42] In addition to material for instructors to use in the classroom, the Citizens Committee offered a movie that provided "a colorful & dramatic picture of the work of the Hoover Commission. . . . The camera takes you to Washington for an intimate sightseeing tour of the sprawling government departments, bureaus, and agencies. . . . It takes you inside for a view of the people at work. . . . It reveals the obsolete equipment, the vast tangle of red tape . . . the overlapping and duplication."[43] Material of this sort sowed doubt about the government's competence and reinforced wartime conservative messaging about the superiority of the private sector. The Citizens Committee sent talking points directly to its student members and encouraged them to proselytize on campus.[44] The Citizens Committee also provided students with a handbook containing clear guidance on how they could organize in support of the Hoover Report on their campuses.[45] By early 1950, the Citizens Committee claimed hundreds of student members, including many of the "top student leaders on each campus."[46] The Citizens Committee's student work was another shrewd investment in the future of the conservative movement.

Following the Freedom Train model on a smaller scale, the Citizens Committee organized a roadshow to dramatize the Hoover Report's findings and recommendations and to build grassroots support for the report's implementation. The "Cracker Barrel Caravan" consisted of a tractor trailer and a station wagon rather than an entire train, traveled a less ambitious itinerary, and drew smaller audiences. But the Citizens Committee considered the Caravan a success, not least because it received ample radio and television coverage and therefore reached more Americans than the "300 to 1,500" people who attended each of the Caravan's eighty-three meetings in 1950.[47]

The Citizens Committee convened conferences at several levels, including a National Reorganization Conference in December 1949.[48] The Citizens Committee saw the first National Reorganization Conference as a way of fostering the impression of widespread grassroots support, noting that one of the conference's objectives was "to bring home to Congress the national support of all groups for the Hoover Report."[49] The Citizens Committee assembled a group of speakers for the first National Reorganization Conference that provided the appearance of bipartisanship—rising Democratic Party star Adlai Stevenson appeared alongside Wisconsin Republican Senator Joseph McCarthy—but that hammered its conservative message home.[50] The contrast with the National Conference on Economic Security Frances Perkins convened in 1934 could not have been more stark.[51] Participants in that earlier conference saw the government as a source of solutions to public problems. The operative assumption of the 1949 National Reorganization Conference was that the government was a source of problems.

Oveta Culp Hobby delivered the first major address of the National Reorganization Conference. In the speech, which Citizens Committee staff helped write, she emphasized the government's intrusiveness: "the Federal Government each day touches our private lives, our homes, our budgets—everything which we eat and use and put on our faces—far more thoroughly and personally than Thomas Jefferson or Benjamin Franklin would ever have envisioned."[52] She said, "Uncle Sam has become a tremendous Paul Pry. He wants to know the size of potatoes, the grade of meat, what the label on the medicine bottle says, what goes into insecticides, cleaning fluid, bread, and so on ad infinitum. He wants to know how many threads are in the sheets we sleep on, the type of construction in our overstuffed chair. He wants to know, before he finances a house, the quality of materials to be used and who is going to live in it."[53] After painting this unflattering picture of an intrusive government, Hobby lamented that "unhappily, the women of the United States seem not to have realized that their relation with the Federal Government is as direct and immediate as a mustard plaster. A woman keeping house for her family may actually see no Federal employee but the postman. Nevertheless, the most homely of her household tasks, the humblest item on her pantry shelf has been an object of Federal interest and concern. Uncle Sam is our nearest and most curious neighbor."[54]

Other parts of Hobby's speech emphasized other long-standing conservative messages, including the notion that the government could not create wealth. On that assumption, Hobby argued for reducing the number of government employees because those people were "needed outside government work to create the national wealth on which our high standard of living rests."[55] Following the pattern established earlier in the conservative persuasion campaign, Hobby also included concrete suggestions for women to act based on the findings of the Hoover Report: "go back to your PTA, your club or your church unit, and form a study group within that organization."[56] And of course, building on the earlier successes of the National Committee to Uphold Constitutional Government, "we must write our Congressmen. Through individual letters and through group resolutions, the American people owe it to their Congressmen to tell them of their interest."[57]

Hobby aimed her speech at women who may already have served as "opinion molders" in their communities. A second speech, delivered by a woman who identified herself as Mrs. Wesley C. Ahlgren, targeted the "average" American woman and cleverly cast doubt on the government's competence. Ahlgren called her address "The Housewife's Point of View" and argued that the housewife and the government performed broadly similar functions but that the manner in which the government went about the job left much to be desired. Ahlgren reported that she was "flabbergasted" to learn from the Hoover Report how the government performed its duties. She then provided some folksy examples.[58] "When you go marketing, you first look to see what is in the cupboard, and make your marketing list accordingly. Not so Uncle Sam. The Hoover Commission estimated that government supplies to a value of probably 29 billion dollars are stored in various offices and warehouses, with no complete inventory of them anywhere."[59] She cited the story, much loved by the Hoover Commission's conservative boosters, that the government paid to ship lumber from Alaska to Seattle and then back again to nearly the same spot.[60] She concluded that she "could continue indefinitely with examples of confusion, overlapping, and waste in our Federal

Government that would produce some mighty unpleasant conversations around the dinner table if they had been duplicated, on a smaller scale, in our own homes."[61]

The Citizens Committee launched two large advertising campaigns to spread this message of government incompetence far and wide. The first campaign, the National Reorganization Crusade, began in 1950 and included print and radio components.[62] The Citizens Committee followed a simple formula in this campaign: emphasize the Hoover Commission's bipartisan credentials and then sow doubt about the government's competence by providing amusing examples—almost always from the domestic policy realm—of government "waste," "red tape," and "inefficiency." One newspaper ad showed a puzzled farmer who received five different responses from five different agencies to a query he sent the government. Another provided a longer list of similar examples of government incompetence.[63] Radio programming highlighted examples of government "waste" and "inefficiency" in vivid terms. "Automobiles are clogging our streets, but Uncle Sam is still using horse-and-buggy methods" said one ad.[64] "Twenty four administrators and supervisors for 25 workers" declared another.[65] The radio content also continued the long-running conservative effort to increase "tax consciousness."[66] "I know a business that's losing over 8 million dollars a day. It's your business ... [the] Federal Government ... your money being lost!"[67] Another radio spot reported that "if you are an average citizen, you work 47 days a year to support this good old Pandemonium on the Potomac known as your Federal Government."[68]

Following the outbreak of the Korean War in June 1950, the Citizens Committee began arguing that the government's incompetence threatened national security. In a widely distributed speech called "Freedom's War on Waste," Citizens Committee public relations mastermind Charles Coates followed the standard formula, touting the commission's bipartisan credentials and then rattling off a litany of examples of government ineptitude and inefficiency compared to the private sector.[69] "If it were any laughing matter," Coates declared, "federal business procedure would be simply hilarious."[70] Coates then said that "every dollar we waste is a gift to the enemies of freedom," adding that "the Russians can exploit our weaknesses. Only we can create them. The Russians can profit from our inefficiencies, only we can correct them."[71] Radio ads developed by the Citizens Committee argued similarly that national security depended on the full and rapid implementation of the Hoover Report.[72] A 1951 solicitation from the committee declared that the "immediate enactment" of the Hoover Report recommendations "is vital to national security."[73] Similarly, the 1951 committee membership card said that members' active participation in the reorganization push would "help strengthen national security."[74]

In 1950, the Citizens Committee persuaded the Ad Council to coordinate a national campaign on behalf of the Hoover Report. Howard Chapin of General Foods—the company that supplied so many leaders of the conservative persuasion campaign—coordinated the Ad Council campaign. The J. Walter Thompson agency prepared the ads.[75] Building on one of the central themes of the 1950 National Reorganization Crusade, the Ad Council campaign dramatized the Hoover Report's vivid accounting of government "waste" and "inefficiency" to sow doubts about the government's competence.

A series of ads designed by J. Walter Thompson depicted Americans talking about various government "boondoggles." One trucker asks another, "Isn't that the load of government lumber I hauled down from Alaska a week ago?" "Yeah," the other trucker replies, "I just got orders to haul it back again!"[76] In another ad, a woman and a man stand outside a new-looking building. The man asks, "Isn't that new government hospital open yet?" The woman replies, "NO. They never even bothered to find out whether they could get enough doctors to staff it!"[77] The selective framing and misrepresentations the Ad Council used to sell the Hoover Report infuriated civil servants like Veterans Affairs official A. W. Woolford. He wrote a series of memos rebutting the "broadsides" against his agency, but he could not compete with the devastating clarity of the Ad Council campaign.[78]

Other ads nudged Americans toward a form of selective anti-statism by encouraging them to support spending for "national security" but to oppose spending for "welfare" programs. These ads accepted higher taxes to pay for physical security but provided vivid examples of why citizens should not want to pay for "wasteful," "bungling" domestic programs.

Here's just one example of waste that's paid for with your tax money. Hoover Report recommendations have cut this waste by billions of dollars. You can help save *more!*

FIGURE 8.1 Truckers Joke about the Government's Incompetence (Courtesy of The Advertising Council, Inc.)

"Defense costs mean higher taxes—no one can help that. But no one wants to pay higher taxes for waste and inefficiency."[79] The headline at the top of one ad declared, "Poor service at prohibitive cost is typical of many government agencies."[80] Another ad compared public insurance programs unfavorably to private ones. Two men watch a woman walk down the street with her two children. The first man says to the other, "We ought to get together and do something for Mrs. Green!" The second man replies, "That's right! Bill died almost 3 months ago and his G.I. insurance hasn't come through yet."[81] The ad noted that "private insurance companies settle most death claims within 15 days."[82]

Other ads charged that through its incompetence the government itself had become a threat to national security. Ad Council ads supporting the Hoover Commission argued that the "red tape," "bottleneck," and "snarl"-filled government operating in "crazy quilt" and "horse & buggy" fashion threatened the country's readiness to deal with foreign threats. The message, as one bold ad headline put it, was that "our national security hangs in the balance" and depended on full implementation of the Hoover Report's recommendations.[83] Conservatives had attacked government programs as wasteful and inefficient in the past, but their critiques were often easily dismissed as self-interested or partisan. They were not dismissed so easily in this instance thanks to the Ad Council's success cultivating a nonpartisan image and to the attention-grabbing message that government incompetence threatened national security.

Although the dramatic reduction of the government's responsibilities Hoover and his conservative allies sought did not happen immediately, what the public relations campaign on behalf of the Hoover Commission accomplished proved significant in the long run. By making a sport out of highlighting examples of government ineptitude, fostering the impression that such ineptitude was widespread, and presenting government incompetence as a threat to national security, the campaign helped transform public perceptions of what the government could and should do.

Meanwhile, conservatives exploited the peculiar economic aftermath of World War II to claim credit for the private sector for what looked like an economic "miracle" that would never end. Government spending remained high, but because large amounts of it went to military contractors the private sector was again able to claim credit for the economic security that flowed from those jobs. At the same time, American companies inherited vast new government-financed production facilities after the war and could run them at capacity because the war had decimated international competitors. With conservatives making progress diminishing public confidence in government, the economy booming, and the private sector ascendant, Americans looked less and less to the government for economic security.[84] Prospects looked remote for expanding economic security programs along the lines liberals thought necessary for lasting national security.

Stoking Fears of Communism to Narrow Political Possibilities

According to conservatives, incompetence wasn't the only way the government under Truman's leadership threatened national security. The onset of the Cold War enabled conservatives to frame Truman's proposals to expand the government's economic security responsibilities, including by establishing national health insurance, as socialist and therefore as a threat to national security. Conservatives like Senator Robert Taft (R-OH) argued that no viable middle ground existed between communism and socialism on the one side and capitalism on the other.[85] "The basic domestic issue today," Taft declared, "is liberty against socialism."[86] The Cold War thus gave conservatives a winning argument against liberal proposals to expand the government's economic security responsibilities. Ironically, it was a reversal of the same argument Franklin Roosevelt used to expand the government's economic security responsibilities in the first place. Roosevelt had said national security required such an expansion because without economic security Americans would turn to alternative ideologies, just like people in other countries. Now, conservatives argued that national security required *halting* the expansion of the government's economic security responsibilities and that failure to do so would amount to surrender to a hostile ideology.[87]

Conservatives seized on the breakdown of the U.S.-Soviet alliance to stoke fears of communism and socialism through their continuing persuasion campaign.[88] Through the National Association of Manufacturers, the U.S. Chamber of Commerce, and the Advertising Council, conservatives worked tirelessly to persuade Americans that communism and socialism threatened both the "American way of life" and Americans individually.[89] That conservative efforts to paint the liberal state-building agenda as socialist predated the Cold War suggests many leading conservatives were not motivated only or even primarily by Cold War anxieties but rather by the desire to limit the government's domestic responsibilities.[90] Efforts to tar economic security programs as socialist worked alongside allegations of government incompetence to help conservatives ensure that Americans' turn away from the government for economic security outlasted the postwar boom.

Throughout the latter half of the 1940s, the NAM and the Chamber of Commerce issued stark warnings about the dangers of communism and socialism through publications like NAM's *Sum & Substance* and the Chamber's *American Economic Security*. The Chamber sounded an alarmist tone about communism in 1946, issuing a lengthy pamphlet on "Communist Infiltration in the United States: Its Nature and How to

Combat It."[91] NAM compared "free enterprise vs. communism" in cartoon form in June 1947, told the American people not to "be a sucker" for collectivism that same year, and compared followers of "isms" to "rabbits" in another pamphlet.[92] The second issue of NAM's *Sum & Substance* included a cartoon that likened the comprehensive national security state liberals wanted to build to prison, complete with a ball and chain that deprived the citizen prisoner of freedom.[93]

The second issue of NAM's *Sum & Substance* also featured an article warning of what conservatives liked to call "creeping socialism": "Many of the measures [the liberal] suggests, when considered singly and apart from the others, do not appear too harmful. But they are all tiles for a mosaic. Each tile appears to be just a little pink. But when they're ultimately put together by the socialist planners, the mosaic will turn out to be deep red."[94] The Chamber of Commerce similarly warned against "The Drive

FIGURE 8.2 The National Association of Manufacturers' Depiction of the Perfect Security State (Courtesy of the National Association of Manufacturers.)

for a Controlled Economy via Pale Pink Pills" in a 1949 pamphlet, presenting the Fair Deal as the legislative road to socialism.[95] The January–February 1950 issue of *American Economic Security* warned that a growing "welfare state" had the potential to lead the country into socialism and included an excerpt from Herbert Hoover on that point.[96] The Chamber again sounded the alarm about socialism in another pair of pamphlets the following month.[97]

Conservatives took particular issue with Federal Security Agency head Oscar Ewing's efforts to persuade the public and members of Congress of the need for national health insurance.[98] The push for what the American Medical Association labeled "socialized medicine" failed in the face of torrents of propaganda, much of which framed national health insurance as a decisive step on the road to socialism and therefore as a threat to national security.[99] The American Medical Association's public relations consultants went so far as to invent a quote from Lenin: "Socialized Medicine is the keystone to the arch of the Socialist State."[100]

In addition to portraying socialism as an existential threat to the United States, conservatives devoted considerable energy to persuading Americans that socialism threatened them individually. The "Freedom Issue" of NAM's *Sum & Substance* filled its pages with bleak portrayals of life in the Soviet Union, drawing parallels between Stalin and Hitler and using cartoons to illustrate key points.[101] NAM's "Startling Facts about Dictatorship" cartoon showed a column of terrified citizens forced to march at gunpoint, with a dead body from one of their ranks who had been shot visible in the center of the frame. It also featured a couple facing a firing squad after their son reported them to the authorities for hiding "part of their crops."[102] The cartoon emphasized that "whatever it's called, any form of collectivism makes the individual a SLAVE to the STATE!!"[103]

The ostensibly nonpartisan Advertising Council also stoked Americans' fears of socialism through its "American Economic System" campaign.[104] The campaign's stated objective was "to bring about an understanding of our system and how it works."[105] The campaign's central narrative was that ever-increasing productivity drove American economic success—and that the government had nothing to do with it. Factors cited in driving productivity gains included "the constantly rising use of machines and power, freedom of individual action, free markets and competition, free collective bargaining, [and] steadily improving methods of distribution."[106] The campaign mentioned none of the many ways in which the government had facilitated the country's development. Similarly, ads accompanying the campaign trumpeted material and consumer progress—things provided by the private sector—as the real markers of the country's advancement, as opposed to the expansion of government-guaranteed economic rights through programs like Social Security.[107] In this way, as it had with the Freedom Train, the Ad Council helped to write the government out of the story of American development.

The Ad Council's American Economic System campaign also continued conservatives' effort to sow doubt about the government's competence. A clever ad designed to undermine public support for Truman's Fair Deal called "How to tune a piano!" featured three men swinging axes wildly at a piano. "The piano's out of tune. So we'll chop it up. Then we'll get a tin horn instead. Sure, these men are crazy. But they're using the same kind of thinking a lot of people have been using on the American economic system lately."[108] Conservatives' ability to pass off this mockery of liberal policy proposals as "public service advertising" showed how much progress the conservative persuasion campaign

How to tune a piano!

FIGURE 8.3 The Ad Council's Portrayal of Truman's Economic Security Proposals (Courtesy of The Advertising Council, Inc.)

had made over the preceding fifteen years in shifting the terms of public debate.

The Ad Council's efforts to stoke fears of communism increased the power of conservatives' messaging. One ad featured a larger-than-life, wild-eyed, and terrifying Russian soldier staring at the reader with the warning that "IVAN is watching you." "IVAN is a dyed-in-the-wool Communist. . . . He's sold to the hilt on Red ideas. Which means he's out to get *you*. He believes it's either you or him . . . that the world is too small for both."[109] Despite the frightening image and emphatic capitalization, the Ad Council's messaging was more sophisticated than the NAM's and the Chamber's. The Ad Council designed the messaging in "Ivan" and other similar ads to do more than merely frighten Americans; it sought also to motivate them to greater productive effort. This spurring made sense during the Korean War as American industry struggled to shift back to military production. But the ads also exhorted Americans to greater production of civilian goods because "we can't allow needless shortages to take prices skyrocketing and lower the value of our dollar."[110]

IVAN is watching you

FIGURE 8.4 The Ad Council's Efforts to Stoke Fears of Communism
(Courtesy of The Advertising Council, Inc.)

This framing pressured labor to produce. It also shifted responsibility for economic security from the government to individuals.

Under the guise of anti-communism, conservatives also collaborated with the new foreign policy–focused national security profession to pound more nails into the coffin containing the liberal vision for national security. Beginning in 1950, the Ad Council launched a campaign supporting the "Crusade for Freedom." The Crusade was a Central Intelligence Agency (CIA)–funded initiative designed to foster the impression that ordinary Americans financed Radio Free Europe, a CIA-backed radio station that broadcast into Eastern Europe.[111] The American Heritage Foundation, which organized the Freedom Train, helped provide cover for the Crusade, and influential conservatives served as the Crusade's foremost backers.[112] They used the Crusade to stimulate anti-communism among Americans.[113]

Millions of Americans participated in the Crusade for Freedom in the early 1950s, signing the "Freedom Scroll"—first principle: "I believe in the sacredness and dignity of the individual"—and sending "Freedom-Grams," donating "freedom dollars" and participating in countless other activities.[114] The Crusade presented the United States as locked in an existential struggle with communism and socialism in which every citizen had a vital role to play. With its unsubtle messaging about the horrors of life under communism and socialism, the Crusade helped bring about the heightened citizen vigilance against government expansion conservatives had long sought. The Crusade also reinforced other conservative messaging about the threat posed by the "creeping socialism" of Truman's economic security agenda.

Truman's Ineffective Response

Harry Truman found conservative messaging both infuriating and difficult to counter. He tried repeatedly to reveal conservative efforts to stoke fears of communism for what they were—a political tactic—but made little headway. On the campaign trail in 1948, Truman said "the Democratic Party has steadily improved the well-being of the American people—the best defense against communism; and we have successfully prevented the spread of communism in this world."[115] He emphasized that "the Democratic Party is for free government and against totalitarianism. We are for free enterprise and against communism."[116] But Truman added that "we are against those who raise the cry of communism to slander and obstruct policies conceived in the people's interest. There is nothing that the Communists would like better than to weaken the liberal programs that are our shield against Communism."[117] In an address at the annual Jefferson-Jackson Day Dinner on February 24, 1949, Truman said conservatives "are again trying to frighten the people with the old, worn-out bugaboo that socialism is taking over Washington. They have been saying that for 16 years, ever since I have been here. Not a word of truth in it, of course. This one-sided barrage of propaganda seems overwhelming at first. There are no full page ads on our side. In fact, all we have on our side is the people. Thank God for that!"[118]

Truman kept trying to neutralize the communism and socialism charges with which conservatives continued to bludgeon liberals. In a March 1950 press conference, Truman accused Republicans of using anti-communism for electoral advantage, arguing that "the Republicans have been trying vainly to find an issue on which to make a bid for the control of the Congress for next year. They tried 'statism.' They tried 'welfare state.' They tried 'socialism.'"[119] He added that "this fiasco which has been going on in the Senate is the very best asset that the Kremlin could have in the operation of the cold war. And that is what I mean when I say that [Senator Joseph] McCarthy's antics are the best asset that the Kremlin can have."[120] On January 23, 1951, Truman tried to take the internal security issue out of politics—or at least out of Congress, where Senator McCarthy (R-WI) and others continued to use the issue as a weapon against liberalism. To do so, Truman announced a Commission on Internal Security and Individual Rights headed by Fleet Admiral Chester Nimitz.[121] The effort failed because Congress refused to exempt commission members from conflict-of-interest statutes. The move smacked of partisan politics—Congress had granted such exemptions to members of the Hoover Commission.[122] The onset of the Cold War had turned the charge of communism and socialism into conservatives' most powerful weapon against liberalism. They were not about to give it up.

Truman fared little better in his effort to neutralize the similarly damaging charge of government incompetence. Although Truman supported the Hoover Commission's work and used it to justify requests for reorganization authority from Congress, he did not appreciate conservatives' use of the commission's findings to undermine public confidence in government. During a press conference on November 30, 1950, Truman said Americans' lack of faith in their government was "one of the things that's the matter with the country" and that "confidence in your Government is the first thing to keep it running as it should."[123] In a speech in Detroit on July 21, 1951, Truman told the crowd, "I say to you that people can trust their Government. . . . Don't let yourselves be confused by the smearers and the slanderers."[124]

Truman tried on many occasions to rebut the charge of government incompetence and wastefulness, but his efforts lacked both the persuasive force of his predecessor and the reach to compete with the conservative persuasion campaign.[125] Roosevelt had leaned on the powerful "security" frame to great effect in his nationally broadcast radio addresses. By contrast, Truman continued to speak of "welfare" to little effect to small audiences. An exception that proved the rule—and showed that Truman was not completely ignorant of the language of security's power—was his rare invocation of national security to try to move his housing bill forward in 1949. In a letter to Speaker Sam Rayburn (D-TX), Truman blasted "the extraordinary propaganda campaign that has been unleashed against this bill by the real estate lobby," whom he chided for being "shortsighted and utterly selfish" and for continuing "to cry 'socialism' in a last effort to smother the real facts and real issues which this bill is designed to meet."[126] Truman declared that "when the actual costs are balanced against the potential benefits to the welfare—and indeed the national security—of our people, I believe there can be only one answer—to enact this legislation."[127]

Truman prided himself on the care with which he managed the public purse, so charges of waste produced forceful replies. But Truman's replies suffered once again from his reliance on the language of "welfare" rather than "security." In a speech on September 11, 1951, Truman said, "I could go on down through every item in the budget and show you that there is a vital reason for its being there. I don't mean to claim that there is not a single dollar wasted. In an operation as big as the Federal Government there are bound to be some cases of waste and extravagance. . . . But the main point I want to make is that, although the Federal expenditures are very large, they are all made for purposes that are necessary to our national welfare; and our budget is as tight and solid as we can make it."[128]

Truman's anger continued to grow as the combined effect of conservatives' charges of incompetence and communism and socialism took their toll. Conservatives, Truman told the National Civil Service League in a feisty speech on May 2, 1952, "know that they cannot persuade the people to give up the gains of the last 20 years. But they think they can undermine those gains by attacking the men and women who have the job of carrying out the programs of the Government. And so they have launched a campaign to make people think that the Government service as a whole is lazy, inefficient, corrupt, and even disloyal."[129] Truman accused conservatives of launching "a personal campaign against the Government worker himself. He is pictured as mediocre, shiftless, lazy, nonproductive, a feeder at the public trough who couldn't get a job anywhere else. At one moment he is berated as a low-salaried nonentity with no standing in his field, and in the next breath he is called a high-salaried drain on the public purse."[130]

Truman charged that conservatives "are engaged in a ruthless, cynical attempt to put over a gigantic hoax and fraud on the American people. They say, 'Let's make the public think that the Government service is full of crooks and thieves. Let's create the impression that all public servants are bad. Let's tell the people that the Government servants are Reds. Let's confuse innuendo with fact, rumor with evidence, charge with guilt. If the real people get mad enough and confused enough, we won't have to take a position on any of the great public policy issues; we can sneak into office by the back door.'"[131] Truman denounced the conservative effort "to gain political ends by the shameful method of defaming and degrading the people who work for the Government of the United States."[132] Truman thundered that "there is no more cancerous, no more corrosive, no more subversive attack upon the great task of our Government today, than that which seeks to undermine confidence in Government."[133] Truman's anger reflected not just what he considered the baselessness and shamefulness of the charges conservatives leveled against the government—but also the fact that the charges seemed to be sticking.

HARRY TRUMAN PROVIDED a first draft of the history of his presidency in his final State of the Union in January 1953. He said his administration had improved both "the people's welfare and security."[134] But even his own listing of accomplishments in those two areas—which, once again, Truman separated—made plain that his administration had made much more progress building a foreign policy–focused national security state than an economic security–focused welfare state.[135] The explosive growth of a national security profession focused on foreign policy during Truman's presidency reinforced the distinction between national security and welfare and pushed domestic policy further from the national security frame. Leading figures within the booming national security establishment like Vannevar Bush continued to claim the mantle of national security exclusively for themselves and warned against broadening the term's scope.[136]

Two acts from the end of Truman's presidency illustrate the extent to which the national security state's responsibilities narrowed on his watch to exclude the economic security component that was once its foundation. In October 1952, Truman signed a memo creating a "National Security Agency" tasked with providing "an effective, unified organization and control of the communications intelligence activities of the United States conducted against foreign governments."[137] It is difficult to imagine Franklin Roosevelt creating a "National Security Agency" so narrowly focused. One of Truman's final acts as president further underscored the narrowing of the national security state's purview on his watch. On his penultimate day in office, Truman issued Executive Order 10431, creating a "National Security Medal" to be "awarded to any person, without regard to nationality, including members of the armed forces of the United States, for distinguished achievement or outstanding contribution on or after July 26, 1947, in the field of intelligence relating to the national security."[138]

As Truman himself had anticipated in 1947, the emergence of separate national security and welfare states negatively affected resource flows to—and public perceptions of—the economic security programs no longer considered part of the government's national security responsibilities. Truman's final budget submission put the material consequences of this shift into stark relief: Truman proposed spending $58.2 billion for national security programs and $2.7 billion for welfare programs.[139] Little evidence suggested the trend would slow or reverse. The national security state continued to benefit from the commanding power of the language of security that surrounded it, developing into one of the most powerful forces in American life. In the "welfare" state, historian Jennifer Klein astutely notes, "the positive language of security [was] replaced by the pejorative nomenclature of dependency."[140] More and more Americans subscribed to a selective anti-statism under which they generally supported national security spending but opposed welfare spending.[141]

By the time Truman left office in January 1953, Franklin Roosevelt's dream of a comprehensive national security state in which the government guaranteed economic as well as physical security was dead for the general public, though service members and veterans enjoyed something close to it through what historian Jennifer Mittelstadt calls the "military welfare state."[142] The conservative persuasion campaign nailed the coffin shut by telling Americans that their government was incompetent and by stoking fears of communism. The consistent repetition of these messages across all forms of media enabled conservatives to cultivate the impression that constructing a comprehensive national security state would amount to financial ruin, surrender to an alien ideology, or both. Along with the separation of the state into distinct national security and welfare components, conservatives' success painting the government as incompetent and tarring domestic policy with the socialist brush shaped American politics for decades.

Epilogue

IN THE YEARS SINCE FRANKLIN ROOSEVELT first put the phrase "national security" at the center of American politics, what counts as a national security matter has determined to a large extent the government's responsibilities and priorities. But since the mid-1940s, national security debates have been limited almost entirely to foreign policy. We have all but forgotten that the original debates over national security ranged across the full terrain of domestic policy—and that foreign policy hardly featured at first. Recovering that history restores a more expansive understanding of national security's possible meanings as we face the great challenges of our times.

To supporters and opponents alike, Roosevelt's success invoking national security to expand the government's responsibilities demonstrated the phrase's unmatched persuasive and institution-building power. During the Great Depression, Roosevelt invoked national security to persuade Americans that preserving capitalism and democracy required making the government responsible for economic security. With the coming of World War II, Roosevelt invoked national security to persuade Americans to abandon a foreign policy based on neutrality. Both cases revealed national security's special power not only to shape public perceptions of what the government *should* do but also to determine what the government *can* do. To the day he died, Roosevelt dedicated himself to building a comprehensive national security state that would protect Americans against hazards—domestic and foreign—against which they could no longer protect themselves in modern times. Ironically, however, Roosevelt's progress toward that goal galvanized the forces that ultimately undermined his vision for national security.

The conservative movement ranks foremost among those forces. People at the time and commentators since have underestimated the conservative movement's role in shaping American politics before the 1950s, primarily because they have overlooked the impact of conservatives' intense effort to shape public opinion beginning in the 1920s. From the 1920s into the 1950s, conservatives sent an ever-increasing and ultimately enormous volume of political messages—billions of them—disparaging domestic programs and sowing doubt about the government's competence.[1] This deluge of conservative messaging demands attention because psychologists established long ago that the frequent repetition of messages shapes what people believe.[2] By the 1940s, conservative messaging swamped messages delivered by the liberal champions of domestic state building. Through the volume of its messaging, the conservative persuasion campaign helped steer the country into a new period of conservatism rather than the "new period of liberalism" Roosevelt confidently predicted to a Denver audience on the campaign trail in 1932.[3]

Most significantly, the conservative persuasion campaign contributed to the emergence of separate "national security" and "welfare" states in the 1940s and to the selective anti-statism that characterized post–World War II American politics. Under this selective anti-statism, many Americans paired support for a robust foreign policy–focused "national security" establishment with disdain for economic security programs considered part of the "welfare" state. This bifurcation of the state had profound consequences at home and abroad. In government, removing economic security from the national security state's purview hardened gender roles among policymakers. Beginning in the 1940s, women were largely excluded from senior national security policymaking positions but accepted in equivalent positions in the welfare state.[4] The almost total exclusion of half the population limited the perspectives available to inform national security policymaking.[5] The number of women serving in senior national security positions has grown in recent times, but the percentage of women in senior positions in the welfare state remained nearly twice as large as late as 2019.[6]

Excluding economic security from what counted as a national security matter also diminished its importance in the eyes of the public, creating a vicious cycle in which the government found it more difficult to address economic insecurity, and these difficulties eroded public confidence in the government, which in turn further reduced public support for economic security programs. During the economic boom that followed World War II, the growing disparity in the capacities of the national security state and the welfare state did not seem to matter. But when the postwar boom ended in the 1960s, widespread economic insecurity returned and the government struggled to address it because Americans no longer saw economic insecurity as a national security issue. As both Franklin Roosevelt and his conservative opponents understood, when it comes to mobilizing public opinion and resources, the term "welfare" just can't compete with "national security."

There is a great irony here. The United States originated the concept of a comprehensive national security state as the way to solve the problem of economic insecurity without abandoning capitalism and democracy. But the United States failed to institutionalize such a state. By contrast, countries like Germany that embraced authoritarianism in the early 1930s became models after World War II of the kind of comprehensive national security state Roosevelt tried and failed to build.[7] The irony doubles because the United States helped underwrite the creation of comprehensive national security states abroad in the same years Americans abandoned that project at home.[8]

Recovering Franklin Roosevelt's vision for national security enables us to rethink what is possible in American politics. The meaning of national security is not fixed, and national security policymaking does not have to be limited to foreign policy. This is just as well, for removing domestic issues from what counted as a national security matter did not make them disappear. Arguably, it only made them more difficult and more expensive to address.[9] In many cases, excluding domestic policy from the national security policymaking toolkit led to the use of the military and foreign policy as an imperfect substitute for domestic policy. During the

1970s energy crisis, for example, Congress could not or would not pass meaningful energy legislation. Instead, Congress allowed President Jimmy Carter to create the precursor to a military command for the Middle East, tasked with ensuring the free flow of energy supplies to the United States.[10] Used this way, foreign policy is a luxury good—a more expensive way of trying to achieve national security than through a mix of domestic and foreign policy.

The unusual prosperity created by World War II enabled the United States to afford a foreign policy–focused approach to national security for a time. But this approach has not served conservatives who worried about the dangers of big government. Given the vast numbers of personnel and resources necessary to manage the foreign policy–focused approach to national security, the size and cost of government have only grown.[11] And those conservatives who worried that Roosevelt's vision for national security would make for an unacceptably intrusive state might wonder at the extent to which the long-standing approach to national security has challenged Americans' civil liberties and personal freedoms. It is no longer clear that the United States can afford a foreign policy–focused approach to national security, or that such an approach can actually deliver national security. In recent times, the Great Recession, the increase in acts of domestic terrorism, and the coronavirus pandemic all showed that some of the most serious national security threats facing the United States must be addressed through domestic policy. Achieving national security in our time will require a blend of domestic and foreign policy.

IN A NEW PERIOD OF CRISIS that creates conditions conducive to expanding the government's domestic responsibilities, another generation of liberals might be tempted to dust off Franklin Roosevelt's playbook and place their domestic agenda under the umbrella of national security. But before they do, they would be wise to learn from Roosevelt's policy design missteps. They should also consider whether security by itself is the right frame for their policies.

Policy design shapes public perceptions of the government no less than the way policies are described. Roosevelt, like most of his predecessors, continued a tradition dating to the Founding of minimizing the appearance of the national government's power by working through state and local governments, as well as through the private sector. The consequences of that policy design choice revealed a fundamental problem with that approach.[12] Keeping the government out of sight can reduce public antipathy toward it, as the Founders intended, but the approach risks diminishing public support for the government and its programs.[13] After all, if people cannot connect government spending to their own economic security or to other desirable outcomes, why should they be expected to support that spending? Relying on the government-owned, contractor-operated model during World War II enabled conservatives to deny the government credit for the "miracle of production" and for the return of prosperity even though both flowed from massive government-funded and government-managed programs. This approach diminished support for economic security programs and made it easier for Americans to accept the rapid buildup of the new foreign policy–focused national security state, because so much of it existed in the private sector.[14] Public perceptions and understanding of government matter. Ultimately, it is in no American's interest for the public to doubt the government's competence, nor does it serve the public interest for such a large extent of the state's essential activities to be obfuscated. Different policy design choices can address both problems.

After decades on the losing side of the framing wars that do much to shape the government's responsibilities, it would be understandable if liberals want to seize the most powerful known weapon in that fight—the language of security and national security—and put it back in the service of their agenda. The language of security has undeniable mobilizing power. But there are drawbacks to framing issues in terms of security. Foremost among them is the infinite expansion problem inherent to security.[15] Political scientist Ole Wæver notes that "security" can easily become "a synonym for everything that is politically good or desirable."[16] The risk is that the unbounded nature of security will prevent those things labeled necessary for national security from being achieved. One could look at Franklin Roosevelt's presidency and see in it evidence of this problem. Unable to deliver national security as he defined it initially, Roosevelt continually expanded the scope of the government's national security responsibilities until they covered the entire world. Set as the country's chief objective, the pursuit of security appeared to be a one-way, ever-expanding project. This was what worried Friedrich Hayek—that the endless pursuit of an unattainable objective ultimately would destroy society.[17] We want security, of course, but we don't want to destroy society in its pursuit.

One answer to this problem is to set something other than security as the government's chief objective and to subordinate the pursuit of security to that larger objective.[18] Conservatives nominated "freedom" for this role, but we have abundant evidence that the government guarantee of freedom does not ensure the equal access to the pursuit of happiness that the Declaration of Independence lists as one of the three "unalienable rights" it is the government's job to secure.[19] When next confronted with challenges on par with the ones Americans faced in the 1930s and 1940s, American policymakers—like their predecessors in the Roosevelt administration—will have an opportunity to redefine the relationship between the government and citizens. They could do so not only in terms of security and freedom but also in terms of justice, on which both security and freedom depend. When the full force of crisis hits, the air will again be thick with the urgent questions Americans asked in the 1930s and 1940s: What are the government's fundamental responsibilities to citizens? Do Americans have economic rights, and, if so, to what extent should the government ensure them? As they seek just answers to those questions, policymakers and the public would do well to remember what Franklin Roosevelt said in 1938: "National security is not a half and half matter; it is all or none."[20]

Abbreviations

APP	American Presidency Project, University of California, Santa Barbara, Santa Barbara, CA
FDRL	Franklin D. Roosevelt Presidential Library and Museum, Hyde Park, NY
GLC	Gilder Lehrman Collection, New York, NY
HIA	Hoover Institution Library & Archives, Stanford CA
HLH	Houghton Library, Harvard University, Cambridge, MA
HML	Hagley Museum and Library, Wilmington, DE
HSTL	Harry S. Truman Presidential Library and Museum, Independence, MO
MAY	Manuscripts and Archives, Yale University, New Haven, CT
MLP	Seeley G. Mudd Manuscript Library, Princeton University, Princeton, NJ
RBML	Rare Book and Manuscript Library, Columbia University, New York, NY
UIA	University of Illinois Archives, Urbana, IL
UKY	University of Kentucky Special Collections Research Center, Lexington, KY
UNDA	University of Notre Dame Archives, Notre Dame, IN
WHS	Wisconsin Historical Society, Madison, WI

Notes

Introduction

1. Throughout this book, "the government" refers to the federal government. Sissela Bok writes that the phrase "national security" creates "a sense of self-evident legitimacy." Daniel Yergin asserts that the phrase "suggests and rationalizes courses of action" and "almost magically puts an end to disputes and debates." James E. Baker argues that "there is no more important assertion of policy validation than an assertion of national security." See Sissela Bok, *Secrets: On the Ethics of Concealment and Revelation* (New York: Vintage, 1989), 115; Daniel Yergin, *Shattered Peace: The Origins of the Cold War* (New York: Penguin, 1990), 196; and James E. Baker, *In the Common Defense: National Security Law for Perilous Times* (New York: Cambridge University Press, 2007), 13–15.

2. On the phrase's timeless quality, see Yergin, *Shattered Peace*, 195.

3. On words as "weapons," see Daniel T. Rodgers, *Contested Truths: Keywords in American Politics since Independence* (Cambridge, MA: Harvard University Press, 1998), 10–11. See also Quentin Skinner's brief essay in Stefan Collini, Michael Bidiss, David Hollinger, Quentin Skinner, J. G. A. Pocock, Bruce Kuklick, and Michael Hunter, "What Is Intellectual History?" *History Today* 35, no. 10 (October 1, 1985): 51.

4. Franklin D. Roosevelt, "Chicago, Illinois—Acceptance Speech on Receiving Nomination," July 2, 1932, MSF, Box 9, (483), FDRL, http://www.fdrlibrary.marist .edu/_resources/images/msf/msf00493 and https://www.fdrlibrary.org/documents /356632/405112/afdr005.mp3/c73e0261-b0fc-41b7-a278-35f6031752ce.

5. Franklin D. Roosevelt, "Fireside Chat #2—'Outlining the New Deal Program,'" May 7, 1933, MSF, Box 14, (627), FDRL, http://www.fdrlibrary.marist.edu/_resources/images /msf/msf00646 and https://www.fdrlibrary.org/documents/356632/405112/afdr014.mp3 /943f2504-4303-4303-bbff-8a72b13db2ca.

6. Franklin D. Roosevelt, "Fireside Chat #16," December 29, 1940, MSF, Box 58, (1351A), FDRL, http://www.fdrlibrary.marist.edu/_resources/images/msf/msf01403 and https://www.fdrlibrary.org/documents/356632/405112/afdr223.mp3/a70c292d-eb42-4412-81e8-5c9f1fe6e70b.

7. Franklin D. Roosevelt, "Annual Message to Congress—State of the Union," January 11, 1944, MSF, Box 76, (1501), FDRL, http://www.fdrlibrary.marist.edu/_resources/images/msf/msfb0129 and https://www.fdrlibrary.org/documents/356632/405112/afdr285.mp3/0f815ba6-8388-4c66-88b8-66b40572950c.

8. Ibid.

9. For a wide-ranging philological study of the language of security, see John T. Hamilton, *Security: Politics, Humanity, and the Philology of Care* (Princeton, NJ: Princeton University Press, 2013).

10. See, for example, Alexander Hamilton, *The Federalist* No. 1, October 27, 1787, https://avalon.law.yale.edu/18th_century/fed01.asp, and John Jay, *The Federalist* No. 3, November 3, 1787, https://avalon.law.yale.edu/18th_century/fed03.asp.

11. On the language of security, see Hamilton, *Security*, 7–24; David A. Baldwin, "The Concept of Security," *Review of International Studies* 23 (1997): 5–26; Michael Dillon, *Politics of Security: Towards a Political Philosophy of Continental Thought* (London: Routledge, 1996), 120–128; Anthony Burke, *Beyond Security, Ethics and Violence: War Against the Other* (London: Routledge, 2007), 27–53; Barry Buzan and Lene Hansen, *The Evolution of International Security Studies* (New York: Cambridge University Press, 2009), 214; Itty Abraham, "Segurança/Security in Brazil and the United States," in *Words in Motion: Toward a Global Lexicon*, Carol Gluck and Anna Lowenhaupt Tsing, eds. (Durham, NC: Duke University Press, 2009), 21–23; Mark Neocleous, *Critique of Security* (Montreal: McGill-Queen's University Press, 2008); and James Der Derian, *Critical Practices in International Theory: Selected Essays* (London: Routledge, 2009), 149–166.

12. Among many works, see John Lewis Gaddis, *The United States and the Origins of the Cold War, 1941–1947* (New York: Columbia University Press, 1972); Yergin, *Shattered Peace*; John Lewis Gaddis, *Strategies of Containment: A Critical Appraisal of American National Security Policy during the Cold War* (New York: Oxford University Press, 1982); Melvyn P. Leffler, "The American Conception of National Security and the Beginnings of the Cold War, 1945–48," *American Historical Review* 89, no. 2 (April 1984): 346–381; Melvyn P. Leffler, *A Preponderance of Power: National Security, the Truman Administration, and the Cold War* (Stanford, CA: Stanford University Press, 1992); Michael J. Hogan, *A Cross of Iron: Harry S. Truman and the Origins of the National Security State, 1945–1954* (New York: Cambridge University Press, 1998); John A. Thompson, "Conceptions of National Security and American Entry into World War II," *Diplomacy and Statecraft* 16, no. 4 (2005): 671–697; Andrew Preston, "Monsters Everywhere: A Genealogy of National Security," *Diplomatic History* 38, no. 3 (2014): 477–500; and John A. Thompson, *A Sense of Power: The Roots of America's Global Role* (Ithaca, NY: Cornell University Press, 2015). On the instrumental use of a term to explain the past, see Daniel T. Rodgers, "Republicanism: The Career of a Concept," *Journal of American History* 79, no. 1 (June 1992): 11–38.

13. For instance, see Michael S. Sherry, *Preparing for the Next War: American Plans for Postwar Defense, 1941–1945* (New Haven, CT: Yale University Press, 1977); Yergin, *Shattered Peace*; and Leffler, "The American Conception of National Security and the Beginnings of the Cold War, 1945–48."

14. See, for example, Laura K. Donohue, "The Limits of National Security," *American Criminal Law Review* 48 (2011): 1573–1756; Aziz Rana, "Who Decides on Security?" *Connecticut Law Review* 44, no. 5 (July 2012): 1417–1490; Joseph Masco, *The Theater of Operations: National Security Affect from the Cold War to the War on Terror* (Durham, NC: Duke University Press, 2014); and Aziz Rana, "Constitutionalism and the Foundations of the Security State," *California Law Review* 103, no. 2 (April 2015): 335–386.

15. Two works took important first steps toward filling this gap. See Mark Neocleous, "From Social to National Security: On the Fabrication of Economic Order," *Security Dialogue* 37, no. 3 (September 2006): 363–384, and Mariano-Florentino Cuéllar, *Governing Security: The Hidden Origins of American Security Agencies* (Stanford, CA: Stanford University Press, 2013).

16. Michael Sherry calls national security a "slippery term." See Michael S. Sherry, *In the Shadow of War: The United States since the 1930s* (New Haven, CT: Yale University Press, 1995), xi.

17. Arnold Wolfers, "'National Security' as an Ambiguous Symbol," *Political Science Quarterly* 67, no. 4 (December 1952): 481.

18. P. G. Bock and Morton Berkowitz, "The Emerging Field of National Security," *World Politics* 19, no. 1 (October 1966): 122–136.

19. Yergin, *Shattered Peace*, 462n3.

20. Melvyn P. Leffler, "National Security," *Journal of American History* 77, no. 1 (June 1990): 143–152, and Howard Jones and Randall B. Woods, "Origins of the Cold War in Europe and the Near East: Recent Historiography and the National Security Imperative," *Diplomatic History* 17, no. 2 (1993): 251–276.

21. Emily S. Rosenberg, "Commentary: The Cold War and the Discourse of National Security," *Diplomatic History* 17, no. 2 (1993): 283, and Anders Stephanson, "Commentary: Ideology and Neorealist Mirrors," *Diplomatic History* 17, no. 2 (1993): 285–295. Robert Latham and Ole Wæver have also argued against that ahistorical approach. See Robert Latham, *The Liberal Moment: Modernity, Security, and the Making of the Postwar International Order* (New York: Columbia University Press, 1997), 92–94, and Ole Wæver, "Security: A Conceptual History for International Relations," working paper dated November 2012, 3.

22. This is true even of Ole Wæver's brilliant "Security: A Conceptual History for International Relations," which, as the title implies, privileges international relations and discounts domestic policies that did not figure into the ultimately triumphant American conception of national security. As Wæver writes, "the object of study should be restricted to those places, times and contexts where a concept of security was articulated which flows into our current concept." See Wæver, "Security: A Conceptual History for International Relations," 25. Similarly, Andrew Preston states up front in his important article "Monsters Everywhere: A Genealogy of National Security" that his

objective is to "trace the emergence of national security as a foreign policy doctrine." He succeeds brilliantly but leaves important parts of the history of national security and the evolution of the national security state unexplained. See Preston, "Monsters Everywhere," 479 and generally. See also Wolfers, "'National Security' as an Ambiguous Symbol"; Rosenberg, "Commentary: The Cold War and the Discourse of National Security"; Sherry, *In the Shadow of War*; Wæver, "Security: A Conceptual History for International Relations"; Thierry Balzacq, "Qu'est-ce que la sécurité nationale?" *Revue Internationale et Stratégique* 52 (2003/4): 33–50; and Alexandre Rios-Bordes, "When Military Intelligence Reconsiders the Nature of War: Elements for an Archaeology of 'National Security' (United States, 1919–1941)," *Politix* 104 (2013/4): 105–132.

23. David Green warns that there is great risk when "a discipline designed to investigate political phenomena takes its intellectual categories, and authority structure, directly from the political arena it is supposed to be investigating." With "national security," scholars have long been stuck in what Robert Latham calls an "auto-referential paradigm." See David Green, *The Language of Politics in America: Shaping Political Consciousness from McKinley to Reagan* (Ithaca, NY: Cornell University Press, 1987), 13–14, and Latham, *Liberal Moment*, 93–94.

24. On the merits of looking forward from the past through the eyes of historical actors, see Thomas K. McCraw, *The Founders and Finance: How Hamilton, Gallatin, and Other Immigrants Forged a New Economy* (Cambridge, MA: Harvard University Press, 2012), 348.

25. An example that appears surprising in retrospect but that makes sense looking forward from the past is Margaret Sanger's 1935 article "National Security and Birth Control" in which she argued that "national planning for economic and social security can, in the long run, produce no real benefits unless such plans be based upon the cornerstone of family security through family planning." See Margaret Sanger, "National Security and Birth Control," *Forum and Century* 93, no. 3 (March 1935): 139–141. Other topics that since the mid-1940s have not been considered related to national security—conservation and land use, for instance—were also once in that frame. See, for example, Richard F. Hammatt, "Forest Conservation and National Security," *Scientific Monthly* 49, no. 2 (August 1939): 120–134.

26. On the benefits of focusing on historical processes, see David Hackett Fischer, *Historians' Fallacies: Toward a Logic of Historical Thought* (New York: Harper, 1970), 280. The process of "securitization" is an important concept within the international relations subfield of political science. Among many works, a good starting point is Ole Wæver, "Securitization and Desecuritization," in *On Security*, Ronnie D. Lipschutz, ed. (New York: Columbia University Press, 1995), 46–86.

27. Green, *Language of Politics in America*, 127. On the value of paying close attention to political language in American history, see also Rodgers, *Contested Truths*.

28. This is a fundamental element of the German approach to conceptual history, *Begriffsgeschichte*. For an English-language overview, see Melvin Richter, *The History of Political and Social Concepts: A Critical Introduction* (New York: Oxford University Press, 1995).

29. Other scholars have called attention to Franklin Roosevelt's use of the language of security to justify domestic policy during his first term but, relying on published primary sources, suggest erroneously that Roosevelt did so only beginning in 1934 in

"an attempt to outflank critics." See Neocleous, "From Social to National Security," 368. See also Jennifer Klein, *For All These Rights: Business, Labor, and the Shaping of America's Public-Private Welfare State* (Princeton, NJ: Princeton University Press, 2003), 80. Klein's and Neocleous's reliance on published primary sources may have led them to overlook Roosevelt's earlier uses of the language of security. For example, Neocleous makes much of the absence of "security" from the first volume of Roosevelt's memoirs, an omission perhaps better explained by Samuel Rosenman's authoring Roosevelt's memoirs at a time when Rosenman was not close to what was happening in the administration. On Rosenman's being out of the loop, see Samuel I. Rosenman, *Working with Roosevelt* (New York: Harper, 1952), 94. On Roosevelt's tendency to deviate from prepared texts, see The Reminiscences of Samuel I. Rosenman, Oral History Research Office, Columbia University, 1960, 141, and Laura Crowell, "Word Changes Introduced *Ad Libitum* in Five Speeches by Franklin Delano Roosevelt," *Speech Monographs* 25, no. 4 (November 1958): 229–242. All quotations from Roosevelt's speeches cited in this book are transcribed from the audio recordings if they exist.

30. The most useful of these records are in Raymond Moley's papers at the Hoover Institution in Stanford, California. Moley was Roosevelt's closest advisor during the 1932 campaign and lead speechwriter until 1935. Moley's papers at the Hoover Institution document the evolution of Roosevelt's thinking down to the level of word choice during this crucial period.

31. On the origins and development of the conservative movement and the persuasion campaign at its center, see Peter Roady, "Selling Selective Anti-Statism: The Conservative Persuasion Campaign and the Transformation of American Politics since the 1920s," *Modern American History* 6, no. 1 (March 2023): 21–43. On the role of these business leaders, see Fredrick Rudolph, "The American Liberty League, 1934–1940," *American Historical Review* 56, no. 1 (October 1950): 21–22, 32; George Wolfskill, *The Revolt of the Conservatives: A History of the American Liberty League, 1934–1940* (Westport, CT: Houghton Mifflin, 1962); Robert F. Burk, *The Corporate State and the Broker State: The Du Ponts and American National Politics, 1925–1940* (Cambridge, MA: Harvard University Press, 1990); Kim Phillips-Fein, *Invisible Hands: The Businessmen's Crusade Against the New Deal* (New York: Norton, 2009); Julian Zelizer, "Rethinking the History of American Conservatism," *Reviews in American History* 38, no. 2 (June 2010): 370; and Julia Bowes, "'Every Citizen a Sentinel! Every Home a Sentry Box!' The Sentinels of the Republic and the Gendered Origins of Free-Market Conservatism," *Modern American History* 2, no. 3 (November 2019): 270–273. For overviews of the extensive literature on American conservatism, see Zelizer, "Rethinking the History of American Conservatism," 367–392; Kim Phillips-Fein, "Conservatism: A State of the Field," *Journal of American History* 98, no. 3 (December 2011): 723–743; and Elizabeth Tandy Shermer, "Whither the Right? Old and New Directions in the History of American Conservatism," *Reviews in American History* 44, no. 4 (2016): 644–652. Other authors who have written about elements of the conservative campaign include S. H. Walker and Paul Sklar, *Business Finds Its Voice: Management's Effort to Sell the Business Idea to the Public* (New York: Harper & Brothers, 1938); Wolfskill, *Revolt of the Conservatives*; Richard S. Tedlow, "The National

Association of Manufacturers and Public Relations during the New Deal," *Business History Review* 50, no. 1 (Spring 1976): 25–45; Robert Griffith, "The Selling of America: The Advertising Council and American Politics, 1942–1960," *Business History Review* 57, no. 3 (Autumn 1983): 388–412; Burk, *Corporate State and the Broker State*; Elizabeth A. Fones-Wolf, *Selling Free Enterprise: The Business Assault on Labor and Liberalism, 1945–1960* (Urbana: University of Illinois Press, 1994); Stuart Ewen, *PR!: A Social History of Spin* (New York: Basic Books, 1996), 288–336; Roland Marchand, *Creating the Corporate Soul: The Rise of Public Relations and Corporate Imagery in American Business* (Berkeley: University of California Press, 1998), 202–248; William L. Bird Jr., *"Better Living": Advertising, Media, and the New Vocabulary of Business Leadership, 1935–1955* (Evanston, IL: Northwestern University Press, 1999); Wendy L. Wall, *Inventing the "American Way": The Politics of Consensus from the New Deal to the Civil Rights Movement* (New York: Oxford University Press, 2008); Allan J. Lichtman, *White Protestant Nation: The Rise of the American Conservative Movement* (New York: Grove Press, 2008); Phillips-Fein, *Invisible Hands*; Marjorie E. Kornhauser, "Shaping Public Opinion and the Law: How a 'Common Man' Campaign Ended a Rich Man's Law," *Law and Contemporary Problems* 73, no. 1 (Winter 2010): 123–147; Kevin M. Kruse, *One Nation Under God: How Corporate America Invented Christian America* (New York: Basic Books, 2015); Mark R. Wilson, *Destructive Creation: American Business and the Winning of World War II* (Philadelphia: University of Pennsylvania Press, 2016); Bowes, "'Every Citizen a Sentinel! Every Home a Sentry Box!'" 269–297; Lawrence B. Glickman, *Free Enterprise: An American History* (New Haven, CT: Yale University Press, 2019); Charlie Whitham, *Corporate Conservatives Go to War: How the National Association of Manufacturers Planned to Restore American Free Enterprise, 1939–1948* (Cham, Switzerland: Palgrave Macmillan, 2020); and Naomi Oreskes and Erik M. Conway, *The Big Myth: How American Business Taught Us to Loathe Government and Love the Free Market* (New York: Bloomsbury, 2023).

32. On conservatism as a "big tent movement," see George H. Nash, *The Conservative Intellectual Movement in America since 1945* (Wilmington, DE: ISI Books, 2006), xiv–xv, and Jennifer Burns, "In Retrospect: George Nash's *The Conservative Intellectual Movement in America Since 1945*," *Reviews in American History* 32, no. 3 (September 2004): 453.

33. Adam J. Berinsky, Eleanor Neff Powell, Eric Schickler, and Ian Brett Yohai, "Revisiting Public Opinion in the 1930s and 1940s," *PS: Political Science and Politics* 44, no. 3 (July 2011): 516. See also Sarah Igo, *The Averaged American: Surveys, Citizens, and the Making of a Mass Public* (Cambridge, MA: Harvard University Press, 2007), 127–131.

34. Exceptions include Betty Houchin Winfield, *FDR and the News Media* (Urbana: University of Illinois Press, 1990); Robert J. Brown, *Manipulating the Ether: The Power of Broadcast Radio in Thirties America* (Jefferson, NC: McFarland & Co, 1998); Griffith, "Selling of America"; Fones-Wolf, *Selling Free Enterprise*; Wall, *Inventing the "American Way"*; and Wilson, *Destructive Creation*. Jill Lepore provides a useful example of the value of paying greater attention to big efforts to shape public opinion by centering some such efforts in her synthesis of American history. See Jill Lepore, *These Truths: A History of the United States* (New York: Norton, 2018).

35. For instance, see Lynn Hasher, David Goldstein, and Thomas Toppino, "Frequency and the Conference of Referential Validity," *Journal of Verbal Learning and Verbal Behavior* 16, no. 1 (February 1977): 107–112; Lisa K. Fazio, Nadia M. Brashier, B. Keith Payne, and Elizabeth J. Marsh, "Knowledge Does Not Protect Against Illusory Truth," *Journal of Experimental Psychology: General* 144, no. 5 (2015): 993–1002; and Lisa K. Fazio, David G. Rand, and Gordon Pennycook, "Repetition Increases Perceived Truth Equally for Plausible and Implausible Statements," *Psychonomic Bulletin & Review* 26 (October 2019): 1705–1710.

36. Done well, persuasion campaigns exploit the human brain's effort to remain on autopilot, which requires less energy than thinking. Among many works on this topic, a useful summary is Daniel Kahneman, *Thinking, Fast and Slow* (New York: Farrar, Straus and Giroux, 2011), 19–49. Persuasion campaigns also contribute to what psychologist Jerome Bruner called "the narrative construction of reality." See Jerome Bruner, "The Narrative Construction of Reality," *Critical Inquiry* 18, no. 1 (Autumn 1991): 1–21.

37. Brian Balogh, *A Government Out of Sight: The Mystery of National Authority in Nineteenth-Century America* (New York: Cambridge University Press, 2009), 52.

38. Starting in the 1940s, the public relations professionals running the conservative persuasion campaign tracked the number of "impressions" their messages received. For a message delivered by radio, for example, they defined a "listener impression" as "one message heard once by one listener." See *Ad Council Annual* Report, 8th, "How Business Helps Solve Public Problems," 1949–1950, Advertising Council Archives, 13-2-207, Box 7, File 503, University of Illinois Archives [hereafter UIA].

39. On "loss frames," see Amos Tversky and Daniel Kahneman, "The Framing of Decisions and the Psychology of Choice," *Science* 211, no. 4481 (January 30, 1981): 453–458. Political scientists Barry Buzan, Lene Hansen, and Ole Wæver have shown that "securitizing" something changes the rules of the political game. See Buzan and Hansen, *Evolution of International Security Studies*, 214, and Wæver, "Security: A Conceptual History for International Relations," 6n11.

40. On this point, see Gary Gerstle, *Liberty and Coercion: The Paradox of American Government from the Founding to the Present* (Princeton, NJ: Princeton University Press, 2015), 206–207.

41. On Roosevelt's appropriation of "liberalism," see Green, *Language of Politics in America*, chapter 5, and Gerstle, *Liberty and Coercion*, 187. On Roosevelt's use of the language of security to justify expanding the federal government, see Cuéllar, *Governing Security*, 191.

42. Based on text mining of congressional and executive branch documents going back to the country's birth. For instance, George Washington wrote in 1783 that "I cannot hesitate to contribute my best endeavours, toward the establishment of the National security." See From George Washington to Elias Boudinot, August 26, 1783, Founders Online, National Archives, https://founders.archives.gov/?q=%22national%20security %22&s=1111311111&sa=&r=8&sr=, quoted in Alexandra Ouyang, "Security," *Critical Quarterly* 58, no. 3 (December 22, 2016): 107–109. For a broader discussion of earlier appearances of the phrase "national security," see Donohue, "The Limits of National

Security." Mark Shulman's discovery of a World War I–era organization called the "National Security League" led him to claim genealogical importance for that entity in the emergence of the phrase "national security" in American political discourse. The organization's choice of name certainly implies some understanding of the phrase's rhetorical value. But the infrequency with which the organization used the phrase in its activities and advocacy—preferring the words "preparedness" and "defense"—suggests that the organization did not grasp the full potential of "national security" as a tool of persuasion. On the National Security League, see Mark R. Shulman, "The Progressive Era Origins of the National Security Act," *Dickinson Law Review* 104, no. 2 (Winter 2000): 289–330; John Carver Edwards, *Patriots in Pinstripes: Men of the National Security League* (Washington, DC: University Press of America, 1982); and Robert D. Ward, "The Origin and Activities of the National Security League, 1914–1919," *The Mississippi Valley Historical Review* 47, no. 1 (June 1960): 51–65. In his conceptual history of "security" in international relations, Ole Wæver also concludes that the group's choice of name was incidental and not part of a rhetorical strategy. See Wæver, "Security: A Conceptual History for International Relations," 66.

43. On "corner stone," see Franklin Roosevelt, "Statement upon Signing the Social Security Act," August 14, 1935, MSF, Box 22, (791), FDRL, http://www.fdrlibrary.marist .edu/_resources/images/msf/msf00814.

44. Green, *Language of Politics in America*, 162–163. Historians have noted the pitfalls associated with using the term "conservative," which, as Elizabeth Tandy Shermer points out, did not take hold everywhere at the same time. Because the characters in this story did embrace the "conservative" label for themselves and for their movement, I feel that using the term conforms with Kim Phillips-Fein's sound advice to let historical actors define themselves. For thoughtful reflections on the labeling issue, see Green, *Language of Politics in America*, 162–163; Phillips-Fein, *Invisible Hands*, 321–322; and Elizabeth Tandy Shermer, *Sunbelt Capitalism: Phoenix and the Transformation of American Politics* (Philadelphia: University of Pennsylvania Press, 2013), 7. Given the range of people involved, the term "conservative movement" adds problems of its own. Here, I follow George Nash's suggestion that we see modern American conservatism as a big tent movement. See Nash, *Conservative Intellectual Movement in America since 1945*, xiv–xv, and Burns, "In Retrospect: George Nash's *The Conservative Intellectual Movement in America Since 1945*," 453.

45. Isaiah Berlin, "Two Concepts of Liberty," in *Liberty: Incorporating Four Essays on Liberty*, 2nd ed. (New York: Oxford University Press, 2002), 166–217.

46. Roosevelt, "Annual Message to Congress—State of the Union," January 11, 1944, FDRL.

47. The phrase "selective anti-statism" comes from sociologist Allen Hunter. See Allen Hunter, "Virtue with a Vengeance: The Pro-Family Politics of the New Right," (Ph.D. diss., Brandeis University, 1985), 271. On other strands of selective anti-statism, see Matthew D. Lassiter, "Political History beyond the Red-Blue Divide," *Journal of American History* 98, no. 3 (December 2011): 763–764, and John S. Huntington, *Far-Right Vanguard: The Radical Roots of Modern Conservatism* (Philadelphia: University of Pennsylvania Press, 2021), 4.

1. Campaigning on the Promise of Security

1. Franklin D. Roosevelt, "Chicago, Illinois—Acceptance Speech on Receiving Nomination," July 2, 1932, MSF, Box 9, (483), FDRL, http://www.fdrlibrary.marist .edu/_resources/images/msf/msf00493 and https://www.fdrlibrary.org/ documents/356632/405112/afdr005.mp3/c73e0261-b0fc-41b7-a278-35f6031752ce.

2. On the worldwide nature of the Great Depression, see Kiran Klaus Patel, *The New Deal: A Global History* (Princeton, NJ: Princeton University Press, 2016), 2. On the comparatively greater severity of the Depression in the United States, see Daniel T. Rodgers, *Atlantic Crossings: Social Politics in a Progressive Age* (Cambridge, MA: Harvard University Press, 1998), 412. On the viability and compatibility of capitalism and democracy, see Sheri Berman, *The Social Democratic Moment: Ideas and Politics in the Making of Interwar Europe* (Cambridge, MA: Harvard University Press, 1998), 3, and Alonzo L. Hamby, *For the Survival of Democracy: Franklin Roosevelt and the World Crisis of the 1930s* (New York: Free Press, 2004), 3.

3. Lepore, *These Truths*, 425.

4. Ibid.

5. For an evocative portrait of this grim period, see Arthur M. Schlesinger Jr., *The Crisis of the Old Order, 1919–1933: The Age of Roosevelt, Vol. 1* (Boston: Mariner Books, 2003), 166–176.

6. Franklin D. Roosevelt, "Pittsburgh, Pennsylvania—Campaign Address," October 1, 1936, MSF, Box 27, (930), FDRL, http://www.fdrlibrary.marist.edu/_resources/images /msf/msf00955 and https://www.fdrlibrary.org/documents/356632/405112/afdr061 .mp3/ec397ff3-6133-4376-87b1-63dbf356aa38.

7. Roosevelt, "Chicago, Illinois—Acceptance Speech on Receiving Nomination," July 2, 1932, FDRL.

8. Ibid.

9. Ibid.

10. Ibid.

11. For varying judgments, see Ernest K. Lindley, *The Roosevelt Revolution: First Phase* (New York: Viking, 1933), 6–13; Schlesinger Jr., *Crisis of the Old Order*, chapters 32–33; Clinton L. Rossiter, "The Political Philosophy of F. D. Roosevelt: A Challenge to Scholarship," *Review of Politics* 11, no. 1 (1949): 87–95; William E. Leuchtenburg, *Franklin D. Roosevelt and the New Deal, 1932–1940* (New York: Harper, 1963), 33; James MacGregor Burns, *Roosevelt: The Lion and the Fox, 1882–1940* (New York: Open Road, 2012), 144, 151–156; Rodgers, *Atlantic Crossings*, 437–438; David M. Kennedy, *Freedom from Fear: The American People in Depression and War, 1929–1945* (New York: Oxford University Press, 1999), 99–103; Eric Rauchway, *Winter War: Hoover, Roosevelt, and the First Clash over the New Deal* (New York: Basic Books, 2018), 14–18; and Cass R. Sunstein, *The Second Bill of Rights: FDR's Unfinished Revolution and Why We Need It More Than Ever* (New York: Basic Books, 2004), 65.

12. Eric Rauchway debunks the long-standing view that Roosevelt either lacked a coherent philosophy or failed to articulate one. See Rauchway, *Winter War*, 7–8, 14–18.

13. In a 1932 message to the New York State Legislature, then-Governor Roosevelt said that Americans were "fortunate that our fathers provided systems . . . which permit peaceful

change by intelligent and representative leadership to meet changing conditions of human society." See Franklin D. Roosevelt, "Albany, New York—Message to the Legislature," January 6, 1932, MSF, Box 9, (457), FDRL, http://www.fdrlibrary.marist .edu/_resources/images/msf/msf00467.

14. See Franklin D. Roosevelt, "University of Virginia, Charlottesville, Virginia," July 6, 1931, MSF, Box 8, (435), FDRL, http://www.fdrlibrary.marist.edu/_resources/images /msf/msf00441, and "FDR address on Excessive Cost of Local Government," July 6, 1931, Moley Papers (68008), Box 283, (FD Roosevelt Schedule A), (Folder 30), HIA.

15. Roosevelt, "Albany, New York—Message to the Legislature," January 6, 1932, FDRL.

16. See Franklin D. Roosevelt, "Troy, New York," March 3, 1912, MSF, Box 1, (14), FDRL, http://www.fdrlibrary.marist.edu/_resources/images/msf/msf00015. James MacGregor Burns dismisses this speech as "pretentious nonsense," but other historians, including Arthur Schlesinger Jr. and Jean Edward Smith, give the speech the weight it deserves. See Burns, *Roosevelt: The Lion and the Fox*, 53; Schlesinger Jr., *Crisis of the Old Order*, 336–338; and Jean Edward Smith, *FDR* (New York: Random House, 2007), 84.

17. Roosevelt, "Troy, New York," March 3, 1912, FDRL.

18. Franklin D. Roosevelt, "Albany, New York—Radio Address Social Welfare and Government," October 13, 1932, MSF, Box 11, (552), FDRL, http://www.fdrlibrary .marist.edu/_resources/images/msf/msf00564.

19. On Eleanor Roosevelt's influence on Franklin Roosevelt, see Blanche Wiesen Cook, *Eleanor Roosevelt: Volume One, 1884–1933* (New York: Viking, 1992); Blanche Wiesen Cook, *Eleanor Roosevelt: Volume Two, The Defining Years, 1933–1938* (New York: Penguin, 1999); Doris Kearns Goodwin, *No Ordinary Time: Franklin & Eleanor Roosevelt: The Home Front in World War II* (New York: Simon & Schuster, 1995); and Joseph P. Lash, *Eleanor and Franklin* (New York: Norton, 1971), 431–435, 575–577. On Perkins's influence on Franklin Roosevelt, see Kirstin Downey, *The Woman Behind the New Deal: The Life of Frances Perkins, FDR's Secretary of Labor and His Moral Conscience* (New York: Doubleday, 2009), and Adam Cohen, *Nothing to Fear: FDR's Inner Circle and the Hundred Days That Created Modern America* (New York: Penguin, 2009), 157–247. On Perkins's push for social insurance, see Downey, *Woman Behind the New Deal*, 109–110; Kennedy, *Freedom from Fear*, 99; and Roosevelt, "Albany, New York—Message to the Legislature," January 6, 1932, FDRL.

20. See Roosevelt, "Troy, New York," March 3, 1912, FDRL. On Roosevelt's embrace of planning, see Philip W. Warken, "A History of the National Resources Planning Board, 1933–1943," (Ph.D. diss., The Ohio State University, 1969), 15, and Patrick D. Reagan, *Designing a New America: The Origins of New Deal Planning, 1890–1943* (Amherst: University of Massachusetts Press, 1999).

21. Franklin D. Roosevelt, "Informal remarks following visit to Home Subsistence Exhibition Auditorium of the Commerce Building," MSF, Box 17, (695), April 24, 1934, http://www.fdrlibrary.marist.edu/_resources/images/msf/msf00715.

22. Ibid.

23. Among many works on this topic, see Richard R. John, "Government Institutions as Agents of Change: Rethinking American Political Development in the Early Republic, 1787–1835," *Studies in American Political Development* 11, no. 2 (October 1997): 347–380, William J. Novak, "The Myth of the 'Weak' American State," *American*

Historical Review 113, no. 3 (June 2008): 752–772, and Balogh, *A Government Out of Sight*. On the choices the Founders made in an effort to create a "light and inconspicuous" federal government, see Max Edling, *A Revolution in Favor of Government: Origins of the U.S. Constitution and the Making of the American State* (New York: Oxford University Press, 2003), 224–225.

24. For a sense of his thinking on the importance of planning, see Roosevelt Handwritten notes for January 7, 1931, annual message to the New York State Legislature, n.d. [January 1931], Tully Collection, Box 13, (Speech Drafts-Annual Message to the Legislature, January 7, 1931), FDRL, http://www.fdrlibrary.marist.edu/_resources /images/tully/13_05.pdf.

25. Roosevelt, "Albany, New York—Message to the Legislature," January 6, 1932, FDRL.

26. Ibid. See Roosevelt's handwritten draft on p. 2 of the PDF. On the aperture-opening effects of the Depression, see Rodgers, *Atlantic Crossings*, 412–416.

27. On "reconstruction," see, for example, Roosevelt, "Chicago, Illinois—Acceptance Speech on Receiving Nomination," July 2, 1932, FDRL. On taking a long time, see Franklin D. Roosevelt, *Whither Bound?* (Cambridge, MA: The Riverside Press, 1926), 15.

28. On the growing importance of expertise in this period, see Rana, "Who Decides on Security?" 1452–1458.

29. For a short history of planning in the United States, see Warken, "A History of the National Resources Planning Board," 4–37. For a longer history of planning in the United States that traces its evolution from the local and state level in the 1890s to the national level in the 1920s and 1930s, see Reagan, *Designing a New America*. A National Economic and Social Planning Association—later renamed, tellingly, the National Planning Association and then, more tellingly, the National Policy Association—was founded in 1934. See National Policy Association Records Finding Aid, Walter P. Reuther Library, Wayne State University, https://reuther.wayne.edu/files/LR001816 .pdf.

30. Frances Perkins, Part 3, Session 1, Columbia University Oral History Research Office, 1955, 602–603, http://www.columbia.edu/cu/lweb/digital/collections/nny/perkinsf /transcripts/perkinsf_3_1_602.html.

31. Blanche Wiesen Cook, "Introduction," in *My Day: The Best of Eleanor Roosevelt's Acclaimed Newspaper Columns, 1936–1962*, ed. David Emblidge (Boston: Da Capo Press, 2001), xiii.

32. Frank Freidel, *Franklin D. Roosevelt: The Apprenticeship* (Boston: Little, Brown, 1952), 148–149. On Howe, see also Lela Stiles, *The Man Behind Roosevelt: The Story of Louis McHenry Howe* (Cleveland, OH: The World Publishing Company, 1954); Alfred B. Rollins Jr., *Roosevelt and Howe* (New York: Alfred A. Knopf, 1962); and Julie M. Fenster, *FDR's Shadow: Louis Howe, the Force That Shaped Franklin and Eleanor Roosevelt* (New York: St. Martin's Press, 2009).

33. Robert Schlesinger, *White House Ghosts: Presidents and Their Speechwriters* (New York: Simon & Schuster, 2008), 5.

34. Raymond Moley, *After Seven Years* (New York: Harper & Brothers, 1939), 5–34; Raymond Moley, *The First New Deal* (New York: Harcourt, Brace & World, 1966), 14–16; Lindley, *Roosevelt Revolution*, 25–41; and James Kieran, "The 'Cabinet' Mr. Roosevelt Already Has," *New York Times*, November 20, 1932. For a chronology of the

Brain Trust's work, see Rexford G. Tugwell, *The Brains Trust* (New York: Viking Press, 1968), xv–xviii.

35. Moley, *First New Deal*, 15–16.

36. Rosenman, *Working with Roosevelt*, 56–66.

37. Tugwell, *Brains Trust*, 31; Moley, *After Seven Years*, 11; Reminiscences of Adolf Berle, Part 2, Oral History Project, Columbia University, 1970, 171–173.

38. Reminiscences of Adolf Berle, Part 2, Oral History Project, Columbia University, 1970, 186. Moley and Tugwell had similar realizations. See Raymond Moley to Eva Moley, July 27, 1932, Moley Papers, Box 1, (1932), FDRL, and Tugwell, *Brains Trust*, 19, 31.

39. On Roosevelt's learning style, see Kennedy, *Freedom from Fear*, 112–113.

40. Moley, *After Seven Years*, 11, and R. G. Tugwell, "The Preparation of a President," *Western Political Quarterly* 1, no. 2 (1948): 132.

41. Reminiscences of Adolf Berle, Part 2, Oral History Project, Columbia University, 1970, 173.

42. Ibid., 172.

43. Moley, *After Seven Years*, 20.

44. Tugwell, *Brains Trust*, 169.

45. Moley, *After Seven Years*, 11.

46. On the preparation of Roosevelt's speeches, see Moley, *After Seven Years*, 22, 44–45, 55–56; Grace G. Tully, *F. D. R., My Boss* (New York: C. Scribner's Sons, 1949), 94–100; Marguerite "Missy" LeHand, Draft Article about FDR and Working in the White House, n.d. [1937–1938], Tully Collection, Box 10, (Writings: Draft Article about FDR and Working in the White House, ca. 1937–1938), FDRL, http://www.fdrlibrary.marist .edu/_resources/images/tully/10_48.pdf (see pp. 61–63 of the PDF); Rosenman, *Working with Roosevelt*, 1–13 and generally; Robert E. Sherwood, *Roosevelt and Hopkins: An Intimate History* (New York: Harper, 1948), 183–184, 195–196, 212–219, 265–267; and Halford R. Ryan, *Franklin D. Roosevelt's Rhetorical Presidency* (New York: Greenwood Press, 1988), 161–167.

47. Lindley, *Roosevelt Revolution*, 21–26; Moley, *After Seven Years*, 21; Moley, *First New Deal*, 14–17. On Rosenman's appointment to the New York Supreme Court, see Rosenman, *Working with Roosevelt*, 59–60.

48. See, for example, Moley handwritten notes on 1932 campaign, n.d. [1932], Moley Papers (68008), Box 282, (FD Roosevelt Schedule A), (Folder 13), HIA. See also Moley, *After Seven Years*, 35, and Moley, *First New Deal*, 97.

49. Moley, *After Seven Years*, 22, 26, 44–45, 55.

50. Ibid.

51. See Moley, *After Seven Years*, 27, 44–45, 55, 291, and Moley, *First New Deal*, 97.

52. Lindley, *Roosevelt Revolution*, 265.

53. Moley told public relations legend Edward Bernays that the public opinion course he taught at Columbia in the 1920s was "altogether the most satisfying and helpful course—to myself, at any rate—that I ever gave." See Moley to Bernays, April 24, 1937, Moley Papers (68008), Box 5, (Bernays, Edward L.), HIA. On Roosevelt's careful monitoring of public opinion, see Richard W. Steele, "The Pulse of the People: Franklin D. Roosevelt and the Gauging of American Public Opinion," *Journal of*

Contemporary History 9, no. 4 (October 1974): 195–216; Winfield, *FDR and the News Media*, 215–229; and James T. Sparrow, *Warfare State: World War II Americans and the Age of Big Government* (New York: Oxford University Press, 2011), 29–41. On Roosevelt's feel for public opinion judged by another master of it, see Reminiscences of Edward L. Bernays, Oral History Project, Columbia University, 1971, 227–228.

54. On Roosevelt's reliance on public opinion polling, see Robert M. Eisinger and Jeremy Brown, "Polling as a Means Toward Presidential Autonomy: Emil Hurja, Hadley Cantril and the Roosevelt Administration," *International Journal of Public Opinion Research* 10, no. 3 (Fall 1998): 237–256, and Melvin G. Holli, *The Wizard of Washington: Emil Hurja, Franklin Roosevelt, and the Birth of Public Opinion Polling* (New York: Palgrave, 2002), 39–80.

55. Eleanor Roosevelt, *This I Remember* (Westport, CT: Greenwood Press, 1949), 73. For an example of how Franklin Roosevelt inserted easy-to-understand analogies into his speeches, see Roosevelt marked-up third draft of fireside chat, n.d. [April 1935], Moley Papers (68008), Box 290, (FD Roosevelt Schedule A), (Folder 13), HIA,14–15, in which Roosevelt inserted a handwritten paragraph comparing the construction of his administration's domestic programs to the building of a great oceangoing ship. Roosevelt noted that when looking at the early stages of the shipbuilding process, it was sometimes hard to see how the various pieces would fit together—but that they were nevertheless part of a plan that would be comprehensible once construction was further along.

56. For Moley's objections to the speechwriter label, see Moley, *First New Deal*, 17, 96–97, and Moley, *After Seven Years*, 55. On the speeches being "Roosevelt's," see, among many examples, Tully, *F. D. R., My Boss*, 87–88, 94–100.

57. Rosenman, *Working with Roosevelt*, 8–9. Rosenman added a caveat to this statement in his 1960 Columbia oral history interview, noting that the speechwriters' influence on policy was somewhat less on occasions when Roosevelt told the speechwriters what policy he wished to announce. See The Reminiscences of Samuel I. Rosenman, Oral History Research Office, Columbia University, 1960, 138. See also Halford Ryan, "Franklin Delano Roosevelt: Rhetorical Politics and Political Rhetorics," in *Presidential Speechwriting: From the New Deal to the Reagan Revolution and Beyond*, Kurt Ritter and Martin J. Medhurst, eds. (College Station: Texas A&M University Press, 2003), 21–24.

58. On the importance of this type of overlooked figure, see Green, *Language of Politics in America*, 19–20.

59. On "four years," see Moley, *After Seven Years*, 55.

60. Moley, *After Seven Years*, 3. For additional background on Moley, see Lindley, *Roosevelt Revolution*, 298–304, and Cohen, *Nothing to Fear*, 46–83.

61. Moley, *After Seven Years*, 1–12.

62. Rosenman, *Working with Roosevelt*, 61. Rosenman noted on another occasion the ease with which Moley wrote, saying that Moley "had a very facile pen." See The Reminiscences of Samuel I. Rosenman, Oral History Research Office, Columbia University, 1960, 113.

63. Frank Freidel foreword to Moley, *The First New Deal*, vii–xiv.

64. Lindley, *Roosevelt Revolution*, 23. On Moley's importance to Roosevelt, see also Kenneth S. Davis, *FDR: The New York Years, 1928–1933* (New York: Random House, 1985), 265–266, and Davis W. Houck, *Rhetoric as Currency: Hoover, Roosevelt, and the Great Depression* (College Station: Texas A&M Press, 2011), 116.

65. On Moley's eagerness to work on Roosevelt's campaign, see Moley, *After Seven Years*, 2–5.

66. Moley's delicate constitution comes through most clearly in the letters Moley wrote to his wife Eva during the 1932 campaign. The portrait of Moley that emerges from these letters at the Roosevelt Library is somewhat different—and less flattering—than the picture presented in his *After Seven Years* and his papers at the Hoover Institution, perhaps because he did not curate the papers at the Roosevelt Library. See Moley Papers, Box 1, (1932), FDRL. On "Wild days and nights of work," see Moley, *After Seven Years*, 22.

67. Among many examples in the Moley Papers at the Hoover Institution, see Moley handwritten notes on 1932 campaign, n.d. [1932], Moley Papers (68008), Box 282, (FD Roosevelt Schedule A), (Folder 13), HIA.

68. Almost all of Moley's papers are at the Hoover Institution, but these letters are at the FDR Library, perhaps because they were donated by his first wife Eva, who divorced Moley in 1948. Moley's letters to Eva provide unique insight into the development of Roosevelt's and his advisors' thinking in 1932—a fact Moley himself acknowledged in one letter in which he asked his wife to save the correspondence because of its value to the historical record. See Raymond Moley to Eva Moley, August 24, 1932, Moley Papers, Box 1, (Correspondence—1933–1934), FDRL.

69. Lindley, *Roosevelt Revolution*, 302; The Reminiscences of Samuel I. Rosenman, Oral History Research Office, Columbia University, 1960, 113; Tugwell, *Brains Trust*, 154–155.

70. For representative photographs of Moley, see the opening photo in his *After Seven Years* and several of the others included in that book. See also the opening photo in his *The First New Deal*.

71. For Roosevelt's observation, see Tugwell, *The Brains Trust*, xxviii.

72. See, for example, Moley, *After Seven Years*, 310–312.

73. Raymond Moley to Eva Moley, November 8, 1932, Moley Papers, Box 1, (1932), FDRL.

74. Moley, *After Seven Years*, 5, 11, and Moley, *First New Deal*, 15.

75. Franklin D. Roosevelt, "Albany, New York—Radio Address re a National Program of Restoration," April 7, 1932, MSF, Box 9, (469), FDRL, http://www.fdrlibrary.marist.edu/_resources/images/msf/msf00479 and https://www.fdrlibrary.org/documents/356632/405112/afdr004.mp3/aa876539-0aa5-4039-9dd1-8dd52f7ccab6.

76. Ibid.

77. Ibid.

78. Ibid.

79. On the time limitations of the persuasive power of justifications based on emergency, see Aaron L. Friedberg, *In the Shadow of the Garrison State: America's Anti-Statism and Its Cold War Grand Strategy* (Princeton, NJ: Princeton University Press, 2000), 26.

80. Tugwell, *Brains Trust*, 21–26, 41–50.

81. Ibid., 26; Moley, *After Seven Years*, 15; Davis, *FDR: The New York Years, 1928–1933*, 271–276.

82. Moley, *After Seven Years*, 15.

83. Tugwell, *Brains Trust*, 66–68, and The Reminiscences of Samuel I. Rosenman, Oral History Research Office, Columbia University, 1960, 113.

84. Brain Trust handwritten and typed drafts of recovery program, n.d. [1932], Moley Papers (68008), Box 282, (FD Roosevelt Schedule A), (Folder 4), HIA. The text does not indicate authorship, but the language and ideas expressed—a "national economic council" and a "concert of interests," for instance—match Tugwell's writing.

85. There are conflicting accounts of the timing of Berle's joining. I have relied on Moley's account from 1939 because he kept excellent records and was writing closer to the time of the events in question than when Berle sat for his Columbia oral history interviews in 1969 and 1970. See Moley, *After Seven Years*, 18. Tugwell also dates Berle's "acquisition" to between April 7 and April 18, 1932. See Tugwell, *Brains Trust*, xv. On Berle's tendency to dominate conversations, including the Brain Trust discussions, see Tugwell, *Brains Trust*, 44, 132. On Berle generally, see Jordan A. Schwarz, *Liberal: Adolf A. Berle and the Vision of an American Era* (New York: Free Press, 1987), and Davis, *FDR: The New York Years, 1928–1933*, 276–288.

86. On Tugwell's prior study of the problems, see Tugwell, *Brains Trust*, 12–26.

87. In his Columbia oral history interviews, Berle contradicted himself on when the discussion group formed—saying in 1969 that the group began meeting in late 1931 and saying in 1970 that it had met for "a couple of years" before 1932. The exact timing is less important than that Berle was deeply engaged on the question of the causes and remedies of the Depression before he joined the Brain Trust. See Reminiscences of Adolf Berle, Oral History Project, Columbia University, 1969, 1, and Reminiscences of Adolf Berle, Part 2, Oral History Project, Columbia University, 1970, 167. On Berle's age, see Burns, *Roosevelt: The Lion and the Fox*, 154.

88. Reminiscences of Adolf Berle, Part 2, Oral History Project, Columbia University, 1970, 167.

89. Adolf A. Berle and Louis Faulkner, "The Nature of the Difficulty," May 1932, reproduced in Beatrice Bishop Berle and Travis Beal Jacobs, eds., *Navigating the Rapids, 1918–1971: From the Papers of Adolf A. Berle* (New York: Harcourt Brace Jovanovich, 1973), 32–50, hereafter Berle and Faulkner, "The Nature of the Difficulty."

90. On the drafting of the speech, see Moley, *After Seven Years*, 12, and Tugwell, *Brains Trust*, 50.

91. Franklin D. Roosevelt, "St. Paul, Minnesota—Jefferson Day Dinner Address," April 18, 1932, MSF, Box 9, (473), FDRL, http://www.fdrlibrary.marist.edu/_resources/images /msf/msf00483. For Moley and Tugwell's handwritten draft containing the "real security" phrase, see p. 5 of Moley and Tugwell handwritten speech fragments, n.d. [April 1932], Moley Papers (68008), Box 284, (FD Roosevelt Schedule A), (Folder 1), HIA. It is not clear whether Moley and Tugwell drafted that phrase on their own or in conversation with Roosevelt. The page is in Moley's handwriting and is labeled "Insert A," which often—but not always—indicated that it was a Roosevelt dictation, or something Roosevelt and his speechwriters concocted together while polishing a speech.

92. Roosevelt, "St. Paul, Minnesota—Jefferson Day Dinner Address," April 18, 1932, FDRL.

93. Ibid. The language is again largely Moley's. See p. 7 of Moley and Tugwell handwritten speech fragments, n.d. [April 1932], Moley Papers (68008), Box 284, (FD Roosevelt Schedule A), (Folder 1), HIA.

94. For instance, Roosevelt's speech before a civic club in Troy, New York, on March 3, 1912—though far less eloquent than his presidential addresses—shows how his views on the meaning of liberty remained much the same. See Roosevelt, "Troy, New York," March 3, 1912, FDRL.

95. Based on a reading of Roosevelt's 1910 campaign speeches and keyword searches of subsequent speeches available in the Franklin D. Roosevelt Presidential Library's Master Speech File, the most extensive collection available of Roosevelt's speeches and speech drafts dating to 1898: http://fdrlibrary.marist.edu/archives/collections/franklin /index.php?p=collections/findingaid&id=582. The term "security" also does not appear in the second volume, covering 1905–1928, of the collection of Roosevelt's personal letters that his son Elliott published. See Elliott Roosevelt, ed. *F. D. R., His Personal Letters, 1905–1928* (New York: Duell, Sloan and Pearce, 1970). In his 1930 Armistice Day speech in Boston, Roosevelt juxtaposed the people like him who believed in using the state to better "the safety, security, and happiness of every individual in the Nation" against "the forces of conservatism, of selfishness, of greed." See Franklin D. Roosevelt, "Boston, MA—Armistice Day Speech," November 11, 1930, MSF, Box 8, (410), http://www.fdrlibrary.marist.edu/_resources/images/msf/msf00415.

96. Moley, Tugwell, and Berle all later recalled that "security" was the common denominator as early as the 1932 campaign. See Tugwell, *Brains Trust*, 157; Moley, *After Seven Years*, 310; Adolf A. Berle, "Intellectuals and New Deals," *The New Republic*, March 7, 1964.

97. Rosenman, *Working with Roosevelt*, 64; Moley, *After Seven Years*, 22–23.

98. Brain Trust handwritten and typed drafts of recovery program, n.d. [1932], Moley Papers (68008), Box 282, (FD Roosevelt Schedule A), (Folder 4), HIA.

99. Rosenman, *Working with Roosevelt*, 65.

100. Ibid.

101. Ernest Lindley, a journalist who was also an admirer and occasional advisor, drafted the speech and Roosevelt delivered it largely as written. On Lindley and his role in the Oglethorpe speech, see Rosenman, *Working with Roosevelt*, 65–66; Tugwell, *Brains Trust*, 93–95, 103–105; Schlesinger Jr., *Crisis of the Old Order*, 402; and Alonzo L. Hamby, *Man of Destiny: FDR and the Making of the American Century* (New York: Basic Books, 2015), 148.

102. Franklin D. Roosevelt, "Atlanta, Georgia—Oglethorpe University Commencement Address," May 22, 1932, MSF, Box 9, (476), FDRL, http://www.fdrlibrary.marist.edu /_resources/images/msf/msf00486.

103. Ibid.

104. Ibid.

105. Ibid.

106. Ibid.

107. Ibid.

108. Reminiscences of Adolf Berle, Part 2, Oral History Project, Columbia University, 1970, 169.

109. Tugwell, *Brains Trust*, xvi, and Berle and Jacobs, eds., *Navigating the Rapids, 1918–1971*, 32.

110. Berle and Faulkner, "The Nature of the Difficulty," 34, 43.

111. Ibid., 33.

112. Ibid., 43.

113. Not counting an eighth appearance in its adjectival, financial sense: "security holdings." Moley and FDR marked up draft of 1932 Democratic nomination acceptance speech, n.d. [July 1932], Moley Papers (68008), Box 284, (FD Roosevelt Schedule A), (Folder 6), HIA. On Moley's drafting of the speech, see Moley, *After Seven Years*, 25–27.

114. Moley, *After Seven Years*, 26–34; Rosenman, *Working with Roosevelt*, 67. For marked up drafts of the speech, see Moley and FDR marked up draft of 1932 Democratic nomination acceptance speech, n.d. [July 1932], Moley Papers (68008), Box 284, (FD Roosevelt Schedule A), (Folder 6), HIA; Roosevelt, "Chicago, Illinois—Acceptance Speech on Receiving Nomination," July 2, 1932, FDRL; and Franklin D. Roosevelt, "Chicago, Illinois—Acceptance Speech for Presidential Nomination," July 2, 1932, MSF, Box 9, (483A), FDRL, http://www.fdrlibrary.marist.edu/_resources/images/msf/msf00494.

115. Schlesinger Jr., *Crisis of the Old Order*, 313.

116. Hamby, *Man of Destiny*, 153.

117. Roosevelt, "Chicago, Illinois—Acceptance Speech on Receiving Nomination," July 2, 1932, FDRL.

118. Ibid.

119. Ibid.

120. Ibid.

121. Berle and Faulkner, "The Nature of the Difficulty," 43.

122. Roosevelt, "Chicago, Illinois—Acceptance Speech on Receiving Nomination," July 2, 1932, FDRL.

123. Ibid.

124. Ibid.

125. On the content of the address, see Tugwell, *Brains Trust*, 372–385.

126. Franklin D. Roosevelt, "Albany, New York—Radio Address—The Democratic Platform," July 30, 1932, MSF, Box 10, (488), FDRL, http://www.fdrlibrary.marist.edu/_resources/images/msf/msf00500 and https://www.fdrlibrary.org/documents/356632/405112/afdr006.mp3/2a470a45-9806-4a02-bf27-c56e64805f0e.

127. Raymond Moley to Eva Moley, August 1, 1932, Moley Papers, Box 1, (1932), FDRL.

128. Roosevelt, "Albany, New York—Radio Address—The Democratic Platform," July 30, 1932, FDRL.

129. Ibid.

130. Tully, *F. D. R., My Boss*, 88–89, and Lepore, *These Truths*, 428.

131. Lepore, *These Truths*, 422.

132. Susan J. Douglas, *Listening In: Radio and the American Imagination* (Minneapolis: University of Minnesota Press, 2004), 128, 131; Hadley Cantril and Gordon Allport, *The Psychology of Radio* (New York: Harper, 1935), 14.

133. Brown, *Manipulating the Ether*, xi.

134. Douglas, *Listening In*, 4.

135. Ibid., and generally.

136. Anthony Storr, *Music and the Mind* (New York: Free Press, 1992), 26, quoted in Douglas, *Listening In*, 23.

137. Douglas, *Listening In*, 5.

138. On "imagined community," see Benedict Anderson, *Imagined Communities: Reflections on the Origins and Spread of Nationalism* (New York: Verso, 1983). Douglas expands on Anderson's work by arguing that radio superseded newspapers as the primary means by which "imagined communities" were constructed. See Douglas, *Listening In*, 23.

139. On the narrative construction of reality, see Bruner, "The Narrative Construction of Reality."

140. Eleanor Roosevelt, *This I Remember*, 73–74.

141. Douglas, *Listening In*, 8.

142. Frances Perkins, *The Roosevelt I Knew* (New York: Viking, 1946), 69–70.

143. Ibid., 70–71.

144. Quoted in Brown, *Manipulating the Ether*, 27.

145. Roosevelt, "Albany, New York—Radio Address—The Democratic Platform," July 30, 1932.

146. Herbert Hoover, "Address Accepting the Republican Presidential Nomination," August 11, 1932, APP, https://www.presidency.ucsb.edu/node/207366.

147. Franklin D. Roosevelt, "Columbus, Ohio—Campaign Speech," August 20, 1932, MSF, Box 10, (490), FDRL, http://www.fdrlibrary.marist.edu/_resources/images/msf/msf00502.

148. Ibid.

149. Ibid.

150. Ibid.

151. On "educational trip for me," see Franklin D. Roosevelt, "Goodland, Kansas—Extemporaneous remarks," September 15, 1932, MSF, Box 10, (500), FDRL, http://www.fdrlibrary.marist.edu/_resources/images/msf/msf00512. On the real purpose of the trip, see Franklin D. Roosevelt, "Denver, Colorado—Extemporaneous remarks at dinner in his honor—8:00 p.m.," September 15, 1932, MSF, Box 10, (503), FDRL, http://www.fdrlibrary.marist.edu/_resources/images/msf/msf00515.

152. Moley handwritten notes on 1932 campaign, n.d. [1932], Moley Papers (68008), Box 282, (FD Roosevelt Schedule A), (Folder 13), HIA.

153. Moley, *After Seven Years*, 52–56.

154. Franklin D. Roosevelt, "Topeka, Kansas—Campaign Speech," September 14, 1932, MSF, Box 10, (498), FDRL, http://www.fdrlibrary.marist.edu/_resources/images/msf/msf00510.

155. Franklin D. Roosevelt, "Salt Lake City—Speech at Mormon Temple," September 17, 1932, MSF, Box 10, (508), FDRL, http://www.fdrlibrary.marist.edu/_resources/images/msf/msf00520.

156. Ibid.

157. Roosevelt, "Denver, Colorado—Extemporaneous remarks at dinner in his honor—8:00 p.m.," September 15, 1932, FDRL.

158. Ibid.

159. Ibid.

160. Ibid.

161. Ibid.

162. Franklin D. Roosevelt, "San Francisco, California—Commonwealth Club Speech," September 23, 1932, MSF, Box 10, (522), FDRL, http://www.fdrlibrary.marist.edu /_resources/images/msf/msf00534.

163. Ibid.

164. Ibid.

165. Ibid.

166. Ibid.

167. Ibid.

168. See Roosevelt, "Troy, New York," March 3, 1912, FDRL.

169. Roosevelt, "San Francisco, California—Commonwealth Club Speech," September 23, 1932, FDRL. Roosevelt's Commonwealth Club speech differed in tone from most of his other campaign addresses and has been a source of disagreement among historians ever since, some of whom have dismissed it as an aberration that reflected Adolf Berle's views rather than Roosevelt's. Although it is true that Berle provided the first draft of the speech, it was not an aberration but a synthesis of the conclusions that Roosevelt and the Brain Trust had formed over the preceding months. On the speech, see also Schlesinger Jr., *Crisis of the Old Order*, 426; Kennedy, *Freedom from Fear*, 123; Moley, *After Seven Years*, 57–58; and Robert Eden, "On the Origins of the Regime of Pragmatic Liberalism: John Dewey, Adolf A. Berle, and FDR's Commonwealth Club Address of 1932," *Studies in American Political Development* 7, no. 1 (1993): 74–150.

170. It is no exaggeration to suggest, as David Green has, that "in transforming the popularly accepted meaning of the word 'liberal,' Roosevelt transformed people's expectations of government." Green, *Language of Politics in America*, 120.

171. Moley draft of FDR Milwaukee campaign speech, September 30, 1932, Moley Papers (68008), Box 287, (FD Roosevelt Schedule A), (Folder 10), HIA.

172. Roosevelt, "Albany, New York—Radio Address Social Welfare and Government," October 13, 1932, FDRL.

173. Green, *Language of Politics in America*, 120.

174. Moley to Farley, September 27, 1932, Moley Papers (68008), Box 284, (FD Roosevelt Schedule A), (Folder 8), HIA.

175. Ibid.

176. Herbert Hoover, "Address at Madison Square Garden in New York City," October 31, 1932, APP, https://www.presidency.ucsb.edu/node/208073.

177. Ibid.

178. Ibid.

179. Ibid.

180. Ibid.

181. Ibid. On Hoover's expansion of the federal government's responsibilities, see Kennedy, *Freedom from Fear*, 81–85. Eric Rauchway is right to emphasize that "the contest between [Hoover and Roosevelt] had deep roots in stark philosophical differences that they clearly expressed on the campaign trail." See Rauchway, *Winter War*, 14–15.

182. Moley, *After Seven Years*, 64.

183. Franklin D. Roosevelt, "Boston, Massachusetts—Campaign Address from Boston Arena," October 31, 1932, MSF, Box 12, (582), FDRL, http://www.fdrlibrary.marist.edu /_resources/images/msf/msf00594.

184. Ibid., 37.

185. Ibid., 37–38.

186. Ibid., 39.

187. Tugwell, *Brains Trust*, 484.

188. Franklin D. Roosevelt, "New York City, New York—Address Republican for Roosevelt League," November 3, 1932, MSF, Box 12, (583), FDRL, http://www.fdrlibrary.marist .edu/_resources/images/msf/msf00595.

189. Reminiscences of Frances Perkins, Part 3, Session 1, Columbia University Oral History Research Office, 1955, 463, http://www.columbia.edu/cu/lweb/digital/collections/nny /perkinsf/transcripts/perkinsf_3_1_463.html. For the date of Perkins's speech, which is not given in her oral history interview, see "Baker Urges Election of Roosevelt: Says Republican Tariff Policy Has Caused Intense Economic War with Rest of World," *Hartford Courant*, November 3, 1932.

190. Reminiscences of Frances Perkins, Part 3, Session 1, Columbia University Oral History Research Office, 1955, 463, http://www.columbia.edu/cu/lweb/digital/collections/nny /perkinsf/transcripts/perkinsf_3_1_463.html.

191. So did the immediate reaction of Harvard Law professor and fellow Roosevelt advisor Felix Frankfurter, who—in the gushing style of flattery that was his custom—"came rushing forward, grabbed me by both hands, kissed me and said, 'Frances, you have invented a new political speech." Reminiscences of Frances Perkins, Part 3, Session 1, Columbia University Oral History Research Office, 1955, 463–464, http://www .columbia.edu/cu/lweb/digital/collections/nny/perkinsf/transcripts/perkinsf_3_1_463 .html.

192. Hoover, "Address at Madison Square Garden in New York City," October 31, 1932, APP.

193. Lindley, *Roosevelt Revolution*, 34.

194. Schlesinger Jr., *Crisis of the Old Order*, 438.

195. Hamby, *Man of Destiny*, 163.

2. The Domestic Policy Origins of the National Security State

1. The Twentieth Amendment, which moved presidential inaugurations to January, did not come into force until the next election cycle.

2. Kennedy, *Freedom from Fear*, 132.

3. On "Security of Savings," see Berle and Faulkner, "The Nature of the Difficulty," 34.

4. Kennedy, *Freedom from Fear*, 132–133.

5. "Technical Note: Labor Force, Employment, and Unemployment, 1929–1939: Estimating Methods," U.S. Bureau of Labor Statistics, 1948, https://www.bls.gov/opub /mlr/1948/article/pdf/labor-force-employment-and-unemployment-1929-39-estimating -methods.pdf. On "Security of Work," see Berle and Faulkner, "The Nature of the Difficulty," 43.

6. Kennedy, *Freedom from Fear*, 87.

7. Franklin D. Roosevelt, "Washington, D.C.—Inaugural Address," March 4, 1933, MSF, Box 13, (610), FDRL, http://www.fdrlibrary.marist.edu/_resources/images/msf /msf00628 and https://www.fdrlibrary.org/documents/356632/405112/afdr012.mp3 /92b01969-c0ce-4e37-ad86-2a1fd78f39f7. The preparation of Roosevelt's first inaugural address has generated much confusion, some of it perpetuated by those who may have wished Roosevelt had written the entire thing himself. Raymond Moley provides a full account of how he drafted the speech and then polished it with Roosevelt, with Louis Howe adding the line about "fear" for which the speech became famous. See Moley, *First New Deal*, 96–119. For a detailed examination of the speech, see also Davis W. Houck, *FDR and Fear Itself: The First Inaugural Address* (College Station: Texas A&M University Press, 2002).

8. Roosevelt, "Washington, D.C.—Inaugural Address," March 4, 1933, FDRL. On the attendance at the inaugural and the size of the radio audience, see Ryan, *Franklin D. Roosevelt's Rhetorical Presidency*, 81.

9. Corcoran quoted in Ken Burns, *The Roosevelts: An Intimate History*, Episode 4, September 14, 2014, http://www.pbs.org/kenburns/the-roosevelts.

10. On Roosevelt's use of military language in his first inaugural address, see Ryan, *Franklin D. Roosevelt's Rhetorical Presidency*, 77–78 and 81–84.

11. Roosevelt, "Washington, D.C.—Inaugural Address," March 4, 1933, FDRL.

12. Ibid.

13. Ibid.

14. Franklin D. Roosevelt, "Advisory Council of the National Conference on Economic Security," November 14, 1934, MSF, Box 20, (746), FDRL, http://www.fdrlibrary.marist .edu/_resources/images/msf/msf00767.

15. On "Security of Savings" and "Security of Work," see Berle and Faulkner, "The Nature of the Difficulty," 34, 43.

16. Franklin D. Roosevelt, "Fireside Chat #2—'Outlining the New Deal Program,'" May 7, 1933, MSF, Box 14, (627), FDRL, http://www.fdrlibrary.marist.edu/_resources/images /msf/msf00646 and https://www.fdrlibrary.org/documents/356632/405112/afdr014 .mp3/943f2504-4303-4303-bbff-8a72b13db2ca.

17. Franklin D. Roosevelt, "Statement upon Signing the Social Security Act," August 14, 1935, MSF, Box 22, (791), FDRL, http://www.fdrlibrary.marist.edu/_resources/images /msf/msf00814 and https://www.fdrlibrary.org/documents/356632/405112/afdr025 .mp3/1ca81dab-949d-4beb-8bf1-74f3364d703d.

18. Roosevelt, "Washington, D.C.—Inaugural Address," March 4, 1933, FDRL.

19. Kennedy, *Freedom from Fear*, 135.

20. On the banking crisis, see Kennedy, *Freedom from Fear*, 131–137; Arthur M. Schlesinger Jr., *The Coming of the New Deal, 1933–1935: The Age of Roosevelt, Vol. 2* (Boston: Mariner Books, 2003), 4–8.

21. Kennedy, *Freedom from Fear*, 135.

22. Ibid., 135–136.

23. Ibid.

24. On the use of language to transform the public's expectations of government, see Green, *Language of Politics in America*, 120.

25. Franklin D. Roosevelt, "Fireside Chat #1—The Banking Crisis," March 12, 1933, MSF, Box 14, (616a), FDRL, http://www.fdrlibrary.marist.edu/_resources/images/msf /msf00635 and https://www.fdrlibrary.org/documents/356632/405112/afdr013.mp3 /097bd699-7563-49a0-8191-0db3bf313d4b.

26. Ibid.

27. On Roosevelt's tone, see Ibid. On the speech, see also Moley, *First New Deal*, 195–196, and Kennedy, *Freedom from Fear*, 136.

28. Kennedy, *Freedom from Fear*, 136–137.

29. Davis Houck rightly notes that "confidence and legislation . . . were . . . symbiotic." See Houck, *Rhetoric as Currency*, 179.

30. For drafts of the speech, see Moley notes for FDR speech, May 6, 1933, Moley Papers (68008), Box 289, (FD Roosevelt Schedule A), (Folder 8), HIA, and Roosevelt, "Fireside Chat #2—'Outlining the New Deal Program,'" May 7, 1933, FDRL.

31. Roosevelt, "Fireside Chat #2—'Outlining the New Deal Program,'" May 7, 1933, FDRL.

32. Ibid.

33. Ibid.

34. Ibid.

35. Ibid.

36. Andrew Preston similarly emphasizes that Roosevelt's use of the term "national security" here had nothing to do with foreign relations. See Preston, "Monsters Everywhere," 489–490.

37. Moley, *After Seven Years*, 189.

38. On Moley's level of involvement in each speech, see Moley, *First New Deal*, 194–196, 290, 477.

39. For Moley's draft, see Roosevelt, "Fireside Chat #2—'Outlining the New Deal Program,'" May 7, 1933, FDRL, 24–42. For Moley's handwritten notes on the speech, see Moley notes for FDR speech, May 6, 1933, Moley Papers (68008), Box 289, (FD Roosevelt Schedule A), (Folder 8), HIA.

40. Roosevelt, "Fireside Chat #2—'Outlining the New Deal Program,'" May 7, 1933, FDRL, 29.

41. Ibid., 12.

42. Ibid. Roosevelt added "well-rounded" when he delivered the address.

43. Berle and Faulkner, "The Nature of the Difficulty," 43.

44. On the Agricultural Adjustment Act, see Kennedy, *Freedom from Fear*, 139–144.

45. For a concise summary of the National Industrial Recovery Act, see Kennedy, *Freedom from Fear*, 151–152.

46. On the relationship between the AAA and the NIRA, see Kennedy, *Freedom from Fear*, 151–152. For an early critique of the administration's initial approach to delivering economic security, see Frederick Horner Bunting, "Two Roads to National Security," *Sewanee Review* 42, no. 1 (January–March 1934): 80–88. Bunting agreed with the administration's objectives but argued that the administration's approach to economic insecurity amounted to a policy of nationalism that would ultimately fail.

47. Roosevelt, "Albany, New York—Message to the Legislature," January 6, 1932, FDRL.

48. Tugwell handwritten speech fragment, n.d. [April 1932], Moley Papers (68008), Box 284, (FD Roosevelt Schedule A), (Folder 1), HIA. The handwriting appears to be

Tugwell's, but the language sounds like Roosevelt. The people working with Roosevelt on his speeches often took dictation from him, and it is possible that Roosevelt dictated this text to Tugwell.

49. Franklin D. Roosevelt, "Washington, D.C.—Annual Message to Congress," January 3, 1934, MSF, Box 17, (673), FDRL, http://www.fdrlibrary.marist.edu/_resources/images /msf/msf00693.

50. For speech notes, outlines, and drafts, see Moley Papers (68008), Box 289, (FD Roosevelt Schedule A), (Folders 15–16, 18), HIA; Franklin D. Roosevelt, "Message to Congress in re the Recovery Program," June 8, 1934, MSF, Box 18, (710), FDRL, http:// www.fdrlibrary.marist.edu/_resources/images/msf/msf00730; Franklin D. Roosevelt, "Message to Congress in re the Drought," MSF, Box 18, (711), FDRL, http://www .fdrlibrary.marist.edu/_resources/images/msf/msf00731; and Franklin D. Roosevelt, "Fireside Chat #5," MSF, Box 18, (713), FDRL, http://www.fdrlibrary.marist.edu /_resources/images/msf/msf00734. For Moley's recollections on working on the messages, see Moley, *After Seven Years*, 291, and Moley, *First New Deal*, 520–522.

51. On the drafting process, see Moley, *After Seven Years*, 291–292. For the many notes, drafts, and revisions of these important messages, see Moley Papers (68008), Box 289, (FD Roosevelt Schedule A), (Folders 16 and 18), HIA.

52. Moley draft fragments on security for FDR's "security" speech, June 8, 1934, Moley Papers (68008), Box 289, (FD Roosevelt Schedule A), (Folder 16), HIA.

53. Moley typed draft fragments for FDR's "security" speech, June 8, 1934, Moley Papers (68008), Box 289, (FD Roosevelt Schedule A), (Folder 16), HIA.

54. Uncorrected Moley first draft fragments of FDR's "security" speech, June 8, 1934, Moley Papers (68008), Box 289, (FD Roosevelt Schedule A), (Folder 16), HIA.

55. Moley outline for FDR's "security" fireside chat, June 28, 1934, Moley Papers (68008), Box 289, (FD Roosevelt Schedule A), (Folder 18), HIA, and Moley draft speech fragments, n.d. [1934], Moley Papers (68008), Box 283, (FD Roosevelt Schedule A), (Folder 26), HIA.

56. Moley typed draft fragments for FDR's "security" speech, June 8, 1934, Moley Papers (68008), Box 289, (FD Roosevelt Schedule A), (Folder 16), HIA.

57. Franklin D. Roosevelt, "Message to Congress—Control and Development of Water Resources," June 4, 1934, MSF, Box 18, (709), FDRL, http://www.fdrlibrary.marist .edu/_resources/images/msf/msf00729.

58. Ibid.

59. Roosevelt, "Message to Congress in re the Recovery Program," June 8, 1934, FDRL.

60. Ibid.

61. Ibid.

62. Ibid.

63. Ibid.

64. Ibid.

65. Franklin D. Roosevelt, "Informal remarks to the National Emergency Council," June 26, 1934, MSF, Box 18, (712a), FDR, http://www.fdrlibrary.marist.edu/_resources /images/msf/msf00733.

66. Ibid.

67. Roosevelt, "Fireside Chat #5," June 28, 1934, FDRL.

68. Ibid.

69. Ibid.

70. "Social Security History: FDR's Statements on Social Security," Social Security Administration, https://www.ssa.gov/history/fdrstmts.html#exec. See also Franklin D. Roosevelt, Executive Orders and Presidential Proclamations, 1933–1936, Series 1, 6757, FDRL. The text of the order, as signed by Roosevelt, is available on page 3 of http://www.fdrlibrary.marist.edu/_resources/images/eo/eo0021.pdf.

71. Ibid.

72. Perkins, *Roosevelt I Knew*, 269.

73. Reminiscences of Frances Perkins, Part 3, Session 1, Columbia University Oral History Research Office, 1955, 569, http://www.columbia.edu/cu/lweb/digital/collections/nny/perkinsf/transcripts/perkinsf_3_1_569.html.

74. Ibid., 600–602, and Downey, *Woman Behind the New Deal*, 11.

75. Perkins, *Roosevelt I Knew*, 266.

76. Perkins to McIntyre, December 22, 1933, PPF 1820, Box 1, (Speech Materials and Suggestions, 1933), FDRL.

77. Downey, *Woman Behind the New Deal*, 265.

78. Perkins, *Roosevelt I Knew*, 266.

79. Ibid., 268.

80. Edwin Witte, "Birth and Early Days of Social Security in the U.S.," Social Security History, October 1955, https://www.ssa.gov/history/ew25.html.

81. Franklin D. Roosevelt, "Bonneville, Oregon—Informal remarks," August 3, 1934, MSF, Box 18, (718), FDRL, http://www.fdrlibrary.marist.edu/_resources/images/msf/msf00739.

82. Franklin D. Roosevelt, "Fireside Chat #6 Moving Forward to Greater Freedom and Greater Security," September 30, 1934, MSF, Box 19, (740), FDRL, http://www.fdrlibrary.marist.edu/_resources/images/msf/msf00761 and https://www.fdrlibrary.org/documents/356632/405112/afdr019.mp3/024ad358-afb9-4bb9-8d7f-f8668dfe4266.

83. Ibid.

84. Ibid.

85. Ibid.

86. Donald R. Richberg, "The National Emergency Council," *Vital Speeches of the Day* 1, no. 2 (October 22, 1934): 57.

87. Kennedy, *Freedom from Fear*, 215.

88. Hopkins quoted in Sherwood, *Roosevelt and Hopkins*, 65.

89. "Security," November 24, 1934, Moley Papers (68008), Box 118, (Indexed Subject File), (Folder 1), HIA, 5.

90. Ibid.

91. Ibid.

92. Roosevelt, "Fireside Chat #6 Moving Forward to Greater Freedom and Greater Security," September 30, 1934, FDRL and "Security," November 24, 1934, Moley Papers (68008), Box 118, (Indexed Subject File), (Folder 1), HIA.

93. "Security," November 24, 1934, Moley Papers (68008), Box 118, (Indexed Subject File), (Folder 1), HIA, 6.

94. Ibid., 29.

95. Roosevelt, "Advisory Council of the National Conference on Economic Security," November 14, 1934, FDRL.

96. Ibid.

97. Franklin D. Roosevelt, "Message to the Congress on the State of the Union," January 4, 1935, MSF, Box 20, (759), FDRL, http://www.fdrlibrary.marist.edu/_resources/images /msf/msf00780.

98. Ibid.

99. Ibid.

100. Ibid.

101. Ibid.

102. Thomas H. Eliot, *Recollections of the New Deal: When the People Mattered* (Boston: Northeastern University Press, 1992), 101, and Witte, "Birth and Early Days of Social Security in the U.S."

103. Perkins, *Roosevelt I Knew*, 273; The Development of the Social Security Act: An Interview with Dr. Edwin E. Witte, Social Security History, August 12, 1955, https:// www.ssa.gov/history/witte2.html; Kennedy, *Freedom from Fear*, 262.

104. Witte, "Birth and Early Days of Social Security in the U.S."; Eliot, *Recollections of the New Deal*, 100–104.

105. U.S. Congress, House, *Economic Security Act: Hearings before the Committee on Ways and Means*, 74th. Cong., 1st sess., January 21, 22, 23, 24, 25, 26, 28, 29, 30, 31 and February 1, 2, 4, 5, 6, 7, 8, and 12, 1935, 170.

106. U.S. Committee on Economic Security, Report to the President of the Committee on Economic Security (Washington, DC: Government Printing Office, 1935), 1–2, https:// hdl.handle.net/2027/mdp.39015023138301.

107. Ibid., 2.

108. Franklin D. Roosevelt, "Message to Congress re Economic Security Program," January 17, 1935, MSF, Box 20, (761), FDRL, http://www.fdrlibrary.marist.edu /_resources/images/msf/msf00782.

109. Ibid.

110. Witte, "Birth and Early Days of Social Security in the U.S."

111. Eliot, *Recollections of the New Deal*, 110.

112. Kiran Klaus Patel offers the interesting hypothesis that the change in name reflected the desire of Perkins and other "New Dealers" to "broaden[] their concept of security beyond the economic realm and immediate emergency legislation, while carefully avoiding identification with the idea of 'welfare' more broadly." See Patel, *New Deal*, 201.

113. Franklin D. Roosevelt, "Fireside Chat #7—Works Relief Program," April 28, 1935, MSF, Box 21, FDRL, http://www.fdrlibrary.marist.edu/_resources/images/msf /msf00799 and https://www.fdrlibrary.org/documents/356632/405112/afdr022.mp3 /5aec1343-21e2-4ce9-aa49-9c8d72d1a599.

114. Ibid.

115. Ibid.

116. Roosevelt, "Fireside Chat #7—Works Relief Program," April 28, 1935, FDRL.

117. Kennedy, *Freedom from Fear*, 273.

118. Press Conference 209, May 31, 1935, http://www.fdrlibrary.marist.edu/_resources /images/pc/pc0022.pdf, 17.

119. Ibid.

120. Eliot, *Recollections of the New Deal*, 95.

121. Burns, *Roosevelt: The Lion and the Fox*, 267. For a thoughtful exploration of the intellectual origins and development of Social Security, see Rodgers, *Atlantic Crossings*, 428–446.

122. Roosevelt, "Statement upon Signing the Social Security Act," August 14, 1935, FDRL.

123. On the belief among liberals that the Social Security Act was merely an important first step and that health security would come next, see Klein, *For All These Rights*, 116, and Patel, *New Deal*, 202.

124. Roosevelt, "Statement upon Signing the Social Security Act," August 14, 1935, FDRL.

125. See Sarah E. Igo, "Social Insecurities: Private Data and Public Culture in Modern America," in *Shaped by the State: Toward a New Political History of the Twentieth Century*, Brent Cebul, Lily Geismer, and Mason B. Williams, eds. (Chicago, IL: University of Chicago Press, 2019), 35–44.

126. On Lange's photo, see Dan Bouk, *How Our Days Became Numbered: Risk and the Rise of the Statistical Individual* (Chicago, IL: University of Chicago Press, 2015), 209–236.

127. Igo, "Social Insecurities," 39.

128. Ibid., 37. On the exclusion of many Americans from Social Security's original benefit structure, see (among many sources) the clear summary in Alice Kessler-Harris, *In Pursuit of Equity: Women, Men, and the Quest for Economic Citizenship in 20th-Century America* (New York: Oxford University Press, 2001), 88–100.

129. Patel, *New Deal*, 201.

130. Franklin D. Roosevelt, "Radio Address to Young Democratic Clubs of America Convention," August 24, 1935, MSF, Box 22, (795), FDRL, http://www.fdrlibrary .marist.edu/_resources/images/msf/msf00818 and https://www.fdrlibrary.org /documents/356632/405112/afdr027.mp3/4797a03b-44ad-4700-89e0-51647c60ae22.

131. Ibid.

132. Ibid.

133. FDR notes dictated for 1935 Western trip speeches, September 22, 1935, Moley Papers (68008), Box 291, (FD Roosevelt Schedule A), (Folder 9), HIA.

134. Franklin D. Roosevelt, "Los Angeles, California—Address from Memorial Coliseum," October 1, 1935, MSF, Box 23, (806), FDRL, http://www.fdrlibrary.marist.edu /_resources/images/msf/msf00829.

135. Franklin D. Roosevelt, "San Diego, California—Address at San Diego Exhibition," October 2, 1935, MSF, Box 23, (807), FDRL, http://www.fdrlibrary.marist.edu /_resources/images/msf/msf00830.

136. Roosevelt, "Fireside Chat #7—Works Relief Program," April 28, 1935, FDRL.

137. Ibid.

138. Ibid.

139. Ibid. For Roosevelt's handwritten insertion into the speech, see p. 2 of FDR marked-up fourth draft of fireside chat, n.d. [April 1935], Moley Papers (68008), Box 290, (FD Roosevelt Schedule A), (Folder 13), HIA.

140. Cook, "Introduction," in Emblidge, ed., *My Day*, xiv.

141. Emblidge, ed., *My Day*, 14.

142. For the phrase, see Eleanor Roosevelt, "My Day," October 5, 1936, The Eleanor Roosevelt Papers, Digital Edition, https://www2.gwu.edu/~erpapers/myday/displaydoc .cfm?_y=1936&_f=md054453.

143. For a concise summary of the program's origins and functioning and to see the resulting works, see The FSA-OWI, Photogrammar, http://photogrammar.yale.edu /about/fsa_owi/. For a summary of historians' interpretations of the program, see Jillian Russo, "Photogrammar: A New Look at New Deal Photography," *American Quarterly* 68, no. 2 (June 2016): 441–442.

144. E. Pendleton Herring, "Official Publicity under the New Deal," *The Annals of the American Academy of Political and Social Science* 179 (May 1935): 167–175. Ewen cites the same quote in his history of public relations. See Ewen, *PR!*, 289–290.

145. Herring, "Official Publicity under the New Deal," 171.

146. On Hanson, see Edwin Emery, *History of the American Newspaper Publishers Association* (St. Paul: University of Minnesota Press, 1950), 221–244, and Samuel T. Williamson, *Frank Gannett: A Biography* (New York: Duell, Sloan & Pearce, 1940), 209–210.

147. Elisha Hanson, "Official Propaganda and the New Deal," *Annals of the American Academy of Political and Social Science* 179, no. 1 (May 1935): 176.

148. Ibid.

149. Ibid., 186.

3. The Conservative Counteroffensive

1. On the size of the crowd and Barton's speech, see Felix Bruner, "Trade Chiefs Gather to Ask Government for Freedom," *Washington Post*, December 4, 1935; "Barton Outlines Plan for Fight on Politicians," *New York Herald Tribune*, December 5, 1935; and Marchand, *Creating the Corporate Soul*, 202–203.

2. Bruce Barton, "Business Can Win Public from Politician," *Printers' Ink* 173, no. 11 (December 12, 1935): 17.

3. Barton, "Business Can Win Public from Politician," 17.

4. Ibid., 20.

5. Ibid.

6. Ibid., 24.

7. Ibid., 24.

8. Ibid., 20.

9. Existing works on aspects of the NAM campaign include Walker and Sklar, *Business Finds Its Voice*; Congress, Senate, Subcommittee of the Committee on Education and Labor, Violations of Free Speech and Rights of Labor- Hearings Pursuant to S. Res. 266, 74th–76th Congs., 1936–1940, Part III, hereafter "LaFollette Committee Report"; Richard W. Gable, "A Political Analysis of an Employers' Association: The National Association of Manufacturers," (Ph.D. diss., University of Chicago, 1950); Tedlow, "The National Association of Manufacturers and Public Relations during the New

Deal"; Colleen Ann Moore, "The National Association of Manufacturers: The Voice of Industry and the Free Enterprise Campaign in the Schools, 1929–1949," (Ph.D. diss., University of Akron, 1985); Ewen, *PR!*, 299–322; Fones-Wolf, *Selling Free Enterprise*, 24–29; Andrew Workman, "Manufacturing Power: The Organizational Revival of the National Association of Manufacturers, 1941–1945," *Business History Review* 72, no. 2 (Summer 1998); Bird Jr., *Better Living*, 53–117; Wall, *Inventing the "American Way,"* 34–35, 48–62, 129–131; Phillips-Fein, *Invisible Hands*, 13–15; Wilson, *Destructive Creation*, 92–252; Jennifer Delton, *The Industrialists: How the National Association of Manufacturers Shaped American Capitalism* (Princeton, NJ: Princeton University Press, 2020), 107–110 and 136–140, and Whitham, *Corporate Conservatives Go to War*, 32–36 and generally.

10. On NAM as the "spearhead," see Wall, *Inventing the "American Way,"* 53, and Phillips-Fein, *Invisible Hands*, 13–15.

11. Among many examples of works presenting the conservative movement as a reaction against the New Deal, see Kennedy, *Freedom from Fear*, 214; Donald T. Critchlow, *The Conservative Ascendency: How the GOP Right Made Political History* (Cambridge, MA: Harvard University Press, 2007), 1–14; Phillips-Fein, *Invisible Hands*, generally; Kathryn S. Olmsted, *Right Out of California: The 1930s and the Big Business Roots of Modern Conservatism* (New York: The New Press, 2015), 7; and Huntington, *Far-Right Vanguard*, 4. Other scholars date the emergence of the conservative movement later, to the late 1940s, the 1950s, or the 1960s. See, for example, Nash, *Conservative Intellectual Movement in America since 1945*; Patrick Allitt, *The Conservatives: Ideas and Personalities Throughout American History* (New Haven, CT: Yale University Press, 2009), 2, 159; Rick Perlstein, *Before the Storm: Barry Goldwater and the Unmaking of the American Consensus* (New York: Hill and Wang, 2001); Lisa McGirr, *Suburban Warriors: The Origins of the New American Right* (Princeton, NJ: Princeton University Press, 2001); Elizabeth Tandy Shermer, "Origins of the Conservative Ascendancy: Barry Goldwater's Early Senate Career and the De-Legitimization of Organized Labor," *Journal of American History* 95, no. 3 (2008): 678–709.

12. These business leaders served as what Julian Zelizer calls "the money-men of the Right." There were, of course, many other people who could claim leadership roles in the nascent conservative movement—but most of them depended on the financial resources and organizational abilities of these business leaders. Zelizer, "Rethinking the History of American Conservatism," 370. On the role of these business leaders, see also Rudolph, "The American Liberty League, 1934–1940," 21–22, 32; Wolfskill, *Revolt of the Conservatives*; Burk; *Corporate State and Broker State*; Phillips-Fein, *Invisible Hands*, 58, 86, and generally; and Bowes, "Every Citizen a Sentinel! Every Home a Sentry Box!"

13. For other efforts to date the origins of the modern American conservative movement before the wave of New Deal reaction, see Lynn Dumenil, "'The Insatiable Maw of Bureaucracy': Antistatism and Education Reform in the 1920s," *Journal of American History* 77, no. 2 (1990): 499–524; Donald T. Critchlow, "Rethinking American Conservatism: Toward a New Narrative," *Journal of American History* 98, no. 3 (December 2011): 753–754; Romain D. Huret, *American Tax Resisters* (Cambridge,

MA: Harvard University Press, 2014); Nelson Lichtenstein and Elizabeth Tandy Shermer, "Introduction," in *The Right and Labor in America: Politics, Ideology, and Imagination*, eds. Nelson Lichtenstein and Elizabeth Tandy Shermer (Philadelphia, 2012), 4; J. Casey Sullivan, "Way before the Storm: California, the Republican Party, and a New Conservatism," *Journal of Policy History* 26, no. 4 (2014): 568–594; James Casey Sullivan, "Against the Tendencies of the Times: The Republican Party and the Roots of Modern Conservatism, 1900–1930," (Ph.D. diss., University of California, Davis, 2016); and Bowes, "Every Citizen a Sentinel! Every Home a Sentry Box!"

14. "A 1943 Platform for the National Industrial Information Committee," April 28, 1943, NAM Records (1411), Box 1093, (NIIC Administrative—NIIC Program Committee 4-29-43—1943), HML, 4.

15. Berlin, "Two Concepts of Liberty," 166–217.

16. James McKay, "Crusading for Capitalism: Christian Capitalists and the Ideological Roots of the Conservative Movement," (Ph.D. diss., The University of Wisconsin-Madison, 2015), 151–152.

17. Burk, *Corporate State and the Broker State*, 29–30.

18. Ibid. On the role that Prohibition played in the growth of the government's domestic responsibilities, see Lisa McGirr, *The War on Alcohol: Prohibition and the Rise of the State* (New York: W. W. Norton, 2016).

19. Burk, *Corporate State and the Broker State*, 30.

20. Ibid, 30–31.

21. Pierre du Pont quoted in Ibid, 38. On the takeover of the AAPA, see *Report to the Directors, Members, and Friends of the Association Against the Prohibition Amendment, 1928* (Washington, DC: 1929), 1–8, and Fletcher Dobyns, *The Amazing Story of Repeal: An Exposé of the Power of Propaganda* (Chicago: Willet, Clark, 1940), 8–15.

22. On the du Ponts' motivations, see Pierre S. du Pont, *Eighteenth Amendment Not a Remedy for the Drink Evil* (Washington, DC: Association Against the Prohibition Amendment, 1926), 8; Dobyns, *Amazing Story of Repeal*, 17–28; and Burk, *Corporate State and the Broker State*, 35–37.

23. Pierre du Pont quoted in Burk, *Corporate State and the Broker State*, 48. On the fight over the government's responsibilities in the period between 1913 and 1933, see Jesse Tarbert, *When Good Government Meant Big Government: The Quest to Expand Federal Power, 1913–1933* (New York: Columbia University Press, 2022).

24. *Report to the Directors, Members, and Friends of the Association Against the Prohibition Amendment, 1928* (Washington, DC: Association Against the Prohibition Amendment, 1929), 24–31; *Annual Report to the Directors, Members, and Friends of the Association Against the Prohibition Amendment, 1931* (Washington, DC: Association Against the Prohibition Amendment, 1932), 18–9; *32 Reasons for Repeal* (Washington, DC: Association Against the Prohibition Amendment, 1932). For examples of AAPA anti-Prohibition propaganda, see Association Against the Prohibition Amendment postcards and stationery, HML, https://digital.hagley.org/2005204.

25. Burk, *Corporate State and the Broker State*, 57–59. For a useful discussion of the "grassroots" and the "grasstops," see Shermer, *Sunbelt Capitalism*, 2. For Shermer, the "grasstops" includes "the local elites."

26. Burk, *Corporate State and the Broker State*, 107.

27. Phillips-Fein, *Invisible Hands*, xi, 6, and Burk, *Corporate State and the Broker State*, 122.

28. On their lack of interest in ceding power, see Tedlow, "The National Association of Manufacturers and Public Relations during the New Deal," 32, and Phillips-Fein, *Invisible Hands*, xi.

29. "A 1943 Platform for the National Industrial Information Committee," April 28, 1943, NAM Records, HML, 4.

30. "AAPA Board of Directors Resolution," December 6, 1933, quoted in Wolfskill, *Revolt of the Conservatives*, 54.

31. Roosevelt, "Fireside Chat #5," June 28, 1934, FDRL.

32. On the discussions, see Burk, *Corporate State and the Broker State*, 134–138.

33. "Platform and Organization of the American Liberty League," 1934, Raskob Papers (0473), Box 61, (American Liberty League (Charter)), HML and "American Liberty League," Statement by Jouett Shouse at the time of the announcement of the formation of this organization, August 23, 1934, Jouett Shouse Collection (American Liberty League Pamphlets), Special Collections Research Center, University of Kentucky [hereafter Shouse Collection, UKY]. See also Wolfskill, *Revolt of the Conservatives*, 20; Arthur M. Schlesinger Jr., *The Politics of Upheaval, 1935–1936: The Age of Roosevelt, Vol. 3* (Boston: Mariner Books, 2003), 32; Jared A. Goldstein, "The American Liberty League and the Rise of Constitutional Nationalism," *Temple Law Review* 86, no. 2 (Winter 2014): 294; and Patrick C. Patton, "Standing at Thermopylae: A History of the American Liberty League," (Ph.D. diss., Temple University, 2015).

34. William H. Stayton quoted in Wolfskill, *Revolt of the Conservatives*, 111.

35. Wolfskill, *Revolt of the Conservatives*, 22, and Burk, *Corporate State and the Broker State*, 134–142.

36. Wolfskill, *Revolt of the Conservatives*, 62–64, and Phillips-Fein, *Invisible Hands*, 10–13.

37. Eunice Barnard, "Dr. Counts Assails 'Liberty's Enemies,'" *New York Times*, February 24, 1936, quoted in Wolfskill, *Revolt of the Conservatives*, 210–211.

38. See Richard S. Tedlow, *Keeping the Corporate Image: Public Relations and Business, 1900–1950* (Greenwich, CT: JAI Press, 1979), 30, 39–40; Jackson Lears, *Fables of Abundance: A Cultural History of Advertising in America* (New York: Basic Books, 1995), 218–233; and Ewen, *PR!*, 3, 10–11, and 116–127.

39. Edward Bernays, *Propaganda* (New York: Ig Publishing, 2004), 47–61. See also Ewen, *PR!*, 192–196, and generally.

40. Bernays, *Propaganda*, 49.

41. Burk, *Corporate State and the Broker State*, 164.

42. *Bulletin of the American Liberty League* 1, no. 1 (August 1935), Shouse Collection, UKY, 3.

43. Wolfskill, *Revolt of the Conservatives*, 66.

44. Ibid, 67.

45. Ibid.

46. See, for example, *Bulletin of the American Liberty League* 1, no. 5 (December 1935), Shouse Collection, UKY, 3.

47. Wolfskill, *Revolt of the Conservatives*, 263.

48. Franklin D. Roosevelt, "Philadelphia, Pennsylvania—Acceptance of Re-nomination," June 27, 1936, MSF, Box 25, (879), FDRL, http://www.fdrlibrary.marist.edu/_resources /images/msf/msf00903 and https://www.fdrlibrary.org/documents/356632/405112 /afdr049.mp3/1cd96a6f-4fef-4fcc-baaa-d52b9e45f3fb.

49. Ibid.

50. See, for example, p. 62 and p. 81 of http://www.fdrlibrary.marist.edu/_resources /images/msf/msf00903.

51. Roosevelt, "Philadelphia, Pennsylvania—Acceptance of Re-nomination," June 27, 1936, FDRL.

52. Ibid.

53. Ibid.

54. Ibid.

55. Ibid.

56. Ibid.

57. Charlotte A. Twight, *Dependent on D.C.: The Rise of Federal Control over the Lives of Ordinary Americans* (New York: St. Martin's Press, 2002), 64–66.

58. Alfred M. Landon, "I Will Not Promise the Moon," September 26, 1936, *Vital Speeches of the Day* 3, no. 1 (October 15, 1936): 26.

59. Ibid.

60. Ibid.

61. On the extent to which this speech backfired, see Kenneth S. Davis, *FDR: The New Deal Years, 1933–1937* (New York: Random House, 1986), 643.

62. For instance, see American Liberty League Document No. 72, "Dangerous Experimentation: A Discussion of Policies and Performances Apparently Based upon the Belief that Perpetual Motion Is Progress and Involving the Squandering of Public Money upon Socialistic Undertakings of Doubtful Constitutionality," October 28, 1935, Shouse Collection, UKY and American Liberty League Document No. 133, "Federal Bureaucracy in the Fourth Year of the New Deal: A Study of the Appalling Increase in the Number of Government Employees," August 23, 1936, Shouse Collection, UKY.

63. *Webster's Third New International Dictionary of the English Language Unabridged* (New York, 2002), 254, and "Deutsch Gets Boon-Doggle—the Real Thing," *New York Times*, April 11, 1935.

64. On how the Roosevelt administration countered charges of boondoggling, see Jason Scott Smith, *Building New Deal Liberalism: The Political Economy of Public Works, 1933–1956* (New York: Cambridge University Press, 2005), 141–149.

65. "Relief Dancing Stirs Laughter of New Yorkers: Outsiders Do Most of the Teaching," *Chicago Tribune*, April 4, 1935.

66. "A Nation of Boon-Doggles," *Wall Street Journal*, April 5, 1935.

67. American Liberty League Document No. 128, "The New Deal vs. Democracy, Speech of Jouett Shouse, broadcast over the National Broadcasting Company network," June 20, 1936, Shouse Collection, UKY, 5.

68. "The New Deal Boondoggling Circus," May 27, 1936, Jouett Shouse Papers, Box 16, Folder 28, UKY and American Liberty League Document No. 78, "Work Relief: A

Record of the Tragic Failure of the Most Costly Governmental Experiment in All World History," November 25, 1935, Shouse Collection, UKY, 15–18.

69. An ngram chart illustrates the term's increasingly frequent appearance in print beginning in the mid-1930s: https://books.google.com/ngrams/graph?content =boondoggle&year_start=1800&year_end=2019&corpus=26&smoothing=3&di rect_url=t1%3B%2Cboondoggle%3B%2Co#t1%3B%2Cboondoggle%3B%2Cco. The New York *Daily News,* the country's most popular newspaper and a vehicle for conservative messaging, picked up the phrase. On the paper, see Matthew Pressman, "The New York *Daily News* and the History of Conservative Media," *Modern American History* 4, no. 3 (October 2021): 219–238. Influential conservative radio pioneer Clarence Manion also delighted in talking about government "boondoggles" during his multidecade broadcasting career from 1954 to 1979. See, for example, *Manion Forum* No. 302, July 10, 1960, Clarence Manion Papers, PMMN 1/07, #302, University of Notre Dame Archives [hereafter Manion Papers, UNDA]; *Manion Forum* No. 628, October 16, 1966, Manion Papers, PMMN 1/14, #628, UNDA; and *Manion Forum* No. 1277, April 1, 1979, 3. https://archive.org/details/sim_manion-forum_1979-04-01_1277/page /n3/mode/2up?q=boondoggle. On Manion's influence, see Nicole Hemmer, *Messengers of the Right: Conservative Media and the Transformation of American Politics* (Philadelphia: University of Pennsylvania Press, 2016).

70. Franklin D. Roosevelt, "Newark, New Jersey—State Emergency Council Meeting— Remarks," January 18, 1936, MSF, Box 24, (838), FDRL, http://www.fdrlibrary.marist .edu/_resources/images/msf/msf00862.

71. Franklin D. Roosevelt, "Syracuse, New York—Democratic State Convention," September 29, 1936, MSF, Box 27, (924), FDRL, http://www.fdrlibrary.marist.edu /_resources/images/msf/msf00949 and https://www.fdrlibrary.org/documents /356632/405112/afdr060.mp3/dd62233e-4a37-4b3a-8683-c9d00e12e5e7.

72. Ibid.

73. Ibid.

74. Ibid.

75. For drafts of the speech, see Franklin D. Roosevelt, "Wichita, Kansas—Western Campaign Trip—Campaign Address," October 13, 1936, MSF, Box 28, (960), FDRL, http://www.fdrlibrary.marist.edu/_resources/images/msf/msf00985.

76. Roosevelt, "Wichita, Kansas—Western Campaign Trip—Campaign Address," October 13, 1936, FDRL.

77. Ibid.

78. Ibid.

79. Ibid.

80. See the attachments to Daniels to Rosenman, October 21, 1944, Rosenman Papers, Box 19, (Speech Material, 1944 Campaign), FDRL.

81. Franklin D. Roosevelt, "Wilkes-Barre, Pennsylvania—Campaign Address" October 29, 1936, MSF, Box 29, (1003), FDRL, http://www.fdrlibrary.marist.edu/_resources/images /msf/msf01029. On the speech, see Burns, *Roosevelt: The Lion and the Fox*, 282.

82. Franklin D. Roosevelt, "New York City, New York—Madison Square Garden—Address," October 31, 1936, MSF, Box 30, (1007A), FDRL, http://www.fdrlibrary.marist.edu

/_resources/images/msf/msf01033 and https://www.fdrlibrary.org/documents
/356632/405112/afdr067.mp3/692aee38-3ddd-4f8f-9032-683cd72aa8b2.

83. Franklin D. Roosevelt, "Worcester, Massachusetts—New England Campaign Swing—Address," October 21, 1936, MSF, Box 29, (991), FDRL, http://www.fdrlibrary.marist.edu/_resources/images/msf/msf01017 and https://www.fdrlibrary.org/documents/356632/405112/afdr064.mp3/71e77a09-9b11-4c17-a476-78cc1d2216b6.

84. Franklin D. Roosevelt, "Detroit, Michigan—Western Campaign Trip—Campaign Address," October 15, 1936, MSF, Box 29, (974), FDRL, http://www.fdrlibrary.marist.edu/_resources/images/msf/msf01000.

85. On the magnitude of Roosevelt and his party's victory in 1936, see George Wolfskill and John A. Hudson, *All but the People: Franklin D. Roosevelt and His Critics* (New York: Macmillan, 1969), 168, and Kennedy, *Freedom from Fear*, 286.

86. On the Liberty League's importance in the development of the conservative movement, see Patton, "Standing at Thermopylae," 10–17, and generally; Phillips-Fein, *Invisible Hands*, 15; Burk, *Corporate State and the Broker State*, 193; and Wolfskill, *Revolt of the Conservatives*, 65.

87. Barton, "Business Can Win Public from Politician," 17.

88. The most comprehensive account of NAM's origins is Delton, *The Industrialists*.

89. Tedlow, "The National Association of Manufacturers and Public Relations during the New Deal," 29.

90. On the "Brass Hats" and the takeover of NAM, see Ibid., 29–32, and Workman, "Manufacturing Power," 286–288. On the broader history of NAM's leadership, see Phillip H. Burch Jr., "The NAM as an Interest Group," *Politics & Society* 4, no. 1 (Fall 1973): 97–129.

91. Burch Jr., "The NAM as an Interest Group," 110–112 and 110n34–112n35.

92. Tedlow, "The National Association of Manufacturers and Public Relations during the New Deal," 29–30, and LaFollette Committee Report, 44–47. Jennifer Delton also lists J. Howard Pew among the Brass Hats. See Delton, *Industrialists*, 108.

93. For example, Ernest T. Weir was a member of both groups and went on to head NAM's National Industrial Information Committee. For his participation in the Brass Hats discussions, see Tedlow, "The National Association of Manufacturers and Public Relations during the New Deal," 28. For his participation in the du Pont group discussions, see Wolfskill, *Revolt of the Conservatives*, 25. For his leadership of the NIIC, see "Re-Selling the American Way to America," 1939, NAM Records (1411), Box OS 4, (Miscellaneous NIIC Material, 1938–1940), HML. On the broader point about the role of interlocking directorates in the nascent conservative movement, see Burk, *Corporate State and the Broker State*, 153–154, and Burch Jr., "The NAM as an Interest Group," 97–129.

94. Henderson quoted in LaFollette Committee Report, 44.

95. Lund quoted in Tedlow, "The National Association of Manufacturers and Public Relations during the New Deal," 31.

96. Ibid.

97. Marchand, *Creating the Corporate Soul*, 206.

98. Tedlow, "The National Association of Manufacturers and Public Relations during the New Deal," 31.

99. Weisenburger's name is misspelled as "Weisenberger" in much of the literature. For the correct spelling, see, for example, Walter B. Weisenburger, "Your Day in the Court of Public Opinion," December 3, 1942, NAM Records (1411), Box 1095, (NIIC Subject-'Key Documents'—Basic Memos—1942–1945), HML. On Weisenburger's hiring, see Workman, "Manufacturing Power," 288. See also LaFollette Committee Report, 46–47, and Tedlow, "The National Association of Manufacturers and Public Relations during the New Deal," 32. For a biographical sketch of Weisenburger, see "W. Weisenburger, NAM Official, 59: Executive Vice President and Leading Publicist Is Dead—Developed Recent Program," *New York Times*, June 24, 1947.

100. "James P. Selvage of Publicity Firm," *New York Times*, December 2, 1975. On Selvage's hiring, see Tedlow, "The National Association of Manufacturers and Public Relations during the New Deal," 32.

101. Tedlow, "The National Association of Manufacturers and Public Relations during the New Deal," 33.

102. On the tone of Liberty League messaging, see Wolfskill, *Revolt of the Conservatives*, 258. On the moderating influence of the public relations professionals running the NAM campaign, see Workman, "Manufacturing Power," 288–293, and Delton, *Industrialists*, 136–138.

103. Objectives, Strategy and Techniques of the NIIC Public Information Program, March 23, 1943, NAM Records (1411), Box 1093, (NIIC Administrative—NIIC Program Committee Mtg. 3-23-43—1943), HML. See also Gable, "A Political Analysis of an Employers' Association," 323–324.

104. "Meeting of the Advisory Committee, NAM Committee on Public Relations," March 17, 1939, NAM Records (1411), Box 143, (Committee - Public Relations Advisory Committee - General, 1939), HML.

105. National Industrial Information Committee, *Your Public Information Program in Action, Annual Report for 1942*, n.d. [1942], NAM Records (1411), Box 1093, (NIIC Administrative—Annual Reports—NIIC—1942), HML.

106. See, for example, "Conference on Public Relations," November 30–December 1, 1942, NAM Records (1411), Box 143, (Public Relations—Conference on Public Relations, Nov. 30–Dec. 1, 1942), HML and *Proceedings of the Second Annual Public Relations Conference Sponsored by the National Association of Manufacturers*, December 6 and 7, 1943, NAM Records (1411), Box 144, (Meetings—Public Relations—General—1943), HML.

107. Tedlow, *Keeping the Corporate Image*, 73.

108. On the importance of women to the conservative movement, see McGirr, *Suburban Warriors*, 87; Michelle Nickerson, "Women, Domesticity, and Postwar Conservatism," *OAH Magazine of History* 17, no. 2 (January 2003), 17–21; Donald T. Critchlow, *Phyllis Schlafly and Grassroots Conservatism: A Woman's Crusade* (Princeton, NJ: Princeton University Press, 2005), 7–8; June Melby Benowitz, *Days of Discontent: American Women and Right-Wing Politics, 1933–1945* (DeKalb: Northern Illinois University Press, 2002); Kirsten Delegard, *Battling Miss Bolsheviki: The Origins of Female Conservatism in the United States* (Philadelphia: University of Pennsylvania Press, 2012); and Michelle Nickerson, *Mothers of Conservatism: Women and the Postwar Right*

(Princeton, NJ: Princeton University Press, 2012). On youth, see John A. Andrew III, *The Other Side of the Sixties: Young Americans for Freedom and the Rise of Conservative Politics* (New Brunswick, NJ: Rutgers University Press, 1997), and Gregory L. Schneider, *Cadres for Conservatism: Young Americans for Freedom and the Rise of the Contemporary Right* (New York: New York University Press, 1999).

109. *Report of the National Industrial Information Committee for the Year 1941*, n.d. [1941], NAM Records (1411), Box 1093, (NIIC Administrative—Annual Reports—NIIC—1941–1943), HML. Among others, the organization relied on the services of Elmo Roper and Claude Robinson, the latter a conservative-minded pioneer in public opinion research who wrote one of the first books on public opinion polling. See Claude E. Robinson, *Straw Votes: A Study of Political Prediction* (New York: Columbia University Press, 1932).

110. "A 1943 Platform for the National Industrial Information Committee," April 28, 1943, NAM Records, HML, 4.

111. Ibid., 9.

112. An ngram chart illustrates the uptake of the term "government intervention": https://books.google.com/ngrams/graph?content=%22government+intervention%22&year_start=1800&year_end=2019&corpus=28&smoothing=3&direct_url=t1%3B%2C%22%20government%20intervention%20%22%3B%2Cc0#t1%3B%2C%22%20government%20intervention%20%22%3B%2Cc0.

113. Historians Howell John Harris, Robert Griffith, Elizabeth Fones-Wolf, and James T. Patterson all have argued, as Griffith puts it, that "given their overlapping membership, financial support, and shared assumptions" the differences between these organizations "have probably been exaggerated." See Robert Griffith, "Forging Americas Postwar Domestic Order: Domestic Politics and Political Economy in the Age of Truman," in *The Truman Presidency*, Michael J. Lacey, ed. (Washington, DC: Woodrow Wilson International Center for Scholars, 1989), 67; Howell John Harris, *The Right to Manage: Industrial Relations Policies of American Business in the 1940s* (Madison: University of Wisconsin Press, 1982); Fones-Wolf, *Selling Free Enterprise*, 36–37; and James T. Patterson, *Grand Expectations: Postwar America, 1945–1974* (New York: Oxford University Press, 1996), 58.

114. Tedlow, "The National Association of Manufacturers and Public Relations during the New Deal," 32.

115. Ibid.

116. On the number of attendees, see for example, NAM, "Press Release Summarizing Remarks of Henry N. Wriston," December 11, 1943, NAM Records (1411), Box 104, (Free Enterprise- General—1949–1940), HML, which says about four thousand people attended the 1943 Congress of American Industry.

117. Fones-Wolf cites a Nash-Kelvinator ad as an example. See Fones-Wolf, *Selling Free Enterprise*, 27.

118. On Chester's role in the nascent conservative movement, see Walker and Sklar, *Business Finds Its Voice*, 54–55.

119. "Meeting of the Advisory Committee, NAM Committee on Public Relations," March 17, 1939, NAM Records, HML.

120. Ibid.

121. Workman, "Manufacturing Power," 288, and Phillips-Fein, *Invisible Hands*, 14.

122. "Meeting of the Advisory Committee, NAM Committee on Public Relations," March 17, 1939, NAM Records, HML, 4.

123. Quoted in Gable, "A Political Analysis of an Employers' Association," 369.

124. "Meeting of the Advisory Committee, NAM Committee on Public Relations," March 17, 1939, NAM Records, HML, 14.

125. For estimates of the campaign's reach at various points, see Report of the National Industrial Information Committee for the Year 1941, HML; Report on the 1945 NAM Public Relations Program (NIIC) and Preview for 1946, undated [1945], NAM Records (1411), Box 1097, (NIIC Subject- Public Relations- Aug. 1945–1946), HML; and NAM Salesletter, January 17, 1949, NAM Records (1411), Box 141, (Public Relations Div. Programs, 1949–1948), HML. For an outside assessment of the NAM campaign's reach, see Senate, Subcommittee of the Committee on Education and Labor, Violations of Free Speech and Rights of Labor—Hearings Pursuant to S. Res. 266, 74th-76th Congs., 1936–1940, Parts 17 and 18.

126. *A Day in the Life of an Average American*, undated [1939], NAM Records (1411), Box 1096, (NIIC Subject- Misc. NIIC Material—1940), HML.

127. Ibid.

128. For instance, see Hasher et al., "Frequency and the Conference of Referential Validity," and Fazio et al., "Repetition Increases Perceived Truth Equally for Plausible and Implausible Statements."

129. Gable, "A Political Analysis of an Employers' Association," 344.

130. On Roosevelt's belief in the power of keeping his radio appearances somewhat scarce, see Roosevelt to Leffingwell, March 16, 1942, reproduced in *F. D. R.: His Personal Letters, 1928–1945*, Volume 4, ed. Elliott Roosevelt (New York: Kraus Reprint Co., 1970), 198–199, and Richard W. Steele, *Propaganda in an Open Society: The Roosevelt Administration and the Media, 1933–1941* (Westport, CT: Greenwood, 1985), 22. On NAM's ability to get free airtime, see Gable, "A Political Analysis of an Employers' Association," 343.

131. *A Day in the Life of an Average American*, NAM Records, HML and *Industry Must Speak!*, 1937, NAM Records (1411), Box 1095, (Committee—NIIC Booklets, 1937), HML. On *The American Family Robinson*, see Elizabeth Fones-Wolf, "Creating a Favorable Business Climate: Corporations and Radio Broadcasting, 1934 to 1954," *Business History Review* 73, no. 2 (Summer 1999): 230–236, and Bird Jr., *Better Living*, 53–61.

132. Gable, "A Political Analysis of an Employers' Association," 344.

133. *A Day in the Life of an Average American*, NAM Records, HML, and Gable, "A Political Analysis of an Employers' Association," 343–344.

134. *A Day in the Life of an Average American*, NAM Records, HML.

135. Tedlow, "The National Association of Manufacturers and Public Relations during the New Deal," 35.

136. *Industry Must Speak!*, 1937, NAM Records, HML. See also Gable, "A Political Analysis of an Employers' Association," 344.

137. On providing news commentators with material, see *Industry Must Speak!*, 1937, NAM Records, HML. Andrew Workman writes that the "NAM hired Robert J. Smith Associates," which "managed to insinuate material, often just as written, into a wide variety of entertainment and news programs." Workman, "Manufacturing Power," 312.

138. Tedlow, "The National Association of Manufacturers and Public Relations during the New Deal," 33.

139. Gable, "A Political Analysis of an Employers' Association," 332–333. These nonattributed pieces amounted to "puffery," which Richard Tedlow defines as "the publication of items in the news columns which appear to be normal reportage, but which are in fact thinly disguised advertisements." See Tedlow, *Keeping the Corporate Image*, 7.

140. *Industry Must Speak!*, 1937, NAM Records, HML.

141. *A Day in the Life of an Average American*, NAM Records, HML.

142. Gable, "A Political Analysis of an Employers' Association," 335.

143. "Meeting of the Advisory Committee, NAM Committee on Public Relations," March 17, 1939, NAM Records, HML, 14.

144. "Re-Selling the American Way to America," NAM Records, HML.

145. *Proceedings of the Second Annual Public Relations Conference Sponsored by the National Association of Manufacturers*, December 6 and 7, 1943, NAM Records, HML, 86.

146. Ibid.

147. See, for example, *Service for Plant Publications*, no. 86, August 1943, NAM Records (1411), Box 144, (Public Relations—Service for Plant Publications, Jan. 1941–Oct. 1944), HML.

148. *A Day in the Life of an Average American*, NAM Records, HML.

149. National Industrial Information Committee, *Your Public Information Program in Action, Annual Report for 1942*, n.d. [1942], HML, 30.

150. "Meeting of the Advisory Committee, NAM Committee on Public Relations," March 17, 1939, NAM Records, HML, 15.

151. Gable, "A Political Analysis of an Employers' Association," 335.

152. See, for example, McGirr, *Suburban Warriors*, 87; Nickerson, "Women, Domesticity, and Postwar Conservatism," 18; and Critchlow, *Phyllis Schlafly and Grassroots Conservatism*.

153. James Bell to General Mills stockholders, July 26, 1935, Moley Papers (68008), Box 283, (FD Roosevelt Schedule A), (Folder 29), HIA.

154. Ibid.

155. *Industry Must Speak!*, 1937, NAM Records, HML.

156. *A Day in the Life of an Average American*, NAM Records, HML. See also LaFollette Committee Report, 165, 173–175.

157. "Meeting of the Advisory Committee, NAM Committee on Public Relations," March 17, 1939, NAM Records, HML, 6.

158. "The NAM Story: Speech Material Covering NAM Structure, Activities, Services, and the 1948 Public Relations Program," May 10, 1948, NAM Records (1411), Box 141, (Public Relations Div. Programs, 1949–1948), HML, 10. See also Gable, "A Political Analysis of an Employers' Association," 352.

159. "Meeting of the Advisory Committee, NAM Committee on Public Relations," March 17, 1939, NAM Records, HML, 6.

160. National Industrial Information Committee, *Your Public Information Program in Action, Annual Report for 1942*, n.d. [1942], NAM Records, HML, 25.

161. "N.A.M. Will Survey School Textbooks," *New York Times*, December 11, 1940, 29.

162. "Meeting of the Advisory Committee, NAM Committee on Public Relations," March 17, 1939, NAM Records, HML, 7.

163. Ibid.

164. Selvage quoted in Congress, Senate, Subcommittee of the Committee on Education and Labor, Violations of Free Speech and Rights of Labor—Hearings Pursuant to S. Res. 266, 74th-76th Congs., 1936–1940, Part III, 165.

165. "Meeting of the Advisory Committee, NAM Committee on Public Relations," March 17, 1939, NAM Records, HML, 7.

166. On "conspicuously successful," see Adams to Sloan Jr., June 21, 1943, NAM Records (1411), Box 1093, (NIIC Administrative—Governing Board Meeting—10-25-43—1943), HML, 5.

167. Holcombe Parkes, "Merchandising Free Enterprise," December 6, 1946, NAM Records (1411), Box 104, (Free Enterprise- General—1949-1940), HML, 14.

168. *A Day in the Life of an Average American*, NAM Records, HML. See also *Industry Must Speak!*, 1937, NAM Records, HML.

169. On the World War I "Four-Minute Men," see Ewen, *PR!*, 102–104, 116–120.

170. Wallace F. Bennett, "The Bridge," April 8, 1949, NAM Records (1411), Box 2, (Freedom—General (1 of 2)), HML.

171. *A Day in the Life of an Average American*, NAM Records, HML.

172. Phillips-Fein, *Invisible Hands*, 14.

173. "Theme of 1939–1940 Program," n.d., NAM Records (1411), Box 143, (Committee—Public Relations—General, 1939), HML. See also Tedlow, "The National Association of Manufacturers and Public Relations during the New Deal," 34.

174. "Living Is Better in America series, poster #1, n.d. [1940], NAM Records (1411), Series 1, HML, https://digital.hagley.org/LMSS_1411_Living_01.

175. See, for example, "Living Is Better in America series, poster #2," n.d. [1940], NAM Records (1411), Series 1, HML, https://digital.hagley.org/LMSS_1411_Living_02, and "Living Is Better in America series, poster #5," n.d. [1940], NAM Records (1411), Series 1, HML, https://digital.hagley.org/LMSS_1411_Living_05.

176. "Theme of 1939–1940 Program," NAM Records, HML.

177. See Marchand, *Creating the Corporate Soul*, 241–244.

178. Ibid.

179. Raymond Moley, "How Much Regulation Can Business Stand?" October 9, 1936, *Vital Speeches of the Day* 3, no. 2 (November 1, 1936): 40. Moley told his first wife Eva that he broke with Roosevelt in 1936 because of a difference of opinion on foreign policy. Moley supported neutrality and believed the president did not. But Moley also increasingly opposed efforts to transform American political economy along the lines advanced by some of Roosevelt's other advisors, who were gaining influence. See Raymond Moley to Eva Moley, n.d. [late November 1935], Moley Papers, Box 1,

(Correspondence—1935), FDRL; Moley to Tugwell, February 19, 1934, Tugwell Papers, Box 15, (Moley, Raymond), FDRL; Moley to Tugwell, February 6, 1939, Tugwell Papers, Box 15, (Moley, Raymond), FDRL; Moley to Tugwell, June 8, 1939, Tugwell Papers, Box 15, (Moley, Raymond), FDRL; and Tugwell, *Brains Trust*, xxvi–xxvii.

180. Barton, "Business Can Win Public from Politician," 17.

181. See Reeves to Harrison, May 11, 1945, NAM Records (1411), Box 1097, (NIIC Subject-Public Relations Policy Cmte.—Jan.–May 1945), HML.

182. Wolfskill, *Revolt of the Conservatives*, 110.

183. Gable, "A Political Analysis of an Employers' Association," 351.

184. James P. Warburg, "What of 1936?" *Vital Speeches of the Day* 2, no. 9 (January 27, 1936): 269.

185. Pew to Link, July 24, 1951, J. Howard Pew Papers (1634), Box 28, (B), HML. Pew believed the quest for "security destroys freedom."

186. "A 1943 Platform for the National Industrial Information Committee," April 28, 1943, NAM Records, HML.

4. The First Battle over the Government's National Security Responsibilities

1. Franklin D. Roosevelt, "Message to Congress—State of the Union," January 6, 1937, MSF, Box 31, (1028), FDRL, http://www.fdrlibrary.marist.edu/_resources/images/msf/msf01057 and https://www.fdrlibrary.org/documents/356632/405112/afdr076.mp3/2c6eec18-6883-4c7e-9480-d2ee53927716.

2. Ibid.

3. Ibid.

4. Franklin D. Roosevelt, "Inaugural Address," January 20, 1937, MSF, Box 31, (1030), FDRL, http://www.fdrlibrary.marist.edu/_resources/images/msf/msf01059 and https://www.fdrlibrary.org/documents/356632/405112/afdr077.mp3/c8f20f82-d06f-4866-b154-55d6ed4c7402. On the weather, see Justin Grieser, "Washington, D.C. Presidential Inauguration Weather History," *Washington Post*, January 16, 2013, https://www.washingtonpost.com/blogs/capital-weather-gang/post/washington-dc-presidential-inauguration-weather-history/2013/01/16/5def1200-5ff3-11e2-b05a-605528f6b712_blog.html.

5. Roosevelt, "Inaugural Address," January 20, 1937, FDRL.

6. Ibid.

7. See Chapter 1.

8. Roosevelt, "Informal remarks following visit to Home Subsistence Exhibition Auditorium of the Commerce Building," April 24, 1934, FDRL.

9. Ibid.

10. Roosevelt often talked at length about planning in his press conferences. See, for example, Press Conference 84, January 3, 1934, FDRL; Press Conference 85, January 5, 1934, FDRL; Press Conference 97, February 14, 1934, FDRL; Press Conference 336, January 11, 1937, FDRL; Press Conference 339, January 26, 1937, FDRL; Press Conference 343, February 9, 1937, FDRL; Press Conference 400, October 6, 1937,

FDRL; Press Conference 589, October 17, 1939, FDRL; Press Conference 602, December 1, 1939, FDRL; Press Conference 616, January 19, 1940, FDRL; Press Conference 880, February 16, 1943, FDRL; Press Conference 883, March 12, 1943, FDRL; Press Conference 907, July 9, 1943, FDRL. All available here: http://www.fdrlibrary.marist.edu/archives/collections/franklin/?p=collections/findingaid&id=508.

11. Roosevelt, "Inaugural Address," March 4, 1933, FDRL.

12. Franklin D. Roosevelt, "Message to Congress re Tennessee Valley Authority," April 10, 1933, MSF, Box 14, (622), FDRL, http://www.fdrlibrary.marist.edu/_resources/images/msf/msf00641.

13. Warken, "History of the National Resources Planning Board," 1–2.

14. Ibid., 1.

15. On Mitchell, see Reagan, *Designing a New America*, 82–110.

16. Reagan, *Designing a New America*, 1, 93, 106.

17. Warken, "History of the National Resources Planning Board," 2.

18. See National Planning Board, *Final Report—1933–1934* (Washington, DC, 1934), 17–38.

19. Ibid., 35. See also Warken, "History of the National Resources Planning Board," 2, and Schlesinger Jr., *Coming of the New Deal*, 349–351.

20. Franklin D. Roosevelt, "Executive Order 6777 Establishing the National Resources Board," June 30, 1934, APP, https://www.presidency.ucsb.edu/node/208466.

21. Warken, "History of the National Resources Planning Board," 2.

22. Roosevelt, "Executive Order 6777 Establishing the National Resources Board," June 30, 1934, APP.

23. Ibid. For concise biographies of Delano, Merriam, and Mitchell, see Reagan, *Designing a New America*, 2–4.

24. National Planning Board, *Final Report—1933–1934*, 22.

25. National Resources Board, *A Report on National Planning and Public Works in Relation to Natural Resources and Including Land Use and Water Resources with Findings and Recommendations* (Washington, DC, 1934), 82.

26. Ibid., 83.

27. Ibid.

28. Ibid., 84.

29. Ibid.

30. National Resources Board, *A Report on National Planning and Public Works*, 84.

31. Ibid.

32. Excerpts from Gilbert Chinard on the Declaration, PPF 1820, Box 1, (Speech Materials and Suggestions, 1934 Mar-Sept), FDRL.

33. Pendleton Herring, "A Prescription for Modern Democracy," *Annals of the American Academy of Political and Social Science* 180 (July 1935): 138–148.

34. See, for example, Press Conference 156, November 7, 1934, FDRL. Roosevelt told reporters, "We will have to find a new word that is different from 'planning.'" See also Press Conference 880, February 16, 1943, FDRL. Roosevelt said, "I know 'planning' is not a popular term."

35. Franklin D. Roosevelt, "Richmond, Virginia—Address to Governors' Conference," April 27, 1932, MSF, Box 9, (475), FDRL, http://www.fdrlibrary.marist.edu/_resources

/images/msf/msf00485. For additional drafts of this speech, including many handwritten chunks in Roosevelt's script, see Drafts of Address before the Conference of Governors, n.d. [April 1932], Tully Collection, Box 13, (Speech Drafts-Tribute to George Washington, Address before the Conference of Governors, Richmond, Virginia, April 27, 1932), FDRL, http://www.fdrlibrary.marist.edu/_resources/images/tully/13_07.pdf.

36. National Planning Board, *Final Report—1933–1934*, 19.

37. National Resources Board, *A Report on National Planning and Public Works*, 80.

38. Ibid.

39. Ibid., 81–82.

40. Ibid., 82.

41. Franklin D. Roosevelt, "Message to the Congress on the State of the Union," January 4, 1935, MSF, Box 20, (759), FDRL, http://www.fdrlibrary.marist.edu/_resources/images/msf/msf00780.

42. Ibid.

43. Ibid.

44. Ibid.

45. Robert L. Lund, "'Measured by Deeds, New Deal Has Failed,' Says Lund," *Los Angeles Times*, August 18, 1935.

46. Ibid.

47. Ibid.

48. Ibid.

49. Marion Clawson, *New Deal Planning: The National Resources Planning Board* (New York: RFF Press, 1981), 46.

50. Peri E. Arnold, *Making the Managerial Presidency: Comprehensive Reorganization, 1905–1996, Second Edition, Revised* (Lawrence: University Press of Kansas, 1998), 90–91.

51. Moley, *After Seven Years*, 79–80.

52. Ibid., 81.

53. Franklin D. Roosevelt, "Letters to Congressional Leaders Concerning Reorganization of the Executive Branch," March 22, 1936, APP, https://www.presidency.ucsb.edu/node/208709.

54. Ibid.

55. Franklin D. Roosevelt, "Announcement of a Committee to Plan for the Reorganization of the Executive Branch," March 22, 1936, APP, https://www.presidency.ucsb.edu/node/208704. On the Brownlow Committee, see Arnold, *Making the Managerial Presidency*, 93–107.

56. Roosevelt, "Letters to Congressional Leaders Concerning Reorganization of the Executive Branch," March 22, 1936, APP.

57. Press Conference 318, September 8, 1936, FDRL, http://www.fdrlibrary.marist.edu/_resources/images/pc/pc0038.pdf. See pp. 47–48 of the PDF.

58. Ibid.

59. Ibid.

60. Ibid.

61. Franklin D. Roosevelt, "Olathe, Kansas—Western Campaign Trip—Informal remarks," October 13, 1936, MSF, Box 28, (957), FDRL, http://www.fdrlibrary.marist.edu/_resources/images/msf/msf00982.

62. James W. Fesler, "The Brownlow Committee Fifty Years Later," *Public Administration Review* 47, no. 4 (July–August 1987): 291–296.

63. Press Conference 336, January 11, 1937, FDRL, http://www.fdrlibrary.marist.edu /_resources/images/pc/pc0042.pdf.

64. Franklin D. Roosevelt, "Message to Congress—Administrative Management," January 12, 1937, MSF, Box 31, (1029), FDRL, http://www.fdrlibrary.marist.edu/_resources/images /msf/msf01058, and Franklin D. Roosevelt, "Summary of the Report of the Committee on Administrative Management," January 12, 1937, APP, https://www.presidency.ucsb.edu /node/209074. On Roosevelt's efforts to reorganize the executive branch, see Richard Polenberg, *Reorganizing Roosevelt's Government: The Controversy over Executive Reorganization, 1936–1939* (Cambridge, MA: Harvard University Press, 1966).

65. Arnold, *Making the Managerial Presidency*, 108–109.

66. Polenberg, *Reorganizing Roosevelt's Government*, 166.

67. Rep. Eaton, speaking on April 9, 1937, 74th Cong., 1st sess., *Congressional Record* 81, pt. 3:3338.

68. Arnold, *Making the Managerial Presidency*, 107, and James T. Patterson, *Congressional Conservatism and the New Deal* (Lexington: University of Kentucky Press, 1967), 214–218.

69. Arnold, *Making the Managerial Presidency*, 108.

70. Ibid., and Patterson, *Congressional Conservatism and the New Deal*, 218–219.

71. On "dictatorial powers," see Ronald Steel, *Walter Lippmann and the American Century* (New Brunswick, NJ: Transaction Publishers, 2008), 300.

72. Angus Burgin, *The Great Persuasion: Reinventing Free Markets since the Depression* (Cambridge, MA: Harvard University Press, 2012), 55, and Steel, *Walter Lippmann and the American Century*, 322–326.

73. Franklin D. Roosevelt, "Statement on a Report of the National Resources Committee," September 20, 1937, APP, https://www.presidency.ucsb.edu/node/208752.

74. Ibid.

75. Ibid.

76. On Gannett and the National Committee to Uphold Constitutional Government, see Polenberg, *Reorganizing Roosevelt's Government*, 55–78; Wolfskill and Hudson, *All But the People*, 168; Samuel T. Williamson, *Frank Gannett: A Biography* (New York: Kessinger, 1940), 174–216; and Joanne Dunnebecke, "The Crusade for Individual Liberty: The Committee for Constitutional Government, 1937–1958," (M.A. thesis, University of Wyoming, 1987).

77. Quoted in Wolfskill and Hudson, *All But the People*, 168.

78. On this point, see Wolfskill, *Revolt of the Conservatives*, 209–213.

79. On the du Pont brothers' contributions, see Polenberg, *Reorganizing Roosevelt's Government*, 235n112.

80. On the National Committee's membership, see Williamson, *Frank Gannett*, 180–181; Polenberg, *Reorganizing Roosevelt's Government*, 56; and Dunnebecke, "The Crusade for Individual Liberty," 46, 55–56.

81. Polenberg, *Reorganizing Roosevelt's Government*, 71. See also Williamson, *Frank Gannett*, 182–183, and Committee for Constitutional Government, *Needed Now— Capacity for Leadership, Courage to Lead* (New York, 1944), 6.

82. Quoted in Polenberg, *Reorganizing Roosevelt's Government*, 72.

83. Polenberg, *Reorganizing Roosevelt's Government*, 71–72.
84. Congress, Senate, Special Committee to Investigate Lobbying Activities, 75th Cong., Third session, 1938, Parts 7–8, 2111, hereafter "Senate Lobbying Hearings."
85. Ibid.
86. Historians have noted the importance to the conservative movement of direct mailings but have focused more on the work of Richard Viguerie beginning in the 1960s. Rumely's earlier and effective use of direct mail was an important forerunner of those later efforts. On Viguerie, see Rick Perlstein, *The Invisible Bridge: The Fall of Nixon and the Rise of Reagan* (New York: Simon & Schuster, 2014), 452.
87. Polenberg, *Reorganizing Roosevelt's Government*, 171–172. It was so effective that it provoked a Senate investigation and a memorable hearing in which Rumely refused to comply with what his lawyer, Elisha Hanson, called a "dragnet subpoena." See Senate Lobbying Hearings, 2098–2148.
88. Harold Ickes, "Mail Order Government," *Collier's* 103, no. 7 (February 18, 1939): 48, cited in Williamson, *Frank Gannett*, 186.
89. Ickes, "Mail Order Government," 48.
90. Gannett to Schwellenbach, March 17, 1938, reproduced in Senate Lobbying Hearings, 2112.
91. Ibid.
92. Quoted in Polenberg, *Reorganizing Roosevelt's Government*, 70–71.
93. Polenberg, *Reorganizing Roosevelt's Government*, vii, 55, 141, 164–165, 171–172.
94. Ibid., 165–166.
95. "American Deadlock," *Economist*, April 16, 1938, 130–131.
96. Ibid.
97. Ibid.
98. Rosenman, *Working with Roosevelt*, 172.
99. Ibid., 172–173. For the draft, see Draft #1, Tully Collection, Box 13, (Speech Drafts-Fireside Chat on Economic Conditions, April 14, 1938), FDRL, http://www.fdrlibrary .marist.edu/_resources/images/tully/13_41.pdf.
100. See p. 13 of Draft #1, Tully Collection, Box 13, (Speech Drafts-Fireside Chat on Economic Conditions, April 14, 1938), FDRL, http://www.fdrlibrary.marist.edu /_resources/images/tully/13_41.pdf.
101. Franklin D. Roosevelt, "Fireside Chat #12—New Spending Program," April 14, 1938, MSF, Box 38, (1129A), FDRL, http://www.fdrlibrary.marist.edu/_resources/images /msf/msf01163 and https://www.fdrlibrary.org/documents/356632/405112/afdr107.mp3 /8e0f2105-18e4-423a-9c8d-53608bcaf52b.
102. Ibid.
103. Ibid.
104. Ibid.
105. Ibid. Andrew Preston also calls attention to Roosevelt's effort in this fireside chat to use events abroad to justify policy proposals. See Preston, "Monsters Everywhere," 491.
106. Roosevelt, "Fireside Chat #12—New Spending Program," April 14, 1938, FDRL.
107. Ibid.
108. Ibid.
109. Ibid.

110. Ibid.
111. Polenberg, *Reorganizing Roosevelt's Government*, 181–182.
112. Gannett quoted in Ibid., 182.
113. Polenberg, *Reorganizing Roosevelt's Government*, 181–184.
114. Roosevelt, "Radio Address on 3rd Anniversary of Social Security Act," August 15, 1938, FDRL.
115. Ibid.
116. See Roosevelt, "Chicago, Illinois—Acceptance Speech on Receiving Nomination," July 2, 1932, FDRL.
117. Franklin D. Roosevelt, "Radio Address on 3rd Anniversary of Social Security Act," August 15, 1938, MSF, Box 41, (1166), FDRL, http://www.fdrlibrary.marist.edu /_resources/images/msf/msf01203 and https://www.fdrlibrary.org/documents/356632 /405112/afdr121.mp3/f52072f3-4d06-498c-a780-5c89e98430b3.
118. Ibid.
119. Ibid.
120. Ibid.
121. Franklin D. Roosevelt, "Statement on Signing Amendments to the Social Security Act," August 11, 1939, APP, https://www.presidency.ucsb.edu/node/209866.
122. Franklin D. Roosevelt, "Message to Congress—Reorganization Plan No. 1," April 25, 1939, MSF, Box 46, (1220), FDRL, http://www.fdrlibrary.marist.edu/_resources/images /msf/msf01259. On rapid congressional approval, see Robert C. Albright, "President Wins Congress to Reorganization with Mild Approach," *Washington Post*, May 14, 1939.
123. Roosevelt, "Message to Congress—Reorganization Plan No. 1," April 25, 1939, FDRL.
124. Ibid.
125. Ibid. For a summary of the planning-related aspects of the plan, see Reagan, *Designing a New America*, 212–213.
126. Reagan, *Designing a New America*, 213.
127. Roosevelt, "Message to Congress—Reorganization Plan No. 1," April 25, 1939, FDRL.
128. Ibid. Mariano-Florentino Cuéllar's important book *Governing Security* rescued the Federal Security Agency from historical obscurity.
129. Draft executive branch organization chart, n.d. [1939], PPF 1820, Box 4, (Speech Materials and Suggestions, 1939 Sept-Dec), FDRL.
130. See also Cuéllar, *Governing Security*, 64–65, 191.
131. For Roosevelt's 1937 comment, see pp. 20–21 of http://www.fdrlibrary.marist.edu /_resources/images/pc/pc0042.pdf.
132. Cuéllar, *Governing Security*, 117.
133. Franklin D. Roosevelt, "Executive Order 8248 Reorganizing the Executive Office of the President," September 8, 1939, APP, https://www.presidency.ucsb.edu/node/210008.
134. Warken, "A History of the National Resources Planning Board," 107.
135. On the National Resources Planning Board and its work, see also Edwin Amenta and Theda Skocpol, "Redefining the New Deal: World War II and the Development of Social Provision in the United States," in *The Politics of Social Policy in the United States*, Margaret Weir, Ann Shola Orloff, and Theda Skocpol, eds. (Princeton, NJ: Princeton University Press 1988), 87–94.

136. "House Decides to Continue Planning Unit: Reverses Stand After Urgent Plea from Roosevelt," *Washington Post*, April 13, 1940.

137. Ibid.

138. See, for example, Hammat, "Forest Conservation and National Security."

5. Foreign Policy as a National Security Matter

1. Franklin D. Roosevelt, "Message to Congress—The State of the Union," January 4, 1939, MSF, Box 43, (1191B), FDRL, http://www.fdrlibrary.marist.edu/_resources /images/msf/msf01229, 147, and https://www.fdrlibrary.org/documents/356632/405112 /afdr134.mp3/59e90862-0ef4-443d-be5d-5b9afde5d03f.

2. Ibid.

3. Ibid., 150–151.

4. Ibid., 147.

5. Ibid., 148–149.

6. Ibid., 147.

7. Ibid., 153.

8. Ibid. Historian Michael Sherry also calls attention to the way Roosevelt "wove together" his domestic and foreign policies in this speech, though Sherry does not see them both, as Roosevelt did, as parts of a broader national security whole. See Sherry, *In the Shadow of War*, 30–44, 78–80.

9. Roosevelt, "Message to Congress—The State of the Union," January 4, 1939, FDRL.

10. Arthur Krock, "Critics Move to Split Dual Executive Policy," *New York Times*, January 8, 1939, 71.

11. Ibid.

12. Ibid.

13. Diplomatic historians have written extensively on Roosevelt's efforts to reorient American foreign policy. Starting points include David Reynolds, *From Munich to Pearl Harbor: Roosevelt's America and the Origins of the Second World War* (Chicago: Ivan R. Dee, 2001); Robert Dallek, *Franklin D. Roosevelt and American Foreign Policy, 1932–1945* (New York: Oxford University Press, 1995), 171–313; and Anders Stephanson, "Fourteen Notes on the Very Concept of the Cold War," in Gearóid Ó Tuathail and Simon Dalby, eds., *Rethinking Geopolitics* (London: Routledge, 1998), 61–62.

14. Franklin D. Roosevelt, "West Point, New York—Commencement Exercises—Address," June 12, 1939, MSF, Box 47, (1229), FDRL, http://www.fdrlibrary.marist.edu /_resources/images/msf/msf01268 and https://www.fdrlibrary.org/documents /356632/405112/afdr148.mp3/5dd9a3c5-63e3-4fd8-9d78-0bf686bcca36.

15. Franklin D. Roosevelt, "Message to Congress on Neutrality Laws," July 14, 1939, APP, https://www.presidency.ucsb.edu/node/209730.

16. On Roosevelt's unsuccessful efforts to persuade Congress to modify neutrality legislation during the spring and summer of 1939, see Dallek, *Franklin D. Roosevelt and American Foreign Policy*, 187–192, 199–200.

17. On the fall of France as a turning point, see Stephen Wertheim, *Tomorrow, the World: The Birth of U.S. Global Supremacy* (Cambridge, MA: Harvard University Press, 2020), chapter 2.

18. Franklin D. Roosevelt, "Fireside Chat #14—War in Europe," September 3, 1939, MSF, Box 47, (1240), FDRL, http://www.fdrlibrary.marist.edu/_resources/images/msf/msf01279 and https://www.fdrlibrary.org/documents/356632/405112/afdr149.mp3/087b6d22-f1c3-4c43-8652-914c4c43a529.

19. Ibid.

20. Ibid.

21. Ibid.

22. Franklin D. Roosevelt, "Message to Congress at Extraordinary Session to Amend Neutrality," September 21, 1939, MSF, Box 48, (1243), FDRL, http://www.fdrlibrary.marist.edu/_resources/images/msf/msf01282 and https://www.fdrlibrary.org/documents/356632/405112/afdr150.mp3/993bb15b-f400-4d56-8515-15154a3df83d.

23. Ibid.

24. See Arthur Krock, "In the Nation: Sacrifices for National Security in Pittman Bill," *New York Times*, September 26, 1939, 20, and Arthur Krock, "In the Nation: The Pro-Embargo Bloc and Old Mother Hubbard," *New York Times*, September 27, 1939, 23.

25. Arthur Krock, "In the Nation: Pittman Bill Amendments, Though Risky, Are Indicated," *New York Times*, September 28, 1939, 24. In his column a week later, Krock again used national security as a framing device, arguing that in the debate over neutrality legislation, "the real issue is over national security, and whether it is better guarded by repeal or retention." See Arthur Krock, "In the Nation: The Senate Seemingly Is Getting Down to Cases," *New York Times*, October 5, 1939, 20.

26. Arthur Krock, "'Moderates' Are Wary in Presidential Truce," *New York Times*, October 15, 1939, 77.

27. Franklin D. Roosevelt, "Message to Congress—State of the Union Address," January 3, 1940, MSF, Box 49, (1262), FDRL, http://www.fdrlibrary.marist.edu/_resources/images/msf/msf01301 and https://www.fdrlibrary.org/documents/356632/405112/afdr157.mp3/7a9ae484-c676-465e-8817-c026094c0cba.

28. For the first three drafts, see Ibid., 44–184.

29. Franklin D. Roosevelt, "Radio Message to the White House Conference on Children in a Democracy," January 19, 1940, MSF, Box 50, (1268), FDRL, http://www.fdrlibrary.marist.edu/_resources/images/msf/msf01309 and https://www.fdrlibrary.org/documents/356632/405112/afdr159.mp3/7ec8fae7-9ab1-4be2-b637-f3bd94d10ed5.

30. Ibid. Roosevelt added that question and answer—which he probably invented—to the draft of the speech prepared for him by the Labor Department, illustrating the value he saw in trying to use the international crisis to justify the furtherance of his domestic agenda in the name of national security. The spot where Roosevelt added the question and answer is marked (A) on the Labor Department draft. See Ibid., 29.

31. Arthur Krock, "In the Nation: An Epistolary Account of the Situation," *New York Times*, May 24, 1940, 18.

32. Ibid.

33. Ibid.

34. Ibid.

35. Franklin D. Roosevelt, "Fireside Chat #15," May 26, 1940, MSF, Box 51, (1283A), FDRL, http://www.fdrlibrary.marist.edu/_resources/images/msf/msf01325 and https://

www.fdrlibrary.org/documents/356632/405112/afdr169.mp3/416d1c68-9694-4fb3-8fe6
-fa024a8aa500.

36. Ibid.

37. Ibid.

38. The many drafts are filed in "Fireside Chat #15," MSF, Boxes 51–52, (1283A-D), FDRL,
http://www.fdrlibrary.marist.edu/_resources/images/msf/msf01325; http://www
.fdrlibrary.marist.edu/_resources/images/msf/msf01326; http://www.fdrlibrary.marist
.edu/_resources/images/msf/msf01327; and http://www.fdrlibrary.marist.edu
/_resources/images/msf/msf01328.

39. Roosevelt, "Fireside Chat #15," May 26, 1940, FDRL.

40. Franklin D. Roosevelt, "University of Virginia—Address," June 10, 1940, MSF, Box 52,
(1285), FDRL, http://www.fdrlibrary.marist.edu/_resources/images/msf/msf01330 and
https://www.fdrlibrary.org/documents/356632/405112/afdr170.mp3/7d78933a-17ef
-4afe-bb0a-227027aa0624.

41. Ibid.

42. Ibid.

43. Arthur Krock, "In the Nation: Now Is the Time for All Good Men, Etc.," *New York
Times*, July 12, 1940, 14.

44. Franklin D. Roosevelt, "Radio Message Accepting 3rd Term Nomination," July 19,
1940, MSF, Box 52, (1291), FDRL, http://www.fdrlibrary.marist.edu/_resources/images
/msf/msf01336 and https://www.fdrlibrary.org/documents/356632/405112/afdr171.mp3
/c0f1cc1b-044c-459c-a5f2-374686dea52d.

45. Ibid.

46. Ibid.

47. Ibid.

48. Ibid.

49. Arthur Krock, "Democratic Strategy Risks Counter-Attacks," *New York Times*,
September 1, 1940, E3.

50. See, for example, Arthur Krock, "Actions of President Open Issue for Willkie," *New
York Times*, September 8, 1940, 75, and Arthur Krock, "Campaign Arguments on
Indispensable Man," *New York Times*, September 15, 1940, 75.

51. For the handwritten drafts, see Roosevelt, "Radio Message Accepting 3rd Term
Nomination," July 19, 1940, FDRL, 137–138.

52. Roosevelt, "Radio Message Accepting 3rd Term Nomination," July 19, 1940, FDRL.

53. Ibid.

54. Ibid.

55. Ibid.

56. Arthur Krock, "In the Nation: A Halt to Defense Which Could Quickly Be Removed,"
New York Times, August 21, 1940, 18.

57. Franklin D. Roosevelt, "Executive Order 8568 Establishing the St. Lawrence River
Advisory Committee," October 17, 1940, APP, https://www.presidency.ucsb.edu/node
/209261.

58. Wendell Willkie, "Address Accepting the Presidential Nomination in Elwood, Indiana,"
August 17, 1940, APP, https://www.presidency.ucsb.edu/node/275905.

59. Ibid.

60. Letter from Albert Culbertson to Eleanor Roosevelt, Sep. 21, 1940, PPF 1820, Box 4, (Speech Materials and Suggestions: 1940 Aug-Sept), FDRL.

61. On Willkie's views, see Kennedy, *Freedom from Fear*, 455.

62. Although it was not his primary motivation in seeking increases in the production of military materiel, Roosevelt hoped privately that the policy would pay domestic political dividends. As Treasury Secretary Henry Morgenthau summarized Roosevelt's thinking, "These foreign orders mean prosperity in this country and we can't elect a Democratic Party unless we get prosperity and these foreign orders are of the greatest importance." In the final days of the campaign, Roosevelt even appealed directly by radio to people living in areas where increased weapons production had reduced unemployment. See Kennedy, *Freedom from Fear*, 464.

63. See Alan Brinkley, *The End of Reform: New Deal Liberalism in Recession and War* (New York: Vintage, 1995), 155.

64. O. J. Arnold, "Our National Security," *Vital Speeches of the Day* 7, no. 1 (October 15, 1940): 22.

65. Ibid.

66. Ibid.

67. Ibid.

68. Ibid.

69. Ibid.

70. Ibid.

71. Ibid.

72. Raymond Moley, "Perspective: On All Fronts," *Newsweek* 15, no. 22 (May 27, 1940): 68.

73. "A 1943 Platform for the National Industrial Information Committee," April 28, 1943, NAM Records, HML, 5.

74. Ibid.

75. On the evolution of persuasion from fact-based appeals to the fostering of impressions, see Ewen, *PR!*, 192–196, and generally.

76. *Primer for Americans*, 1940, NAM Records (1411), Box 1097, (Primer for Americans -1940-1941), HML, 43.

77. Ibid., 43–44.

78. Ibid., 44.

79. Ibid., 44.

80. Ibid., 56.

81. Ibid.

82. Ibid.

83. Ibid., 57.

84. Ibid.

85. Ibid.

86. Lawson to Weisenburger, November 13, 1940, NAM Records (1411), Box 144, (Public Relations—Memo to Lawson from Weisenburger, Nov. 13, 1940), HML, 8.

87. *Primer for Americans*, 1940, NAM Records, HML, 4.

88. Ibid.

89. Ibid.

90. Rosenman, *Working with Roosevelt*, 258.

91. Sherwood to Winchell, October 2, 1938, PPF 7356, (Sherwood, Robert E.), FDRL.

92. Sherwood Diary, January 21, 1940, Robert E. Sherwood Additional Papers, (89M-66), (1940), Houghton Library, Harvard University.

93. Ibid. On Hopkins's influence, see Cohen, *Nothing to Fear*, 56; Goodwin, *No Ordinary Time*, 37; and The Reminiscences of Samuel I. Rosenman, Oral History Research Office, Columbia University, 1960, 169.

94. Sherwood to Roosevelt, January 25, 1940, Robert E. Sherwood Papers, 1917–1968 (MS Am 1947), (1468), Houghton Library, Harvard University. For Sherwood's recollections of the beginnings of his career as a Roosevelt speechwriter, see Sherwood, *Roosevelt and Hopkins*, 183–184.

95. On Sherwood's selection, see Rosenman, *Working with Roosevelt*, 228–234, and The Reminiscences of Samuel I. Rosenman, Oral History Research Office, Columbia University, 1960, 134, 181–183.

96. Sherwood's handwritten speech fragments from 1940 and 1941 in his papers at Harvard's Houghton Library make this clear. Sherwood also wrote to Roosevelt on July 12, 1941, "the only thing anybody will fight for in the world today is peace and security." Sherwood to Roosevelt, July 12, 1941, Robert E. Sherwood Papers, 1917–1968 (MS Am 1947), (1468), Houghton Library, Harvard University. Sherwood expanded on the point in a ten-page speech draft. See Sherwood on security, n.d., Robert E. Sherwood Papers, 1917–1968 (MS Am 1947), (1468), Houghton Library, Harvard University.

97. Winfield, *FDR and the News Media*, 219. See also Steven Casey, *Cautious Crusade: Franklin D. Roosevelt, American Public Opinion, and the War Against Nazi Germany* (New York: Oxford University Press, 2001), 19.

98. See the many public opinion surveys and reports saved in PPF 1820, Box 4, FDRL.

99. Rowe to Roosevelt, August 9, 1940, OF 857, Box 2, (Straw Votes, 1947–1940), FDRL. Note that this version of the origins of Cantril's work for the Roosevelt administration differs from the account in J. Michael Sproule, *Propaganda and Democracy: The American Experience of Media and Mass Persuasion* (New York: Cambridge University Press, 1997), 183–185, but the two accounts are not mutually exclusive. Given Cantril's desire to influence the course of American foreign policy, it is likely that he was working several angles to get to the president. Cantril provides a high-level overview of his work for Roosevelt in Hadley Cantril, *The Human Dimension: Experiences in Policy Research* (New Brunswick, NJ: Rutgers University Press, 1967).

100. On Bruner's role in Cantril's operation, see Niles to Roosevelt, March 15, 1943, OF 857, Box 2, (Straw Votes, 1943–1945), FDRL.

101. On Cantril's involvement with the British, see Hadley Cantril, https://ropercenter.cornell.edu/pioneers-polling/hadley-cantril, November 14, 2019. On Sherwood's involvement with British intelligence, see British Security Coordination, *The Secret History of British Intelligence in the Americas, 1940–1945* (New York: Fromm International, 1999), 17.

102. William Boyd, "The Secret Persuaders," *The Guardian*, August 19, 2006, https://www.theguardian.com/uk/2006/aug/19/military.secondworldwar.

103. British Security Coordination, *The Secret History of British Intelligence in the Americas, 1940–1945*, xxvi. This is the official, little-known history of British Security Coordination, written by BSC personnel in 1945 and released to the public only in 1998. In the intervening years, a handful of accounts of BSC's work appeared, but they are filled with so many errors, omissions, and exaggerations that they should not be relied upon. On those works, see Nigel West's introduction to the published official history.

104. British Security Coordination, *The Secret History of British Intelligence in the Americas, 1940–1945*, 16.

105. Ibid., 102.

106. Ibid., 11.

107. Ibid. Sherwood did not hide his collaboration with British intelligence personnel. He even invited two of them to join him as guests of the president during delivery of a February 1942 fireside chat. See Rosenman, *Working with Roosevelt*, 344.

108. For Rosenman's arrival, see December 26th, 1940, FDR: Day by Day, FDRL, http://www.fdrlibrary.marist.edu/daybyday/daylog/december-26th-1940/. For Sherwood's arrival, see December 27th, 1940, FDR: Day by Day, FDRL, http://www.fdrlibrary.marist.edu/daybyday/daylog/december-27th-1940/.

109. Ira Chernus has argued Roosevelt's use of the term "national security" is a story of accident and unintended consequences. One can make a good case for the latter point, but the archival record makes clear Roosevelt's use of the term was no accident. See Ira Chernus, "Franklin D. Roosevelt's Narrative of National Insecurity," *Journal of Multicultural Discourses* 11, no. 2 (2016): 135–148.

110. For the first draft, see Franklin D. Roosevelt, "Fireside Chat #16," December 29, 1940, MSF, Box 58, (1351A), FDRL, http://www.fdrlibrary.marist.edu/_resources/images/msf/msf01403, 48–49.

111. Rosenman, *Working with Roosevelt*, 259.

112. Ibid.

113. For the opening of the second draft, see Roosevelt, "Fireside Chat #16," December 29, 1940, MSF, Box 58, (1351A), FDRL, 32–35.

114. Ibid. For the opening of the third draft, see Ibid., 48–51. For the opening of the fourth draft, see Ibid., 52–54.

115. For Sherwood's insight, see Sherwood to Roosevelt, July 12, 1941, Robert E. Sherwood Papers, 1917–1968 (MS Am 1947), (1468), Houghton Library, Harvard University. For the opening of the fifth draft, see Roosevelt, "Fireside Chat #16," December 29, 1940, MSF, Box 58, (1351A), FDRL, 98.

116. For the sixth draft, see Marked up sixth draft of Dec. 29, 1940 fireside chat, Hopkins Papers, Box 97, General Correspondence, 1939–1940 (Roosevelt, Franklin D.) (F.D.R. Speech, 12-29-40), FDRL.

117. Franklin D. Roosevelt, "Fireside Chat #16," December 29, 1940, MSF, Box 58, (1351A), FDRL, http://www.fdrlibrary.marist.edu/_resources/images/msf/msf01403 and https://www.fdrlibrary.org/documents/356632/405112/afdr223.mp3/a70c292d-eb42-4412-81e8-5c9f1fe6e70b.

118. Ibid.

119. See Franklin D. Roosevelt, "Fireside Chat #2—'Outlining the New Deal Program,'" May 7, 1933, MSF, Box 14, (627), FDRL, http://www.fdrlibrary.marist.edu/_resources /images/msf/msf00646 and https://www.fdrlibrary.org/documents/356632/405112 /afdr014.mp3/943f2504-4303-4303-bbff-8a72b13db2ca.

120. See, for example, Franklin D. Roosevelt, "White House Correspondents Dinner Address," March 15, 1941, MSF, Box 59, (1361A), FDRL, http://www.fdrlibrary.marist .edu/_resources/images/msf/msf01418 and https://www.fdrlibrary.org/documents /356632/405112/afdr230.mp3/b519d068-3d9c-4867-a900-f9106a5c6090. Robert Sherwood was present when Roosevelt dictated the relevant text. See Sherwood Diary, March 12–16, 1941, Robert E. Sherwood Additional Papers, (89M-66), (1941), Houghton Library, Harvard University.

121. Roosevelt, "Fireside Chat #16," December 29, 1940, MSF, Box 58, (1351A), FDRL.

122. Ibid.

123. Ibid.

124. Ibid. For Roosevelt's personal involvement in shaping these words, see Roosevelt's handwriting on the fourth draft on Ibid., 70.

125. For a retrospective analysis of the increase in public support for aid to Britain, see Berinsky, Powell, Schickler, and Yohai, "Revisiting Public Opinion in the 1930s and 1940s," 519–520.

126. America Faces the War, n.d. [1940–1941], OF 857, Box 2, (Straw Votes, 1943–1945), FDRL, 4.

127. Ibid.

128. Ibid., 28.

129. On Lend-Lease, see Warren F. Kimball, *The Most Unsordid Act: Lend-Lease, 1939–1941* (Baltimore: Johns Hopkins University Press, 1969).

130. Roosevelt, "Fireside Chat #16," December 29, 1940, MSF, Box 58, (1351A), FDRL.

6. Roosevelt's Unrealized Vision for a Comprehensive National Security State

1. Franklin D. Roosevelt, "Annual Message to Congress—State of the Union," January 11, 1944, MSF, Box 76, (1501), FDRL, http://www.fdrlibrary.marist.edu/_resources/images /msf/msfb0129 and https://www.fdrlibrary.org/documents/356632/405112/afdr285.mp3 /0f815ba6-8388-4c66-88b8-66b40572950c.

2. Frederick C. Crawford, "The Next Fifty Years," January 25, 1945, NAM Records (1411), Box 104, (Free Enterprise- General—1949–1940), HML, 2.

3. Franklin D. Roosevelt, "Message to Congress—The State of the Union," January 6, 1941, MSF, Box 58, (1353A), FDRL, http://www.fdrlibrary.marist.edu/_resources /images/msf/msf01407 and https://www.fdrlibrary.org/documents/356632/405112 /afdr224.mp3/c07a0140-51a9-43ce-b192-a703f65c8f19.

4. Ibid.

5. Ibid. For a careful study of how this speech came together, see Laura Crowell, "The Building of the 'Four Freedoms' Speech," *Speech Monographs* 22, no. 5 (November 1955): 266–283, https://www.tandfonline.com/doi/abs/10.1080/03637755509375153.

6. See, for example, Franklin D. Roosevelt, "Wichita, Kansas—Western Campaign Trip—Campaign Address," October 13, 1936, MSF, Box 28, (960), FDRL, http://www .fdrlibrary.marist.edu/_resources/images/msf/msf00985.

7. For an insightful exploration of the ideas in the Four Freedoms speech, see Elizabeth Borgwardt, *A New Deal for the World: America's Vision for Human Rights* (Cambridge, MA: Harvard University Press, 2005).

8. This discussion builds on the ideas expressed in Berlin, "Two Concepts of Liberty" and James M. McPherson, *Battle Cry of Freedom: The Civil War Era* (New York: Oxford University Press, 1988), 865–867. See also Rossiter, "The Political Philosophy of F. D. Roosevelt," 90.

9. See, for example, Sparrow, *Warfare State*, 21; Neocleous, "From Social to National Security"; and Andrew Preston, "Liberalism, War, and the Invention of 'National Security,'" talk delivered at the Clements Center at the University of Texas at Austin, May 1, 2019, https://warontherocks.com/2019/05/horns-of-a-dilemma-past-and -present-how-the-idea-of-national-security-has-shifted-over-time/.

10. Press and Radio Conference #929, December 28, 1943, Press Conferences of President Franklin D. Roosevelt, 1933–1945, Series 1, (926–929), FDRL, http://www.fdrlibrary .marist.edu/_resources/images/pc/pc0155.pdf, 44–48. On Roosevelt's hope that the comment would neutralize criticism, see Warren F. Kimball, *The Juggler: Franklin Roosevelt as Wartime Statesman* (Princeton, NJ: Princeton University Press, 1991), 61. John Jeffries and Elizabeth Borgwardt also suggest that historians have interpreted Roosevelt's comment in ways that have led them to overlook his continued focus on domestic policy. See John W. Jeffries, "The 'New' New Deal: FDR and American Liberalism, 1937–1945," *Political Science Quarterly* 105, no. 3 (Autumn 1990): 397, and Borgwardt, *New Deal for the World*, 50.

11. Roosevelt, "Message to Congress—The State of the Union," January 6, 1941, FDRL.

12. Ibid.

13. Ibid.

14. For drafts, see Franklin D. Roosevelt, "Message to Congress—The State of the Union," January 6, 1941, MSF, Box 58, (1353A), FDRL.

15. Currie to Roosevelt, December 2, 1940, PPF 1820, Speech Material and Suggestions, Box 18, (Annual Message to Congress, 1941), FDRL.

16. McNutt to Roosevelt, January 3, 1941, PPF 1820, Box 18, (Annual Message to Congress, 1941), FDRL.

17. Roosevelt, "Message to Congress—The State of the Union," January 6, 1941, FDRL. Benjamin V. Cohen helped shape that line. For Cohen's input, see Ibid., 79–82.

18. Roosevelt, "Message to Congress—The State of the Union," January 6, 1941, FDRL.

19. Ibid.

20. For Roosevelt's dictation, see Ibid., 77–78.

21. Franklin D. Roosevelt, "Pan American Union Address Proclaiming an Unlimited National Emergency," May 27, 1941, MSF, Box 60, (1368A), FDRL, http://www.fdr library.marist.edu/_resources/images/msf/msf01426 and https://www.fdrlibrary.org /documents/356632/405112/afdr234.mp3/d3a79519-b8ac-4f9c-b1e4-f3b76b9f58df.

22. Ibid.

23. Ibid.

24. Ibid.

25. Ibid.

26. Ibid.

27. Ibid.

28. Reagan, *Designing a New America*, 218.

29. Ibid.

30. Franklin D. Roosevelt, "Statement on the Atlantic Charter Meeting with Prime Minister Churchill," August 14, 1941, APP, https://www.presidency.ucsb.edu/node/209814. Samuel Rosenman credits the NRPB's work on a second Bill of Rights with influencing the content of the Atlantic Charter. See Interviews with Louis Brownlow and Luther Gulick, June 1, 1949, Rosenman Papers, Box 1, (Gulick, Dr. Luther), FDRL.

31. Memorandum for the President, December 4, 1941, PSF, Box 175, (Post-War Planning—Subject File), FDRL, http://www.fdrlibrary.marist.edu/_resources/images/psf/psfc0005.pdf, 4.

32. Ibid., 10.

33. Ibid., 10–11.

34. See Franklin D. Roosevelt, "State of the Union Address to Congress (2 parts)," January 6, 1942, MSF, Box 65, (1409), FDRL, http://www.fdrlibrary.marist.edu/_resources/images/msf/msfb0015, 54 and https://www.fdrlibrary.org/documents/356632/405112/afdr248.mp3/8700ddb7-f268-40a2-8112-b6bcba5f301b.

35. Roosevelt, "State of the Union Address," January 6, 1942, FDRL, 105.

36. Bruce J. Schulman, *From Cotton Belt to Sunbelt: Federal Policy, Economic Development, and the Transformation of the South, 1938–1980* (Durham, NC: Duke University Press, 1994), 152.

37. NRPB report quoted in Rebecca U. Thorpe, *The American Warfare State: The Domestic Politics of Military Spending* (Chicago: University of Chicago Press, 2014), 53.

38. War Production Board report quoted in Schulman, *From Cotton Belt to Sunbelt*, 101. Schulman argues persuasively that "the Roosevelt administration used the war emergency to develop the South." See Ibid., 100.

39. NRPB Post War Agenda, February 6, 1942, Rosenman Papers, Box 1, (Gulick, Luther), FDRL. On Gulick's hiring, see Reagan, *Designing a New America*, 217.

40. NRPB Post War Agenda, February 6, 1942, Rosenman Papers, FDRL.

41. On the war going badly in the first half of 1942, see Rosenman, *Working with Roosevelt*, 328–329.

42. FDR to Director of the Budget, March 31, 1942, PPF 1820, Box 6, (Speech Materials and Suggestions, 1942 Jan–Nov), FDRL.

43. See Memorandum on the Work Projects Administration, National Youth Administration, and Farm Security Administration attached to FDR to Director of the Budget, March 31, 1942, PPF 1820, Box 6, (Speech Materials and Suggestions, 1942 Jan–Nov), FDRL.

44. Kennedy, *Freedom from Fear*, 637.

45. Ibid., 644.

46. Quoted in Kennedy, *Freedom from Fear*, 644.

47. Reagan, *Designing a New America*, 217.

48. On the NRPB's ineffective public relations efforts, see Jeffries, "The 'New' New Deal," 410–415.

49. See National Resources Planning Board, "After the War—Security," PPF 1820, Box 18, (Speech Material—Suggestions, 1942 and Dec 1942), FDRL.

50. Hamby, *Man of Destiny*, 363.

51. Steele, "The Pulse of the People," 209–210; Eisinger and Brown, "Polling as a Means Toward Presidential Autonomy," 237–256; and Winfield, *FDR and the News Media*, 215–229.

52. On Hurja, see Holi, *Wizard of Washington*. For examples of how the president and his advisors used the Cantril-Lambert operation, see Lambert to Rosenman, September 1, 1943, Rosenman Papers, Box 19, (Speech Material, 1940–1944 (1)), FDRL, and Cantril to Rosenman, October 2, 1943, Rosenman Papers, Box 14, (Princeton Public Opinion Poll (Hadley Cantril)), FDRL.

53. Niles to Tully, December 15, 1942, PPF 8229, (Cantril, Dr. Hadley), FDRL.

54. Roosevelt collected documents related to expanding social security, December 1942, PPF 1820, Box 6, (Speech Materials and Suggestions, 1942 December), FDRL. On American newspaper coverage, see (among many articles) "London Cable," *Wall Street Journal*, December 4, 1942; George Gallup, "The Gallup Poll: Overwhelming Majority of British Public Favors Launching of Social Security Plan," *Washington Post*, December 11, 1942; and Leo Wolman, "British Social Security Plan Aims at Eliminating Want," *Washington Post*, December 18, 1942.

55. See Cox to Hopkins, December 22, 1942, MSF, Box 71, (1447), FDRL, http://www .fdrlibrary.marist.edu/_resources/images/msf/msfb0069, 246. On Cox's liberalism, see Steele, "The Pulse of the People," 212–213.

56. See Cox to Hopkins, December 22, 1942, MSF, Box 71, (1447), FDRL, http://www .fdrlibrary.marist.edu/_resources/images/msf/msfb0069, 246.

57. See Tully to Hopkins, Rosenman, and Sherwood, December 24, 1942, MSF, Box 71, (1447), FDRL, http://www.fdrlibrary.marist.edu/_resources/images/msf/msfb0069, 2.

58. Franklin Roosevelt to Mackenzie King, December 29, 1942, reproduced in *F. D. R., His Personal Letters, 1928–1945, II (Volume 4)*, ed. Elliott Roosevelt (New York: Duell, Sloan, and Pearce, 1970), 1382.

59. See Tully to Hopkins, Rosenman, and Sherwood, December 24, 1942, FDRL, 2–10.

60. On Roosevelt's prior uses of that phrase, see Perkins, *Roosevelt I Knew*, 270–271.

61. Franklin D. Roosevelt, "Message to Congress re The State of the Union," January 7, 1943, MSF, Box 70, (1447), FDRL, http://www.fdrlibrary.marist.edu/_resources/images /msf/msfb0067 and https://www.fdrlibrary.org/documents/356632/405112/afdr269.mp3 /9508f113-c8d9-49c2-94f8-b3855db493d3.

62. Ibid. On Roosevelt's responsibility for that line, see Tully to Hopkins, Rosenman, and Sherwood, December 24, 1942, FDRL, 9.

63. Ibid.

64. Guffey to Roosevelt, January 26, 1943, PPF 1820, Box 6, (Speech Materials and Suggestions, 1943 Mar–April), FDRL.

65. Ibid.

66. Ibid.

67. Ibid.

68. Barry D. Karl, *The Uneasy State: The United States from 1915 to 1945* (Chicago: University of Chicago Press, 1983), 120, and Friedberg, *In the Shadow of the Garrison State*, 29.

69. Gregory Hooks and Brian McQueen, "American Exceptionalism Revisited: The Military-Industrial Complex, Racial Tension, and the Underdeveloped Welfare State," *American Sociological Review* 75, no. 2 (April 2010): 187.

70. See, for example, Rosenman to Roosevelt, July 11, 1943, Rosenman Papers, Box 3, (Roosevelt, Franklin D.), FDRL; Noyes to Byrnes, July 20, 1943, PPF 1820, Box 7, (Speech Materials and Suggestions, 1943 May-July), FDRL; and Lambert to Rosenman, September 1, 1943, Rosenman Papers, Box 19, (Speech Material, 1940–1944 (1)), FDRL.

71. Reagan, *Designing a New America*, 191.

72. The Independent Offices Appropriation Act of 1944 (57 Stat. 169), June 26, 1943 defunded the NRPB and led to its dissolution by the beginning of 1944. See "Records of the National Resources Planning Board (NRPB), 1931–1943," National Archives and Records Administration, https://www.archives.gov/research/guide-fed-records/groups /187.html#187.1.

73. In the second draft of his 1944 State of the Union address, Roosevelt planned to ask Congress for "a regular planning agency" and said that they should "not be afraid of that word 'planning.'" But Roosevelt realized that the issue remained politically toxic and struck those lines. See Roosevelt, "Annual Message to Congress—State of the Union," January 11, 1944, FDRL, 117.

74. Kennedy, *Freedom from Fear*, 784.

75. Sherwood handwritten notes on Roosevelt and NRPB, n.d., Robert E. Sherwood Papers, 1917–1968 (MS Am 1947), (1866 (3 of 6)), Houghton Library, Harvard University.

76. For an example of how Roosevelt's frustration manifested itself privately, see Roosevelt to Rosenman and Sherwood, February 23, 1943, PPF 1820, Box 6, (Speech Materials and Suggestions, 1943 Jan-Feb), FDRL.

77. Untitled NAM-NIIC PR Campaign Plan, n.d. [1943], NAM Records (1411), Box 1094, (NIIC Subject- Advertising- 1943), HML, 26.

78. See, for example, Memo from Weisenburger and Harrison to the Executive Committee, n. d. [1944], NAM Records (1411), Box 1093, (NIIC Administrative—Annual Reports— NIIC—1941–1943), HML. As NAM's PR campaign became more sophisticated in the early 1940s, NAM paid careful attention to the meaning of words and the ways that the public understood specific words like "security." For example, see Semantic Notes Related to NIIC Program, n.d. [1943], NAM Records (1411), Box 1097, (NIIC Subject-Program Semantics—1943), HML; NAM Records (1411), Box 1098, (NIIC Subject—Semantics—1943-1944), HML; and Walter D. Fuller, "Is Free Enterprise Still Free?" May 27, 1941, NAM Records (1411), Box 104, (Free Enterprise- N.A.M.—1938-1949), HML.

79. "Theme of 1939-1940 Program," NAM Records, HML, 5.

80. See Wilson, *Destructive Creation*, 92–138.

81. Lawson to Weisenburger, November 13, 1940, NAM Records, HML.

82. Ibid.

83. Untitled NAM-NIIC PR Campaign Plan, NAM Records, HML, 51.

84. Wilson, *Destructive Creation*, 61–63.

85. Lawson to Ross, January 24, 1941, NAM Records (1411), Box 142, (Public Relations—Service for Plant Publications, Making America Strong, Proof-Sheets, Dec. 1940), HML, 4. Wendy Wall also calls attention to a shift in NAM's approach beginning in 1942. See Wall, *Inventing the "American Way,"* 126, 128–131.

86. H. W. Prentis Jr., "The Way to Freedom," December 4, 1942, NAM Records (1411), Box 2, (Freedom—General (2 of 2)), HML, 12. Glickman cites the same speech in Glickman, *Free Enterprise*, 196.

87. National Industrial Information Committee, *Your Public Information Program in Action, Annual Report for 1942*, n.d. [1942], HML, 7.

88. *A Better America*, December 1943, NAM Records (1411), Box 145, (A Better America), HML, 9.

89. National Industrial Information Committee, *Your Public Information Program in Action, Annual Report for 1942*, n.d. [1942], HML, 8–9.

90. Wilson, *Destructive Creation*, 62–91.

91. Ibid., 73.

92. On the number of employees at the North American Dallas bomber plant, see Department of the Navy, "Integrated Cultural Resource Management Plan: Naval Weapons Industrial Reserve Plant, Dallas, Dallas County, TX," July 2002, 8–32.

93. The reliance on the GOCO model sheds further light on the paradox Lisa McGirr explores in *Suburban Warriors*, with defense plant workers in Southern California playing a leading role in the conservative movement and adopting selectively anti-statist views even though the government was, in effect, paying their wages.

94. On the consequences of policy design choices on public perceptions of the government, see Suzanne Mettler, *The Submerged State: How Invisible Government Policies Undermine American Democracy* (Chicago: University of Chicago Press, 2011).

95. Wilson, *Destructive Creation*, 48–138, 274.

96. "Businessmen Look Ahead," *Service for Plant Publications*, no. 88, October 1943, NAM Records (1411), Box 142, (Public Relations—Service for Plant Publications, Jan. 1941-Oct. 1944), HML.

97. *Service for Plant Publications*, no. 93, March 1944, NAM Records (1411), Box 144, (Public Relations—Service for Plant Publications, Jan. 1941-Oct. 1944), HML.

98. Wall, *Inventing the "American Way,"* 128–129, and Wilson, *Destructive Creation*, 286.

99. *Service for Plant Publications*, no. 64, October 1941, NAM Records (1411), Box 144, (Public Relations—Service for Plant Publications, Jan. 1941-Oct. 1944), HML.

100. *A Better America*, December 1943, NAM Records, HML, 4. On Crawford's background and importance, see Sanford M. Jacoby, *Modern Manors: Welfare Capitalism since the New Deal* (Princeton, NJ: Princeton University Press, 1997), 196–198.

101. *A Better America*, December 1943, NAM Records, HML, 28.

102. Ibid.

103. Ibid., 29.

104. Ibid., 30.

105. Ibid., 29.

106. Ibid., 30.

107. Ibid., 31.

108. Roosevelt to Rosenman and Sherwood, February 23, 1943, PPF 1820, Box 6, (Speech Materials and Suggestions, 1943 Jan-Feb), FDRL.

109. Bowles to Rosenman, December 23, 1943, Rosenman Papers, Box 1, (Bowles, Chester), FDRL.

110. Ibid. Louis Brownlow made similar suggestions. See Rosenman, *Working with Roosevelt*, 425, and Roosevelt to Brownlow, December 29, 1943, PPF 1820, Box 7, (Speech Materials and Suggestions, 1943 Aug-Dec), FDRL.

111. Cantril to Rosenman, January 6, 1944, Rosenman Papers, Box 14, (Princeton Public Opinion Poll (Hadley Cantril)), FDRL.

112. Ibid.

113. See Rosenman to Roosevelt, December 31, 1943, Rosenman Papers, Box 3, (Roosevelt, Franklin D.), FDRL, and Rosenman to Roosevelt, January 5, 1944, Rosenman Papers, Box 3, (Roosevelt, Franklin D.), FDRL. See also Steele, "The Pulse of the People," 214. On Roosevelt's approval, see Rosenman, *Working with Roosevelt*, 426.

114. Bowles to Rosenman, December 23, 1943, Rosenman Papers, Box 1, (Bowles, Chester), FDRL.

115. Ibid.

116. Ibid.

117. James MacGregor Burns reaches a similar conclusion in James MacGregor Burns, *Roosevelt: The Soldier of Freedom*, 1940–1945 (New York: Open Road, 2012), 425–426. See also Sunstein, *Second Bill of Rights*, 94.

118. See Roosevelt, "Annual Message to Congress—State of the Union," January 11, 1944, FDRL, 184–187.

119. Roosevelt, "Annual Message to Congress—State of the Union," January 11, 1944, FDRL.

120. Ibid.

121. Ibid.

122. The stated reason for the departure from recent practice was that the president was recovering from the flu. But Rosenman notes that Roosevelt "seldom hesitated, when necessary, to go over the heads of the Congress and appeal directly to the people" and the tone of parts of the message suggests that he was doing precisely that. See Rosenman, *Working with Roosevelt*, 426.

123. Roosevelt, "Annual Message to Congress—State of the Union," January 11, 1944, FDRL.

124. Ibid., 150.

125. Roosevelt, "Annual Message to Congress—State of the Union," January 11, 1944, FDRL.

126. Burns, *Roosevelt: The Soldier of Freedom*, 426.

127. Rosenman to Roosevelt, February 12, 1944, Rosenman Papers, Box 3, (Roosevelt, Franklin D.), FDRL, and Cantril to Rosenman, January 27, 1944, Rosenman Papers, Box 14, (Princeton Public Opinion Poll (Hadley Cantril)), FDRL.

128. List of proposed messages to congress, n.d. [1944], Rosenman Papers, Box 19, (Speech Material, 1940–1944 (1)), FDRL.

129. Ibid.

130. On "entering wedge," see Rosenman, *Working with Roosevelt*, 395.

131. Alan Brinkley, "The National Resources Planning Board and the Reconstruction of Planning," in *The American Planning Tradition: Culture and Policy*, ed. Robert Fishman (Washington, DC: Woodrow Wilson Center Press, 2000), 183.

132. Rosenman, *Working with Roosevelt*, 395.

133. On the distribution of the GI Bill's benefits and its effects on American society, see Ira Katznelson, *When Affirmative Action Was White: An Untold History of Racial Inequality in Twentieth-Century America* (New York: Norton, 2005), 113–141, and Suzanne Mettler, *Soldiers to Citizens: The G.I. Bill and the Making of the Greatest Generation* (New York: Oxford University Press, 2005). On the effects of what Ira Katznelson calls the "Southern Cage," see Ira Katznelson, *Fear Itself: The New Deal and the Origins of Our Time* (New York: Liveright, 2013) 16 and generally.

134. See Jennifer Mittelstadt, *The Rise of the Military-Welfare State* (Cambridge, MA: Harvard University Press, 2015).

135. Franklin D. Roosevelt, "Statement on Signing the G.I. Bill," June 22, 1944, APP, https://www.presidency.ucsb.edu/node/210867.

136. See, for example, Franklin D. Roosevelt, "Detroit, Michigan—Hamtramck Stadium—Western Campaign Trip—remarks," October 15, 1936, MSF, Box 29, (973), FDRL, http://www.fdrlibrary.marist.edu/_resources/images/msf/msf00999.

137. Correspondence summary, July 5, 1944, PPF 8229, (Cantril, Dr. Hadley), FDRL, and Cantril to Roosevelt, July 5, 1944, OF 857, Box 2, (Straw Votes, 1943–1945), FDRL.

138. Thomas Dewey, "Address Accepting the Presidential Nomination at the Republican National Convention in Chicago, Illinois," June 28, 1944, APP, https://www.presidency.ucsb.edu/node/275898.

139. Ibid.

140. Ibid.

141. Ibid.

142. For an insightful portrait of Dewey, albeit from a later campaign, see Richard H. Rovere, "Letter from a Campaign Train: En Route with Dewey," *The New Yorker*, October 16, 1948, 75–80.

143. Franklin D. Roosevelt, "Chicago, Illinois—Soldier's Field—Campaign Address," October 28, 1944, MSF, Box 83, (1552A), FDRL, http://www.fdrlibrary.marist.edu/_resources/images/msf/msfb0184 and https://www.fdrlibrary.org/documents/356632/405112/afdr302.mp3/07390b9b-afbd-4765-b9fc-b619cc2aa9a7.

144. Ibid.

145. Ibid.

146. Franklin D. Roosevelt, "Radio Address to the Democratic National Convention, accepting Its Nomination for a Fourth Term," July 20, 1944, MSF, Box 79, (1525A), http://www.fdrlibrary.marist.edu/_resources/images/msf/msfb0155 and https://www.fdrlibrary.org/documents/356632/405112/afdr292.mp3/72d0de98-f5ac-40cd-85e2-8ffe6717ed51.

147. Roosevelt, "Chicago, Illinois—Soldier's Field—Campaign Address," October 28, 1944, FDRL.

148. Roosevelt, "Radio Address to the Democratic National Convention, accepting Its Nomination for a Fourth Term," July 20, 1944, FDRL.

149. Dewey quoted in Burns, *Roosevelt: The Soldier of Freedom*, 528.

150. See Voter Turnout in Presidential Elections, The American Presidency Project, https://www.presidency.ucsb.edu/statistics/data/voter-turnout-in-presidential-elections.

151. Burns, *Roosevelt: The Soldier of Freedom*, 528.

152. F. A. Hayek, *The Road to Serfdom: Text and Documents—the Definitive Edition (The Collected Works of F. A. Hayek, Volume 2)*, ed. Bruce Caldwell (Chicago: University of Chicago Press, 2007), 43.

153. Ibid., 174.

154. Ibid., 147.

155. Ibid., 156.

156. Ibid.

157. This paragraph and the one that follows rely on Angus Burgin's insightful analysis of the conservative movement's selective appropriation of Hayek's work. See Burgin, *Great Persuasion*, 87–94.

158. *Reader's Digest* 46, no. 276 (April 1945).

159. Burgin, *Great Persuasion*, 88–89.

160. Ibid.

161. Hayek, *Road to Serfdom*, 133–135. See also Burgin, *Great Persuasion*, 90–91.

162. Hayek, *Road to Serfdom*, 134–135.

163. Compare Hayek, *Road to Serfdom*, 134–135, with the text attributed to Hayek in *Reader's Digest* 46, no. 276 (April 1945).

164. According to Angus Burgin, the magazine's "readership numbered well over eight million." Burgin, *Great Persuasion*, 87.

165. *Reader's Digest* 47, no. 279 (July 1945).

166. Burgin, *Great Persuasion*, 89.

167. Ibid.

168. Ibid.

169. On the book's success, see Nash, *Conservative Intellectual Movement in America since 1945*, 5–7, and Phillips-Fein, *Invisible Hands*, 41.

170. Hayek quoted in Burgin, *Great Persuasion*, 92.

171. "An Advertising Program for the National Association of Manufacturers," n.d. [1944], Brophy Papers, Box 57, (National Association of Manufacturers, 1944–1945), WHS.

172. Henry M. Wriston, "Free Enterprise," December 10, 1943, NAM Records (1411), Box 104, (Free Enterprise- N.A.M.—1938–1949), HML.

173. Breckenridge to Harrison, November 13, 1944, NAM Records (1411), Box 1093, (NIIC Administrative—NIIC Executive Cmte. 11-14-44—1944), HML, 6.

174. "How Americans can EARN MORE, BUY MORE, HAVE MORE," NAM Records (1411), Box OS 5, (Untitled), HML, https://digital.hagley.org/LMSS_1411_863_002 _07?solr_nav%5Bid%5D=f1265f236e7f71250a07&solr_nav%5Bpage%5D=0&solr_nav %5Boffset%5D=5.

175. "GUTS," NAM Records (1411), Box OS 5, (Untitled), HML, https://digital.hagley.org
     /LMSS_1411_863_002_02?solr_nav%5Bid%5D=f1265f236e7f71250a07&solr_nav
     %5Bpage%5D=0&solr_nav%5Boffset%5D=11.

176. Ibid. For an example of how the ad looked in print, see "Display Ad 8—no Title,"
     Chicago Tribune, December 22, 1944, 8.

177. The NAM ran its public relations campaign like a business and used constant public
     opinion polling to gauge return on investment. By the second half of the 1940s, public
     opinion polling led the NAM to conclude that its efforts were succeeding. See, for
     example, Holcombe Parkes, "An Integrated Public Relations Program for the National
     Association of Manufacturers," January 14, 1946, NAM Records (1411), Box 141, (Long
     Range Program), HML, 10.

178. On "too dull, too stuffy," see Brophy to Cox, January 8, 1945, Brophy Papers, Box 57,
     (National Association of Manufacturers, 1944–1945), WHS, and Brophy to Weir,
     January 7, 1945, Brophy Papers, Box 57, (National Association of Manufacturers,
     1944–1945), WHS. On the favorable public reaction to the ads, see Brophy to
     Breckenridge, February 19, 1945, Brophy Papers, Box 57, (National Association of
     Manufacturers, 1944–1945), WHS.

179. Ibid. On the scuttling of the ad campaign, see also Cox to Brophy, February 13, 1945,
     Brophy Papers, Box 57, (National Association of Manufacturers, 1944–1945), WHS.

180. Crawford, "The Next Fifty Years," January 25, 1945, NAM Records, HML, 2.

181. Ibid.

182. Ibid.

183. Franklin D. Roosevelt, "Message to Congress—The State of the Union," January 4,
     1939, MSF, Box 43, (1191B), FDRL, http://www.fdrlibrary.marist.edu/_resources
     /images/msf/msf01229 and https://www.fdrlibrary.org/documents/356632/405112
     /afdr134.mp3/59e90862-0ef4-443d-be5d-5b9afde5d03f.

184. Among many examples, see Purcell to Roosevelt, PPF 1820, Box 6, (Speech Materials
     and Suggestions, 1943 Jan-Feb), FDRL.

185. Andrew Workman argues that "through much of the war, NAM was ignored by the
     administration and widely seen as an ideological dinosaur." See Workman,
     "Manufacturing Power," 281.

186. For concise summaries of the American Liberty League's perceived failure, see
     Phillips-Fein, *Invisible Hands*, 11–13, and Wilson, *Destructive Creation*, 31, 123.

187. Rosenman to Roosevelt, January 5, 1945, Rosenman Papers, Box 3, (Roosevelt,
     Franklin D.), FDRL. On expanding Social Security, see Altmeyer to Rosenman,
     September 6, 1944, Rosenman Papers, Box 19, (Speech Material, 1940–1944 (2)),
     FDRL. On a national health program, see Cox to Rosenman, September 17, 1944,
     Rosenman Papers, Box 19, (Speech Material, 1944 Campaign), FDRL.

188. Arthur Krock, "In the Nation: New Deal's Orchestra Tries Symphonic Blend," *New
     York Times*, October 9, 1938, 73.

7. Separate National Security and Welfare States

1. Harry S. Truman, "Special Message to the Congress: The President's First Economic
   Report," January 8, 1947, APP, https://www.presidency.ucsb.edu/node/232721.

2. Department of Armed Forces, Department of Military Security: hearings before the Committee on Military Affairs, United States Senate, Seventy-Ninth Congress, first session, on S. 84, a bill to provide for a Department of Armed Forces, secretary of the Armed Forces, under secretaries of Army, Navy, and Air, and for other purposes [and] S. 1482, a bill to establish a Department of Military Security, to consolidate therein the military security activities of the United States, and for purposes. October 17, 18, 19, 22, 23, 24, 30, 31, November 2, 7, 8, 9, 14, 15, 16, 17, 23, 29, 30, and December 4, 5, 6, 7, 10, 13, 14, 15, 17, 1945, 98–99, hereafter "Senate Military Affairs Committee Fall 1945 Hearings."

3. For the National Security Resources Board's stated purpose, see the chart in Senate Military Affairs Committee Fall 1945 Hearings, Exhibit 1 (between pages 98 and 99).

4. Although scholars have written about the individual roles played by Earle, Lippmann, Herring, and Eberstadt in the development of the American national security state—or the role that two of the four played together—never, to my knowledge, have scholars evaluated the influence of all four together.

5. Roosevelt to Forrestal, March 31, 1945, GLC, http://www.americanhistory.amdigital.co.uk/Documents/Details/GLC00162.17.

6. See Oral History Interview with George M. Elsey by Jerry N. Hess, July 10, 1969, Harry S. Truman Library [hereafter HSTL], https://www.trumanlibrary.gov/library/oral-histories/elsey4, and Clark M. Clifford with Richard Holbrooke, *Counsel to the President: A Memoir* (New York: Random House, 1991), 74–75.

7. Ibid.

8. Oral History Interviews with Judge Samuel I. Rosenman by Jerry N. Hess, October 15, 1968, and April 23, 1969, HSTL, 55, https://www.trumanlibrary.gov/library/oral-histories/rosenmn.

9. Rosenman tried to resign following Roosevelt's death, but Truman declined to accept Rosenman's resignation letter. See Harry S. Truman, "Letter Declining to Accept Resignation of Samuel I. Rosenman as Special Counsel to the President," June 1, 1945, APP, https://www.presidency.ucsb.edu/node/232926.

10. Oral History Interviews with Judge Samuel I. Rosenman by Jerry N. Hess, October 15, 1968, and April 23, 1969, HSTL, 55.

11. Joanna Grisinger, *The Unwieldy American State: Administrative Politics Since the New Deal* (New York: Cambridge University Press, 2012), 160.

12. Harry S. Truman, "Special Message to the Congress Presenting a 21-Point Program for the Reconversion Period," September 6, 1945, APP, https://www.presidency.ucsb.edu/node/230568.

13. Ibid.

14. Ibid.

15. On tensions between liberals and conservatives within the Truman administration, see Clifford with Holbrooke, *Counsel to the President*, 77–80.

16. Ibid.

17. Ibid., 78.

18. Ibid.

19. Historian Alonzo Hamby calls the speech "the literary equivalent of a copious kitchen sink overflowing with pots, pans, and dinnerware of wildly diverse patterns and

origins." See Alonzo L. Hamby, *Man of the People: A Life of Harry S. Truman* (New York: Oxford University Press, 1995), 363.

20. Oral History Interviews with Judge Samuel I. Rosenman by Jerry N. Hess, October 15, 1968, and April 23, 1969, HSTL, 65.

21. Harry S. Truman, *Memoirs of Harry S. Truman, Volume One: Year of Decisions* (New York: Doubleday, 1955), 691.

22. On the greater persuasive power of loss frames, see Tversky and Kahneman, "The Framing of Decisions and the Psychology of Choice."

23. Harry S. Truman, "Message to the Congress on the State of the Union and on the Budget for 1947," January 21, 1946, APP, https://www.presidency.ucsb.edu/node /231926. For the Advertising Council's summary of the meeting, see Report on Major National Problems, February 1946, Advertising Council Archives, 13/2/207, Box 4, File 317, UIA.

24. Oral History Interviews with Judge Samuel I. Rosenman by Jerry N. Hess, October 15, 1968, and April 23, 1969, HSTL, 65.

25. James Webb Young speech, November 14, 1941, Advertising Council Archives, 13/2/282, Box 1, (James Webb Young (Speeches)), UIA.

26. Ibid. On Young's speech, see also Griffith, "Selling of America," 390. For insight into Young's political views, see James Webb Young, *The Diary of an Ad Man: The War Years June 1, 1942–December 31, 1943* (Chicago: Advertising Publications, Inc., 1944).

27. "The Background and Beginning of the Ad Council," 1952, Advertising Council Archives, 13/2/207, Box 10, File 647a, UIA, 11-6, and Griffith, "Selling of America," 390.

28. For instance, see Young to Pew, October 25, 1945, Advertising Council Archives, 13/2/305, Box 3, (Council Future Plans—1945) (2), UIA, and Barton to Young, September 19, 1946, Brophy Papers, Box 1, (Correspondence, 1946–), WHS.

29. Ad Council Board Minutes, May 11, 1945, Advertising Council Archives, 13/2/201, Box 1, (War Advertising Council Minutes, May–June 1945), UIA.

30. *Which Way Will America Choose?*, undated [1945], Advertising Council Archives, 13/2/305, Box 3, (Council Future Plans—1945), UIA.

31. Wall, *Inventing the "American Way*," 176.

32. See Thomas D'Arcy Brophy, "Advertising in a Mobilized Economy," April 6, 1951, Brophy Papers, Box 25, (Speeches, 1950–1953), WHS, 7.

33. For one year's count, see *Ad Council Annual Report*, 8th, "How Business Helps Solve Public Problems," 1949–1950, Advertising Council Archives, UIA.

34. Griffith, "The Selling of America," 388. On conservatives' growing support for military spending in the decades following World War II, see Jonathan Soffer, "The National Association of Manufacturers and the Militarization of American Conservatism," *Business History Review* 75, no. 4 (Winter 2001): 775–805.

35. Mortimer to Board of Directors, October 30, 1947, Brophy Papers, Box 1, (Correspondence, 1947), WHS.

36. See Griffith, "Selling of America," 400.

37. See Hutton to Brophy, December 29, 1944, Brophy Papers, Box 5, (War Advertising Council, 1944–1945), WHS, and Brophy to Thomas, January 4, 1945, Brophy Papers, Box 5, (War Advertising Council, 1944–1945), WHS.

38. For an example Hutton ad, see Osmer to Hutton, May 29, 1946, Brophy Papers, Box 35, (Hutton, E. F. Correspondence with Brophy, 1944–1947), WHS.

39. For an overview of Kenyon & Eckhardt's relationship with Hutton, see Brophy to Drepperd, July 3, 1946, Brophy Papers, Box 35, (Hutton, E. F. Correspondence with Brophy, 1944–1947), WHS.

40. See Cox to Brophy, December 4, 1946, Brophy Papers, Box 35, (Hutton, E. F. Correspondence with Brophy, 1944–1947), WHS; Brophy to Hutton, March 10, 1947, Brophy Papers, Box 35, (Hutton, E. F. Correspondence with Brophy, 1944–1947), WHS; Brophy to Hutton, July 25, 1946, Brophy Papers, Box 35, (Hutton, E. F. Correspondence with Brophy, 1944–1947), WHS; and Brophy to Hutton, August 29, 1945, Brophy Papers, Box 35, (Hutton, E. F. Correspondence with Brophy, 1944–1947), WHS.

41. See Brophy to Hutton, October 11, 1946, Brophy Papers, Box 35, (Hutton, E. F. Correspondence with Brophy, 1944–1947), WHS.

42. See, generally, Brophy Papers, Box 35, ("I Am An American" Program—1946), WHS, and Wall, *Inventing the "American Way,"* 176.

43. Thomas D'A. Brophy, "A Program to Re-sell Americanism to Americans," November 15, 1946, Brophy Papers, Box 35, ("I Am an American"—1946), WHS, 3.

44. Ibid., 2. On the circulation of Brophy's proposal, see Wall, *Inventing the "American Way,"* 205.

45. Brophy, "A Program to Re-sell Americanism to Americans," November 15, 1946, Brophy Papers, WHS, 2.

46. "Address by Honorable Tom C. Clark at Bill of Rights Luncheon," December 10, 1946, Brophy Papers, Box 25, (Clark, Thomas C., 1946–1958, 1951–1952, 1954, n.d.), WHS, 2.

47. Wall, *Inventing the "American Way,"* 202.

48. Ibid., 203.

49. Ibid.

50. "Balaban Gifts 'Bill of Rights' to U.S. Library," *Variety* 153, no. 1 (December 15, 1943): 1. See also Wall, *Inventing the "American Way,"* 204.

51. Wall, *Inventing the "American Way,"* 203–205.

52. Ibid.

53. Ibid., 205.

54. The information in this paragraph comes from Wendy Wall's impeccably researched chapter on the Freedom Train. See Wall, *Inventing the "American Way,"* 206–208.

55. On Aldrich, see Will Lissner, "Winthrop Aldrich Dead; Banker and Diplomat, 88," *New York Times*, February 26, 1974, 40.

56. On the establishment of the American Heritage Campaign / Foundation and the Freedom Train, see "Address by Honorable Tom C. Clark at Bill of Rights Luncheon," December 10, 1946, Brophy Papers, WHS; Ad Council Board Minutes, December 20, 1946, Brophy Papers, Box 2, (Advertising Council- Minutes, Board of Directors, 1946), WHS; Ad Council Board Minutes, January 31, 1947, Brophy Papers, Box 2, (Advertising Council- Minutes, Board of Directors, 1947), WHS; Ad Council Board Minutes, May 15, 1947, Brophy Papers, Box 2, (Advertising Council- Minutes, Board of Directors, 1947), WHS; Clark to Brophy, June 23, 1947, Brophy Papers, Box 25, (Clark, Thomas C.,

1946–1958, 1951–1952, 1954, n.d.), WHS. For a useful retrospective synopsis of the
American Heritage Foundation's work, see Cox to Seiler, January 19, 1954, Brophy
Papers, Box 32, (Correspondence, S—General File, 1952–1959, 1964), WHS. Among
many secondary accounts that deal with the Freedom Train, good starting points
include Stuart J. Little, "The Freedom Train: Citizenship and Postwar Political Culture
1946–1949," *American Studies* 34, no. 1 (Spring 1993): 35–67, and Wall, *Inventing the
"American Way,"* 201–240.

57. "Conference at the White House—American Heritage Program," May 22, 1947,
　　Advertising Council Archives, 13/2/207, Box 4, File 381, UIA.

58. Ibid., 4.

59. Brophy quoted in Wall, *Inventing the "American Way,"* 207.

60. Wall, *Inventing the "American Way,"* 207.

61. For the list of American Heritage Foundation board members, see "Conference at the
　　White House—American Heritage Program," May 22, 1947, Advertising Council
　　Archives, UIA, 9.

62. Wall, *Inventing the "American Way,"* 205.

63. "Conference at the White House—American Heritage Program," May 22, 1947,
　　Advertising Council Archives, UIA. On the conservatism of the American Heritage
　　Foundation and supporting Ad Council campaign, see Griffith, "Selling of America,"
　　399.

64. Wall, *Inventing the "American Way,"* 206.

65. See Chapter 6.

66. Wall, *Inventing the "American Way,"* 209.

67. Aldrich quoted in Wall, *Inventing the "American Way,"* 209.

68. Wall, *Inventing the "American Way,"* 209–211.

69. "The American Heritage Program for Your Community," n.d. [1947], Brophy Papers
　　Part 3 (MCHC69-051), Box 1, (AHF Freedom Train), WHS. See also Wall, *Inventing
　　the "American Way,"* 209.

70. "The American Heritage Program for Your Community," n.d. [1947], Brophy Papers,
　　WHS, 4.

71. On the document selection process, see Wall, *Inventing the "American Way,"* 211–216.
　　On the document selection committee specifically, see Ibid., 213.

72. "Conference at the White House—American Heritage Program," May 22, 1947,
　　Advertising Council Archives, UIA, 5.

73. On "negative" and "positive" liberty, see McPherson, *Battle Cry of Freedom,* 867.
　　McPherson argues that with the Civil War, "positive liberty . . . became the newly
　　dominant American understanding of liberty." The leaders of the NAM and the Ad
　　Council worked hard to reverse that shift.

74. Little, "Freedom Train," 48–49. See also Griffith, "Selling of America," 396–399; Wall,
　　Inventing the "American Way," 212–213; and Eric Foner, *The Story of American Freedom*
　　(New York: Norton, 1998), 249–252.

75. Little, "Freedom Train," 48–49, and Wall, *Inventing the "American Way,"* 213.

76. To see how the American Heritage Foundation presented the documents it included on
　　the Freedom Train, see Our American Heritage—Documents of Freedom, n.d. [1947],

Brophy Papers Part 3 (MCHC69-051), Box 1, (AHF Freedom Train), WHS. For granular detail on the Freedom Train, see "Freedom Train Timeline," https://www .freedomtrain.org/freedom-train-timeline.htm.

77. For an insightful discussion of the re-separation of political and economic rights in the second half of the 1940s, see Borgwardt, *New Deal for the World*, 50–53.

78. Section 310 of the National Security Act of 1947 specified that it "shall take effect on whichever of the following days is the earlier: The day after the day upon which the Secretary of Defense first appointed takes office, or the sixtieth day after the date of the enactment of this Act." Forrestal was sworn in as the first secretary of defense on September 17, 1947. See Walter Millis, ed. *The Forrestal Diaries* (New York: Viking, 1951), 311. For the language of the original National Security Act, see https://global.oup .com/us/companion.websites/9780195385168/resources/chapter10/nsa/nsa.pdf.

79. National Security Act of 1947, Pub. L. No. 235, 61 Stat. 496 (1947). On "corner stone," see Franklin Roosevelt, "Statement upon Signing the Social Security Act," August 14, 1935, FDRL.

80. Mary Stuckey similarly argues that Roosevelt's "rhetoric of mobilization" "worked to Roosevelt's short-term political advantage" but "helped undergird the creation of the national security state" and made it "difficult to return it to a purely civilian footing." Mary E. Stuckey, *The Good Neighbor: Franklin D. Roosevelt and the Rhetoric of American Power* (East Lansing: Michigan State University Press, 2013), 63.

81. On Lippmann's *Inquiry into the Principles of the Good Society*, see Burgin, *Great Persuasion*, 55–78.

82. It is largely for that reason that historians have credited Lippmann with helping popularize the term "national security," but Lippmann's infrequent use of the term—it appears in his bestselling 1943 book only a handful of times, and in only a small percentage of the hundreds of columns he wrote from the late 1930s through the late 1940s—suggests he may have played a lesser role. For claims of Lippmann's influence, see Yergin, *Shattered Peace*, 194–195; Steel, *Walter Lippmann and the American Century*, 408; and David Milne, *Worldmaking: The Art and Science of American Diplomacy* (New York: Farrar, Straus and Giroux, 2015), 200–203.

83. Milne, *Worldmaking*, 202.

84. Walter Lippmann, *U.S. Foreign Policy: Shield of the Republic* (New York: Little, Brown, 1943), 51. See also Steel, *Walter Lippmann and the American Century*, 408, and Milne, *Worldmaking*, 203.

85. Several scholars have argued that Earle influenced the development of the American national security state by shaping Walter Lippmann's and James Forrestal's thinking. But a careful examination of Earle's interactions and correspondence with those two people raises questions about the extent to which Earle shaped their thinking on or use of the term "national security." For claims of Earle's influence, see Yergin, *Shattered Peace*, 194 and 466n49; Reynolds, *From Munich to Pearl Harbor*, 179; Sherry, *In the Shadow of War*, 36; David Ekbladh, "Present at the Creation: Edward Mead Earle and the Depression-Era Origins of Security Studies," *International Security* 36, no. 3 (Winter 2011/12): 107–141; Preston, "Monsters Everywhere," 494–497; and Dexter Fergie, "Geopolitics Turned Inwards: The Princeton Military Studies Group and the

National Security Imagination," *Diplomatic History* 43, no. 4 (September 2019): 644–670. For a skeptical assessment of Earle's influence, see Rios-Bordes, "When Military Intelligence Reconsiders the Nature of War," 108.

86. Fergie, "Geopolitics Turned Inwards," 651–653.

87. See A. K. Weinberg, "The Meaning of Security (In General and in American History)," with comments, n.d., Earle Papers, Box 33, (Security), MLP, and Poole to Earle, October 22, 1941, Earle Papers, Box 33, (Security), MLP.

88. See Earle comments on Weinberg's definition of national security, n.d., Earle Papers, Box 33, (Security), MLP.

89. Edward Mead Earle, "American Security—Its Changing Conditions," *Annals of the American Academy of Political and Social Science* 218 (November 1941): 189n6.

90. For an example letter to someone Earle considered influential, see Earle to Butler, October 15, 1941, Earle Papers, Box 24, (Princeton Military Studies Group—Seminar Statement, 1941), MLP. For an example journal article, see Edward Mead Earle, "American Military Policy and National Security," *Political Science Quarterly* 53, no. 1 (March 1938): 1–13. For an example talk, see Lecture at Academy of Political Science, November 13, 1940, Earle Papers, Box 37, (Drafts-Transcripts-Lectures-Miscellaneous (1 of 4), 1940–1944), MLP. Earle's book was *Against This Torrent*.

91. It is instructive that the title of a comprehensive account of the development of "security studies" includes "international" in its title. See Buzan and Hansen, *Evolution of International Security Studies*. On Earle's role in the development of academic security studies, see Ekbladh, "Present at the Creation," 107–141.

92. It was only in the years around the dissolution of the Soviet Union that security studies scholars began to revisit Earle's founding assumption. With the lessening of the salience of the physical security and foreign policy concerns that had animated the founders of security studies in the 1940s, international relations scholars (and others) in the 1980s and early 1990s began to "redefine security" and to explore the process by which issues become "securitized." See, for example, Richard H. Ullman, "Redefining Security," *International Security* 8, no. 1 (Summer 1983): 129–153; Barry Buzan, *People, States, and Fear: The National Security Problem in International Relations* (Chapel Hill: University of North Carolina Press, 1983); Jessica Tuchman Mathews, "Redefining Security," *Foreign Affairs* 68, no. 2 (Spring 1989): 162–177; Wade Greene, "An Idea Whose Time Is Fading," *Time* 135, no. 22 (May 28, 1990): 90; Theodore C. Sorensen, "Rethinking National Security," *Foreign Affairs* 69, no. 3 (Summer 1990): 1–18; Graham Allison and Gregory F. Treverton, eds., *Rethinking America's Security: Beyond Cold War to New World Order* (New York: Norton, 1992); Joseph J. Romm, *Defining National Security: The Nonmilitary Aspects* (New York: Council on Foreign Relations Press, 1993); and Wæver, "Securitization and Desecuritization." Notably, however, these works rarely escaped the international relations frame, even in their proposed "widening" of the definition of national security.

93. Rana, "Who Decides on Security?", 1460.

94. In two books he had written over the preceding decade, Herring had advocated the further development of the positive state to ensure the nation's constant preparedness for war. See Herring, *Public Administration and the Public Interest*, and Herring, *The*

Impact of War. Herring further cemented the foreign policy focus of the national security state by supporting the emergence of academic security studies through his later work as the head of the Social Science Research Council. On Herring's experiences at SSRC, see Reminiscences of Edward Pendleton Herring, Carnegie Corporation Project, Oral History Research Office, Columbia University, 1969.

95. On Herring's influence on Eberstadt, see Jeffrey M. Dorwart, *Eberstadt and Forrestal: A National Security Partnership, 1909–1949* (College Station: Texas A & M University Press, 1991), 96. For a detailed discussion of Herring's views, see Rana, "Who Decides on Security?", 1458–1469.

96. See Summary of Report to Hon. James Forrestal, May 10, 1945, Eberstadt Papers, Box 60, (Forrestal, Janes V.—Files—Eberstadt, Ferdinand, 'Eberstadt Report' . . . , October 22, 1945), MLP.

97. Ibid., 7.

98. Ibid.

99. On Forrestal's opposition to unification, see Hogan, *Cross of Iron*, 32–35, 41–53.

100. It is likely not a coincidence that Ferdinand Eberstadt was similarly leaning on the term "national security" in the same period in private correspondence to influential journalists and members of Congress in support of Forrestal's effort to save the navy from unification. See, for example, Eberstadt to Millis, November 13, 1945, Eberstadt Papers, Box 5, (Armed Services Unification Files—Eberstadt, Ferdinand Files—Correspondence, Chronological Files, September-December 1945), MLP, and Eberstadt to Hart, November 13, 1945, Eberstadt Papers, Box 5, (Armed Services Unification Files—Eberstadt, Ferdinand Files—Correspondence, Chronological Files, September-December 1945), MLP.

101. Senate Military Affairs Committee Fall 1945 Hearings, 97.

102. Ibid., 99. For Forrestal's prepared statement omitting that line, see Forrestal Statement before the Senate Military Affairs Committee, October 22, 1945, Eberstadt Papers, Box 60, (Forrestal, Janes V.—Files—Statement, Senate Military Affairs Committee, October 22, 1945), MLP.

103. Senate Military Affairs Committee Fall 1945 Hearings, 117.

104. See, for example, Yergin, *Shattered Peace*, 194, and Fergie, "Geopolitics Turned Inwards," 669.

105. Senate Military Affairs Committee Fall 1945 Hearings, 117.

106. Ibid.

107. Richard E. Neustadt, "Congress and the Fair Deal: A Legislative Balance Sheet," in *Harry S. Truman and the Fair Deal*, ed. Alonzo L. Hamby (Lexington, MA: Heath, 1974), 17.

108. See Yergin, *Shattered Peace*, 193–220; Cecilia Stiles Cornell, "James V. Forrestal and American National Security Policy, 1940–1949," (Ph.D. diss., Vanderbilt University, 1987); Dorwart, *Eberstadt and Forrestal*; and Hogan, *Cross of Iron*, 32–35.

109. Forrestal's consistent omission of topics like economic security previously central to "national security" was an important factor. See, for example, James Forrestal, "Speech before the Economic Club of Detroit," November 19, 1945, Forrestal Papers, Box 157, (19), MLP, https://findingaids.princeton.edu/collections/MC051/c05170. In his

remarks, Forrestal outlined a conception of "all aspects of our national security" that did not include domestic economic security (p. 10 of his remarks; p. 12 of the PDF).

110. Walter Lippmann, "Today and Tomorrow: Soviet-American Military Ideas," *Hartford Courant*, March 21, 1946, 10.

111. On the National Security Act of 1947, see Harold Hongju Koh, *The National Security Constitution: Sharing Power after the Iran-Contra Affair* (New Haven, CT: Yale University Press, 1990), 101–105; Hogan, *Cross of Iron*, 23–68; Amy B. Zegart, *Flawed by Design: The Evolution of the CIA, JCS, and NSC* (Stanford, CA: Stanford University Press, 1999), 54–75 and generally; Leffler, *Preponderance of Power*, 174–179; and Douglas T. Stuart, *Creating the National Security State: A History of the Law That Transformed America* (Princeton, NJ: Princeton University Press, 2008).

112. Two works that deal with both topics are Janet Farrell Brodie, "Learning Secrecy in the Early Cold War: The RAND Corporation," *Diplomatic History* 35, no. 4 (September 2011): 643–670, and Daniel Bessner, *Democracy in Exile: Hans Speier and the Rise of the Defense Intellectual* (Ithaca, NY: Cornell University Press, 2018). Bessner provides helpful lists of the relevant literature on think tanks in his notes. See especially Bessner, *Democracy in Exile*, 238n4, 240n22, 240n23. There is a need for a comprehensive history of the security clearance in the United States, but starting points include Daniel Patrick Moynihan, *Secrecy: The American Experience* (New Haven, CT: Yale University Press, 1998); Hugh Gusterson, *Nuclear Rites: A Weapons Laboratory at the End of the Cold War* (Berkeley: University of California Press, 1996), 68–100; Geoffrey R. Stone, *Top Secret: When Our Government Keeps Us in the Dark* (Lanham, MD: Rowman & Littlefield, 2007); and David Pozen, "The Leaky Leviathan: Why the Government Condemns and Condones Unlawful Disclosures of Information," *Harvard Law Review* 127 (2013): 512–635.

113. On the power and enduring influence of the first and second generation of "national security" professionals, see Richard J. Barnet, *Roots of War* (New York: Penguin, 1972), 48–133.

114. On the backgrounds of these "national security" leaders, see Barnet, *Roots of War*, 48–75, and Godfrey Hodgson, "The Foreign Policy Establishment," in *Ruling America*, eds. Steve Fraser and Gary Gerstle (Cambridge, MA: Harvard University Press, 2005), 215–249. On Forrestal, see Townsend Hoopes and Douglas Brinkley, *Driven Patriot: The Life and Times of James Forrestal* (Annapolis, MD: Naval Institute Press, 1992). On Donovan, see Douglas Waller, *Wild Bill Donovan: The Spymaster Who Created the OSS and Modern American Espionage* (New York: Free Press, 2011). On Lovett and McCloy, see Walter Isaacson and Evan Thomas, *The Wise Men: Six Friends and the World They Made* (New York: Simon & Schuster, 1986).

115. On the Dulles brothers, see Stephen Kinzer, *The Brothers: John Foster Dulles, Allen Dulles, and Their Secret World War* (New York: Times Books, 2013).

116. On the new national security professionals' socioeconomic status, see Dorwart, *Eberstadt and Forrestal*, 7–8, and Michael H. Hunt, *Ideology and U.S. Foreign Policy* (New Haven, CT: Yale University Press, 1987), 150–151.

117. Some of the titles of books about these people are instructive. See, for example, Robert D. Schulzinger, *The Wise Men of Foreign Affairs: The History of the Council on Foreign*

Relations (New York: Columbia University Press, 1984); Isaacson and Thomas, *The Wise Men*; and Evan Thomas, *The Very Best Men: Four Who Dared: The Early Years of the CIA* (New York: Simon & Schuster, 1995).

118. Dorwart discusses Ferdinand Eberstadt's "Good Man" list in Dorwart, *Eberstadt and Forrestal*, 7–9 and generally.

119. James Forrestal, "Princeton University Speech," June 21, 1944, Forrestal Papers, Box 163, (10), MLP, https://findingaids.princeton.edu/collections/MC051/c05253.

120. On this point, see Wilson, *Destructive Creation*, 61–67.

121. Clifford with Holbrooke, *Counsel to the President*, 78. For examples of Forrestal's comments on domestic policy in cabinet meetings, see Millis, ed., *Forrestal Diaries*, 356 and 369.

122. James Forrestal, "Radio Address on the Occasion of the Princeton University Bicentennial Anniversary," November 14, 1946, Forrestal Papers, Box 163, (11), MLP, 14, https://findingaids.princeton.edu/collections/MC051/c05254.

123. On Forrestal, see Hoopes and Brinkley, *Driven Patriot*, 127. On Donovan, see Waller, *Wild Bill Donovan*, generally. On Allen Dulles, who first became addicted to this type of work during World War I, see Kinzer, *Brothers*, 36, 64–65. See also Thomas, *The Very Best Men*, 10.

124. McCloy quoted in Isaacson and Thomas, *Wise Men*, 335.

125. Lovett quoted in Ibid., 735.

126. Hoopes and Brinkley, *Driven Patriot*, 353. On Hoopes's service on Forrestal's staff, see Ibid., 359.

127. Harry S. Truman, "Annual Message to the Congress on the State of the Union," January 6, 1947, APP, https://www.presidency.ucsb.edu/node/232364. Rosenman's papers at the Truman Library indicate that he arrived in Washington in time to work on the draft of the speech in which the paragraph appeared. See Clifford to Rosenman, n.d., Rosenman Papers, Box 9, (1947: Message to Congress, Drafts, January 6, 1947), HSTL, and 2nd Draft of 1/3/47, Truman Papers, PSF, Box 36, (January-March, 1947), HSTL. For drafts of the speech, see Elsey Papers, Box 10, (1947, January 6: State of the Union—Drafts), HSTL. For the increasingly common distinction between "national security" and "welfare" thereafter, see, for example, Harry S. Truman, "Annual Budget Message to the Congress, Fiscal Year 1949," January 12, 1948, APP, https://www.presidency.ucsb.edu/node/232457; Harry S. Truman, "Annual Budget Message to the Congress: Fiscal Year 1950," January 10, 1949, APP, https://www.presidency.ucsb.edu/node/230146; and Harry S. Truman, "Annual Budget Message to the Congress: Fiscal Year 1951," January 9, 1950, APP, https://www.presidency.ucsb.edu/node/230956.

128. See, for example, the 1948 Federal Security Agency annual report, which picked up Truman's rhetorical distinction between "national security" and "welfare." Federal Security Agency, *Annual Report of the Federal Security Agency, 1948* (Washington, DC: United States Government Printing Office, 1949), 489.

129. Harry S. Truman, "Special Message to the Congress: The President's First Economic Report," January 8, 1947, APP, https://www.presidency.ucsb.edu/node/232721. Truman's Council of Economic Advisers, chaired by Edwin G. Nourse, wrote that line. See "Materials Submitted to the President by the Council of Economic Advisers

Relative to the President's Economic Report," December 17, 1946, Clifford Files, Box 4, (Economic Advisers to the President, Council of [10 of 10]; President's Economic Report—January 8, 1947), HSTL, 84.

130. Harry S. Truman, "Excerpts from Annual Message: The President's Economic Report to the Congress," January 14, 1948, APP, https://www.presidency.ucsb.edu/node /229299.

131. Harry S. Truman, "The President's News Conference on the Budget," January 10, 1948, APP, https://www.presidency.ucsb.edu/node/232391.

132. Hassett to Colegrove, December 29, 1950, OF, Box 1766, (OF 2535 The Welfare State), HSTL.

133. Little, "Freedom Train," 35. For a detailed description of the scene at a Freedom Train stop, see Gilbert Bailey, "Why They Throng to the Freedom Train," *New York Times Magazine*, June 25, 1948.

134. Little, "Freedom Train," 35, 51.

135. Michael Hogan notes that at the festivities that accompanied the Freedom Train's stops across the country, "distinguished citizens, often military leaders, wasted no time in stressing key themes in the national security ideology." See Hogan, *Cross of Iron*, 433.

136. Freedom Train Launch Radio Broadcast, September 16, 1947, John Foster Dulles Papers, Box 294, (Speech- Freedom Train, "American Heritage" Program, Radio Broadcast), MLP.

137. Griffith, "Selling of America," 399.

138. Ibid.

139. Ibid.

140. Little, "Freedom Train," 35.

141. See Del Monte to Brophy, July 16, 1948, Brophy Papers, Box 12, (American Heritage Foundation—Correspondence, 1947–1953), WHS.

142. *Real Security*, n.d. [1948], NAM Records (1411), Series 16, Box 218, (NAM Publications-Q-Report to . . .), HML.

143. Ibid.

144. See David G. McCullough, *Truman* (New York: Simon & Schuster, 1992), chapter 14.

145. Harry S. Truman, "Address in Milwaukee, Wisconsin," October 14, 1948, APP, https://www.presidency.ucsb.edu/node/233585.

146. Harry S. Truman, "Address in Oklahoma City," September 28, 1948, APP, https://www.presidency.ucsb.edu/node/233188. On the care and planning that went into this speech, see the extensive correspondence and many marked up drafts in Elsey Papers, Box 19, (1948, September 28: Oklahoma City, Oklahoma), HSTL; Clifford Papers, Box 35, (1948, Campaign Trip, September 28, Oklahoma—Major [address] [Oklahoma City]), HSTL; and Murphy Files, Box 2, (September 28, 1948, Oklahoma City, Oklahoma), HSTL.

147. Truman, "Address in Oklahoma City," September 28, 1948, APP.

148. McCullough, *Truman*, 847.

149. Dewey quoted in Richard H. Rovere, "Letter from a Campaign Train: En Route with Dewey," *The New Yorker*, October 16, 1948, 76.

150. "The NAM Story: Speech Material Covering NAM Structure, Activities, Services, and the 1948 Public Relations Program," May 10, 1948, NAM Records, HML, 14.

8. Cementing a Foreign Policy–Focused National Security State

1. Harry S. Truman, "Address at the 70th Anniversary Meeting of the National Civil Service League," May 2, 1952, APP, https://www.presidency.ucsb.edu/node/230618.
2. Harry S. Truman, "Annual Message to the Congress on the State of the Union," January 5, 1949, APP, https://www.presidency.ucsb.edu/node/230007.
3. Ibid.
4. See Neustadt, "Congress and the Fair Deal: A Legislative Balance Sheet," 15–41, and Amenta and Skocpol, "Redefining the New Deal," 92.
5. Alonzo L. Hamby, "The Vital Center, the Fair Deal, and the Quest for a Liberal Political Economy," *American Historical Review* 77, no. 3 (June 1972): 672.
6. On the "trust in government" question, see "Public Trust in Government: 1958–2019," Pew Research Center, April 11, 2019, https://www.pewresearch.org/politics/2019/04/11/public-trust-in-government-1958-2019.
7. On conservative business leaders' involvement in stoking anticommunism, see Peter H. Irons, "American Business and the Origins of McCarthyism: The Cold War Crusade of the United States Chamber of Commerce," in *The Specter: Original Essays on the Cold War and the Origins of McCarthyism*, eds. Robert E. Griffith and Athan Theoharis (New York: New Viewpoints, 1974), 72–89.
8. Harry S. Truman, "Special Message to the Congress: The President's First Economic Report," January 8, 1947, APP, https://www.presidency.ucsb.edu/node/232721.
9. Interview with Charles B. Coates, November 14, 1967, Herbert Hoover Oral History Program Interviews (XX028), Box 5, (Coates), HIA, 1.
10. Interview with Don K. Price, July 20, 1970, Herbert Hoover Oral History Program Interviews (XX028), Box 19, (Price, Don K.), HIA, 27–30. See also Grisinger, *Unwieldy American State*, 153–154, and Jason Scott Smith, "The Transformation of the Cold War State: From Welfare to Security," in *Liberty and Justice for All? Rethinking Politics in Cold War America*, ed. Kathleen G. Donohue (Amherst: University of Massachusetts Press, 2012), 289.
11. For helpful background on Hoover's post-presidential career, see "Hoover Commissions Sought Government Reforms," *New York Times*, October 21, 1964.
12. Barton to Hoover, August 10, 1948, Barton Papers (U.S. Mss 44AF), Box 29, (Hoover, Herbert, 1929–1964), WHS.
13. "Statement by Herbert Hoover," November 18, 1947, First Hoover Commission Records (XX312), Box 14, (Herbert Hoover Statement's—1st Commission), HIA.
14. James Rowe was a Southern Democrat. Dean Acheson and Joseph Kennedy had fallen out with Roosevelt. Although James Forrestal stayed on better terms with Roosevelt, he was not exactly a New Dealer. For Rosenman's use of the phrase "real liberal," see Rosenman to Roosevelt, March 31, 1944, Rosenman Papers, Box 1, (Bowles, Chester), FDRL.
15. "The Government Can't Do It All," 1949, First Hoover Commission Records (XX312), Box 14, (Herbert Hoover Statement's—1st Commission), HIA.

16. Confidential review of Commission's public position, January 24, 1948, First Hoover Commission Records (XX312), Box 14, (Progress Report), HIA, 2.

17. Interview with Don K. Price, July 20, 1970, Herbert Hoover Oral History Program Interviews, HIA, 29.

18. Interview with Clarence Francis, October 3, 1968, Herbert Hoover Oral History Program Interviews (XX028), Box 8, (Francis, Clarence), HIA, 10–11.

19. Interview with Charles B. Coates, November 14, 1967, Herbert Hoover Oral History Program Interviews, HIA, 1.

20. Interview with Clarence Francis, October 3, 1968, Herbert Hoover Oral History Program Interviews, HIA, 7.

21. Interview with Charles B. Coates, November 14, 1967, Herbert Hoover Oral History Program Interviews, HIA, 1.

22. Press Release [on creation of the Citizens Committee for Reorganization of the Executive Branch of the Government (CCREBG)], April 10, 1949, First Hoover Commission Records (XX312), Box 15, (First Commission—Press Releases), HIA. For background on the Citizens Committee, see Johnson to Brophy, March 23, 1949, Brophy Papers, Box 35, (Hoover Report, 1949–1950), WHS. On the Citizens Committee's finances, see Chester to Presidents of Top Companies, October 6, 1949, CCREBG Records, Box 3, (3), HIA; Johnson to Hardware Companies, October 18, 1950, CCREBG Records, Box 3, (3), HIA; and Colby Chester to Non-Contributing Companies, October 23, 1951, CCREBG Records, Box 3, (1), HIA.

23. For the IRS letter granting tax exempt status, see National Reorganization Crusade, April 21, 1950, CCREBG Records, Box 11, (4), HIA, 8–9.

24. Hobby later served as the head of the Federal Security Agency in the Eisenhower administration. In an ironic twist that further reinforced the separation of "national security" and "welfare" and hardened the gender roles associated with each, it was Hobby who oversaw the transformation of the Federal Security Agency into the Department of Health, Education, and Welfare during the Eisenhower administration. For biographical information on Hobby, see James Barron, "Oveta Culp Hobby, Founder of the WACs and First Secretary of Health, Dies at 90," *New York Times*, August 17, 1995, https://www.nytimes.com/1995/08/17/obituaries/oveta-culp-hobby -founder-of-the-wacs-and-first-secretary-of-health-dies-at-90.html. See also Coates to Hobby, February 3, 1953, CCREBG Records, Box 19, (H (2)), HIA.

25. For biographical information on Johnson, see Albert W. Warburton, "Robert L. Johnson Hall Dedicated at Temple University," *The Emerald of Sigma Pi* 48, no. 4 (Winter 1962): 111–112. For biographical information on McCormick, see Guide to the Robert Louis Laing McCormick Papers, Yale Manuscripts and Archives, http://ead -pdfs.library.yale.edu/4116.pdf. Johnson also served on the board of the Armstrong Cork Company headed by former NAM president Henning W. Prentis Jr. For Johnson's service on the Armstrong Cork board, see Warburton, "Robert L. Johnson Hall Dedicated at Temple University," 112.

26. Chester to Presidents of Top Companies, October 6, 1949, CCREBG Records, Box 3, (3), HIA.

27. At the time, Hanes was working with his close friend and influential conservative John M. Olin to reorganize Olin Industries. For background on Hanes, see George James,

"John Wesley Hanes, Sr., 95, Aide to Roosevelt and Corporate Chief," *New York Times*, December 31, 1987, https://www.nytimes.com/1987/12/31/obituaries/john-wesley-hanes-sr-95-aide-to-roosevelt-and-corporate-chief.html.

28. See the list of board members in Chester to Presidents of Top Companies, October 6, 1949, CCREBG Records, Box 3, (3), HIA.

29. Ade to State Chairmen and Executive Secretaries, November 29, 1949, CCREBG Records, Box 3, (2), HIA.

30. See The Citizens Committee's Legislative Program for 1951, November 30, 1950, CCREBG Records, Box 3, (9), HIA. For the model bills, see Legislative Proposals, March 9, 1951, CCREBG Records, Box 3, (9), HIA.

31. McCormick to the Librarians, July 25, 1951, CCREBG Records, Box 3, (9), HIA.

32. In the twenty-first century, the conservatives behind the American Legislative Exchange Council (ALEC) took this approach to a new level of effectiveness. For an insightful overview and case study of ALEC's influence, see Dan Kaufman, *The Fall of Wisconsin: The Conservative Conquest of a Progressive Bastion and the Future of American Politics* (New York: Norton, 2018), 113-159.

33. Chester to Presidents of Top Companies, October 6, 1949, CCREBG Records, Box 3, (3), HIA.

34. See Speakers Handbook, undated, CCREBG Records, Box 3, (7), HIA; Revised Speakers Handbook, undated, CCREBG Records, Box 3, (6), HIA, 14-6; and Notecard Waste Examples, undated, CCREBG Records, Box 10, (1), HIA.

35. Collection Description, CCREBG Records (52007), HIA.

36. Johnson to Hardware Companies, October 18, 1950, CCREBG Records, Box 3, (3), HIA. For an organization chart, see CCREBG Organization Chart, n.d., CCREBG Records, Box 4, (10), HIA. For a personnel roster, see Citizens Committee for the Hoover Report, National Committee Personnel, 1949, CCREBG Records, Box 9, (5), HIA. For an example of the *Washington Watchdog*, see *Washington Watchdog*, no. 1, October 11, 1950, CCREBG Records, Box 2, (7), HIA.

37. Fell and Stevenson to Fuller, June 2, 1949, CCREBG Records, Box 17, (F), HIA, and Coates to Mortimer, April 5, 1950, Brophy Papers, Box 35, (Hoover Report, 1949–1950), WHS. On J. Walter Thompson, see Coates to Cooperating Organizations, October 21, 1949, CCREBG Records, Box 7, (8), HIA.

38. See Chapter 4.

39. For examples of the material the Citizens Committee provided to facilitate creation of state and local committees, see Organizing a State Committee to Support Hoover Commission Findings, April 8, 1949, CCREBG Records, Box 3, (8), HIA, and Organizing a State Committee to Support Hoover Commission Findings, Supplement II, April 18, 1949, CCREBG Records, Box 3, (8), HIA. For an example of how the national committee solicited feedback from state and local committees, see Ade to State Chairmen and Executive Secretaries, February 21, 1950, CCREBG Records, Box 11, (4), HIA.

40. For a full list of state and local chairmen, see List of Chairmen and Executive Secretaries in Affiliated Committees, March 16, 1950, CCREBG Records, Box 4, (3), HIA.

41. For a synopsis of the Citizens Committee's efforts aimed at students, see Coates to Board of Directors, April 10, 1950, CCREBG Records, Box 11, (10), HIA.

42. See Burns Jr. to McCormick, December 30, 1949, CCREBG Records, Box 11, (10), HIA.
43. Mailing to various college librarians, April 25, 1950, CCREBG Records, Box 11, (10), HIA.
44. See, for example, Burns to Student Members, September 26, 1950, CCREBG Records, Box 11, (10), HIA.
45. 'Telling the Story' of the Hoover Report on America's College Campuses, n.d. [1949], CCREBG Records, Box 11, (10), HIA.
46. White to Members of the Schools and Universities Program Advisory Board, February 6, 1950, CCREBG Records, Box 11, (10), HIA.
47. Ade to State and Local Committees and Board of Directors and Executive Committee, September 8, 1950, CCREBG Records, Box 11, (4), HIA. For a photograph of one of the cars that accompanied the caravan, see https://www.ohiomemory.org/digital /collection/p267401coll32/id/29329.
48. Coates to Chairmen and Executive Secretaries, August 11, 1950, CCREBG Records, Box 3, (2), HIA, 6. On the October 12, 1949 State Chairmen's conference, see Proceedings of Citizens Committee for Reorganization of the Executive Branch of the Government, October 12, 1949, CCREBG Records, Box 8, (3), HIA, and Brief Report of the State Chairmen's Conference, October 12, 1949, CCREBG Records, Box 8, (3), HIA.
49. Johnson to All Members of the National Committee, November 30, 1949, CCREBG Records, Box 3, (2), HIA.
50. National Reorganization Conference Agenda, December 12, 1949, CCREBG Records, Box 9, (5), HIA.
51. See Chapter 2.
52. Text of Speeches Delivered at the National Reorganization Conference, Volume 1, December 12–13, 1949, CCREBG Records, Box 9, (5), HIA, 6. On the drafting of the speech, see Ade to Hobby, November 9, 1949, CCREBG Records, Box 19, (Ho-Hu), HIA.
53. Text of Speeches Delivered at the National Reorganization Conference, Volume 1, December 12–13, 1949, HIA, 6.
54. Ibid., 8.
55. Ibid.
56. Ibid., 9.
57. Ibid.
58. Ibid., 32.
59. Ibid.
60. Ibid.
61. Ibid.
62. For background on the National Reorganization Crusade, see Ade to State Chairmen and Executive Secretaries, February 21, 1950, CCREBG Records, Box 11, (4), HIA, and National Reorganization Crusade, April 14, 1950, CCREBG Records, Box 11, (4), HIA.
63. See the attachments to Johnson to Presidents of Top Companies, April 21, 1950, CCREBG Records, Box 11, (4), HIA.
64. Ferris to State Chairmen, Executive Secretaries and County Chairmen, April 4, 1950, CCREBG Records, Box 11, (12), HIA.

65. Ibid.

66. On earlier conservative efforts to cultivate "tax consciousness," see "Theme of 1939–1940 Program," NAM Records, HML, 9, and Selling America to Americans, undated [1939], NAM Records (1411), Box 141, (Speakers Bureau—Speeches—Our Stake in National Defense), HML, 12. See also Huret, *American Tax Resisters*, 154.

67. Ferris to State Chairmen, Executive Secretaries and County Chairmen, April 4, 1950, CCREBG Records, HIA.

68. Ferris to Members of the National Speakers Bureau, September 28, 1949, CCREBG Records, Box 11, (12), HIA.

69. Ferris to State and Local Chairmen and Executive Directors, October 24, 1950, CCREBG Records, Box 11, (12), HIA.

70. Ibid.

71. Ibid.

72. National Reorganization Crusade Radio Spot Announcements, n.d. [1950], CCREBG Records, Box 11, (4), HIA.

73. Robert L. Johnson to Individual Contributors, March 15, 1951, CCREBG Records, Box 3, (1), HIA.

74. Membership Card, n.d. [1951], CCREBG Records, Box 4, (8), HIA.

75. On the roles of Chapin and J. Walter Thompson in the Ad Council campaign on behalf of the Hoover Report, see Ad Council Monthly Progress Report, June 1950, Jackson Files, Box 15, (Advertising Council--Monthly Summaries of Activities [3 of 3, November 1949–May 1952]), HSTL. See also Coates to Chapin, February 29, 1952, CCREBG Records, Box 16, (C [4]), HIA.

76. Government Reorganization—Hoover Report, 1950, Advertising Council Archives, 13/2/207, Box 8, File 530, UIA.

77. Ibid.

78. For Woolford's memos, see Woolford to All Information Service Representatives, January 25, 1950, CCREBG Records, Box 1, (1), HIA; Woolford to All Information Service Representatives, February 2, 1950, CCREBG Records, Box 1, (1), HIA; and Woolford to All Information Service Representatives, February 23, 1950, CCREBG Records, Box 1, (1), HIA.

79. Government Reorganization—Hoover Report, 1951, Advertising Council Archives, 13/2/207, Box 9, File 585, UIA.

80. Ibid.

81. Ibid.

82. Ibid.

83. Ibid.

84. Patterson, *Grand Expectations*, 59.

85. *The Free Enterprise System*, n.d. [1950], NAM Records (1411), Box 104, (Free Enterprise—General), HML. NAM continued to harp on this point: *Building a Better America*, December 2, 1952, NAM Records (1411), Box 545, (NAM Board of Directors Minutes, September 1952–June 1953), HML.

86. Robert A. Taft, "The Fair Deal Is Creeping Socialism," in *Harry S. Truman and the Fair Deal*, ed. Alonzo L. Hamby (Lexington, MA: Heath, 1974), 42.

87. There are ways in which anti-communism, as Jennifer Delton puts it, "made America liberal" in the sense that it contributed to an expansion of certain rights. Both Delton and Mary Dudziak have shown how some groups, including African Americans, were able to use anti-communism to press for expanded *political* rights, sometimes in the name of national security. But these expansions were generally confined to *political* rather than *economic* rights, a distinction that conservatives sought to maintain and that liberals, led by Roosevelt, had tried unsuccessfully to obliterate. See Mary L. Dudziak, *Cold War Civil Rights: Race and the Image of American Democracy* (Princeton, NJ: Princeton University Press, 2000), and Jennifer A. Delton, *Rethinking the 1950s: How Anticommunism and the Cold War Made America Liberal* (New York: Cambridge University Press, 2013).

88. Fones-Wolf, *Selling Free Enterprise*, 6, 37.

89. On the role of these private organizations in shaping American perceptions of the communist threat, see Marc J. Selverstone, *Constructing the Monolith: The United States, Great Britain, and International Communism, 1945–1950* (Cambridge, MA: Harvard University Press, 2009), 51–52.

90. See Landon R. Y. Storrs, *The Second Red Scare and the Unmaking of the New Deal Left* (Princeton, NJ: Princeton University Press, 2013), 5, 15.

91. Chamber of Commerce of the United States, "Communist Infiltration in the United States, Its Nature and How to Combat It," 1946, NAM Records (1411), Box 1, (Communism—General (2 of 2)), HML.

92. *Free Enterprise vs. Communism,* June 1947, NAM Records (1411), Box 104, (Free Enterprise—General), HML; *Don't be a sucker. . .*, n.d. [1947], NAM Records (1411), Box 150, (NAM Publications—D), HML; and *People vs. Rabbits,* n.d. [1947], NAM Records (1411), Series 16, Box 218, (NAM Publications—P—Postwar—Publics), HML.

93. *Sum & Substance*, Second Issue, n.d. [late 1940s], NAM Records (1411), Series 16, Box 218, (NAM Publications—S-Sl-Su), HML.

94. Ibid.

95. Chamber of Commerce of the United States, "The Drive for a Controlled Economy via Pale Pink Pills," 1949, Chamber Records (1960), Series 4, Box 84, (Publications—1949—A-O), HML.

96. See Chamber of Commerce of the United States of America, *American Economic Security* 7, no. 1, January-February 1950, Chamber Records (1960), Series 4, Box 68, (American Economic Security, 7–8, 1950–1951), HML.

97. Chamber of Commerce of the United States, "7 Doors to Socialism," March 1950, Chamber Records (1960), Series 4, Box 84, (Publications—1950—O-Z), HML, and Chamber of Commerce of the United States, "Socialism in America," n.d. [1950], NAM Records (1411), Box 6, (Socialism—General), HML.

98. On FSA head Ewing's lobbying, see Chamber of Commerce of the United States of America, *American Economic Security* 7 no. 5, August-September 1950, Chamber Records (1960), Series 4, Box 68, (American Economic Security, 7–8, 1950–1951), HML, 1–7.

99. On the role of anti-communism in defeating the Truman administration's national health insurance proposal, see Colin Gordon, *Dead on Arrival: The Politics of Health*

Care in Twentieth-Century America (Princeton, NJ: Princeton University Press, 2003), 141–147; Ellen Schrecker, *Many Are the Crimes: McCarthyism in America* (Princeton, NJ: Princeton University Press, 1998), 383–384; and Jonathan Bell, *The Liberal State on Trial: The Cold War and American Politics in the Truman Years* (New York: Columbia University Press, 2004), 164–174.

100. Quoted in Gordon, *Dead on Arrival*, 144.

101. *Sum & Substance,* Freedom Issue, n.d. [1950], NAM Records (1411), Series 16, Box 218, (NAM Publications—S-Sl-Su), HML.

102. Ibid.

103. Ibid.

104. The effectiveness of the American Economic System campaign was a subject of disagreement even before it concluded. As with earlier National Association of Manufacturers efforts to "mold opinion molders," the Ad Council's American Economic System campaign may have had its greatest impact indirectly, by shaping young minds and influential voices over the medium and long term. For skeptical views of the campaign's effectiveness that focus on the campaign's direct messaging, see Whyte Jr., *Is Anybody Listening?* and John Vianney McGinnis, "The Advertising Council and the Cold War," (Ph.D. diss., Syracuse University, 1991). For a sense of the intense focus the Ad Council placed on this campaign, see the monthly Ad Council activity reports in Jackson Files, Box 15, (Advertising Council—Monthly Summaries of Activities [1 of 3, undated, July 1948–December 1948]), HSTL.

105. Wilson to Brophy, August 26, 1948, Brophy Papers, Box 2, (Advertising Council—Correspondence, 1948–1949), WHS. Conservatives had considered such a campaign since 1946, but it did not get off the ground until after Truman's election. On the origins of the campaign, see McGinnis, "The Advertising Council and the Cold War," 40–53.

106. The American Economic System, 1952, Advertising Council Archives, 13/2/207, Box 10, File 614, UIA.

107. The Miracle of America, 1950, Advertising Council Archives, 13/2/207, Box 6, File 482 UIA.

108. House Magazine copy—American Economic System, Fight Tuberculosis, United America, Traffic Safety, 1949, Advertising Council Archives, 13/2/207, Box 5, File 437a, UIA.

109. American Economic System—Ivan Is Watching You, 1951, Advertising Council Archives, 13/2/207, Box 8, File 524, UIA.

110. Ibid.

111. On the Crusade for Freedom, see Richard H. Cummings, *Radio Free Europe's "Crusade for Freedom"* (Jefferson, NC: McFarland, 2010); Hugh Wilford, *The Mighty Wurlitzer: How the CIA Played America* (Cambridge, MA: Harvard University Press, 2008), 31–40; and Martin J. Medhurst, "Eisenhower and the Crusade for Freedom: The Rhetorical Origins of a Cold War Campaign," *Presidential Studies Quarterly* 27, no. 4 (Fall 1997): 646–661.

112. See, for example, Watson to Boyd, November 12, 1954, Brophy Papers, Box 12, (American Heritage Foundation—Correspondence, 1954), WHS. See also Wall, *Inventing the "American Way,"* 276–277.

113. Cummings, *Radio Free Europe's "Crusade for Freedom,"* 2–3, and Kenneth Osgood, *Total Cold War: Eisenhower's Secret Propaganda Battle at Home and Abroad* (Lawrence: University Press of Kansas, 2006), 41.

114. Ibid. For an example "Freedom Scroll," see Crusade for Freedom, 1950, Advertising Council Archives, 13/2/207, Box 7, File 502, UIA.

115. Harry S. Truman, "Address in Oklahoma City," September 28, 1948, APP, https://www.presidency.ucsb.edu/node/233188.

116. Ibid.

117. Ibid.

118. Harry S. Truman, "Address at the Jefferson-Jackson Day Dinner," February 24, 1949, APP, https://www.presidency.ucsb.edu/node/229922.

119. Harry S. Truman, "The President's News Conference at Key West," March 30, 1950, APP, https://www.presidency.ucsb.edu/node/230873.

120. Ibid.

121. Harry S. Truman, "Statement Upon Issuing Order Establishing the President's Commission on Internal Security and Individual Rights," January 23, 1951, APP, https://www.presidency.ucsb.edu/node/230643.

122. On the episode, see Harry S. Truman, "Letter to the Chairman, Committee on the Judiciary, on the Commission on Internal Security and Individual Rights," May 12, 1951, APP, https://www.presidency.ucsb.edu/node/231051.

123. Harry S. Truman, "The President's News Conference," November 30, 1950, APP, https://www.presidency.ucsb.edu/node/230485.

124. Harry S. Truman, "Address in Detroit at the Celebration of the City's 250th Anniversary," July 28, 1951, APP, https://www.presidency.ucsb.edu/node/230497.

125. As historian Alonzo Hamby puts it, Truman was "always a step or two behind the public-relations curve." Hamby, *Man of the People*, 584.

126. Harry S. Truman, "Letter to the Speaker on the Housing Bill," June 17, 1949, APP, https://www.presidency.ucsb.edu/node/229572.

127. Ibid.

128. Harry S. Truman, "Address at the Cornerstone Laying of the New General Accounting Office Building," September 11, 1951, APP, https://www.presidency.ucsb.edu/node/230759.

129. Harry S. Truman, "Address at the 70th Anniversary Meeting of the National Civil Service League," May 2, 1952, APP, https://www.presidency.ucsb.edu/node/230618. For the many drafts of the speech, see Lloyd Files, Box 10, (Civil Service Speech, May 2, 1952), HSTL, and Murphy Files, Box 18, (May 2, 1952, 70th Anniversary of National Civil Service League), HSTL.

130. Truman, "Address at the 70th Anniversary Meeting of the National Civil Service League," May 2, 1952, APP.

131. Ibid.

132. Ibid.

133. Ibid.

134. Harry S. Truman, "Annual Message to the Congress on the State of the Union," January 7, 1953, APP, https://www.presidency.ucsb.edu/node/231314.

135. Ibid.

136. Chamber of Commerce of the United States of America, *American Economic Security* 7, no. 3, April-May 1950, Chamber Records (1960), Series 4, Box 68, (American Economic Security, 7–8, 1950–1951), HML, 25.

137. Memorandum from President Truman to the Secretary of State and the Secretary of Defense, "Communications Intelligence Activities," October 24, 1952, https://nsarchive2.gwu.edu/NSAEBB/NSAEBB24/nsa02a.pdf.

138. Harry S. Truman, "Executive Order 10431—National Security Medal," January 19, 1953, APP, https://www.presidency.ucsb.edu/node/230910.

139. Harry S. Truman, "Statement by the President Reviewing the 1953 Budget," August 19, 1952, APP, https://www.presidency.ucsb.edu/node/231309.

140. Klein, *For All These Rights*, 14.

141. Roady, "Selling Selective Anti-Statism." See also Schulman, *From Cotton Belt to Sunbelt*, 138, and Michael Brenes, *For Might and Right: Cold War Defense Spending and the Remaking of American Democracy* (New Brunswick: University of Massachusetts Press, 2020).

142. See Mittelstadt, *Military Welfare State*.

Epilogue

1. Starting in the 1940s, the Ad Council tracked the number of "impressions" its messages received. For a message delivered by radio, for example, the Ad Council defined a "listener impression" as "one message heard once by one listener." See Ad Council Annual Report, 8th, "How Business Helps Solve Public Problems," 1949–1950, Advertising Council Archives, 13-2-207, Box 7, File 503, UIA.

2. For instance, see Hasher et al., "Frequency and the Conference of Referential Validity," and Fazio et al., "Repetition Increases Perceived Truth Equally for Plausible and Implausible Statements."

3. Franklin D. Roosevelt, "Denver, Colorado—Extemporaneous remarks at dinner in his honor—8:00 p.m.," September 15, 1932, FDRL.

4. Nancy E. McGlen and Meredith Reid Sarkees, *Women in Foreign Policy: The Insiders* (New York: Routledge, 1993), 2, and Julie Dolan, "Political Appointees in the United States: Does Gender Make a Difference?" *PS: Political Science and Politics* 34, no. 2 (June 2001): 214.

5. On this topic, see Heather Hurlburt and Tamara Cofman Wittes, "The Case for Gender Diversity in National Security," *Lawfare*, July 9, 2019, https://www.lawfareblog.com/case-gender-diversity-national-security.

6. See Rosa Brooks, "Tear Down the Foreign-Policy Glass Ceiling!" *Foreign Policy*, June 25, 2019, https://foreignpolicy.com/2019/06/25/tear-down-the-foreign-policy-glass-ceiling/. For a study of four women who rose to the top of the national security establishment, see Sylvia B. Bashevkin, *Women as Foreign Policy Leaders: National Security and Gender Politics in Superpower America* (New York: Oxford University Press, 2018).

7. See, for example, James J. Sheehan, *Where Have All the Soldiers Gone? The Transformation of Modern Europe* (Boston: Mariner Books, 2009).

8. On the American underwriting of state building abroad, see Ben Zdencanovic, "From Cradle to Grave: The United States in a World of Welfare, 1940–1953," (Ph.D. diss., Yale University, 2019).

9. Both Wendy Wall and Mark Wilson have noted the impact of conservative victories in the fight to shape public opinion in the 1940s on the government's ability to manage economic and social problems thereafter. See Wall, *Inventing the "American Way,"* 12, and Wilson, *Destructive Creation*, 288. Catherine Lutz has also argued that "the legacy and rhetoric of national security . . . has distorted the definition and possibilities for democratic citizenship." See Catherine A. Lutz, *Homefront: A Military City and the American 20th Century* (Boston: Beacon Press, 2001), 3.

10. This was the Rapid Deployment Joint Task Force (RDJTF), which in 1983 became the United States Central Command. On the RDJTF, see Edward C. Keefer, *Harold Brown: Offsetting the Soviet Military Challenge, 1977–1981, Secretaries of Defense Historical Series, Volume IX* (Washington, DC: Office of the Secretary of Defense Historical Office, 2017), 342–349. On the Carter administration's acquiescence to the narrow conception of "national security," see Ullman, "Redefining Security," 129. On the RDJTF's relationship to broader Carter administration foreign policy, see Daniel J. Sargent, *A Superpower Transformed: The Remaking of American Foreign Relations in the 1970s* (New York: Oxford University Press, 2015), 287 and 366n62.

11. On the expense and size of the national security state as it came to be, see (among many works) Ann Markusen, Peter Hall, Scott Campbell, and Sabina Dietrich, *The Rise of the Gunbelt: The Military Remapping of America* (New York: Oxford University Press, 1991); Dana Priest and William M. Arkin, *Top Secret America: The Rise of the New American Security State* (New York: Little, Brown, 2011); Thorpe, *American Warfare State*; and David C. Hendrickson, *Republic in Peril: American Empire and the Liberal Tradition* (New York: Oxford University Press, 2018).

12. On the tradition of minimizing the appearance of national government power, see Edling, *A Revolution in Favor of Government*, and Balogh, *A Government Out of Sight*.

13. See Mettler, *The Submerged State*.

14. On this point, see Linda Weiss, *America, Inc.? Innovation and Enterprise in the National Security State* (Ithaca, NY: Cornell University Press, 2014), and Mark R. Wilson, "Presidents, the Military-Industrial Complex, and the Ascendant Politics of 'Free Enterprise,'" in *The President and American Capitalism since 1945*, eds. Mark H. Rose and Roger Biles (Gainesville: University Press of Florida, 2017), 62–80.

15. Abraham, "Segurança/Security in Brazil and the United States," 22.

16. Wæver, "Securitization and Desecuritization," 47.

17. See Hayek, *Road to Serfdom*.

18. Ole Wæver and Itty Abraham offer similar suggestions. See Ole Wæver, "Securitization and Desecuritization," 56–57, and Abraham, "Segurança/Security in Brazil and the United States," 37.

19. "Declaration of Independence: A Transcription," America's Founding Documents, National Archives, https://www.archives.gov/founding-docs/declaration-transcript.

20. Roosevelt, "Radio Address on 3rd Anniversary of Social Security Act," August 15, 1938, FDRL.

Index